SEXISM

Marielouise Janssen-Jurreit

[Translated from the German by Verne Moberg]

Farrar Straus Giroux

New York

SEXISM

The Male Monopoly on History and Thought

Translation copyright © 1982
by Farrar, Straus and Giroux, Inc.
Originally published in German under the title
Sexismus: Über die Abtreibung der Frauenfrage
© Carl Hanser Verlag München Wien, 1976
All rights reserved
Published simultaneously in Canada
by McGraw-Hill Ryerson Ltd., Toronto
Printed in the United States of America
First edition, 1982
Library of Congress Cataloging in Publication Data
Janssen-Jurreit, Marielouise.
Sexism: the male monopoly on history and thought.
Translation of Sexismus. / Includes bibliographical references.
1. Sex discrimination against women—History.
2. Sexism—History. 3. Feminism—History. I. Title.
HQ1121.J3613 305.4'2'09 80-11657

Thanks are due to the following publishers and authors for permission to quote: *The Elementary Structure of Kinship* by Claude Lévi-Strauss, translation copyright © 1969 by Beacon Press, first published under the title *Les Structures Élémentaires de la Parente*, 1949; *Social Evolution* by V. Gordon Childe, Harry N. Abrams, Inc., 1951; *The Philosophy of Right* by G. W. F. Hegel, Oxford University Press, 1942; *Social Structure* by George Peter Murdock, copyright 1949 by Macmillan Co., Inc, renewed © 1977 by George Peter Murdock; *The Emergence of Modern America: 1865–1875*, by Allan Nevins, copyright 1927 by Macmillan Co., Inc., renewed © 1955 by Allan Nevins; *The Naked Ape* by Desmond Morris, copyright © 1967 by Desmond Morris, McGraw-Hill Book Company; *The Second Sex* by Simone de Beauvoir, translated by H. M. Parshley, copyright 1952 by Alfred A. Knopf, Inc., published in England by Jonathan Cape, Ltd.; *The Decline of the West*, vol. II by Oswald Spengler, copyright 1928, renewed © 1956 by Alfred A. Knopf, Inc., *Unwritten Memories* by Katia Mann, edited by Elisabeth Plessen and Michael Mann, translated by Hunter and Hildegarde Hannum, copyright © 1975 by Alfred A. Knopf, Inc.; *The Evolution of the French People* by Charles Seignobos, copyright 1932, renewed © 1960 by Alfred A. Knopf, Inc.; *The Story of Man* by Carleton S. Coon, copyright © 1954, 1961, 1962 by Carleton S. Coon, Alfred A. Knopf, Inc.; *Married Life in an African Tribe* by Isaac Schapera, Northwestern University Press, 1966, published in England by Faber & Faber, Ltd.; *Man and Woman, Boy and Girl* by John Money and Anke Ehrhardt, copyright © 1972 by The Johns Hopkins University Press; *Conundrum* by Jan Morris, Harcourt Brace Jovanovich, Inc., 1974; *The Dialectic of Sex* by Shulamith Firestone, copyright © 1970 by Shulamith Firestone, William Morrow & Co., Inc.; *Up from the Pedestal* by Aileen S. Kraditor, copyright © 1968 by Aileen S. Kraditor, Times Books, a division of Quadrangle/The New York Times Book Co., Inc.; *Male and Female* by Margaret Mead, copyright 1949 by Margaret Mead, William Morrow & Co., Inc.; *Mein Kampf* by Adolf Hitler, translated by Ralph Manheim, renewed © 1971 by Houghton Mifflin Company; *Myth, Religion, and Mother Right* by J. J. Bachofen, translated by Ralph Manheim, Bollingen Series LXXXIV, copyright © 1967 by Princeton University Press; *The Origin of the Family, Private Property, and the State* by Friedrich Engels, copyright © 1972 by International Publishers; *The Woman in America* by Robert Jay Lifton, copyright © 1964, 1965 by The American Academy of Arts and Sciences, Houghton Mifflin Company

This is a shortened, reworked version of the original German edition.

To my daughter Sarah

Contents

Part One
Sexism and History

1/The Heritage of the Radical Feminist Hedwig Dohm and Her Granddaughter Katia Mann

---

Miller, miller, mill it!
The youths cost a dollar.
The young maids sell for pigeon dirt
that people quickly kick aside.
Miller, miller, mill it!
The maids get a dollar,
The young boys get a saddlehorse,
well worth a thousand dollars.

—*German children's song from the nineteenth*
century

"The first writer I ever saw was my grandmother Hedwig Dohm," Katia Mann wrote in *Unwritten Memories*.[1] Dohm was the first woman in Bismarck's Germany courageous enough to attack the sacred institutions of the Prussian male state: first the Protestant pastors, then the German philosophers, and finally the gynecologists ("I rebel against that category of doctors who see women as nothing more than an instrument for . . . male designs").[2] Yet her granddaughter had not the slightest understanding of the ideas Dohm fought for. Mann wrote of her as "a passionate early champion of women, who really did not have many rights," as "a very small, very droll and, in her way, charming old lady." It is clear from both the condescending, if affectionate, way in which she discusses her grandmother's sense of commitment and personality and the pattern of Katia Mann's life that these rights were hardly important to her.

Katia Mann gained prominence through her husband, the Nobel Prize-winning author Thomas Mann, and from her sons, both writers, as well; Hedwig Dohm's prominence has been erased from the history of political ideas and literature in Germany. Dohm's books endured the same fate as the first feminist movement in general, which dwindled through a regression that Kate Millett aptly termed a backlash period.

This backlash began in the industrialized countries with the adoption of suffrage after World War I, a time of sexual counterrevolution. The granting of equal rights to women was one of society's most convincing lies; under the magic cape of equality, power relationships between the sexes were upheld far more effectively than they had been in the age when political parties, special-interest organizations, and other male groups had frequently fought the woman's demands for equal rights. From this point on, one could always claim slow but continual progress, small improvements and reforms.

Within sixty years after woman suffrage had been introduced in industrialized countries, sexism—the discrimination and exploitation of woman because of her sex—would undergo merely a structural change. The social hierarchy would, on certain issues, be dismantled in public, only to be further reinforced in other more private and more obscure areas, for the first international women's movement could not destroy society's pervasive androcentric thinking.

How could the ideas of the first feminist movement vanish so rapidly? For insight, and perhaps answers, it is interesting to compare the lives of Katia Mann and Hedwig Dohm; this would imply that Mann was the grandmother of Dohm and not the other way around. Their era was one in which the views of such Darwinist doctors as Gustave Le Bon and Theodor Bischoff (who claimed that the female brain diminished in the course of evolution) were accepted unequivocably by even those who considered themselves unprejudiced—for instance, Émile Durkheim, the founder of modern French sociology.[3] But Hedwig Dohm dismissed such speculative scientific hypotheses as anthropological quackery, and in turn she received anonymous abuse and threatening letters.

Even her first pamphlets show great wealth of invention and a temperament that was eager to attack; they are masterpieces of a literary form that is taboo today: the polemic. In the eyes of the public, one pamphlet was virtually a crime against the Kaiser; under the title "Der Jesuitismus im Hausstand" she reprimanded late-nineteenth-century housewives for being excessively thrifty and for exploiting their serving maids by making them work unlimited hours. Did these "priestesses of the house" perhaps fear that the independent and informed professional woman would prevail, that "the cheap naïveté of her daughters would go out of fashion"? Proletarian women were not to be criticized for their lack of commitment to the question of women's rights,

> because they are wanting in judgment and education and because prejudice is generally even stronger among the ignorant than among the educated. The women of the people are incapable of realizing why a place has not been set for them at life's table.[4]

For Dohm, the intolerance of bourgeois women toward even the most modest efforts at emancipation deserved no mercy. The German housewife's dogma of infallibility has never been satirized more cleverly:

> I, Madame Schultz, with all my heart and my strength, believe in me and my kitchen, in my nursery and my laundry, in my drying room and my sewing machine. Everything else, alas, is harmful. I believe that if the dear Lord had a woman, she would have to be exactly like me. I think serving maids are a good-for-nothing race. However, any woman who dares to doubt my infallibility, who opposes my views, or who meddles with so-called ideas, I declare to be an immoral, contemptible emancipated woman, a heretic who by rights must be roasted on a spit—ah, the aroma will smell sweet. Since I have been, and am, and shall be . . . a German housewife.[5]

This campaign against the hypocrisy of the ignorant housewife and mother, persecutor of the domestic servant, became a scandal. Everyone was shocked, men and women alike, the women of the bourgeois women's movement as well as the editors of national newspapers. If it hadn't been for Hedwig Dohm's radical polemics, the testimony of the German women's movement—compared with the political statements by American, English, and French women then—would amount to no more than a paltry collection of provincial literature for the daughters of the upper class.

Hedwig Dohm was born in 1832, the eleventh of eighteen children; she died at the age of eighty-seven in Berlin in 1919, when woman suffrage—which she had been the first in Germany to demand—had become constitutional law. Dohm was rebuked by a sister soldier:

> And if it gets to the point that women are going to the polls and sitting in Parliament—assuming that by this time we don't have a different form of government, which is not an impossibility—it will be thanks to the work and patience of good, modest German women.[6]

Yet, her critic was mistaken, for even in the middle of World War I there were still members of the women's movement—some, good, modest women—who considered the demand for suffrage to be too immodest. In the German nation the demand for political emancipation of women, an important issue in both America and England since the middle of the nineteenth century, was not considered seriously for a long time even by the socialists. At the party congress in Gotha in 1875, woman suffrage was left hanging, despite a supporting petition from the German socialist leader August Bebel. Ferdinand Lassalle, another labor leader (who frequented Hedwig Dohm's house in Berlin), had sought the vote only for male workers, as it was the male who supported the family. Demands for women's work outside the home or even for woman suffrage were unacceptable to the Universal German Workingmen's Association, which Lassalle had founded in May 1863.

In 1876, when Hedwig Dohm declared in her publication "Der Frauen Natur und Recht" that woman's franchise was a goal for all women's political struggles, she made it clear to both female and male adversaries that there was no stopping this timely demand. She wanted woman suffrage to be a self-evident constitutional right within democracy; women were not to be measured by different standards:

> Either a reigning queen is an idea out of a Mardi-Gras, a burlesque notion, and all English citizens who pay homage to the queen and swear allegiance to her are fools . . . or every woman should be endowed·with natural political rights.

Bebel's book *Women under Socialism* appeared three years later, in 1879, with a Swiss publisher, since the Anti-Socialist Laws made its publication impossible in Germany. At the 1891 party congress of the Social Democratic Party of Germany, woman suffrage was elevated to a priority of the party.[7]

Just as important and new as the substance of their demand for suffrage was the way in which it was presented by Hedwig Dohm: with a combination of compelling analysis and polemic agitation, she reversed the weapons of ridicule, time and again aimed at women's emancipation, and used them against the Prussian male state.

> Women don't need the vote. That is to say: men have from time immemorial been so just, so good, so noble that the destiny of half the human race can be placed in their hands. Women don't need the vote . . . it's an idea innate in men, a divine impulse, which drives them—whether their world is barbaric or civilized—to protect women, their rights and their happiness. Women do not need the vote—no—they don't need it . . . in all those fairy tales, never-never lands in which little children and big men sometimes believe. And the meaning of history? The history of women is solely a history of their persecution and lack of rights, and this history

says: men have oppressed women all along in outrageous and unprecedented ways, and human reason ordains: they are going to oppress them until the female sex shares in drafting the laws by which it is governed, for every right not backed up with power is a fantasy, a phantom . . .

How do you get power? Only provisionally and only by the concentration of female strength, prepared to stand up for the political rights of women, through organization and energetic leadership.

She promised no utopian paradise after woman suffrage was won but viewed it rather as only the ineluctable basis for the resolution of coming conflicts over new women's rights in marriage, education, and labor:

> Perhaps the immediate results of suffrage are not what is most important. But the main thing is this: the granting of suffrage is the step across the Rubicon. Only with suffrage for women does agitation begin for those great reforms that are the goal of our endeavors.

Two years earlier, in her publication "Zur wissenschaftlichen Emanzipation der Frau," she had called for the abolition of the division of labor by sex which until then had been regarded as natural. In 1874 Hedwig Dohm stated:

> I believe I can prove that the division of labor is not a privilege for woman but an advantage for man; and that the struggle against women doing professional work begins only at the point when their day's wages amount to more than pennies.

> A picture of women toiling in glassworks, papermills, glue and tobacco factories, etc.; working half bare in fervid cotton mills with suffocating dust and dirt; destroying themselves, contracting consumption in the flaxmill standing in water in the spring of the year. At that time women were already employed in brickworks or stamping down stones; they were metalworkers and miners; stitch by stitch they sewed themselves to death at starvation wages; then, as now, they performed the hardest work in the fields . . . But the female constitution is too delicate—says the patriarch—for the universities to be opened to women![8]

Until she was very old, she defended this stand, sharing it with a group of radical bourgeois women who organized in the nineties.

> The radicals demand all rights and liberties to be unconditional and unlimited, believing that more and more of these "little bits" —a little bit of freedom, a little bit of a profession—will result only

in a piece of patchwork; hence, their main point, and mine, is that without the economic independence of the woman, all other rights are illusory.[9]

. . . sooner or later you are going to see land: the country that, for centuries, indeed for millennia, you have searched for in your heart—the country where women belong not to men but to themselves.

This was Hedwig Dohm's prophecy for all women.[10] Yet, did Katia Mann yearn for this kind of existential freedom, for an experience that would not place her in a permanent relationship with a superior protective male figure? Dohm's demand—"No vote, no right to love!" —affected *her* life, but had little serious effect on the life of her granddaughter. Katia Mann's reminiscences—which she wrote when she was nearly ninety—offer impressive evidence that a family role model (Katia Mann's mother was the favorite daughter of Hedwig Dohm) may accomplish little. The granddaughter's memoirs contain antifeminist passages that the grandmother would have regarded as excellent examples of misogyny and deficient analysis and reflection on her own role in life. Mann begins her account with the sentence: "My father was a professor of mathematics at the University of Munich, my mother was a very beautiful woman." The father was defined by professional position, while only a good appearance characterized the mother, even though she was an actress and a member of the well-known theater troupe of Duke George II of Saxony-Meiningen, the "Meininger."[11]

In February 1905 Katia Pringsheim would wed Thomas Mann, a marriage approved by the family, including even her grandmother. Hedwig Dohm, however, regretted that Katia, who had been among the first generation of female students, would discontinue her studies. Dohm was well aware of the cheap irony writers of the eighteenth and nineteenth centuries used to mock women who made mistakes in writing. Jean Paul writes in *Hesperus, oder 45 Hundsposttage* (1795):

A girl forgets two things most easily: first, how she looks—mirrors were invented for this—and, secondly, the difference between *das* and *daβ* [the German definite article and subordinating conjunction].

The misogynist Ludwig Börne ridicules:

The only woman since the world was created who didn't make spelling mistakes was our mother Eve who hadn't yet learned how to read.

Instruction in the girls' schools, even in the capital city of Berlin, was handled exclusively by old teachers who had been pensioned off and were "already unsuitable for the boys' school."

> The education of women occurs—one knows not how—as if through the atmosphere of imagination, more through living than through the acquisition of knowledge . . .

This opinion of the Prussian national philosopher Hegel on the education of women is not far removed from that of the emancipated journalist Karl Ludwig Börne in its cynicism and arrogance. Hedwig Dohm perceived the ignorance and amused reactions of her male contemporaries as the expression of a nation of violence. She refused to take any responsibility for her inferior school education.

> Isn't it funny, though, that men are ashamed of our ignorance when they are its intellectual authors? Was it perhaps we women who organized the girls' high schools and decided their curriculum? For my part, I disown responsibility for any orthographic, grammatical, or other mistakes that may occur in this paper; I emphatically reject them and lay the blame for them on the shoulders of men. Every punctuation mistake I make is their doing; for every language mistake they incur the disdain of the present generation. I attended the best possible school available in my youth, and it was . . . as poor as it possibly could be.[12]

Granddaughter Katia Mann's mental attitude toward her studies and her special fields, however, shows that more than just the admissions requirements to the schools and universities changed within two generations.

> It was my mother's idea and also my grandmother's that I should have a Gymnasium education. At that time there was no Gymnasium for girls in Munich, and of course no coeducational schools as there are today; consequently, various Gymnasium professors took turns giving me private instruction.

Although she graduated at the top of her class, Katia Mann identified only slightly with her grandmother's concept of education. Studying gave her no trouble whatsoever, and apparently she took little more interest in her privilege than that expected of an obedient daughter.

> Now I was supposed to go to the university. I specialized in the natural sciences: experimental physics with Wilhelm Röntgen and mathematics with my father—calculus and the theory of functions. But I have always felt that I had no special aptitude for

these subjects. One of my brothers, Peter, the second eldest, also studied physics and became a very good physicist. I wasn't predestined for that at all, and Röntgen didn't think much of me either. Once during an experiment I had a minor disaster: I knocked over an apparatus. Röntgen took that rather badly. Probably I would never have excelled in his subject, nor did I find myself very talented in mathematics. I took those courses because of filial attachment, and I've forgotten them all.

Her remoteness from her studies is evident; there is no trace of a goal-oriented will. A remarkable disinterest in graduation, a negative experience with the professor, then the studies interrupted when her children came. Not for one moment did the granddaughter consider combining a profession, marriage, and motherhood—which is what Hedwig Dohm had in mind (an idea which annoyed her contemporaries).

Maybe I would have completed my studies and taken my degree. However, I had studied for only four or six semesters when I got married; soon after that the first baby arrived, and the second one right away, and very soon the third and fourth. That was the end of my studies.

Fifty years earlier her grandmother, as a young girl, had pricked her finger embroidering, dreaming of the deliverance from the empty existence of being the daughter in a bourgeois family.

Never was a girl less destined for or interested in handiwork than I was; for a relatively small sum my mother could have bought a much more beautiful carpet than the one embroidered by me, but still the big lazy girl was supposed to be kept busy doing something useful, and always, as I did my needlework, there was an expectancy in me, an anxious yearning waiting for something extraordinary. Years in the Friedrichstrasse am Halleschen Tor, always embroidering, embroidering without end—but it couldn't go on this way. Something had to happen. When the bell rang, I listened: alert, I waited tensely: who or what would come—maybe a letter or a person, a total stranger who had seen me on the street and wanted to marry me and take me away from this place. The bells, however, brought bills or merchandise and of the letters that came, not one was for me.[13]

After wasted years spent on handiwork, her parents permitted her to attend the teachers' seminary, which consisted of "monotone rote learning of geography, botany, history tables, but, above all, songs from songbooks and Bible sayings." In 1852, at the age of nineteen, and long before her education ended, Hedwig married the thirty-three-year-old writer Ernst Dohm, editor-in-chief of the satirical magazine *Kladderadatsch*. When her first essays on the question of women's rights appeared, she had given birth to five children and was almost forty years old. Ernst Dohm, like herself, was descended from an upper-middle-class Jewish family who had assimilated at the beginning of the century. He was a theology student turned satirist, whose skill in running the editorial office of *Kladderadatsch* was outstanding. For thirty-five years he managed to put together a satirical magazine which had an extraordinary political influence during a period that extended from the reaction to the abortive revolution of 1848 through the proclamation of the German Reich in Versailles' Hall of Mirrors. Little is known of the personal relationship of the Dohms as a married couple. Nevertheless, his carelessness and generosity with money may well have been a burden to the marriage. On several occasions, Ernst Dohm, for years a gambler, escaped debtors' prison thanks only to his publisher. In the end he escaped his creditors by fleeing to Weimar. There, for one year, unmolested, he continued his activity on *Kladderadatsch*. Not until the seventies were his financial affairs in order.

The Dohm house became known for its *jours fixes,* gatherings to which the Berlin intellectuals flocked. No one from this circle of prominent scientists, artists, and socialists appears to have been truly close to the housewife.[14]

In fact, Hedwig Dohm became fair game for ridicule within her own family. She was loved for her goodness, but treated with a lack of seriousness that typified men's feelings about the female sex. Katia Mann wrote of a visit she and her husband made to her grandmother's.

> That was our first trip to Berlin. The second took place when I was already expecting our first child. We visited my grandmother Dohm, the advocate of women's rights, and the way my husband behaved with her wasn't very tactful at all. She asked him, "Well, Tommy, what do you want, a boy or a girl?" He said, "A boy, of course. After all, a girl is not to be taken seriously." That was bad. But in spite of it they got along very well together.

Katia Mann goes on to describe her grandmother as a very "naïve and at the same time gifted woman" who wrote books "which today would probably not be of much current interest." Naïve? Hedwig Dohm, in one of her polemics on the alleged qualities of woman, stated:

> The men believe that they themselves have the qualities they deny to women. They see themselves as actors standing on the stage of life, and the director, the dear Lord, has engaged them to play the heroes' parts, the men of action, the demonic, violent and intellec-

tually strong: the women, however, were left the naïve and senti-
mental roles.[15]

Hedwig Dohm was always citing examples of the disdain elicited
by the birth of a daughter and of the influence of this disparagement
on the self-image of the little girl.

> Not only in antiquity but also in the feudal state was the birth of
> a daughter an affliction. Louis VII, King of France, said in a de-
> cree: Frightened by the great number of our girls, let us ardently
> pray to God that he endow us with more children of a better sex
> *(des enfants d'un sexe meilleur)*. And he granted an annuity to the
> one who would announce to him the birth of a son.[16]

She tried to create a consciousness of the negative assessment of female birth, appealing to the self-esteem of women:

> More pride, you women! How is it possible that you do not rebel
> against the contempt that always greets us? Yes, even today. The
> standing congratulations when a marriage is agreed to in Italy are
> still heard: "Salute e figli maschi" (health and male children). The
> fathers are still disappointed when their first-born is a girl.[17]

Not only among the fathers and not only in Italy and France does
this hold true. Two generations later in this same family, the granddaughter who regarded her grandmother as naïve is unabashedly sexist:

> It turned out to be a girl, Erika. I was very annoyed. I have always
> been annoyed when it was a girl. I don't know why. Altogether we
> had three boys and three girls, so there was a balance. If it had
> been four girls and two boys, I would have been beside myself, but
> this way it was all right. Although he thought a girl wasn't to be
> taken seriously, my husband was more favorably disposed toward
> the girls.

The emotional relations between parents and children in the
Mann family follow the normal pattern of identification in a patriarchal family: the mother favored the sons, the father was more attached to Erika and Elizabeth, who indeed were "nothing serious,"
and hence on more intimate terms with him. The hatred of women
and the woman's rejection of her daughter, apparent in Katia
Mann, are a typical expression of her own tendencies of self-contempt and suggest acted-out inferiority feelings. Unfortunately,
Katia Mann relates too little about her own mother, Hedwig Pringsheim, to include her in this attempt to establish how radical ideas
of the women's movement affected three generations of women in

one family. Katia Mann's memoirs show that the contradiction between women's roles and political powerlessness had never been made clear to her. She does not talk about other women very appreciatively. She gives the impression of being a self-aware, extremely soft, but determined-looking woman, married to a man of somewhat unstable health, a woman who arranges the practical side of life for her husband and, for example, even negotiates with his publisher for him.

Good at getting along in life, realistic, and unconventional in conversation, Katia Mann was still a conformist who questioned nothing. And although she was never sparing with judgments and opinions about individuals, her life story contains hardly any of her own feelings, elation, and pain. Her "reminiscences" reveal an astounding degree of unsentimentality.

Granted, the flashbacks of Katia Mann and Hedwig Dohm would be one-sided if only the granddaughter's immunity to women's rights were discussed and not the remarkably ambiguous behavior of the grandmother. But the fracture of female identity, the schism in the self, takes a different course in the grandmother and granddaughter. Dohm led a psychic double life as a family-oriented mother, beloved grandmother, and the most radical fighter for women's rights of her time. It was she who wrote, "Can we believe that, in this question of enormous import—where it is a matter of eliminating the thinking of thousands of years—the tame propaganda of aesthetic or ethical tea rings or of essays full of poetry will suffice." And yet she was incapable of making a public appearance; she was not good at organizing.

On her eightieth birthday an article appeared in 'the *Berliner Tageblatt* which said: "The most personal and penetrating quality of this unique woman is and was bravery." Her biographer Adele Schreiber portrays the two opposing qualities of her personality in this way:

But this fearless fighter, who drew the sharpest blade in attack, who never eschewed to write the outrageous, with no concern for attacks, ridicule, or defamation, who was never afraid to poke fun at the highest authorities, was personally so modest, indeed, fainthearted, that she could never bring herself to utter in public what she said in such a masterful way with her pen.

And elsewhere:

This shy, polite woman, whom one implicitly believes was afraid to set her serving maid straight, to whom nothing was more embarrassing than to give someone an unfriendly answer—this woman mounted the most daring attacks, fearlessly assailing the most learned authorities when it was a question of standing up for her beliefs, applying her pen to give the lie to injustice.[18]

For Hedwig Dohm's generation it was not possible to synthesize the private person and public militant. But even as an old woman she gave other women courage: the strongest remedy for old age was "the unconditional emancipation of woman and thus the deliverance from the brutal superstition that her right to exist rests solely on sex." She summoned the aging comrades of her sex to skate, bicycle, learn Latin, indeed, even to ride camels through the desert.

> Listen, old woman, to what another old woman is telling you: fight back, have the courage to live. If you only live one day, you have a future in front of you![19]

As far away as America, one saying of eighty-year-old Hedwig Dohm was circulated:

> Long after I am dead and burned, my ashes will glow when the portals of the Reichstag are opened to women.[20]

2/The Exclusion of Women in History

My history books lied to me, they said I didn't exist.

—Alta

The kind of historical thinking that was taught to me in school did not abandon me in the period afterward. Increasingly, world history became for me an inexhaustible source of insights for historical action in the present, as well as for politics.

—Adolf Hitler

The writing of modern history has resulted in a viewpoint that is nothing short of that of a stag party. The history of woman is ignored, hushed up, censored in the most literal sense of the term. This method of eliminating the social and political destiny of half of humanity is the most effective form of supremacy. For a long time the lower class, the poorest social strata—whether the plebeians in Rome, the serfs, or the proletarians at the beginning of the nineteenth century—also had little place in history. Still, it was not possible to write history without going into class differences; they have led to enormous conflicts. However, the history of women is different. Their resistance can be silenced, snuffed out as if it had never existed, because the battle of the sexes is considered a basic fact of nature.

Historiography serves in the self-celebration of man: it is the record of his deeds and the glorification of male values. It is the great vat from which male identity is tapped, and serves the mythification of great men. The image of man that emerges is a composition tailored from the psychological needs of male history consumers; according to the Swiss historian Jacob Burkhardt, true greatness is a mystery. Who

is a great man? "One without whom the world would seem incomplete
to us"?[1]

If so, the world must have been incomplete for those who in the
past were, and even today are, illiterates, or who were ignorant of their
country's leaders. Instead of realistically portraying great men, historiography invents them. Although historians no longer present history the way Burkhardt did, the fundamental ceremony is still preserved: as the act of men bowing to each other.

> History is not dead. We have become what we are through what
> was before us and cannot break away from it. "Drive Nature out
> with a pitchfork, and it will come right back in," says Horace; the
> same is true of the past. Just as the individual is constituted of all
> the experiences of his life from earliest childhood on, the past
> belongs to the present "self" of a people; what memory is to the
> individual, historiography is to the people.[2]

"If a civilization were deprived of any conscious contact with its history, it would not remain in one piece for long," wrote Golo Mann. "In
the process of comparing ourselves historically, we grasp our own
origins, the likeness repeating itself, and also what is unique in our
experience."[3] Mann may not have realized that he, like almost every
historian, had deprived half humanity of its history. His two-volume
history of Germany is a part of today's standard historical literature.
Of various male figures, Mann wrote in his foreword: "Only such
writers, poets, and philosophers were considered representative of the
public spirit; who influence history or are indicative of it."[4]

Wasn't there, in the history of Germany in the nineteenth and
twentieth centuries, a single woman who contemplated, wrote, experienced, or suffered something worth mentioning; women who
willed or brought about something positive, even negative? Historical
comparisons made by both of his volumes, in terms of persons, established facts, and overall conception of history, apply only to men.
Measured even by Golo Mann's own criteria, his choice of persons,
ideas, and social currents representing the nineteenth century does
not appear "objective." For example, in Katia Mann's memoirs, her
private account of a nearly ninety-year-old woman and the subjective
reminiscence of her grandmother become in the works of her son
historian Golo Mann suppressed historical facts, subjected to arbitrary historical perspective. The woman Golo Mann does mention is
Rosa Luxemburg; however, he devotes not even a sentence to her.

> The most radical people lived in Berlin. Here was the loudest talk
> of a "second revolution"; of good, free, courageous people, like the
> socialistic hotspur Ledebour; of fine, tender, bitter theoreticians
> like Rosa Luxemburg; of fanatics obsessed as much with the cause
> as the consciousness of their own mission, such as Karl Lieb-

knecht; of sincere people and of adventure seekers; of demagogues and followers.[5]

Described here in affected adjectives—"fine," "tender," "bitter"— is the woman who, if she had not been murdered by extremists on the right, might have transformed Germany by her goal of humane socialism. On the same page Mann briefly mentions the decrees of the revolutionary government, which took immediate effect in 1918.

Henceforth all political representation was to be chosen by the universal, equal, and secret franchise of all men and women over twenty. Were these not useful reforms, social and democratic innovations?

Were these social and democratic innovations purely a matter of chance, a whim of the new government? Golo Mann offers no explanation. According to him, woman suffrage came out of a historyless vacuum; it fell like a spontaneous idea from heaven.

Unfortunately, the way school books present the introduction of woman suffrage echoes Golo Mann's presentation. In thirty-one German history and social-science books used in academic, technical, and vocational secondary schools in 1973, there is only one sentence on the introduction of woman suffrage among a listing of other reforms such as the eight-hour day and unemployment insurance. Only one book mentions that there were female representatives in the National Assembly, a body which drafted the constitution of the Weimar Republic in 1919; this book also mentions that "Adolf Hitler banned [woman suffrage] again in 1933: politics was men's business!"[6] Although not totally suppressing the women's movement, not one of these history books contains a single correct statement about it. None mentions that there were several factions in the German women's movement fighting for different concepts of the future society: the bourgeois, the radical (the Left feminist wing of the bourgeois women's movement), and the socialist women's movements.

Toward the end of the century, Minna Cauer, one of the more radical women, together with the lawyer Anita Augspurg, published a women's political magazine and supported the union of the Left wing of the bourgeois women's movement with the women of the Social Democratic Party. Minna Cauer also wrote a history of women in the nineteenth century in which she declared: "The women, the working classes, and the Jews: these are the oppressed of this century."[7]

In his portrait of Heinrich Heine, Golo Mann only touches on the Jewish emancipation. Why a whole chapter for Heine and only one single sentence for his friend the emancipated Jew Rahel Varnhagen? As the central figure of a literary salon, she influenced such statesmen as Prince Louis Ferdinand and Friedrich von Gentz. Her male and female friends comprised the intellectual elite of Germany. In her biography, *Rahel Varnhagen: The Life of a Jewish Woman,* Hannah Arendt described what it meant to be Jewish, female, without schooling, and extremely unattractive. Rahel Varnhagen had herself baptized, taking her only chance, as a proper Jew, to assimilate into the bourgeois society. But: "Rahel remained a Jew and pariah. Only because she held fast to both of these did she find a place in the history of Europe's people."[8] Not in Golo Mann's history, however.

Rahel Varnhagen is worth mentioning not only because of her acquaintance and contact with Goethe, Johann Gottlieb Fichte, Friedrich Schleiermacher, and Heinrich Heine, but because in that century the struggle of women against forced marriage—marriage not founded upon free self-determination by both partners—begins with her. This struggle continues throughout the nineteenth century. In the writings of the early socialists, in Marx and Engels's *Communist Manifesto,* in August Bebel's *Woman under Socialism,* in the writings of the national court historian Heinrich von Treitschke, and in Max Weber's writings—not to mention their importance to the women's movement—marriage laws and reforms are discussed. Rahel Varnhagen refused to marry until she found a partner who agreed to her conditions. "The slave trade, war, marriage! And still they're surprised and go on trying to patch everything up," she wrote in 1803 in her diary; deep contempt is manifest in this juxtaposition. "Those married once want to stay married. But no child will ever receive consent from me to marry," she defiantly avowed, as there is no "legal guarantee of a covenant formed in free consent of mutual love, which is the only ethical alternative." Above all, forced sexuality in a union without love was a horror: ". . . an intimate life together without enchantment or delight is more indecent than any kind of ecstasy." On the basis of her thoughts on forced marriage she came to unconditionally reject the distinction of "legitimate" and "illegitimate" children. Long before Johann Jakob Bachofen espoused his theory of mother right, she pleaded: "Children should only have mothers and should bear their names; the mothers should possess the family property and power, since that is as Nature wills."

Rahel Varnhagen said, in reference to the highest manifestation of religion: "Even Jesus had only a mother." And she demanded that for all children ". . . an ideal father should be created and all mothers should be held in honor and be regarded as chaste as Mary."[9]

Varnhagen's views were inspired by Saint-Simonism, ideas popular among members of Young Germany, thanks to Heinrich Heine. The Saint-Simonists Saint-Amand, Bazard, and Le Père Enfantin demanded an androgynous culture and the sexual, economic, and political equality of man and woman. The early Saint-Simonists developed new ideas of God and proclaimed God as "Mapah," as father and mother, and in the beginning of the creation story placed a male-female being they called "Evadam."[10] The history of marriage and marriage law is a subject Golo Mann does not even mention.

The court historian of Wilhelm I, the nationally acclaimed Heinrich von Treitschke, expressed the following opinion on the subject of marriage reform:

> Whatever jeopardizes the whole and lasting community of man and woman falls into moral decay, the well-known free love of the socialists, even as the abortive goddess of the bordello . . . Present-day marriage is the perfect form of marriage, unto the end of history.

Vehemently Hedwig Dohm argued against Treitschke's ideas in an essay which she published at the age of seventy-seven in a socialist journal.

Johann Gottfried Herder, the philosopher of the Enlightenment who, in his *Reflections on the Philosophy of the History of Mankind*, first attempted a study of anthropology, writes:

> The bride . . . quits the house of her parents, as one dead to them for ever, loses her former name, and becomes the property of a stranger, who in all likelihood will treat her as a slave. She must sacrifice to him every thing . . . her person, her liberty, her will, nay probably her life and health . . .

Her sole consolation lies in the fact that she is permitted to listen to man's history of heroic deeds.

> Happy it is, that Nature has endowed and adorned the female heart with an unspeakably affectionate and powerful sense of the personal worth of man. This enables her to bear also the severities . . . [she] is proud, since she is destined to obedience, that she has such a husband to obey.[11]

Golo Mann calls Johann Gottlieb Fichte a "deep and soaring thinker." Fichte decisively influenced the national sensibility of the Germans, but also affected the life of the German woman. Toward the end of the century, when the Civil Code, effective in 1900, was created, the legal texts were based on the views that Hegel and Fichte had expressed on marriage and the family. Even today historiography that ignores the female sex fulfills Fichte's statement:

> The man supersedes her completely; by virtue of her marriage she is, in the eyes of the state, entirely eradicated, of her own essential will, which the state guaranteed. The husband is her guarantee in relation to the state: he becomes her legal guardian; he controls all aspects of her public life; all that is left to her is her life in the home.[12]

The crudity of this allegedly natural domination—necessary for the Christian in him—must be moderated somewhat. Fichte does this by claiming that this domination and natural representation is the married woman's own will. The ideal fusion of female and male wills that Fichte constructed is the absolute dominance of the male will. Fichte allowed women to exert influence on history only through their husbands.

> The women actually practice their franchise in public affairs indirectly, as they are not able to will this without compromising their feminine dignity, but only through the reasonable influence which they have on their husbands through the marriage bond. (The history of all major national changes proves this. Either they derived from women or they were directed and considerably modified by them.)[13]

The results of this loss of identity became apparent in a series of thirty-six famous trials. Many women were subjected to brutal treatment by their husbands; they were betrayed, repudiated, and robbed of children and their property, so to speak, was confiscated by their husbands on the legal grounds of the marriage law. Yet only one woman, the Countess Sophie von Hatzfeld, attempted to defend herself. No historian would have mentioned her if she hadn't eventually found as her attorney a young Jew, gifted at rhetoric, who later became the leader of workers in Germany: Ferdinand Lassalle. In other words, it was not her female destiny, typical of her time, but her union with a famous man that turned her into a historical figure. Golo Mann paints their alliance as an ominous society scandal, and she as a femme fatale: Lassalle "sacrificed years to this peculiar business and spent at least as much energy on it as on politics." The phrase "peculiar business" clearly shows the conservative, patriarchal-tinted world of a historian who will not recognize the larger social and political ramifications intimated in the divorce trial. In his appraisal of Lassalle's role in the Hatzfeld trials, Mann has a famous predecessor, Karl Marx, who, in a letter to Engels, disparagingly judged Lassalle's conduct in this affair: "As if a truly significant person would give up ten years of his life to such a trifle."[14] Mann's statement, and thinking, is more unforgivable, for, unlike Marx, Mann lived at a time when West Germany's constitution guaranteed equality of the sexes.

As a fifteen-year-old, Hedwig Dohm secretly read the rebel poems of Georg Herwegh. During the revolution of 1848 she looked into the eyes of the dead soldier and became a "democrat" and "blood-red revolutionary." Women took part in this revolution, not only at its outbreak, but also in its genesis. The first writings of Luise Otto (the Saxon democrat and militant of 1848)—including a novel entitled *Ludwig der Kellner*—had to be published under the male pseudonym "Otto Stern." Her second novel, *Schloss und Fabrik,* which she wrote under

her own name, was confiscated by the authorities. By means of a
meeting with an official, it was cleared, but to the astounded official
she declared: "Your excellency, I am on principle an opponent of censorship." Her newspaper, the first political women's newspaper in
Germany appearing regularly, was constantly confiscated. As a result
of being interrogated, having her house searched, and being expelled
from or detained in various cities which she was passing through,
Luise Otto found it almost impossible to do her work. The first edition
of the women's newspaper, issued on April 21, 1849, began with a political program:

> The history of all time, and of today most particularly, teaches
> that those who forget to think of themselves will be forgotten!
> . . . In the midst of the great revolution in which all of us find
> ourselves, women are going to find themselves forgotten if they
> forget to think of themselves![15]

These were not merely the lofty freedom phrases found in the
lines of many national poets: behind the words stand immediate political goals—first and foremost, improved working conditions for women
in Saxony. Yet, two years after the revolution, the politicization of
German women was legally called to a halt and their political association made impossible. Minna Cauer:

> For whom is the better age not dawning? In 1850 a law was issued
> on public organization and assembly that read (in clause 8): "No
> female persons may participate in organizations which assemble
> for the purpose of debating political subjects." There was no place
> in the German Fatherland for women. Not a word, not one sen-
> tence, through all the fights and struggles of these decades, urged
> that women be counted as people and citizens of this state—not
> one word; not even from the most noble and best representatives
> of the bourgeoisie.[16]

This law also specified that only men were allowed to publish
periodicals, even women's papers.[17]

In this first attempt in Germany at revolution, in the dream of the
citizens' republic, the contradictions that sever committed women and
sisters-in-arms from the male supporters of the democratic principle
become clear for the first time. Just as women joined the national
cause and advanced to the barricades, they found scarcely an echo of
support among the democrats and Leftists. Renate Möhrmann, author
of a study in literary sociology on literary emancipation attempts by
women prior to the revolution of 1848, writes:

> The same men who proclaim the liberation of the fourth estate,
> of slaves, and of Jews, who inveigh against every form of oppres-

sion and act as attorneys for all humanity, who call themselves Johannes Scherr democrats and leftists, these same men assail the first public steps of women with nothing but ridicule and scorn. Like the most sinister reactionary, Scherr storms against the "taste and shamelessness of the new mothers who wish to extend their traditional rights."

"You could swear," Scherr says, in his reflections on the year 1848,

> that the contingent of women, who, without authorization, were milling about in public, consisted either of hideous and hysterical old virgins—for whom it may be a case of physiological deformity —or of slovenly housewives and negligent mothers whose household accounts, if they keep them at all, are in disarray, whose rooms, kitchens, dining rooms, and linen closets are in topsy-turvy order, whose millinery bills are large but unpaid, and whose children are physically and morally unwashed.[18]

To this Minna Cauer posed a key question that must still be obvious even to a historian today: "if the German bourgeoisie was struggling for the creation of an equitable state, why were the women and the working classes forgotten in the process? This question can be answered only with the charge that the German bourgeoisie did not do its duty . . ."[19]

A later author, Gisela von Streitberg, also made a negative appraisal of the second great national event of the nineteenth century, the founding of the German empire:

> What did women win by the establishment of a united German empire? Absolutely nothing. The social position of woman has since remained unchanged; women's views are not taken into account, their interests are always regarded as being of lesser importance, as they are second-class subjects of the state.[20]

In a section on Bismarck Golo Mann wrote: "He always preserved his personal sphere despite the publicity: a cozy family life." Cozy and preeminently patriarchal.

Bismarck writes to his sister:

> I'm writing a gala letter of congratulations to you for your—let's see, I believe twenty-fourth birthday. You are now of age, or would be, after all, if you hadn't had the bad luck to belong to the female sex, whose members (in the opinion of the attorneys) remain in the minority even when they are mothers of the sturdiest baby boys. Why this arrangement (despite its seeming unfairness) is wise I shall make clear to you, I hope, in two weeks when I have you before me *à portée de voix humaine.*[21]

Other than Countess Sophie von Hatzfeld, Bismarck's wife, Johanna, is the only German woman mentioned in Golo Mann's history of the nineteenth century. (She is given the title of consort.) Golo Mann writes of Bismarck's more appealing qualities:

> His relationship to his wife is splendid even though Johanna von Bismarck does not appear to have been any shining intellect. Such private traits distinguish him from Napoleon as well as from Lenin, the two other political giants with whom he is liable to be compared.[22]

Aside from the fact that the quality of Lenin's relationship to his companion Krupskaya may have been essentially different from that of Bismarck to Johanna, one wonders why Bismarck would spend his life with a woman with little intellect and why she and the Countess von Hatzfeld are the only women of importance in the nineteenth century. What kind of historian would record approvingly the splendid relationship of a statesman and his wife and yet ignore the important women of his country? During the time of Bismarck's reign women were more persecuted and politically oppressed than in any other comparably developed country. The first associations of women workers, which never had contact with the Social Democratic Party, were brutally broken up by the police, although their only political acts consisted of petitioning for admission of women to industrial councils.

> Bismarck never did the slightest bit to elevate and change the social position of women; this was beyond his thinking. Woman existed for him only in the sole relationship in which she exists for all men without exception: as a creature created for man, destined to let her life merge into his.[23]

Thus, if Golo Mann's history of Germans is integrated into the general tradition of historiography, his style of presentation is not especially misogynistic in terms of other historians' works—it contains no stronger invectives against women than do works of nineteenth-century historians.

In its own way, Bruno Gebhardt's *Handbuch der Deutschen Geschichte* is certainly no less important an opinionmaker than the books by Golo Mann. First published in 1891, it has since gone through nine editions and influenced the sense of history of generations of German historians. The publisher's foreword to the ninth edition says (not without a certain pride) that the work "met with favor as a useful tool for the teaching of history in the schools and universities."

In Volume 2 Gebhardt covers the witch hunts with one scant page, without mentioning that the great majority of victims were women. The key sentence of this passage reads:

As a result of gross illegalities, ten thousand people fell victim to this kind of justice, and no age, class, or sex was spared from it: men and women, old and young, peasants and nobility, secular and clerical dignitaries, mayors, chancellors, and canons were accused of witchcraft and killed by fire or sword (children, by opening the arteries, which was considered mild punishment).

Thus, one of the worst chapters in the history of the oppression, torture, and assassination of women becomes an unfortunate mutation—guided from the mysterious depths of the human soul—affecting all in equal degree. Women and their social problems are briefly dealt with if at all, and then only in telegram style.

The anti-feminism of historiography is not unconditionally bound to the sex of the historian: for example, Ricarda Huch, a woman, wrote a classic work of German history, *Der Untergang des Römischen Reiches Deutscher Nation,* which covers up to the end of the eighteenth century. Though in the index of her history book there are a multitude of women's names, they are mainly those of wives, included because marriage signified the alliance of two principalities or empires. In their treatment of women Huch's work and the standard history by Johannes Haller, *Die Epochen der Deutschen Geschichte,* differ only in that Haller mentions Empress Maria Theresa briefly while Ricarda Huch presents a profile:

> Maria Theresa, the last female Hapsburg, resembled her ancestors neither on the surface nor within. Her awareness of her position did not repress her effervescent nature: its current ran a straight course, fresh and strong. On the stage of the great world, in the midst of extremely tangled and fraudulent politics, she spoke the language of a pure, great heart. The letters in which she conveyed requests or appreciation to her generals have the stirring ring of true feeling and yet are full of royal dignity. At the same time she was always completely human and fully a sovereign, since nature created her for this as well.[24]

This stereotyped account stands out in contrast to Ricarda Huch's otherwise fascinating characterizations. Monarchs and politicians are without exception in the middle of extremely tangled and fraudulent politics. In this portrayal Maria Theresa is not depicted as a woman who, perhaps because of her female education, made certain political decisions differently from a man (and this could be substantiated). Rather, since she is a woman, she speaks "the language of a pure, great heart," her letters have "the stirring ring of true feeling," and she is "at the same time . . . always completely human and fully a sovereign." Today, too, we read descriptions of contemporary women politicians who, though committed professionals, are at the same time good mothers.

A history book used today in West German schools describes the Empress:

> Maria Theresa may have been inferior to Frederick the Great in force of intellect, but not in courage or sense of duty. She surpassed him in her feeling for justice and in her unschooled kindness of heart. Through all her work as a reigning monarch she remained the housewife and mother who gave life to sixteen children and a loving wife to her husband. She also interpreted her governing duties as those of the empire's "original and universal mother." Frederick the Great, whom the empress hated all her life, considering him a lawbreaker and robber, admitted: "She brought honor to the throne and to her sex!"[25]

For Ricarda Huch, the Empress embodies the double role of human being and sovereign; in the school-book description, she embodies mother and monarch. Thus, the double role becomes the woman's most important attribute recorded in history.

Ricarda Huch was one of the first German women to receive a doctorate. Nonetheless, she was no champion of women's rights. She had a fascinating talent for relating history, but she did it exclusively from the male's perspective. Of course, in the historiography of her day, this perspective was regarded not as male but as the only admissible and objective one. The paradoxical fact is that, as a woman, she had to fill a historically shaped social role that made it almost impossible for her to formulate history actively—a paradox which was resolved through identification with an aristocratic masculine ideal.

The early-nineteenth-century writer Luise Mühlbach had a female character cry out:

> We have in our government not a single rung, not a single step onto which the female would be able or permitted to climb . . . no single public objective to which the woman could reach up her arms and cry: I will attain you, you shall illumine me and exalt my name! . . . Unfortunate German women, whose only ambition is . . . to go through life unnamed and unknown.[26]

Historians have long been aware of this shortcoming. "Women are rarely shown fighting for anything; their rights have been 'given' to them." This is the gist of a study by Janice Law Trecker on the treatment of women in American high-school history books.[27]

Women played a decisive role in America's history through the second half of the nineteenth century; America had a feminist movement stronger in organization and numbers than that of any European country. Yet, historical accounts devote not much more than marginal comment and footnotes to women. As early as 1922, Arthur M. Schlesinger, Sr., Harvard professor, pleaded for American history to be rewritten and rectified.[28] A few years later he and Dixon Ryan Fox began editing the ambitious twelve-volume series *A History of American Life,* published between 1927 and 1948. He himself wrote one of the two volumes most crucial in assessing the women's movement in America, Volume 10, *The Rise of the City: 1878–1898,* which was first published in 1933.

One chapter entitled "The American Woman" and a series of passages in other chapters concerning the education of women, women's publications, and related themes yield interesting information on woman's life and the conditions of her existence in America during the second half of the nineteenth century, distinguishing this work favorably from its German counterparts. Yet a close examination of the book reveals that Schlesinger falls into the common trap. Information on domestic furnishings and the consumption of candy and chewing gum seems to be linked with the world of women, while the events of world history—wars, national economic developments—were shaped by men. In terms of the historiographical tradition, this chapter works as one of those appendixes of cultural history attached to the general body of history writing.

In some passages Schlesinger sinks to the level of his colleagues. In the last chapter, "Fin de siècle," he deals with neurasthenia, the so-called national disease of Americans around the turn of the century. According to Schlesinger, the fact that women were stricken with particular intensity by such nervous and mental disorders is "undoubtedly the price they had to pay for their ever-increasing participation in activities outside the home." This passage seems to suggest that women would have been spared if, as in previous centuries, they had stayed at home.

> Old notions of family integrity were rudely jarred by the centrifugal forces at work in the home. Outside agencies assumed an ever greater responsibility for the welfare of city children and the nation was startled by the leap in the divorce rate. Yet no finite intelligence could know whether even such changes implied a rise or decline in general ethical standards.[29]

Elsewhere he moralizes even further in commenting on the increase in divorce. Referring to the liberal divorce laws in Nevada, Wyoming, and both Dakotas, he says: "The fruits of the system were scandalous and demoralizing."

> Since twice as many divorces in the period 1878–1898 were granted upon the wife's complaint as on the husband's, it is likely that the increase reflected, in part, a greater self-respect among women and an unwillingness to put up with conditions which their mothers would have accepted in silence.[30]

Here, in the guise of seemingly greater objectivity and depth of research, we see the age-old chain of sexist causality: the progress liberation movements make can never outweigh the guilt these women should feel.

The second volume of this work portrays women in an even worse light. In Allan Nevins's *The Emergence of Modern America,* which deals with the period from 1865 to 1878, there are only a number of disparate, marginal comments which introduce women merely as an arabesque in human history. This is especially evident in the chapter called "Recovery in South and West":

> The freedom of the West offered women new careers and broadened activities, and because women were so badly needed, they attained a new dignity in the social scale. So great was the demand for a feminine element in the Pacific Northwest that a whole shipload of women was sent from New York . . .
>
> Women were "objects of a sort of crude, fierce worship," and were treated not merely as man's equals but "as a strange and costly creation," whose whim ought to be law.[31]

Here the role of woman as precious cult object, not as a subject of history, but as a rare commodity in the Wild West, is presented as something fundamentally more valuable than equality with men.

If women are treated this badly in a fairly large work of history, then it is not surprising if their role in brief presentations is atrophied to a pure shadow existence. Two sentences in the much read *A Pocket History of the United States,* written by Allan Nevins and Henry Steele Commager, characterize the spirit of this history: "This last 'frontier,' like earlier frontiers, was resolutely democratic. Most of the new communities introduced some form of woman suffrage . . ." Resolute democracy is not achieved simply with women winning the same franchise as men; according to Nevins and Commager, it was sufficient to institute "some form of" suffrage. More examples could be discussed, but only one more need be presented. Aileen S. Kraditor, in discussing Ralph Gabriel's *The Course of American Democratic Thought* in which the women's rights movement is not mentioned at all, says: "The seventy-year-old struggle for woman suffrage obviously contributed nothing to the development of American democratic thought."[32]

And so the vicious circle comes to a close in the textbooks. What Janice Trecker says of women's university study also follows for historiography in general:

> The facts that women literally fought their way into colleges and universities, that their admission followed agitation by determined would-be students, and that they were treated as subservient to male students even at such pioneering institutions as Oberlin, are always absent.[33]

The traditional image of woman in history continues:

Even in discussions of reform movements, abolition, labor—areas in which there were articulate and able women leaders—only men are quoted. Even such topics as the life of frontier women are told through the reminiscences of men. When they are included, their profiles and capsule biographies are often introduced in separate sections, apart from the body of the text. While this may simply be a consequence of attempts to update the text without resetting the book, it tends to reinforce the idea that women of note are, after all, optional and supplementary.[34]

Nor is the history writing of European countries any less ignorant of the role of women. In a ten-volume standard work of French history by Ernest Lavisse[35] neither the women's march to Versailles nor the female citizens' manifesto of Olympe de Gouges is mentioned. The universal suffrage in connection with various constitutional projects that he discusses pertains solely to universal suffrage for men. Charlotte Corday, the murderer of Marat, the tyrant of the revolution, is barely mentioned. Madame Roland does not fare much better. According to Lavisse, women were unimportant in the French Revolution.

One of the most widely accepted accounts of French history is *The Evolution of the French People* by Charles Seignobos. The female image conveyed here may be seen in the following quotation, which concerns the gallantry of court life during the twelfth century.

This fashion gave rise to the conventions of gallantry, which became a necessary part of the social equipment of a nobleman. They consisted in the affectation of treating ladies as superior beings, surrounding them with marks of outward respect, kissing their hands, bowing before them, yielding them the place of honour, and giving precedence to them in social assemblies.

This new fashion in manners revolutionized the outward relations between the sexes, which in all countries up to that time had been based upon the precedence of men and the inferior rank of women.[36]

Here one is given the impression that the emancipation of woman was attained back in the Middle Ages. Seignobos does not mention later liberation efforts during the French Revolution or the nineteenth century. That the author carries dichotomous sexual stereotypes to the point of the insufferable is demonstrated with particular clarity in the following quote:

The piety of women was nurtured by reading new devotional works composed for believing Catholics. It was exalted by the practice of prolonged meditation on religious subjects, known as *oraison,* which sometimes reached the pitch of ecstasy. Through women the religious life of France now became permeated with a warmth of loving aspiration which lent French Catholicism a gentle and tender character, more in accordance with the natural instincts of simple souls than the austerity of the Middle Ages had been.

Masculine piety remained more severe in character and did not entirely abandon the ancient practices of mortification of the flesh, fasting, the hair shirt, and even flagellation . . .[37]

When history is written this way, women are nothing more than suffering subjects of male enterprise. The women's "Republican Clubs" of the French Revolution, led and organized by the courageous Rosa Lacombe and the Dutchwoman Etta Palm d'Aelders, like the "Amazon legions" of this period, were returned to "total oblivion." Not even the participation of Frenchwomen in the 1848 revolution, their demands, their efforts to found food cooperatives, their two-fronted battle against the bourgeois reactionaries and the anti-feminism of the proletarian organizations influenced by Pierre Proudhon, or their military participation in the insurrection with the Paris Commune of 1871 (which earned them the name "pétroleuses") are found in the official histories.

The twelve-volume *New Cambridge Modern History* constitutes an exception, to some extent. The chapter entitled "Education" in Volume 2, for example, deals in detail with the problem of girls' education in different countries,[38] covering Germany far more extensively than does Gebhardt's *Handbuch*. Volume 9 includes assessments of the early socialist Flora Tristan and of Olympe de Gouges, neither of whom are included in French history books.[39] Flora Tristan was the first to point out the inaccurate ambiguity of the word *"peuple"* to mean males. In her "Declaration of the Rights of the Woman and Citizen," Olympe de Gouges said that if she has the right to walk the scaffold and fall victim to the Jacobin terror, she must also have the right to mount the speaker's platform.

The *New Cambridge Modern History* includes a discussion of Mary Wollstonecraft's *Vindication of the Rights of Women,* the first comprehensive appeal for woman's equal rights. Issued in 1792, the appeal advocated equal educational opportunity and even coeducation. As with *A History of American Life,* however, these passages are not related to discussions of social issues but are included in a chapter covering literature and ideas. The women's question is presented purely as a problem of fringe groups; the introduction to Volume 2 states that by 1900 the wages of the skilled laborers in Great Britain were already twice as high as those of the unskilled workers. However, the root of the matter—sex discrimination—is not mentioned.

These were years in which the living standard improved, in which gradually it became less necessary to send the children to work, it gradually became less necessary for married women to earn

wages, and gradually became possible to increase leisure time and
shorten working hours.[40]

Thus on the whole, original research in women's history has been
neglected by historians in all countries, and to some extent has been
suppressed systematically.

In a further attempt to defame the emancipation movements of
women, much historiography states that the decline of the state begins
in an age when women demand their rights. Theodor Mommsen, who
received the Nobel Prize for Literature in 1902, believed that the
Roman household, with the omnipotence of the *paterfamilias,* was the
pinnacle in the evolution of family law. "Nothing appeals to the
Roman like the simple but inevitable realization of the legal relationships designed by Nature herself."[41]

The fall of Rome begins with the rise of women's independence.

So begins the emancipation of women. According to old custom
the married woman is by law subject to the control of her husband,
whose authority was equal to that of the father, and the unmarried
female is under the guardianship of her next male relative, who
yielded little of the paternal power. The married woman did not
have assets of her own, and the fatherless maiden and the widow
were not permitted to manage their own funds. But now the
women begin working for the right to dispose of their own income,
in part by devious legal means—especially entering into the fa-
çade of marriage, and thereby releasing themselves from guardianship by their father in order to manage their own property—
in part, in a not much more effective fashion, by divesting marriage of its rigorous legal requirements of the husband's authority
... But in public affairs as well the women's will, and opportunity,
as Cato believed, "to rule the world's rulers" was growing; the
citizen assembly sensed their influence. In the provinces statues
of Roman women had already been erected. Opulence mounted in
dress, ornamentation, and appliances in buildings and in cookery,
especially since the expedition to Asia Minor in the year 190, Asiat-
ic-Hellenic luxury, as it ruled in Ephesos and Alexandria—all this
transmitted to Rome its empty refinement and mercenariness,
corrupting money, time and pleasure. Here, the women were the
cause . . .[42]

Like Mommsen, sociologist Vilfredo Pareto, the Italian "Marx of
the bourgeoisie," expounded on the emergence of women's movements, which he identified with the appearance of wealth:

Among the very poor peoples the woman is treated with less consideration than the housepets; among the civilized peoples (especially among the very rich population of the United States of

America) she has become a luxury object that consumes without producing. Obviously, in order for anything of this sort to be possible, the wealth of the country must be very great. These living conditions affect morals immediately. Feminism is a disease that can occur only among rich people or among the rich portion of a poor people. With the increase of wealth in ancient Rome women's lives grew more depraved. If modern women did not have the money necessary to place their idleness and greed on exhibition, the gynecologists wouldn't be so busy.[43]

When women are portrayed as having political interests, they usually become the instigators of evil events. The Christian historian Arnold J. Toynbee writes in his world history:

> In the heroic age the major catastrophes are usually the work of women, even if the role of women is allegedly passive . . . More commonly: women are the notorious mischiefmakers whose malice drives heroes to kill one another. The legendary clash between Brunhild and Krimhild, which finally ended in the bloodbath in Etzel's hall on the Danube, is part of the authentic events of the battle between the historical Brunhild and her enemy Fredegundis, which cost the Merovingian state succeeding the Roman Empire forty years of civil war.

In Toynbee's view, the heroic age is an interregnum between a primitive state of affairs and a newly emergent culture or higher religion.

> In this transitional state a social vacuum is created in an individualism so absolute that it goes beyond the intrinsic differences between the sexes. It is noteworthy to see this unbridled individualism bear fruit, which scarcely differ from those of a doctrinaire feminism, completely beyond the emotional range and intellectual horizon of the women and men of such a period.

Toynbee's judgment of the unhealthy influence of women, upon whom he inflicts the names Brunhild and Fredegundis, is based on slight and fragmented knowledge of both these women and their motives. At will he scrambles the dice of myth and history. According to him, "we may believe that the pillage of Troy was brought about by the gratification of Paris's longing for Helen."[44]

Just as, according to Toynbee, the major catastrophes are the handiwork of women, so too is there comparable danger developing through women's movements. Catastrophes such as a forty-year civil war, in other words, occur when the intrinsic differences between the sexes are blurred.

Women should exert influence not through their acts or ideas but through their feminine vibrations, in the terms of the Spaniard José Ortega y Gasset, who wrote an essay on the influence of women upon history:

> Incredibly, many people are blind enough to believe that, through the franchise and doctor's degrees, the woman might have an effect on world history as lasting as that which she already exercises through her magic powers to bewitch.[45]

These "feminine vibrations" are echoed in a keynote speech, which Theodor Mommsen delivered at the Berlin Academy of Sciences on March 23, 1876, in honor of the one hundredth anniversary of the Prussian Queen Luise's birthday:

> It was demanded that, through the magic of her personality, she subdue this man—the conqueror of her people, the blasphemer of her honor—and win from him mitigation for the defenseless Prussians at his mercy . . . Luise considered it her duty as the queen to sacrifice even what a woman cannot and may not sacrifice, and for this effort her name stands noted in the annals of that year. She did not enjoy any reigning powers. Not her deeds, but her essence and soul and, one can add, her love and passion, have fixed her memory in the heart of the people.[46]

Mommsen portrayed the Prussian Queen in the style of a women's novel à la Hedwig Courths-Mahler. By love, passion, and self-sacrifice the woman can gain a foothold on the lowest rung of history; not so, however, if she has entered into government business. The Prussian Queen, Mommsen naturally neglects to tell us, would scarcely have had the opportunity to be politically active, since her schooling was interrupted, like that of the majority of women of her time. The political rules of the game, the basic fundamentals of government business, were no more familiar to her than historical events or foreign words:

> Childishly she asks in her correspondence to her old friend, defense councillor Scheffner, what is actually meant by "hierarchy" and when the Greek uprisings and Punic Wars were; "however, if one does not ask," she continues, "and feels ashamed of one's naïveté in front of everyone else, one remains stupid forever, and I hate stupidity."[47]

Even the typically feminine love of peace can keep important men from performing feats worthy of world history. Time and again, Bismarck suspects ladies of the court—especially the Queen—of nearly keeping him out of his great empire-uniting war against France. In his reminiscences Bismarck writes of the sovereign:

He was seventy-three years old, peace-loving, and disinclined to risk the laurels of 1866 in a new battle; yet were he free of feminine influence, the sense of honor he felt as heir to Frederick the Great and the Prussian officers would always remain crucial for him.

He suspected the Queen of biasing the King against declaring war on France "with the fearfulness entitled to her by gender and her lack of national feeling."

It was told to me that the Queen Augusta, before her departure from Ems to Berlin, had sworn in tears to prevent the war—in memory of Jena and Tilsit. I consider this information plausible except for the tears.[48]

The psychological substructure of history writing has remained the same as in societies with exclusively oral traditions. Myths, the whole treasury of opportunities for identification, are woven by men who are initiated into the tribal secrets. Women are aware of the secrets but are excluded. Thus, the perspective and content of history are defined by men. Without institutions and ceremonies to pass their history along, women are not able to confront their own myths, their own history.

The effect of all this is a constant lack of female role models. The suppression of women's movements in history isolates every woman; there is nothing by which she can orient herself to bring her personal experience into continuity with the past.

A great number of psychological studies popular in the twenties, in which children were asked about their models, show that boys identify more strongly than girls with political leaders of the past or with other historical figures. Historiography thus becomes an agent which, on one hand, produces a closed male solidarity and precludes a female one; and yet, on the other hand, also produces a solidarity among women based on male values. The bombastic patriotism of women who sacrifice themselves or their sons to the fatherland is the result of accepting a national role history's authors have created. The interpretation of history, and the mode of writing it, are always methods of making history. The exclusion of the woman, the systematic deletion of her contribution, is a means of subjugation, depriving her of opportunities to identify with other women, forcing her to identify with males.

Learning history means seeking and finding the forces which, as causes, lead to the effects which we then see before our eyes as historical events . . .

The man who wrote this held the following view of the history teaching he had enjoyed in his high school. The teacher was ostensibly able to implant in even small boys a strong sense of their historical mission:

> What made our fortune all the greater was that this teacher knew how to illuminate the past by examples from the present, and how from the past to draw inferences for the present . . . it was then that I became a little revolutionary. For who could have studied German history under such a teacher without becoming an enemy of the state which, through its ruling house, exerted so disastrous an influence on the destinies of the nation?[49]

These quotations from Adolf Hitler's *Mein Kampf* are striking evidence of the degree to which the intermediary of history functions as a political stimulant. As long as historiography unilaterally provides for identification with male hero and leader roles, it will remain the instrument of patriarchal propaganda, teaching little boys to subdue and destroy the world of which, they feel, they are the sole owners.

3 / The Woman Cult and National Sentiment

German women, German trust,
German wine and German song
in the world shall go on sounding
out their lovely olden strains,
us to noble deed inspire
ever through our whole life long . . .
—*Hoffmann von Fallersleben*

A characteristic feature of nationalist thought found in the most diverse cultures is the symbolization of people and country in a mother's, or woman's, embrace. Even the nationally minded prophets of the Old Testament roused Israel by comparing the people with a woman: the "daughter of Zion" or the "maiden Jerusalem" who is "fallen" (Amos) or who acts like a whore in the presence of Jehovah, should be dissuaded from her infidelity. Assimilation into alien cultures, collaboration with the enemy, the worship of foreign gods, and adoption of foreign customs are equated by the Jewish prophets with whoredom and a lack of sexual restraint.

The image of woman that the nationalist projects of people and state presents a different stereotype. De Gaulle, for example, spoke of La France as his "princess." This evokes a chivalric idea of submission to the wishes of the woman that has its roots in Romance traditions, in which the capricious, eccentric woman, with the secretive aura of illogic, is adored. The worship of woman is a part of the Romance style of women's oppression. Even African poets compare their country to a woman. In many poems Léopold Senghor compares Africa with a queen, or he speaks of Africa as "a pitiable princess in agony."[1]

The idealized image of a woman's eternal traits and qualities is a medium through which to express or produce the solidarity and unity of male groups. They need a female to symbolize what they are fighting, or a woman whose defilement and dishonor they can avenge as the Jews did their foreign rulers. The creators of national identity maintain a metaphoric-sexual relationship with their country and people.

Germania, the allegorical female figure personifying Germany, is part of the national symbolism that was to convey to Germans of the nineteenth century the sense of their unity and greatness. In German patriotism, women, as national cult objects, play a role that is far more important than, and also different from, that in other European countries. The role's origins were presented in Germania by the conservative Roman historian Tacitus. In Germany one of the most effective weapons in the fight against the ideas of women's liberation was the ever-recurring allegation that the German man treated his woman better than did the men of other peoples and nations. The old Teuton had supposedly respected his wife as the companion and sacred keeper of the flock, the mother of his children. He had followed her wise, womanly advice, which she, as priestess or prophetess, conferred upon him. The Teutons had been the first to view the woman not only as property and slave, as did other barbaric or civilized peoples, but with respect. Nor did Johann Gottfried Herder forget to give the old Teutons due praise, contrasting them to the brutal races and barbarians:

> The old German, even in his rugged forests, recognized the noble quality of the woman and enjoyed in her the loveliest attributes of her sex: prudence, fidelity, courage, and modesty; indeed, even her atmosphere, her genetic character, her whole way of life. He and his wife grew, like the oaks: slow, indestructible, powerful; the charm of seduction is lacking in his country . . .

Urgently he appealed to female contemporaries to render themselves worthy of the German woman's history:

> Daughter of Germania, feel the glory of your primeval mother and apply yourself with zeal to it. Among few peoples does history laud what it commends in you; among few peoples has the man esteemed the virtue of the woman seen in ancient Germania. The women of most nations are slaves; your mothers were advice-giving friends, and every noble woman among you still is.[2]

In addition to Herder, German philologist and folklorist Jakob Grimm produced a scholarly basis for the national woman cult through the explication of the Germanic and Icelandic sources. Among barbarian peoples German women were supposed to have been priestesses and prophetesses able to interpret oracles.

In the German view, utterances of destiny appear to gain greater sanctity in the mouths of women; prophecy and magic in the good as well as the evil sense are the special gift of women . . .[3]

The fact that a wide-ranging and painstaking scholar like Jakob Grimm held such an uncritical stance toward the ethnographic digression of Tacitus on German men and their women may have reflected his own problematical mother relationship. The prominent scholar painted a picture of woman whose contradictions must have been obvious to any scientific thinker. The Germanic woman appeared as prophetess, enchantress, and priestess of sacrificial offering, yet, although Grimm knew very well she had practically no rights, he still believed that she exerted a "significant influence on the people." Tacitus—who elsewhere in his history thunders out against shameless hussies, rabble, and women who meddle in the business of war—wanted to preach a morality sermon to the Romans, who in his view were effete and corrupt, outlining an alternative program for a pure, strong, uncorrupted people of nature. In the eighteenth century, philosopher Jean Jacques Rousseau, among others, wrote about the natural South Sea islander:

Nature builds their bodies strong, gives them moral powers, lets the talent they deserve by birth emerge in them. The fertile Poseidonic mind is rendered with the tendentiousness of a Tacitus: The attitude of surreptitious hostility to culture makes possible passing shots at the Romans, their old wives' ways, their effeminacy, their early moral depravity. The sketch of German circumstances is not important here, the only thing important is the opposite image of the Roman circumstances.[4]

Just as Tacitus wrote polemics against the liberation endeavors of the women and certain minorities in ancient Rome, the German Romantics and their successors, who reveled in nationalist ideas, later used Tacitus' pamphlet as a tool of struggle against the civil rights demands and emancipation efforts of German women. In 1974, Reinhard Bruder came to the conclusion that "none of the evidence studied was able to prove that Germanic women had an effect on public affairs, that their position was respected, or that they served in an intermediary function between gods and humans."[5]

Bruder also clears away another cliché that evolved from the Tacitus reading: that the brave German man went to any extreme to protect wife and child because marriage and the family were so sacred. Wife and children were considered negotiable property. In bad times, when the Germans were conquered by the Romans, men sold the Romans their wives:

It seems to me . . . no longer possible to maintain the view expressed by Tacitus and his Germanistic interpreters concerning the high regard for the women in relation to the position of hostages and slaves. Certainly, the German man is reluctant to part with his women and daughters, but not on account of their talents and personalities, but because he loses with them his most precious and well-protected property.[6]

In the nineteenth century, Wilhelm Heinrich Riehl compared the Germanic woman favorably not only to Oriental women but also to Greek women. He wrote:

The women of the Orient and of classical antiquity wander about as in a dream world; only the man works. The German men were the first in the Western world who believed in the dignity of women and respect toward women.

There was nothing emancipated or "mannish" about the German woman:

It is one of the most significant cultural historical aspects of the German people, as the most family-oriented, that the goddesses of the German Olympus are thought of as only divine mothers of the household. Where the Greek goddesses wield the spear, the German woman wields the distaff.

Only with the entry of the German people into world history, do the women become truly free and individual; the full consciousness of profession and position of man and wife was first kindled brightly by the Germans.

According to Riehl, the Germans' taste for the dignity of the woman and the sanctity of the family is "a divine inborn gift." The German people understand the true idea of the place of the two sexes, conveyed here from its primeval home in obscure Asia, like an heirloom from the lost paradise. Only the synthesis of Germanhood and Christianity could substantiate the cultural pinnacle of the relationship of the sexes. "To the German mind, the opposition of the sexes became one of the granite pillars on which the great epoch of the new Christian-German cultural life was based,"[7] and "one of the granite pillars" of National Socialism.

Bad but nationalistic poets such as Hoffmann von Fallersleben placed German women alongside such national virtues and treasures as "German trust, German wine and German song." Bismarck saw "in the domestic tradition of the German woman and mother a more solid guarantee for our future than in any bastion of our for-tification."[8] He said this in Kissingen in 1892, twice politely begging the ladies' pardon for speaking of political matters in their presence.

Contemporary authors spoke of Bismarck in the same terms that proponents of National Socialism used for the Führer a half century later. In a brochure entitled "Bismarck and Women," Berlin author Adolf Kohut wrote:

> The German women, past and present, celebrate in the sovereign Bismarck not only the immortal statesman, the renown of Germany, the perfection of German chivalry, but also the protector and guardian of the beloved domestic hearth and the model of German moral purity.[9]

Kohut, the propagandist of Germanic manhood, portrays Bismarck as an Aryan angel of innocence who "never had Gallic liaisons, flirtations, relationships, or any other euphemism customarily applied to the moral transgressions." Gisela von Streitberg ridicules such moral glorification:

> Certainly there was a time in his youth when even he, like other German lads, sowed his wild oats. Germanic moral purity requires this kind of transitional period as due preparation for the state of holy matrimony. When he proposed to Johanna von Puttkamer, her father refused to accept the "crazy Bismarck" as son-in-law since he had created such a scandal among old ladies and gentlemen . . .[10]

Not only the radical women's emancipationists, but the Social Democratic Party, which supported the women's franchise and equal rights in employment, was charged with the alleged decline of German family life. In the Brandenburg provincial diet, the Kaiser told the Social Democrats:

> We shall not fail to liberate our land from this pestilence [the threat of revolution], which not only ravages our people, but also aspires to undermine the most sacred thing we Germans know, the rank of woman.[11]

Reinhold Bruder summarizes, aggressively opposing the statements by Tacitus on the conduct of the German woman:

> The women following the events of the war are free of anxiety and fear about its outcome. While the man wields the weapons, bringing his trained body into action with the utmost courage, the woman constitutes a kind of spiritual background, from which the man continuously renews his powers. The men's battle surges

back and forth; the conviction of the women remains unshakably firm. The men's feats become possible through the spirit of the women. This is the imposing and grandiose image of the German woman that Tacitus projects.[12]

At the outbreak of the First World War it became clear that a great portion of the bourgeois women's movement identified with this chauvinistic image of women derived from Tacitus. The magazine *Frauenkapital,* founded in Berlin two years before the war, emerged as a reservoir of popular sentiment on women couched in unbearable, blood-curdling lyricism. Again and again the conservative-reactionary authors conjured up the image of the Germanic woman who had climbed the barricades of chariots and cheered on the combatants.

> Think of our heroic mothers in the age when Germania joined world history—the peace was disrupted by rapacious invading hordes. Man, accustomed to battle and hunt, clasps the spear; the soil-tilling, herd-keeping woman mounts the wagon barricade, restoring the warriors, goading and urging them on against the enemy when a suddenly rising fear of the far superior enemy tried to drive them back.

The first year of the war saw a women's reserve corps drawn from the bourgeois women's movement. It was teeming with "young Teutonesses" who extended their arms, clenched their fists, and insisted on joining in—"pure German blood, the vital effluence of the primeval mother of our people." Instead of destroying the patriarchal culture's image of the female, these women epitomized it. Prophetically, Marie Raschke said in her appeal for a women's reserve corps: "No woman on earth loves her fatherland so ardently as do the daughters of Germany!"

Thus, true to Tacitus, she paints the picture of the German woman who would rather die than surrender: "Valkyrie soul, German pride suffers no servitude. When iron will urges on the invincible, immortal component of German blood" even a weak female body accomplishes the heroic, the superhuman.

> You will not employ underhanded cunning in aiming weapons at those conquered or in your role as conquering enemy. You will use the weapons when the watch demands it. You will stand on the barricades in a fashion similar to that of our ancestors.[13]

In a story entitled "Germania," a German woman becomes the revelation of a fatherland vision for a fading warrior.

> A song of defiance surges forth. The watch on the Rhine . . . Raw soldiers' gullets, soft women's voices . . . A blonde girl, grown tall,

takes the helm . . . Soldiers strap the knapsack on her back, put a rifle in her hand, on its path are roses gleaming . . . It is as if she were growing. Her figure becomes powerful, her attributes grow large; through the heavy seriousness of her eyes flashes godlike fire. "Germania!" A hundred, five hundred pairs of lips have called it out, the symbol of the hour is found. "Hail, Germania!" Throughout this quarter of the city the anthem rolls: "Deutschland, Deutschland über alles, über alles in der Welt!"

This Germania becomes the focal point of a sado-masochistic hero cult. The soldier, who fights in the battle, imagines that on his return he becomes the creator of an oversized bronze monument meant to represent Germania.

Germania, the redeemed one, the trustworthy, helmeted goddess, upon your altar, palms of peace dipping, a counterpart to the monument from the Niederwald will rise up as a memory to the conflagration of 1914 on the banks of the Rhine, on the heights of the Baskenwald—and he will become the creator of this people's monument . . . Mammoth, larger than life . . . Surrounded by an image of God, a breath of eternity, menacing in glory against the enemy, but embracing the son of the homeland with the woman's undying mercy.

He thinks of his bride, whom he wishes to exalt: For thee, for thee! As thou art more than the love of other soldiers—thou art Germania, the spirit of the holy fatherland become visible in a pledge.

And if I return home, thou willst wait for me. Still I know thee not. And know, yet, who thou art. As thou wert, before I saw the light of this earth, Mother Germania—stern and benevolent lady!

When this hero is hit by a French bullet, "he cries with twisted mouth, 'Hurrah, Germania!' "[14]

The seamy side of the cult of German women reveals inflammatory slogans against women liberating themselves or writing; the sexism acquires racist qualities. In the years before the revolution of 1848 some women in Berlin—including the wife of the young Hegelian Max Stirner ("St. Max," as Karl Marx titled him in his famous pamphlet)—began to wear trousers and smoke in public. Rather than stay at home evenings these women went out with their lovers and husbands to cafés to talk and drink champagne, behavior which was looked down upon. They were influenced by the ideas of George Sand on marriage, socialism, and free love; when some of them publicly declared themselves atheists, the Prussian authorities deported the writer Luise Aston. Women who wore trousers were for years subjects for cartoons in the newspapers of Vienna, Paris, and Berlin.

However, men like Riehl, who was a member of the Frankfurt parliament, were rabid in their invectives against the "women with German names and French manner" who "showed the whole German public the likes of an emancipated woman, drinking and having scandal with the police."

In such spectacles as Luise Aston we see the fruit of our unwholesome literary developments. Out of hyperfemininity, the woman copies the man, while at the same time showing men how feminine *they* have become. The woman possesses a much more powerful instinct to imitate than the man. He must partially compensate for her lesser creative power. The avidity with which so many literary women devote themselves to imitating precisely the most blasé, most confused, the most utterly worthless poetry of the age, reminds me of the Russian poets and artists, who are also wont to imitate only the sort of West European creations that have been corrupted with a vengeance by the ineluctably depraved culture.

It is very tempting to draw a parallel here between Slavs and women. Slavs are a good-natured, home-loving people, content in self-restraint in just the same kindly way as the women; they sing gladly and well and dance even better, they keep to their fathers' customs and have a good deal of passive courage, all of which is supposedly true of good women. But they lack the self-creating genius for invention and art. This is why they, like women, are great virtuosos at imitation.[15]

The fact that sexism and racism are analogous ideological phenomena was one of the first insights of the American women who fought for the emancipation of slaves and females in the nineteenth century. Riehl, who wanted to write a "natural history of people," represented the majority of the spectrum of German opinion; he transferred a negative stereotype of the Slavic people—as being uncreative, good-natured, but pathological in imitation of that which they could never attain: German originality and inventive genius—to the German women and thereby founded a kind of racist inferiority of the German woman. This viewpoint led to the eradication and stigmatization of the intellectual woman.

Wilhelm Heinrich Riehl was knighted in 1883 for such views. He was professor of political economy and later of cultural history in Munich. His book *Die Familie,* published in 1855, was supposed to be the first sociological study of people in groups. (By 1882 the book had already appeared in its ninth edition.) He believed the foundation of the state was the family and its strict role divisions.

An equally sensational publishing success, founded on the connection between sexism and racism, was Otto Weininger's *Sex and Character.* It came out in 1903, was in its fifth edition by 1905, and in

1947, after the Germans had six million Jews on their conscience, was issued in its eighth edition. This adolescent product of a Jewish philosopher who committed suicide at the age of twenty-three differs from Hitler's anthropology of race only in its impressive stylistic qualities. From a commentary on the fifth edition of his book in *The Documents of Socialism,* edited by Eduard Bernstein (Volume 5, Berlin, 1905):

> Weininger, who basically has not and could not have the faintest notion of the Jewish people, of their longing or of their truly tragic flight—that is, in the proper sense of the term—wants to test the validity of the race spectre on the much-abused Jews. Judaism is a spiritual orientation that is closely allied with that of the woman. There are Aryans who are more Jewish than the Jews ... The Jew who is impregnated with femininity exists in the race. He prefers movable goods ... Despite his special sense for business, the need for property, in its stable form, is foreign to the Jew. "This is related to the fact that the Jews turn to communism in such numbers. Socialism is Aryan; communism, Jewish and Russian." ... Moreover the Jew is alleged to be an enemy of the state ... The Jew recognizes no higher authority above himself. He is supposed to be more lecherous, more lascivious, if also less sexually potent... Pandering was an organic predisposition in the Jew ... In agreement with Chamberlain, Weininger declares the Jew to be irreligious. The Jew is in the most profound sense nothing, because he believes nothing ... The goal of existence consists in the conquest of "The Jew" and "The Woman." All fecundity is merely nauseating; and no human being, if he asks himself honestly, feels it his duty to worry about the continuing existence of the human race.[16]

The popularity of Weininger's writings still lingers. A 1966 guide to the psychology of personality by the Mainz psychology professor Albert Wellek covers Weininger's theses on female attributes.[17]

For Nietzsche, however, the subjugation of the woman was not a result of good-natured Germanic manhood; he recommends that German men follow Oriental models in the treatment of women. The famous passages in *Beyond Good and Evil* were impaled by Hedwig Dohm in her portraits of "Antifeminists":

> One reads there: "Her first and last profession should be to bear children"; and further: "A man with depth can think of the woman only in the oriental way ... he must conceive of the woman as a possession, as lock-and-key property, as something predetermined to bondage ...

Because it is only with sexism that racism is developed into a culture, the racist stereotypes are projected back again onto women as a group, yielding a confusion of the roots of sexism and racism. All the qualities that are ascribed to women in a Christian patriarchal culture—incessant sexual seducibility, childishness, negligible intellectual powers, unoriginality, ample emotional life, and limited self-discipline—have time and again been applied to ethnic minorities as well as to oppressed majorities. The Jews, the Italians, the French, and the Slavs were considered by the Germans to have feminine qualities.

Jewish self-contempt led some Jewish writers in Germany to make statements which helped to lay the groundwork for the racist doctrine of the Third Reich. Inasmuch as, in the estimation of the racists, a woman ranked lower than the Jewish male, qualities regarded as Jewish, such as lust and instability, were applied to all women. Walter Rathenau, of a well-to-do Jewish family, later foreign minister of the Weimar Republic, blames the decline of German family life on the idleness of the feminized man whom the woman

> seduced to superficial play, to a pleasure in things, to a craving for pleasure; rousing the unstable sensuality of the girl that slumbers in every woman, and converting it to the sensuality of a streetwalker, thus killing the soul. He bears the blame that Negroid primeval lusts, tamed through thousands of years, have incited in the life of women of our age, whose shame and destitution will shock descendants.[18]

Intellectual—effeminized or womanly: these qualities describe the influence that (in the view of the national thinkers) women with schooling exert upon men and culture. Riehl stated: "The women are getting into all kinds of male art and science and have consequently made our intellectual life womanly . . ."

At the beginning of World War I, Lily Braun, one of social democracy's most contradictory women's emancipationists, lamented:

> If only the word "Dame" ["lady"] had been the first foreign word to be sacrificed on the altar of the fatherland and the lovely old German word "Weib" ["woman"], on the other hand, would come back into favor again!

And eighteen years later, in a sad fashion, her dream was realized:

> . . . the German culture that is to come will be completely liberated from all the painful manifestations of effeminization of the past and will be expressly masculine in the best sense of the term. All that is womanish will be nipped in the bud; everything feminine, however, will be granted infinite scope.[19]

Among the important components of this German national cult
of women is the notion that the women of other countries have fewer
good qualities, are less attractive, and have no feeling for what it
really means to be a woman. Bismarck's state and the Kaiser's empire attacked the Russian women, the first to have fought their way
into universities. The English women and, until today, the American
women, whose civil rights involvement and feminism have always
been a thorn in the side of German men, offer a larger target. German women should have nothing to do with Russian women nihil-
ists or American women raging for emancipation. On the other
hand, the Swiss socialist Anton Dodel, a professor at the University
of Zürich, told the German women to be thankful to the Russian
women:

> The Russian woman remains the unwavering champion of
> women's rights, of the Western woman as well. This should not be
> forgotten when one day the German institutions of higher learn-
> ing open their doors to the German woman.[20]

Out of the ninety thousand Russian students enrolled by 1914, as many
as 23 percent were women—a proportion reached in West Germany
only long after the Second World War.[21]

A decade earlier Wilhelm Heinrich Riehl was still nursing the
hope that university study would bypass the German women:

> Spectacles such as the Russian women nihilist votes or the spiritu-
> ally kindred Paris citoyennes still strike us Germans, though, as
> being very alien, thank God.

He blamed the emancipation ideas on the influence of socialists
and foreigners:

> A woman who thinks of the equality of her sex with the men must
> have read a great many books. The ideas of "women's emancipa-
> tion" would never occur to a German woman on her own.[22]

An early bit of crushing criticism of the women in the United
States appeared in the *Frauen-Anwalt,* a paper of the moderate
women's movement. The male author was worried that American
ideas might encroach on German women's organizations, such as the
Letteverein.

> I doubt the general superiority of such mannish womanhood com-
> pared to the softer essence of a good German woman . . . What
> makes the spectacle especially repugnant to educated Germans,
> however, is the impudence it shows in bringing everything out
> into the open. It is not enough that the American woman in fact

henpecks her husband when the curtains are drawn—now she wants to meddle and henpeck indiscreetly in public too.[23]

With later authors the anti-Americanism grows sharper. The American woman is, in fact, to blame for Germany's women's movement.

The American women's movement was from the start an emancipation movement and a result of the deterioration of the character of the sex. It was natural that the favored position of the American woman aroused the jealousy and the avarice of certain women's circles of other peoples. American women agitators, who, untiringly, incited their European sisters to demand the same "human rights," were stretching their point.[24]

In the introduction of a 1903 Schopenhauer brochure, printed in an edition of fifty thousand and sold cheaply as a polemic against feminism, the editor, Benedikt Friedländer, wrote:

Indeed, the increasing gynecocracy of the German petticoat government is a deep-seated evil common to the whole white race . . . Leading the march in the feminization process is the United States, which would truly be doing us a favor by tipping over their famous Statue of Liberty into the New York harbor, for the sovereign Yankee people have fallen to the most abusive and ridiculous of all kinds of slavery: submission to their own wives. In second place come England and France; then behind, however—unfortunately, with giant steps—follows Germany, whose rising Americanization, all in all, is proverbial, whose moral corruption is obvious, and whose swiftly increasing feminization is only all too clear to the sharp eye.[25]

A German correspondent in America describes the view of the American:

The despotic domination of the woman in public life has until now been regarded as a special American achievement in which infinite pride was taken, and which distinguished America from allegedly backward Europe with its barbaric androcracy.

The same author was critical that American women "have left a feminist imprint on everything to do with love." The sexism of this article turns into racist ideas on the inferior quality of American artists.

This is my explanation for the absence of truly great, monumental achievements in art: the male brain that performs these achievements elsewhere is castrated in America.

The decline of the American nation cannot be far off.

> The excessive feminism in America is adverse to culture and a national disgrace. What is more, it could threaten the continued existence of the people if America ever had to fight a serious war and were forced to pit effeminate males against an enemy with uncorrupted men.[26]

The kind of anti-feminist counter-explanation which in no country was stated so openly or widely as it was in Germany created an instrument for the immunization of women and men against feminist ideas. This was accomplished primarily by means of its pseudo-Germanic-nationalistic component with its allegation that the Germans (unlike peoples of other ancient cultures) had respected the woman highly. The notion that patriarchal rule in Germany was attached to a special esteem for the woman is indelible. Even today those who are serious about resolving sex roles accept this uncritically.

The connection of racist and sexist stereotypes is certainly a universal phenomenon, but only in Germany did it lead to consequences wherein the "biologically inferior" peoples were exterminated and the women were degraded to child-bearing robots denied any human individuality by the Nazis. Adolf Hitler articulated this quite openly:

> If the earlier programs of the liberal intellectualistic women's movements included many, many points, which originated in so-called intellect, the program of our National Socialist women's movement actually contained only one point, the child.[27]

Part Two
Evolutionism as a
Dead End

4/Johann Jakob Bachofen's Mother Right

The work of Johann Jakob Bachofen must be protected so that the women's rights women (the real enemies of men) do not exploit it for their own purposes.

—*Georges Devereux*

It would make more sense to turn this sentence around. Feminism must be protected from the ideas of an inhibited eroticist who, only because of the inaccessible esotericism and unreadability of his writings, has been turned into a legend for having written a work that served the liberation of women. Moreover, it can be shown that Bachofen's mysticism and mother veneration inspired a number of Fascist writers, thereby damaging the women's cause in a variety of ways. Most of his audience, including scholars, know him only secondhand, through summaries of his findings.

The most important and widely known thesis that Bachofen propounded in *Mother Right* is that an age of women's rule, which he called "gynecocracy," preceded patriarchal rule. A form of sexual relationship existed before this women's rule that Bachofen unappetizingly calls *"Sumpfzeugung"* or swamp generation. Because human beings practiced unregulated sexual intercourse without taboos, a practice repugnant to the woman, women induced a matriarchal era, based on marriage. Though Bachofen never left Europe, he generalized about all cultures, extinct and extant. He believed the sexual conduct of barbaric peoples indiscriminate: they copulated like animals, without inhibition or reserve. Women, however, want marriage, fidelity, security, and stability—thus, according to Bachofen, women are to blame for the invention of marriage.

Friedrich Engels also believed that the woman was the first to be drawn to marital intercourse, for it was sexually less degrading. In his work *The Origin of the Family, Private Property, and the State*, we read:

> Bachofen is also perfectly right when he consistently maintains that the transition from what he calls "hetaerism" or "Sumpf-zeugung" to monogamy was brought about primarily through the women. The more the traditional sexual relations lost the naïve primitive character of forest life, owing to the develop-ment of economic conditions with consequent undermining of the old communism and growing density of the population, the more oppressive and humiliating the women felt them to be, and the greater their longing for the right of chastity, of temporary or permanent marriage with one man only, as a way of release . . . it has never occurred to them, even to this day, to renounce the pleasures of actual group marriage. Only when the women had brought about the transition to pairing marriage were the men able to introduce strict monogamy—though only for women.[1]

When Bachofen developed his theory of mother right, there were already countless travel reports from missionaries and diaries of world travelers who had visited the peoples of North and South Amer-ica and Africa since the sixteenth century. Until then no one realized that these peoples' kinship developed according to rules different from the Europeans'. There was talk of female rule; Christoph Meiners, who planned to write a world history of the female sex and brought out the first volume around 1790, had reported that there were some Negro tribes in which the princesses executed unlimited power. The reports of Herodotus, Strabo, and Diodorus of the Egyptians and other peoples were familiar to educated male contemporaries, almost all of whom had mastered Greek. Bachofen did not view the customs of these people as isolated phenomena but constructed a whole epoch in which the women ruled, because motherhood vested in them an aura of power and glory. At that time the connection between sexual inter-course, procreation, and pregnancy was unknown; the concept of fa-therhood did not yet exist.

Bachofen based his theory of mother right on some passages of the Greek historiographers and travelers who had established that other cultures had a law of succession different from their own, and that daughters had rights of inheritance.[2] Bachofen constructed a law of succession that passed exclusively from the mother to the daughter. He used the Greek myths and heroic legends, especially Heracles' and Achilles' fights with the Amazons, but included no pre-cise facts, documentation, lists of references or evidence. His theory of the beginning of history was a new myth that developed from his own inner turmoil: a tormented relation to his beautiful young mother. The "mother right" meant liberation from this. The detailed phrasing of this theory, its formal expression, its metaphors, and also its idea of motherhood had long since been formulated in the writings of the Romantics. The National Socialist Alfred Bäumler, one of the most ecstatic Bachofen worshippers of the twentieth century, recognized this:

> When in the dim, sublime wilderness of his soul Bachofen found the word "mother," he had unknowingly found the blue flower that the Romantics had been searching for.

All that the Romantics were seeking, desiring, aspiring to, was embraced in the word "mother," for the Romantics were a

> countermovement against the paternal idealism on which Fichte placed far too much stress. They wanted to see the rights of the violated mother, of the Nature Fichte despised . . . restored.[3]

Bachofen confronts the creation myth of the Old Testament with his own: In the Old Testament Eve is made from Adam; in Bachofen's theory man is created from woman. Bachofen's theory fits into Freud's developmental psychology, but as an allegation of natural science in the age of Darwin, it was a ridiculous thesis. Though Bachofen rarely relied on facts, he was not consistent enough to renounce the demands of science. Bachofen wrote:

> woman and man do not appear simultaneously, and are not formed together . . . the woman is formed earlier, the man relates to her as a son; the woman is the given, the man is that which first came into being through her . . . the woman is unchangeable; the man is becoming, and therefore always falling to ruin . . . This is the model and foundation of matriarchy.[4]

> The man emerges from the woman through a wonderful metamorphosis of Nature, repeating itself in the birth of every baby boy.[5]

This incredible miracle of nature exists only for the self-celebration of the son, whose birth is a proper historical event. The issue for Bachofen is not motherhood but the self-definition of a son, and here he reveals his own very graphic boy's dreams.

> From the womb of the woman the man is born, and the mother is astounded by the new phenomenon. For she recognizes in the creation of the son the impregnating force to which she owes her motherhood. With delight her gaze lingers on the form. The man becomes her darling, the he-goat her bearer, the phallus

her constant companion . . . This is the highest expression of matriarchy . . .[6]

The mother knew no man before her son; this is the important "realization" that Bachofen wants to impart.

But the first manifestation of male power on earth is the figure of the son. The father is judged by the son; in the son the existence and nature of male power is first visible.[7]

Only later does the complete fantasy become clear: the son wanted to be his own father. And as his own father he wanted to impregnate his mother, she who cannot get enough of the son's phallus, her constant companion.

And so the son himself becomes husband, and fructifier of the mother, and he himself becomes the father . . . having been the son, he becomes the fructifier of the mother; having been the begotten, he himself becomes the begetter. And always in relation to the same woman—sometimes as mother, sometimes as wife. The son becomes his own father.[8]

This is Bachofen's real message: the son has acquired his all-powerful double role in which he himself becomes the be-all and end-all. Now that the eye of the mother, with unspeakable delight, rests upon her darling, the son-spouse and his magnificent phallus, he can allow her to choose her own husband.

The dominion of the woman begins with her own choosing. The woman does the courting, not the man. The woman gives herself in marriage, she makes the agreement . . . The property law of gynecocracy stems from women's independence.[9]

In such sexual relations as Bachofen describes, there are naturally only the noble, the morally pure, the powerful. The female rule that he contrived did not oppress man or turn him into a henpecked husband, but made him an outright hero.

How can the present-day situation be gauged by those of ancient times, especially those of Germanic peoples? The consciousness of supremacy and aptitude for power purifies body and soul, supplants the base desires and sensations, banishes the sexual excesses and assures the birth force and heroic character.[10]

Such tones appeal only to the sexually inhibited, the Puritans. In the youth of human history people were pure and good and brave, mighty warriors who knew no fear.

Far from precluding warlike bravery, matriarchy vastly encourages it. At all times chivalry has gone hand in hand with the cult of the woman. Courage in battle and the veneration of women have always been qualities of virile, youthful peoples.[11]

He also accounts for the heroic deeds of the Romans by the fact that this "heroic people descend from the Sabine women of quite Amazon appearance." For the Sabines had a definite taste for heroes.

Such women cannot bear any weaklings or glittering libertines. Infidelity, which for the most part has its origin in the contempt of man, remains unknown to such women. For that reason, female rule of any age far from diminishes the men's gallantry . . . and so it becomes increasingly clear that the reputation for joyful prosperity has indeed been rightfully bestowed upon the female-governed peoples of ancient times.[12]

However, female rule also had another dimension: the economic one. The description of the economic relationship of the sexes certainly indicates a naïveté one would not believe possible of the son of a Swiss patrician.

Hunting, warring and pillaging filled the life of the men, keeping them far from the women and children. The family, the cart, the hearth, the slaves were entrusted to the women. And here lay the root of their dominant social position and exclusive claim to inheritance. The son was expected to maintain himself by hunting and warfare. The daughter, excluded from these opportunities, was dependent on the family wealth. She alone inherited; the man had his weapons, his bow and his spear were his livelihood. He acquired wealth for his wife and daughter, not for himself or his male descendants. Thus matriarchy and warlike life are concomitant.[13]

One can assume that his readings on the Spartans fostered these statements; Spartan women of the aristocracy managed the property while their husbands devoted themselves to military service. Bachofen writes:

Effect becomes cause and cause effect. The man's exclusion from all inheritance spurred him on to warlike undertakings; his release from all domestic cares enabled him to maintain himself by distant expeditions of rapine and conquest.[14]

That Bachofen expresses affirmation of the martial life and of the capture of slaves and then in another passage contradicts himself is not surprising in view of his characteristic predilection for the irrational.

> A great number of profound national characteristics reappear with astonishing uniformity in all tribes and states in which life is based on the principle of motherhood . . . The preference for a peaceful form of life, the reputation for technological proficiency and much practical training, an essentially conservative way of thought, a higher degree of religious absorption, heartfelt devotion in the mystery and the hopes of reaching beyond, disinclination to deeds of violence, attachment to democracy in its old simplicity, subordination of the whole way of thinking to the manifestations of natural law . . .[15]

Bachofen did not circulate this story to give women back their history but to oppose contrapuntally the maternal rule of the woman —a material one from a lower stage of development—with the definitive rule of the son. As *"Sumpfzeugung,"* a principle of unspirituality, she must be subdued by the hero sons borne by her. At this point the matriarchy was transformed into a realm of Amazons that battled the new elements of religion men created. The legends of Heracles, Dionysius, and Apollo furnish Bachofen with the material for the conquest of these women, who became Amazons.

> They are defeated not only by the Amazons but also by marital matriarchy. They elevate fatherhood from the hordes of the material to the power of the sun and by this means provide it with the uncorporeal higher nature with which it can achieve lasting superiority over the motherhood that is rooted in the material.[16]

The heroes also achieve an act of sublimation in developing the spiritual principle in the culture, though Bachofen could not specify what form this spiritual endeavor takes in the strong-armed heroes and adversaries of the Amazons, Heracles and Achilles. The issue is, of course, that they are conquered. And expressed in this myth, the issue is even more horrible, for man can only love a woman if he kills and destroys her. Bachofen writes:

> As Penthesilea dies in his arms, Achilles perceives her beauty and is smitten with passion for his defeated foe. Here and in many variants of the same motif the idea is always the same. The woman recognizes the higher strength and beauty of the man and gladly inclines to the victorious hero. Weary of her Amazonian grandeur, which she can sustain only for a short time, she willingly bows down to the man who gives her back her natural vocation. She realizes that not warfare against man but love and fertil-

ity are her calling. Thus she willingly follows him who has redeemed her by his victory.[17]

The message of this passage can no doubt be interpreted only as
a warning. Women are able to resist men for only a short time; they
must be defeated, their death is a certainty.

> She also rouses the love of the man, who only now perceives her
> full beauty, and on account of the mortal wounds, which he him-
> self inflicted, is touched by melancholy sadness. Not strife and
> murder—no, love and marriage should reign between them. The
> woman's natural disposition requires it so.[18]

This is, as Bachofen says further, "the restoration of natural relations."

Even to Heracles, the other conqueror of the Amazons, and to his
superior strength "the woman yields gladly. In the subordination of
love, she now recognizes her true destiny."[19]

According to Bachofen, fatherhood managed to evolve fully
through Heracles. "The greater strength that his feats proclaim manifest the divine spirit of Zeus, and in this alone rest full human
rights."[20]

Since the woman now perceives herself as inferior to the man,
she, the material one, submits gladly to his spiritual principle. Finally
the world is put in order; the story is finished.

> Only now is the true equality of the sexes, the lasting peace be-
> tween them, established: only now is the cosmic law realized
> among humans. The moon eternally follows the sun; by itself it
> does not shine, it borrows all its light from the higher star. So too
> is it with the woman and the man. The material one, like the
> moon, is the woman; the spiritual, like the sun, is the man . . . the
> man's spiritual principle dominates. The woman realizes that she
> must borrow her loveliest luster from him.[21]

It is a part of Bachofen's nonsense that he offers no explanation
of this spiritual principle. However, the high point in *Myth, Religion,
and Mother Right* is a legendary confrontation he describes between
Alexander the Great and the Meroëtic Queen Candace. Candace is
confronted by Alexander's "higher intelligence."

> First an adversary, she finally appears to be a spirited supporter
> of the king, whom she has brought up unharmed, and whom she
> herself wanted for a son. However, now it is not the magnificence
> of the man's phallus, but his spiritual splendor which elicits admi-
> ration and affection. In wisdom the king and the queen compete:
> the man's final victory rests in his spirituality. The woman is

pleased at the higher light . . . the woman brings death; the man conquers it through the spirit.[22]

Thus, according to Bachofen the man: "elevated the sex life of woman out of the swamps of impure matter and ruin, across the path of light, to a higher physical existence."[23]

Aside from all the untraceable references and enigmatic Greek or Latin quotations containing no concrete evidence for his theory of matriarchy, there is only one example from literature that supports Bachofen's thesis of the decline of mother right. This is the famous passage from Aeschylus' *Orestes,* on the myth of Clytemnestra's murder of her husband and of the revenge of her son, Orestes, upon his mother. The myth is well known. Agamemnon, the husband of Clytemnestra, has sacrificed his daughter Iphigenia to appease the rage of Poseidon, who stilled his wind and kept his fleet from sailing. Clytemnestra slays her husband on his return. Thereupon Orestes murders his mother, avenging his father. The Furies follow him. However, in a trial which the goddess Athena attends, administering justice, Orestes is acquitted. Athena's birth from the head of her father Zeus is cited as an example of the fact that a son is directly related to his father, while the mother plays little part in the birth of a child. Thus, the murder of the husband carried more weight than the murder of the mother.

This argument from the Aeschylus drama is cited by Bachofen as proof that the issue was a showdown between mother right and father right. Father right triumphed by necessity, for it was of a higher nature. Revenge is an obligation only to those to whom one is related. Because Orestes traces his kinship from his father only, the murder of his mother becomes legitimate. Orestes' matricide is celebrated by Bachofen as a victory of higher principle; Clytemnestra's murder of her husband, however, is condemned, for she belongs to the lower sphere of the material life.

> The maternal blood revenge she pursues belongs to the law of maternal birth, for which motherhood finds its great model in the earth . . . It is the bloodiest of all rights, the physical mother right.[24]

By killing his mother, Orestes, Bachofen believes, also subjugates the goddess Artemis (the goddess of the hunt who until then had power equivalent to her brother Apollo) to the "higher, milder Apollonic" law. Bachofen neglects to say, though, what this subordination to the brother consists of.

Bachofen's interpretation of *Orestes* has been accepted uncritically time and again by all adherents of the matriarchy theory. Friedrich Engels is especially guilty of this; in the foreword to the fourth edition of his book *The Origin of the Family, Private Property, and the State,* he writes that it involved a "new, but definitely correct interpretation of Orestes." Engels boosted Bachofen stock even further with his statement: "The history of the family dates from 1861, from the publication of Bachofen's *Mother Right.*"[25]

While Engels calls the Scottish prehistorian J. F. MacLennan a dry-as-dust jurist, he extols Bachofen as a "mystic of genius." The summary Engels gives of Bachofen's statements is a highly condensed version and does not match Bachofen's intentions. Engels summarizes Bachofen as if women

> as the mothers, the only parents of the young generation known for certain, were paid a higher degree of respect and regard, which according to Bachofen's conception intensified to the point of complete female rule (matriarchy).[26]

Engels did not criticize Bachofen's essential messages, namely the superiority of an allegedly spiritual father principle incarnate in *"Sumpfzeugung."* Engels, who so disapproved of the rise of exogamy, obviously made a deliberate effort to spare Bachofen. It is unclear why, while believing that Bachofen's views would lead to pure mysticism, Engels attributed to them such high scientific value. In prehistory women had occupied a higher social position that originated in their motherhood.

> Bachofen did not put these statements as clearly as this, for he was hindered by his mysticism. But he proved them; and in 1861 that was a real revolution.[27]

Engels did not mention that Bachofen had provided no scientific proof, only a new myth: that of the higher spiritual development and intellectual superiority of the man, who by historical necessity must subdue the material manifestation of woman, who is oriented to childbearing. This is why Bachofen believed the highest development in human history was the Roman Empire. His achievement amounts to the pure and simple fact that he discovered a rule of descent that did not conform to that of the patrilinear European family and clan. He interpreted this rule of descent as the state of universal female rule.

Let us for the time being set aside the question of whether a female government has ever preceded the patriarchal societies as we know them today and, like the male rule today, encompassed all societies and constituted a long period of history. Bachofen provided no proof of this. Of course, there is no evidence to the contrary available either. But let us analyze the myth that Bachofen proposed: the initial dominance of the woman and her inevitable conquest, by which humanity transcends the material. What he presents is a history with a definite moral: the invincibility of male rule.

5/The Errors of the Evolutionists

The history of the human race shows the same beginnings, the same experiences, the same development everywhere. Just as human beings are similar in thinking ability and physical form—as a result of their common origin—so too has their culture been essentially the same everywhere always.

—*Lewis H. Morgan*

"What is the relation of woman to man in the natural state? This is the way one usually begins the questioning . . ." wrote the patriotic poet Ernst Moritz Arndt in 1810.[1] His was a question of this century, even if in answering it Arndt remained faithful to eighteenth-century thinking. Women of all societies and cultures had been slaves in comparison to the civilized Christian-Western societies. Originally,

> the poor woman is a slave, for she can be nothing else. She must not be permitted to walk around free because then there would be nothing but conflict and murder, so little are people the masters of their passions. If the woman were the stronger, she would have locked up men, just as she herself is now locked up.[2]

With the nineteenth century came an attempt at rational explanations of nature and society. Among the evolutionists were a motley collection of philosophers of history—historians, the first ethnologists, and the Darwinists. Common to all was the question of the origin of human social institutions. From the development of these institutions —marriage, the family, the state, private property, political and legal institutions, the military—they tried to extract a design for future society. Since marriage and family were no longer regarded by them as God-given, but rather as historical phenomena, the question of the origin of the relationship between the sexes and the subordination of the woman to the man inevitably arose.

Of all the difficulties that kept the nineteenth- and twentieth-century women's movement from formulating a feminist theory of its own, the errors of the evolutionists were undoubtedly of especially grave consequence. This sounds like a paradox, for the most influential evolutionists promoted the view that women had played a dominant role in the original society. A matriarchy in early history or an equal status of the sexes in prehistoric times was especially attractive to the women's movement, for it would provide scientific proof that woman's oppression was historical and not biological. Moreover, the theses of the evolutionists kindled hope for a restoration of the original state of the sexes. The new international women's movement revived the concept of matriarchy.[3] Since now there is adequate scientific proof that women's oppression is not a "natural order," a simple analogical line of thought that reaches from one matriarchy in prehistory to another in the future can lead only to a theoretical blind alley. This happened earlier to the evolutionists of the nineteenth century, whose theories were founded on a simple intellectual construction.

And yet two distinctly different models of development emerge here. One was more in accord with the thinking of liberal intellectuals: At the beginning of history people were barbarians ruled by brute force. The state of civilization achieved in the nineteenth century, however, guaranteed the progress of humanity, the expansion of human rights, and the end of such abominations as slavery, war, and male supremacy. Ultimately, the highest development of humanity would be reached. The other evolutionist line stated that in the beginning of social development human beings were equal, their social life was peaceful, and they would return to this state at the end of society, only on a higher level, attaining complete control of nature without the inconveniences of primitive life.

The Englishman and liberal Herbert Spencer compared society with the growth of an organism which at each stage of development integrates that which is inferior. Darwin's theory of the evolution of organisms led Spencer to the idea

> that a universal law was put forward that was applicable to all ranges of phenomena: "Whether it is a matter of the evolution of the earth, the evolution of life on the face of the earth, or in the evolution of society, state, industry, of trade, languages, literature, science, or art—all fields are based on the same evolution from simple to complex through successive differentiation.[4]

This principle of development was realized in the development of religious ideas which led humanity from primitive superstition to one central concept of God. For Spencer, primitive society was militaristic, defined by violence and conquest. It was gradually replaced by a peaceful industrial society in which the social barriers and the predominance of the military were reduced in the same way as was man's domination of woman. In his book *Social Statics,* published in the beginning of the 1850s, he claimed that male and female rights could be deduced from legal authority, "and that the objections that are usually raised against granting political power to women are founded on notions and prejudices that will not hold up under close examination."

He asked:

> Who can tell us where the sphere of the woman actually lies? Considering that the customs of people differ from each other so widely, I would like to know how it can be proved that the sphere we assign to her really is here, that the limits we set on her activity are exactly the proper bounds?[5]

According to Spencer the demand for equal rights was applicable to the whole of humanity, male and female.

The other line of evolutionism tried to close a gap between the social and sexual conduct of animals (particularly the various ape families) as well as of humans. Sexual intercourse among apes is completely indiscriminate; if humans and ape families had the same ancestors, the first humans must have lived in promiscuity. In other words, other circumstances must have preceded monogamous marriage. The evolutionists tried to discover remnants of promiscuity, group marriage, polygamy, or polyandry in reports about an aboriginal society.[6]

The most important attempt to draw a line from the dawn of humanity to civilization originated with the American Lewis H. Morgan's book *Ancient Society.*[7] He divided human history into three stages, which he called savagery, barbarism, and civilization, and each of these stages was divided into a lower, middle, and upper stage. Savagery is characterized by the first use of fire, the utilization of fish for nourishment, and articulated speech. The invention of the bow and arrow and the art of pottery appear at the end of this stage. For Morgan the art of pottery is the most definite distinguishing feature of the boundary between savagery and barbarism. In the stage of barbarism begin the breeding of domestic animals, the cultivation of plants, the use of stones in building houses, and the processing of iron. Civilization begins with the invention of a phonetic alphabet and the use of writing. Parallel to technological-economic development runs the development of the forms of the human family, which, according to Morgan, begins with incest between brothers and sisters and reaches its pinnacle in monogamous marriage of the civilized world. He wrote:

Five different and consecutive forms of the family can now be distinguished, each of which is particular to a special form of marriage. They are the following:

I. The consanguine family based on group marriage of brothers, own and collateral, with their sisters.

II. The punaluan family based on the group marriage of several, own and collateral, sisters with their husbands, in which the husbands were not necessarily related to each other. Likewise, in the group marriage of several own and collateral brothers to their wives, in which these women were not necessarily related to each other, although in both cases this frequently occurred. In each case the group of men was married to the group of women.

III. The syndiasmic or pairing family based on marriage between single couples, but without complete marital fidelity. The duration of the marriage was left to the discretion of the husbands.

IV. The patriarchal family based on the marriage of one man to several women, generally resulting in the strict seclusion of the woman.

V. The monogamous family founded on marriage between single couples based on complete marital fidelity.[8]

According to Morgan the form of the family changes in response to the state of human technological development. The first three forms of family and marriage were concerned only with succession and clan affiliation in the family of the mother: kinship and succession were matrilinear. The increased development from the common property of the gentile society to private property brought with it the transformation from the matrilineal to the patrilineal clan. This transformation was associated with a weakening in the female status.

Even Morgan himself got into theoretical troubles upholding this view, for among the North American Indian tribes were the Iroquois, for example, who were organized matrilinearly, who knew agriculture, and who—compared with other Indian tribes—possessed a highly developed political organization (the confederation of several tribes). On the other hand, in the midst of these matrilinear tribes were tribes that were organized patrilinearly and were at a far lower stage of technological, economic, and political development. Morgan noticed this, for instance, among the Winnebago Indian tribe.

It is astonishing that so many branches of this original tribe substitute descent by maternal succession with paternal succession since, during the switch, the idea of property was still undeveloped; thus, inheritance scarcely could have been the motive, as it was with the Greeks and Romans.[9]

However, Morgan did not take the trouble to clear up this obvious contradiction in theory. Moreover, the enthusiastic assimilation of his research by Karl Marx and Friedrich Engels transformed Morgan's research hypotheses into solid components of a political-economic theory and denied them further scientific study. In the years 1880–81 Marx excerpted *Ancient Society.* After his death his extracts were assimilated into Engels's theories.[10] Later in the course of the socialist movement the periodization of history established by Morgan and its reworking by Engels became dogma, which essentially supported the socialists' belief in progress.

As a result of the unassailability of Morgan's periodization of the family, a major portion of socialist research cut itself off from the further development of ethnographic knowledge and the new Anglo-Saxon trend in social anthropology.[11]

The basic concept of evolutionism was a unilinear development of culture. All peoples on earth strive toward civilization and, in their development, move in one and the same direction. Consequently, modern European civilization becomes a barometer of all development, since its productive forces are most highly developed.

The evolutionists claimed that in human history there were universally valid sequences of evolution in which the lower forms of society, the less complicated technology, and the simpler culture preceded the more complicated, complex, and higher forms.[12] Certainly, this sequence of development holds true for nearly all technological invention. In the history of human development the processing of stones into tools precedes the making of iron tools and weapons. However, it is not always possible to prove that the older an object is, the more primitively it is made. One example is the throwing knife from the Congo. There were forms of these throwing knives with one, two, three, and more points. It was thought that the knife with one point, as the simplest version, would be the oldest form. When researchers found all forms of this knife at one native smith's and inquired whether the simplest form was the oldest, they were told it was merely the cheapest. The more expensive the knife, the more complicated the form. Another equally familiar example comes from North America. The settled prairie tribes who tilled the soil switched over to the nomadic life of the buffalo hunter after the Europeans had introduced the horse. In the chronological sequence of the evolutionists, however, the nomad comes before the farmer. The reprimitivization or modification of the modes of production beyond the chronological patterns projected by them was not anticipated. Thus, one must deal with a profusion of autonomous cultural influences in the development of societies without always being able to account for them.

Not only in the fields of economics and technology are there examples refuting the evolutionistic conception, but also in the sphere of culture. The most important medium of a culture is its language. A language's richness in form and possibilities of expression are in many primitive languages a contrast to their primitive tools. Franz Boas writes:

Many primitive languages are complex. Slight differences in opinion are expressed through grammatical forms. The grammatical categories of Latin and to an even greater extent those of modern English seem crude when compared to the variety of psychological and logical forms which are at the disposal of primitive languages and yet which remain unobserved in our forms of expression. On the whole the development of languages appears to proceed in such a way that the finer distinctions disappear; the language begins with complex forms while simpler forms are at the end of the development. Certainly contradictory tendencies exist here.[13]

A characteristic which, according to its periodization, belonged to an earlier stage, is regarded as "atavistic." Thus, for example, any ethnological detail, any part of wedding traditions or ceremonies in which women were equal to men or had special rights, were interpreted as "atavistic" of the matriarchy.

Naturally, it is equally foolish to regard the Christian-Germanic form of the family as absolute, as it is the old Roman form or the old Greek one or the Oriental one, which for that matter together form a sequence of historical development.[14]

This sentence comes not from Engels but from Karl Marx, showing that he, too, thought in terms of a single line of development.

Another part of evolutionistic thinking is the widely disseminated idea that history develops according to the same principle as the life of a human being. Hegel promoted the popular nineteenth-century notion that history can be classified into ages of childhood, youth, manhood, and senility.

The evolutionistic acceptance of a matriarchy at the beginning of history, together with communistic householding, was long a keystone of historical materialism and turned many women into avid supporters of the socialist idea of women's emancipation. Since the end of the Stalin era, however, the theory of matriarchy has overtly or covertly been called into question by Communist scholars of prehistory.

Morgan explains that the family developed only partially out of economic necessities. The hypothetical original family, group incest by brothers and sisters, and also the punaluan family, are developed from purely sexual ideas. Only the patriarchal and the monogamous family are clearly based on economic arguments. Even early socialist family theorists in the first two decades of this century had pointed out the contradictions in Engels's derivation of the family form.[15] The matriarchy was due to a non-economic cause, through the connection of sexual intercourse and the procreation of children. In Morgan's and Bachofen's theses on early promiscuity, Engels makes a special point of clarifying the fact that, in this kind of sexual life, the mother could not determine her children's father. This is the origin of the predominance of the woman in ancient society, the matriarchy, and the insignificance of the father. Thus, the European image of fatherhood was not absolutely pertinent for all societies of Africa, America, and Oceania.

Biological fatherhood was important for the European man; the great Aristotle had noticed that the spermatozoon came from the man while the female provided only the receptacle. Such an obsession with biology, complemented by the virginity cult, made it enormously important for European men to be the biological father of their children. Earlier, however, Germany would allow an impotent or sterile man to engage his brother as a proxy with his wife in order to beget children.

The evolutionists' most plausible argument for the matriarchy consisted in the fact that, in early society, people were ignorant of the connection between sexual intercourse, procreation, and pregnancy and had learned of it only gradually by observation. However, a number of Australian tribes who disputed the existence of a causal connection between sexual intercourse and pregnancy followed the patrilinear rules of descent.

In a number of African and American societies aware of the connection between sexual intercourse and pregnancy, the illegitimate children of a married woman are readily claimed by her husband as their social father. Biological kinship gives way to the consideration of posterity as property.

By the end of the nineteen-sixties even socialist research admitted that the uncertainty over the connection of sexual intercourse and birth by no means ruled out the social existence of the father and his role.

> Among various Australian aborigines the connection between sexual intercourse and the birth of children is unknown. The birth of children is regarded as the consequence of a spirit child that penetrates the woman. The only role that the man plays in this, if he has any at all, consists in clearing the way for the spirit child. Even where the knowledge of the biological role of the man is present—for example, in Arnhem Land—the old belief is retained as theological dogma.
>
> It appears probable that the knowledge of the connection between sexual intercourse and the birth of children was not acquired until relatively late in the history of homo sapiens. For the first humans who did not possess this knowledge, a woman, in contrast to a man, is a creature who at certain intervals through a long period of her life bears children.[16]

If Friedrich Engels had examined in further detail the three-volume history of marriage by Edward Westermarck, he would at least have come to question this thesis of the unlimited promiscuity of the original society and of group marriage. Westermarck had also already established that in the majority of societies the rule of descent from the mother, matrilinearity, was associated not with the predominance of the woman but rather with a predominance of the mother's brother, who in place of the father exercises authority over his sister's children.[17]

In the sixties the evolutionistic model of development was slowly revised by socialist research.

> Uncritically, Engels took over the evolutionistic methods that Morgan had used. In the development of human society he regarded both production, on the one hand, and biological factors, on the other hand, as independent elements. As evidence one can cite what he wrote on the development from the "original condition of unregulated intercourse" through the consanguine family and the punalua family to the pairing family. Engels adopted first an inherent principle of development in the evolution of the family: the progressive avoidance of incest (in fact, he wrote of a "dark pressure to limit inbreeding"); secondly, he accepted unilinearity in the development of the family; thirdly, he accepted the investigation methods of natural science and of course biology, including the interpretation of phenomena as "atavistic."[18]

Irmgard Sellnow, the leading ethnologist of the German Democratic Republic, admitted "that the family is not suited to a periodization or at least not to the formation of a historical sequence."[19] Nonetheless, even Sellnow tries to prove that the patrilinearity of the Australian aborigines is not as old as the matrilinearity.

In 1967 the Russian scholar J. U. I. Semenov wrote:

> Therefore all that Morgan wrote on the rise of the family and on the foregoing forms (a horde living in promiscuity, the consanguine family, the punalua family) has a purely hypothetical character.[20]

Author Rudolph Feustel makes a similar statement. The periodization he deals with is based on archaeological material which determines the state of technological development. However:

> The specific social structure—the horde state, gentile society, promiscuity, matriarchy, patriarchy, etc.—are observed, of course, but they can serve as a basis only conditionally, since they cannot be proven concretely. For the most part, we still find ourselves on the level of scientific speculation, of disputed hypotheses.[21]

Feustel also objects to the old notions of the evolutionists that there was an inherent and unilinear principle of development.

The concrete historical event is not a compact, one-track, homogeneous complex leading straight from lower to higher, but rather a mosaic whose individual parts rapidly or slowly rise and fall, and from which parts break away and new ones emerge, and which in itself changes . . . The concrete road of history is many-laned and tortuous.[22]

The thesis of the unlimited sex life of ancient society was dealt a menacing blow by the Catholic school of ethnology, which formed in Vienna around the figure of Father Wilhelm Schmidt at the beginning of the twentieth century. In 1910, in his book *Die Stellung der Pygmä-envölker in der Entwicklungsgeschichte des Menschen*, he proved that monogamy was the prevailing form of marriage among the pygmy peoples. Monogamous marriage was later also found among the Andamanese, the bushmen of the Kalahari in South Africa, the Wedda of Ceylon, the Negritos in the Philippines, and the inhabitants of Tierra del Fuego. The school of Father Wilhelm Schmidt developed yet another theory of primitive times: In the beginning of human history man and woman entered into marriage by free choice and practiced lifelong monogamy, a theory corresponding to the Catholic doctrine of natural law.[23]

In his primary work *Primitive Society,* the North American ethnologist R. H. Lowie wrote: "Sexual communism as a substitute for individual marriage exists nowhere at present; and the proof for its earlier existence must be rejected as being inadequate."[24] Of the individual family he says: "In short, the bilateral family, consisting of man and wife and their children, is an absolutely universal unit of human society."[25]

Over twenty years later another social anthropologist, the American George Peter Murdock, once again corroborated this finding. He had tackled what was the largest project up to that time in comparing primitive societies and their social structures with each other. Through years of labor he compiled a representative sample of 250 societies on all continents (a World Ethnographic Sample), not including industrial societies. Murdock writes that in this sample only "a handful of tribes" practiced group marriage, and these were exceptions. The most important example of this was the Kaingang in Brazil, a tribe with especially loose sexual bonds. A statistical analysis of Kaingang genealogies over a period of a hundred years showed, however, that only 8 percent of all alliances were group marriages. In 14 percent one woman had several husbands (polyandry); in 18 percent the man was married to several women (polygyny); the majority—60 percent—were monogamous.[26] Thus, he concluded: "Group marriage, though figuring prominently in the early theoretical literature of anthropology, appears never to exist as a cultural norm."

6/Misconceptions in the Theories of Matriarchy and Patriarchy

It is a mistake to assume that we can understand society's institutions in isolation, without taking the time to study coexisting and comparable institutions . . .

There are false notions associated with this differentiation of societies into matriarchal and patriarchal that must be dispelled before we attempt to proceed further.

Extreme patrilinear systems are comparatively rare, and extreme matrilinear systems perhaps even more rare.

—A. R. Radcliffe-Brown

In the investigation of the earliest human cultures there is a sort of Heisenberg uncertainty principle. The archaeological exploration of the actual remains of such cultures provides reliable information on housing, tools and other implements, as well as on the style of burial. However, there is no reliable data on what the Marxists call "phenomena of the superstructure," the religious ideas, relationships of domination, and, above all, the relation of the sexes for those cultures who left no written record. V. Gordon Childe, the famous British scholar of early history, has discussed theories of the existence of an early matriarchy as an almost unsolvable problem.

> In any case, the archaeologist could not hope to recognize the supposed prerogatives of matriarchy. Yet small effigies of a female personage have been taken as indications of such . . . Not only the numerous figurines of Ishtar from Babylonia and Assyria and those of Venus from Greece and Rome, but also contemporary statuettes of the Virgin can be traced back directly to the prehistoric figurines of the Neolithic age at least. Whether the latter indicate the worship of a goddess conceived in female form, as their historical descendants undoubtedly do, may reasonably be questioned . . . As neither male personages nor phalli were thus represented in Paleolithic and early Neolithic cultures, it may be assumed that, as among some contemporary tribes, the part of the father in reproduction had not yet been appreciated . . . But in themselves are female figurines any better evidence for matriarchy than are the Venus figures and Virgins of undeniably patriarchal societies?[1]

From the written testimony at hand, the patriarchal period of humanity, spanning four thousand years, need not represent the norm for the hundred thousand years preceding it. In these hundred thousand years, from the Neanderthal stage up to the Neolithic economy of arable farming and the first urban societies, a great number of cultures and adaptations to changed living conditions arose. The thesis of a universal patriarchy, from the start of human history to the present, is every bit as questionable and incredible as that of the universal matriarchy assumed by the evolutionists. Neither can ever be completely verified, or discredited.

In our own civilization, power shifts and historical processes in the formulation of sexual relationships can be traced from century to century, from generation to generation, and from land to land. In an area of New Guinea where some hundred developing societies on the same technological level exist side by side, there is nonetheless a wide range of differentiation in the relationships of men and women. The famous study by Margaret Mead on marital relationships in several South Sea societies was the first to point out such differences.[2]

Grave findings of early history as well as the later cave drawings offer a multitude of almost insoluble contradictions. In the earliest period there is already evidence of some double burials in which a much older man was found in a grave together with a younger woman. Even the socialist scholars have long assumed that this was a case of suttee (widow suicide).[3] On the other hand, an abundance of cave drawings almost exclusively of women have been traced to the Magdalenian period. And in the Neolithic Age, when arable farming began, there are further indications of women's prominence, such as the excavation of Çatal Hüyük in Anatolia, of which the German scholar Karl J. Narr wrote:

> Nothing in the substance of mother right institutions, necessarily or with any degree of probability, lends itself to tangible objects which have been preserved. One such exception, however, are the remarkable finds of Çatal Hüyük.[4]

In Çatal Hüyük men and women were buried separately. The children's skeletons, however, were normally buried together with the mother's. Women were always buried in the same place inside the building on a large platform, while the male skeletons were found on a smaller platform in various places. Narr writes:

> The fact that children were buried alone or with the woman, but never with the man, contrasts sharply to the circumstances in cemeteries of the Mesolithic period or among later hunters and gatherers. This suggests at least a special stress on mother-child relationships, which also implies consequences for the kinship system and matrilinearity . . . That the male burial place is less specific is a further implication of this.[5]

Narr draws a careful comparison to the Pueblos in North America: women own the houses and the fields and pass them on to their daughters, while the men are politically dominant.

Prehistorians usually theorize with a one-sided focus on men. The American scholar Carleton S. Coon is guilty of this in *The Story of Man:*

> One fact about the life of a hunter which all who have lived among such people have noticed is that hunting is fun. Hunters take pleasure in their work. Human beings have been hunters for a long time, and our physiology is adjusted to this kind of life. As E. J. Faris has shown, a man is at his best from the standpoint of fertility if he is away from home a night or two at a time, giving his sperm cells a chance to accumulate. Hunting gives him just these little absences. Hunting exercises the whole body, as few other occupations do. It places a premium on keen eyesight . . . Hunting develops the muscles and tissue of his hands properly, instead of deforming and thickening them as farming and unskilled labor may do.
>
> It also places a premium on the capacity to make quick decisions, to act quickly, and to work in teams. Obedience and leadership can be developed in no better school . . . In our society, the men who find fun in their work and need no hobbies or vacations

are the scientists and research men, including the archaeologists and anthropologists, who have carried the hunting spirit into new fields.[6]

Descriptions like this, coming from an internationally known expert, clearly show the perspective of anthropology focused exclusively on the man. Even the anatomical development of the male hunter becomes a gauge of general human development. "As the result of a process of natural selection, the human being is created perfectly for the hunt."

Those who deal with ancient history have not always been able to resist the temptation of pure speculation. Ernest Borneman provides the best and, at the same time, the most forbidding recent evidence of counterfeit archaeological knowledge in his *Das Patriarchat.* In 1936, Childe, whom Borneman expressly designated as his teacher, originated the concept of the "Neolithic Revolution." In view of the unheard-of abundance of technical discoveries in the New Stone Age, which can be backed by available finds, Childe selected this concept in order to describe a phenomenon comparable only to the Industrial Revolution at the start of the nineteenth century. For Borneman this becomes "a counter-revolution, a scheming rebellion of men, a kind of primeval coup," or, elsewhere, "a kind of Putsch-type power grab just before the time of history."[7] He goes even further: In his opinion "the sexual relationships" can be detected "with relative certainty" from skeletal finds, graves, etc. On the sexual sensations of humans of the Old Stone Age he reports that they were not "genitalized":

> It was a sexuality that did not have to end in coitus but was gratified in body contact, handholding, embracing and being embraced, in breast contact and breast sucking . . .[8]

Without written documents, this is, of course, only supposition. But we will never be able to know anything about heartfelt sensations or sexual practices of lost cultures without writing; even the artistic evidence—statuettes or drawings—admits only suppositions.

Ernest Borneman was not alone in his attempt to resuscitate evolutionistic theories trying to corroborate Friedrich Engels's doctrine on the rise of family, state, and private property. The American Marxist and member of the women's movement Evelyn Reed voiced a different theory of the early evolution of women through the introduction of private property in ancient society.[9] She echoed the English writer Robert Briffault, who in the twenties published a three-volume work entitled *The Mothers.*[10] Briffault's thesis is that the female sex, even among animals, had stronger social capabilities and, therefore, was the ruling sex among the most primitive humans. The reconstruction of female history, the justified suspicion of suppression, one-sided male research trends, and the lack of female figures in history are certainly among the reasons why some American women writers have begun to fill the historical gaps. However, Evelyn Reed goes far beyond what can legitimately be allowed in the formulation of theory. She eventually falls into sexist conceptions leveled against men. Although it is scarcely possible to make any statement about the social life of people in the transition between animal and human form, Evelyn Reed contends that women were the more social sex and the males were pure cannibals.

> Thus, far from being handicapped by its biology, the female sex was in fact the biologically advanced sex. To be sure, primate males are often larger and stronger than females and possess fighting equipment in their canine teeth. But the females with a capacity for cooperation and collective action had a strength superior to that of any single individual. In addition, as mothers, they wielded their socializing influence over the young males for a longer period than among anthropoids. These advantages enabled women to institute the prohibitions and restraints required for social life.[11]

Such contentions offer a new interpretation to the social interaction pattern of mother and baby. They are just as much pure imagination, though, as the thesis of the genetically determined ability of man for cooperation that was propounded by authors Lionel Tiger and Robin Fox.[12]

According to Reed, the first male hunters could not distinguish the young of their own species from other kinds of animals, and so killed and ate them. This is why the females introduced totemistic taboos, a form of belief of primitive peoples in which certain animals, plants, or objects are regarded as relatives and therefore are spared. As proof of her thesis of male cannibalism, Reed says that in a great number of societies women and men did not eat together; after a hunting expedition or a war campaign, the men had to go through certain purification rites. Women are characterized as the good, non-aggressive sex that, unlike men, eats no flesh but lives on a diet of vegetables. Her thesis is astonishing, for the very literature on hunters and gatherers that she cites says that women generally gathered or killed the small animals—mice, rats, frogs, birds' nests. That males were cannibals and females vegetarians is pure legend.

What we know of cannibalism indicates not that men systematically hunted other members of the human race for food but that cannibalism went hand in hand with religion.[13] Even Herodotus reported that among some Asiatic tribes the corpses of dead persons were not cremated, as in Greece, but were ritually consumed by the members of the tribe. In South Australia some aborigines are supposed to have eaten the dead out of piety: this both prevented the dead person's flesh from decaying and united the living with the dead physically and spiritually. Women of the Tukinamba in South America ate the flesh and fat of a dead enemy probably in order to stay healthy. Infants were also involved, for the mother rubbed her breast with the blood of the enemy. Among the Kubeo, another South American Indian tribe, a fertility cult was obviously linked with anthropophagy. At the end of the cannibalistic meal, the wife of the chieftain ate the penis of the slain man to enhance her fertility.[14]

While until recently Marxist scholarship stubbornly clung to the idea that humanity had developed from a matrilinear to a patrilinear kinship order, culminating today in a bilateral kinship, the Anglo-Saxon scholars attempted to prove the opposite. The school of the ethnologist Franz Boas was characterized by its battle against evolutionism. Boas and his students believed that at the start of society not matrilineal descent but a bilateral kinship system had prevailed; that descent was governed by both father and mother. The anti-evolutionists posed the following: Evolution began with the bilateral descent rule, followed by the patrilinear, and then the matrilinear. For American ethnologists, such as George Peter Murdock, this became "dogma," just as the thesis of the priority of the matriarchy had been the doctrine of socialist scholarship.

In fact, a whole generation of scholars tried to prove that the patrilinearly and bilaterally related Indian tribes of North America were at a more primitive stage of development than the matrilinear ones.[15] Yet Boas managed to produce persuasive evidence that matrilinearly organized societies were no more primitive than the patrilinear, and that their property structures were just as pronounced. His theory, however, shows an empirical weakness. As far back as antiquity there were many examples of transition from a matrilinear to a patrilinear state, but none in which a patrilinear society turned into a matrilinear one. Although Boas attempted with, for example, the Kwakiutl in British Columbia to trace a society from a patrilinear into a matrilinear form, he, too, reached a dead end.[16]

The evolutionists had overlooked the fact that family and kinship systems could not evolve according to the same principles as those of technological knowledge and accomplishments in mastering nature. This knowledge is cumulative; over long periods of time technology and knowledge can be improved and furthered. However, social systems, like the family and larger group formations, cannot be judged according to the model of higher or lower development.

Among the errors of the evolutionists was their failure to understand the function of descent and residency rules, kinship, family form, laws of succession, and the political-economic organization; to some degree they subjected these to moralistic appraisal. A rule of descent brings every individual into temporal continuity with ancestors; within this genealogical line the legal, economic, and religious rights and duties of a person are established. Descent is established in two possible ways. A genealogy can be originated either from the husband's ancestors or from the wife's. In patrilinear societies sons and daughters belong to the line of the father, but only the sons continue the line, since the daughters marry into another line. In matrilinear societies sons and daughters belong to the mother's line. The husband has his legal, economic, and political rights in the line of his sisters. In patrilinear societies the continuity of the generation derives from a common male ancestor; in matrilinear, from a common female ancestor.

In a comprehensive sample of 860 primitive societies, 46 percent follow patrilinear descent, 14 percent matrilinear.[17] A very small number of societies (4 percent) guarantee an individual rights in two separate lines (double descendance). However, much greater than the number of matrilinear or double-descendance groups is the number of bilateral societies that form no genealogical lines. This group encompasses 36 percent of the sample. Here descent is established not only from the father's side but from the mother's. This usually means that the bilateral kinship will not extend for more than three generations. A longer line of ancestors would create an immense number of kinship relations and obligations, since in each generation the relatives must be established on both the mother's and the father's sides. The most important function of a "kinship line"—the definite establishment of solidarity and loyalty toward one exclusive kinship group with unified economic interests—can be performed in a bilateral kinship system only when the circle of living relatives is kept numerically small. More complex societies based on bilateral kinship systems have been formed only among the Germans.[18]

However, all this does not answer the question of why the majority of societies with a patrilinear rule of descent have dominated those with matrilinear descent. Moreover, the question of which rule of descent emerged first in human history (or whether all forms were developed alongside each other) remains unanswered. One group of researchers, including the German Richard H. Thurnwald and the Englishman A. R. Radcliffe-Brown, advanced the view that only unilinear descent was founded on sociological necessities: "Unilinear kinship groups arise out of the need to formulate rights precisely in order to avoid unsolvable conflicts, and out of the need for the continuity of the social structure."[19]

It is clear that the social importance of such kinship groups, which organized into tribes and clans, depends on the existence of inheritable property or inheritable rank or title; these connect generations. Game-hunting societies seldom form such lineages, since the solidarity of kin within a larger political group is unimportant in terms of their economy. Thus, the Austrian priest Wilhelm Schmidt believed that matrilinear descent and clan formation first developed through the female invention of hoeing and the cultivation of tuberous fruit, while patrilinear society began with the introduction of cattle breeding, a male task.[20] He believed in a mother right with a social leadership role for the woman, which was not destroyed until the brother eventually gained power, again passing rights of subjugation and disposal into male hands. He characterized social forms in which the mother's brother dominates as "masculinized mother right." Poignant detachment from and ignorance of the conditions of capitalist industrial production appear in the following quotation from Father Schmidt's *Das Mutterrecht:*

> Women wishing to invoke the mother right had to be made aware of the fact that, although there is a development of mother right, this development shows phases, such as masculinized mother right, which could do little to serve their goals. Nonetheless, it had to be emphasized that the mother right that first developed into a matriarchy emerged from the cultivation of roots, tubers, and leafy fruits and for a long time was dependent on this farming. If nothing else the scanty gardens on the outskirts of our large cities offer moving testimony for the longing of many women to contribute products of their own gardening to daily meals; the stone deserts of the cities are broken up by gardens in which women of all classes carry out their contribution. Moreover, in addition to the money that the man earns, the profits of this garden could be the basis of a moderate new mother right that, now elevated from the gathering to the production stage, would renew the old equality of man and woman in the ancient culture. This would prevent the risk of excessive father and mother right and permit neither patriarchy nor matriarchy, which have generally become unhealthy for both marriage and family and thus for the society.[21]

In 1949 George Peter Murdock brought the discussion to a temporary halt by advancing the theory that primitive societies, over long periods of time, are able to move back and forth between different means of establishing descent.[22] According to Murdock, the determining factors for the transition from one system of descent to another are the residence rule and the historical division of labor. The young married couple can move to the family of the husband (patrilocality) or to the family of the wife (matrilocality) or form a new household (neolocality), which is selected independent of the place of residence of the bride and the bridegroom's family. Sometimes the young couple can choose between residing with the husband's parents or with the wife's parents (ambilocality). In addition, there are two further possibilities: the married couple may move in with the husband's maternal uncle (avunculocality) or establish no common household at all (duolocality) by each marriage partner residing with his/her family. In 69 percent of 859 representative societies, the residence rule of the young couple was determined by the young man; only 13 percent were determined by the wife.[23]

Normally, matrilinear descent is associated with a matrilocal rule for site of residence, the patrilinear with patrilocal place of residence. In three of six regions—Africa, the Mediterranean, and the Pacific islands—there are more societies with patrilocal site of residence than with patrilinear descent. In South America, where only 8 percent of the societies are organized patrilinearly, 32 percent have a site-of-residence rule that forces the husband to move in with his wife. Among the North American tribes, of which 19 percent are organized patrilinearly, 44 percent have a virilocal rule of residence: the woman must move in with the husband.[24]

For the degree of female influence the matrilocal site-of-residence rule is a very decisive factor. In a society that is organized matrilinearly and matrilocally, sisters of a family remain together, while their brothers, although they have their economic, religious, and political obligations in the village of their sisters, must move in with their wives. Thus, women are able to utilize the male power vacuum in their own interest.

According to Murdock, the factors that lead to a break in a residency rule are famines, epidemics, wars, population increases, and changes in the form of the economy. A long-term change of the rule of descent is possible. Everything in a society that serves to promote the influence of the man—the absence of movable property (cattle, goat herds, camels, slaves), the introduction of a new faith, wars to acquire additional women and booty, or political alliances—favors the transition to a patrilinear kinship system. On the other hand, essential new activities of the woman—for example, in farming—favor matrilocality. Even among hunting and gathering peoples Murdock sees such tendencies at work. For example, the Crow Indians, once part of a farming tribe organized matrilocally, later switched to buffalo hunting, changing their residency rule to patrilocality, though their kinship still followed a matrilinear line.

While, according to Murdock, a society with matrilinear and matrilocal form can immediately turn into a patrilocal or avunculocal system, a patrilinear society must first go through a neolocal or bilocal site-of-residence rule in order to become a matrilinear kinship system. Only rare exceptions exist.

> The observation has often been made that in many parts of the world patrilinear and matrilinear peoples are found side by side in restricted areas with cultures showing unmistakable evidences of historical connections. It should now be clear that wherever such a situation exists, if the two types of structure are in fact genetically related, the patrilineal tribes must have evolved from matrilineal organization, and not *vice versa*. It must likewise hold true that in all societies with full-fledged double descent the matrilineal kin groups were the first to be evolved, the rule of patrilineal descent representing a secondary development. These generalizations, of course, can in no way be taken as supporting the evolutionist theory of the universal priority of the matrilineate. On the contrary, since the ancestors of nearly all groups which have survived until today must have undergone many changes in social organization during the long course of human history, the

fact that the last transition in a particular series has been from matrilineal or double descent by no means implies that the matrilineate came first in the entire series.[25]

Kinship organizations, according to Murdock, can change under outside influences, but only in such a way that the social order in these transitions remains balanced. He compares this slow shift with linguistic trends. A language also forms a relatively independent system, which can change over a long period through outside influences, but only in specific ways.

Murdock explains the pendulum between matri- and patrilinear organization of society as well as bilateral kinship systems as mainly the result of new economic developments. His thesis, however, does not offer any comprehensive answer. According to his theory, societies in which women made a major economic contribution should be matrilinear and matrilocal. Cattle breeding and hunting societies, on the other hand, should be patrilinear and patrilocal. In societies in which the economic contribution of both sexes is approximately equal, the consequence would be a bilateral kinship system. But there are large geographical areas in which this does not hold true. Some of the South American game-hunting tribes, in which both sexes make an approximately equal contribution to survival, are matrilinearly organized. In New Guinea, the majority of tribes are patrilinear, although women garden and herd pigs. Many African societies, in which women do much of the field work, are patrilinear. On the other hand, one of the most famous examples of mother right comes from a cattle-tending nomad society, the Tuareg, who today, as a result of Algerian politics, are almost extinct. They are matrilinear and trace their descent from a female ancestor of the fourth and fifth centuries. Although they accepted the Islamic faith, they have remained monogamous. The Tuareg women possess political rights in the tribal council. They master the old Berber writing and pass this knowledge on to their daughters.[26] According to the studies of two American ethnologists, Melvin and Carol R. Ember, only two factors in Murdock's thesis actually influence residence decisions: cattle-tending and political structures. In fact, their studies show that the sexual division of labor plays little role in these decisions.[27] However, the evolutionists believed that matrilinearly organized tribes granted women the same or more rights than men, guaranteed by the kinship line. There are many exceptions to the evolutionists' theory, though. In patrilinear societies women marrying into a family often possess property rights that would not hold in matrilinear societies.[28] H. Baumann points out:

The majority of African mother righters do not participate in inheritance at all, or, if so, from an almost hopeless position; it is always the men of the mother tribe who have the privilege of acquiring wealth.[29]

In a number of patrilinear societies women collect the net profits of their crop yield or handmade products and retain the inheritance right in their father's line. Although some societies—for example, the North American Iroquois—are organized matrilinearly and matrilocally with a markedly high economic and political status for women, the kinship order never denotes any conclusive evidence on the sex-specific division of power in a society.

The relationship of the sexes in a society must be judged from a cultural, economic, religious, and historical standpoint. Special, individual tendencies stand in direct contradiction to the old evolutionist plan. When Bachofen wrote about matriarchy, permanent female rule in a society, he could never have imagined that this would be tied into a patrilinear and patrilocal social system. Yet, this fact applied to the Lovedu 150 years ago, while Bachofen was living. The Lovedu are a people of forty thousand in the northeast Transvaal of South Africa who live mainly by farming and use cattle only as a means to pay the bride price.[30] Since the middle of the nineteenth century women have reigned. However, unlike queens in monarchical systems, the queens here are not surrogate men. They have a religious function as rain-makers. The kingdom is divided into districts and the male or female chiefs send their women for the harem. The queen must not marry, but can have a lover and children. The women of her harem are the connecting links for the alliance with the local and district chieftains, male or female, whose daughters they can marry off. From these marriages, in turn, the queen can claim one of the daughters. In her capacity as highest judge in the land, she has support from the "mothers of the kingdom," who represent individual districts and are appointed by the queen to function as contact persons between her and the inhabitants of the district. The first queen in this line, Mujaji I, who died in 1894, was so famous that even in neighboring tribes first queens suddenly appeared.[31]

This example shows that there is no simple justification for drawing conclusions on the sexual power relationships in a society on the basis of rules of descent. The old question of the nineteenth century —whether there was a matriarchy at the beginning of human evolution—can therefore not be answered definitively by the ethnographic means of descendency research. Though it is awkward to do so, the women's movement will probably have to resign itself to the fact that, in this question of such central significance for self-understanding, there are no unequivocal conclusions yet. This may, however, be an advantage rather than a disadvantage: after what is by now thousands of years of oppression, what help is it for women to console themselves with the fact that once, at the beginning of human history, they ruled over men? Women must incorporate only historical facts in their argument. Their oppression is easy to document and this is more than sufficient to substantiate their demands.

7/Oppression
in Classless Societies

The aboriginal woman always resembles a plodding draft animal with her burden of food, water, or firewood, always in search of edibles with, whenever possible, a baby on her back and a small child at her heels. But a white woman on a hot shopping day, pushing a carriage loaded with baby and a variety of packages, with a child pulling at her coattail, disconcerted and also impeded by her clothes and tight, sweaty corset, on the lookout for favorable prices as she makes her way through an unfriendly crowd, then struggles to get on a bus . . . Anyone critically observing her may be pardoned for asking whether she is really any better off than the naked but gloriously slim, healthy, and gracious aboriginal woman who is eminently adjusted to her environment. On the whole, it appears as if the lot of women in all societies is about equal.

—A. A. Abbie

On the lower Darling River in Australia a fire site dating from 16,800 B.C. was found. Other excavations were made in Queensland. In central East Australia there have been inhabitants for almost nineteen thousand years, and farther north for even longer.[1] The aboriginal inhabitants of Australia, the pygmies of the African rain forest, the bush people of the Kalahari in South Africa, the Negrito tribes on the Malayan peninsula and in the Philippines, and the Fuegians, as well as to some extent the Eskimo tribes—all these people were the "human museum" that was supposed to provide European ethnographers with information about the social relationships of humans during the Stone Age or the Mesolithic Age. Ethnographers thought the idea of human equality was realized in these classless, game-hunting societies. The socialistic prehistorians and ethnographers hoped to find in them their original societies. Another Western school of ethnography that adhered to Christian ideals, that of the priest Wilhelm Schmidt, claimed that these societies were, as when they came from God's hand, initially good. Members of this school found new support for this after discovering that monogamous marriage prevailed among these people, and the majority of such people believed in a single divine being (unlike the polytheistic farming groups). A rich religious life, monogamy, and brotherly sharing within the community—in this they saw the original image of humankind. In these societies the socialist scholars found neither their thesis of promiscuity and group marriage nor the concept of the matrilinearity of primitive cultures confirmed.

These game-hunting societies were classless in both the Marxist and bourgeois senses. The question was: were the relationships of the sexes equal before the fall from grace to private property and the formation of class conflicts? According to Friedrich Engels, there could be no oppression of women in those societies ignorant of private property. Marxists believe the rise of private property coincided with the enslavement of woman, who from then on was condemned to be a machine for producing heirs, an instrument of pleasure and housework.

Naturally, there were also property definitions in these game-hunting societies. Individuals had rights to objects they made themselves, to killed game or fruit trees marked by the discoverer. However, the yield from hunting, gathering, and picking was divided among all members, even those who were too old or too sick to contribute.[2]

Men in the Australian game-hunting societies are specialists at hunting; with sticks the women dig for tubers, roots, and seeds. At certain times of the year they collect mussels and catch lizards, turtles, small snakes, rats, and mice. The men hunt the larger kill, kangaroos, geese, and emus.[3] The results of the hunt depend on luck and chance; on the other hand, the food that the women supply provides a continual basis for existence, true for all game-hunting tribes. The psychoanalyst and ethnologist Géza Róheim, who in 1929 spent time with tribes in Central Australia, wrote:

> The women are, on the whole, more greedy and selfish than the men. It is well known that there is no society which carries altruism so far as that of the Australian native. He will literally give

the last bit of "damper" or of meat to his neighbor, and even a baby will pass on the sugar he has got from the white man—just for the asking.[4]

Yet, despite the altruism, despite the absence of private property and social classes, despite the equivalent contributions to daily life sustenance and the fair distribution of food, women of the Australian aborigines are no less oppressed or discriminated against within their society than are women in societies with private property and class structures.

It is often pointed out that the Australian tribes have a geronto-cratic system. However, old men are not political leaders. They are respected because they have the greatest knowledge of the religious rituals, the myths of the tribe, the watering places, and the diplo-matic relations between neighboring tribes, all of which gives them the right to divide up the flesh of a kangaroo or an emu, and reserve for themselves the treasured fatty portions. However, the tribes' government is not based on the younger men's duty to obey. Men control women. Among other game-hunting tribes, such as the pygmies and the bushmen or the Selk'nam in Tierra del Fuego, young women and men are able to choose their own marriage part-ners.[5]

Usually the betrothal of children among the Australian aborigines is of young girls, and occasionally of unborn daughters. While the girl's mother may voice her opinion, the father or the mother's brother chooses the daughter's husband. With the betrothal, the future hus-band, much older than the girl, must regularly offer gifts to his bride, to her father, and also often to her uncle.[6] According to Géza Róheim, the tribes in Central Australia lay the greatest stress on

> overcoming the resistance of the girl. That is how they explain the custom that the man is grown up and the girl is a baby when they are engaged. It is advisable for him to bring her up from babyhood to woman's estate so that she gets used to him, and becomes friendly. However, she grows up, and continues to be afraid of him.[7]

The marriage proceeds in stages. The husband makes a fire out-side the camp.

> She ought to come now, but if she does not he tells her to come. Then her *kami* brings her, and they sit down together beside the man. Some *inyuta* men (non-marriageable ones) come and tell her, "You two sleep together. Don't run away." The man holds her arm and they sit down.

She begins to cry or scream:

> Now he has had enough and says: "Don't cry or I will beat you!"
> But when he falls asleep she runs back to her mother. The next
> night the same thing happens. He goes and calls her. "Here is
> some meat for your mother." Then she brings some wood and
> makes a fire. They sleep with their backs to each other and a fire
> between them. She scratches a hole for herself in the sand, and
> holds her legs close together. While she sits watching the man, she
> scratches the hole under her body with her hands. He calls her; at
> last she comes walking on all fours. When the hymen is torn she
> groans.

This is, as far as I know, one of the few human groups in
which the normal form of sexual approach is rape.[8]

In many cases men drag little girls out of camp. According to Róheim,
the term for marriage, rape, and sexual intercourse is identical.

Through marriage the husband has acquired sexual rights to his
wife's body. In western Arnhem Land there are stories which serve as
instruction to women:

> Never refuse the sexual requests of a husband; he is entitled to
> them as your protector. Should you refuse him, he is justified in
> taking what actions he thinks necessary.[9]

A number of legends threaten punishment if the woman refuses
her husband; one legend says women will urinate blood and die. The
Australian researchers Ronald M. and Catherine H. Berndt interpret
these myths as a warning to women:

> It is unusual for a wife to refuse her husband his marital rights.
> Such behavior on her part is said to be understandable only during
> pregnancy, menstruation, or illness.[10]

However, not only can the husband constantly exploit his wife's
body, but he can also lend his wife to others. In order to make peace
between two conflicting groups, it is common for women of one band
to be dispatched to the other. If the enemy sleep with them, the dispute
is settled. If they send them back untouched, the hostilities continue.
Australian ethnologist A. P. Elkin, who spent forty years studying the
native population of his country, believes that this practice of lending
women would perhaps end if all the aborigines realized the connection between sexual intercourse and procreation.

At present the physical act is a source of pleasure or a means of expressing or renewing friendship, warding off hostilities, or putting others under an obligation. But this is almost solely the man's point of view; it is not concerned with the offspring and implies that woman is but an object to be used in certain socially established ways. The fact that woman may often not object does not justify the custom.[11]

Elkin points out that many women "live in terror of the use which is made of them at some ceremonial times."[12]

The temporary relinquishment of the wife, which, before the confrontation of the aborigines with the European settlers, was practiced only to form alliances between men, has today taken other forms. Elkin writes: "Wife-lending is associated with the readiness of natives to prostitute their womenfolk in order to get material goods from white or yellow men."[13]

There is in existence only one very rare ceremony, in which the woman has the official right to choose a lover without her husband objecting. According to Róheim, the old women delight in reminiscing over these romantic occasions. Usually, if their husbands treat them badly, they have the opportunity to leave and start a new relationship. The husband, however, can leave at any time or give her to another man. Australian men practice polygamy, which becomes possible in view of the approximate parity of the sexes only when much older men marry much younger women. Because polygamy is connected with a systematic sexual preference for the woman last acquired, constant struggles develop among the women, occasionally ending in the famous women's duels: playing by firmly established rules, women strike each other on the skull with sticks.

What is the function or form of a power structure that is not based on property and in which the man nonetheless has a right to the woman's body, thus oppressing her? Before the development of ethnology and sociology, it was believed all social relationships among barbaric peoples were based on the right of the strongest. Over the long run, though, physical superiority would be of little use to the individual. The exercise of power in human societies rests on the ability to form groups within the group, to associate with others who have essentially the same interests. Some key means of building alliances are propaganda, ideology, common experiences, emotional dependence, and common secrets.

In many primitive classless societies there are respected persons and leaders, often the oldest members, who have no physical power. The power the Australian aborigines hold over women exists for various reasons, most importantly because males control the passing of myths concerning the history and foundations of the tribe, the ceremonies and rituals, the religious performances. Initiation rites and the

secrets of the tribe are men's concerns. Through these rites and ceremonies, the older men recruit males coming of age. Thus, a power
structure is produced among men. Frequently, initiation celebrations
begin with group masturbation of the novices. The clipped-off foreskin is eaten by the older brother or the brother-in-law as a symbolic
bond. Stories of a male ancestor of the tribe, who left many spirit
children behind him wherever he stayed, accompany the ceremony.
When the penis heals, the novice must again appear before the elders
and confess his past misdeeds.[14]

In these ceremonies women have an important role: they must
appear to be impressed by the event. They may participate in the
long initiation rites, though only at a distance, uninvolved. Only the
old men oversee and govern the rites. In some areas of northern Central Australia only women have secret myths and ritual dances
which reinforce their own solidarity. British anthropologist Phyllis
Kaberry believes these embody a fertility cult.[15] Male ceremonies,
however, are more important and more extensive. Religious and
ideological advantages of men are apparent, for example, in the following case: Upon the death of a man, a tribe in Victoria observes a
number of ceremonies. When a woman or child dies, only the close
relatives mourn.

The great dilemma of ethnological, as well as of empirical, social
research stems from never having established uniform criteria for the
comparisons of the status of men and women in primitive societies, or
for determining which forms of domination women were subjected to.
In societies without extreme forms of domination or in those without
political authority—such as the game hunters with their primitive
style of economy, producing no surplus—lie the greatest differences in
assessing the relationship between the sexes. (This often reflects nothing but the prejudices of the researchers, male or female.) According
to an observation by the famous British anthropologist Bronislaw
Malinowski, one should ensure the credibility of ethnological studies
and travel reportage by never believing their generalizations unless
they give a concrete example on which the generalization rests.

Frequent ethnological reports of the equal rights of woman con-
tradict the simultaneous account of daily life in these societies. As the
Berndts write of the sex life of the Australians in western Arnhem
Land:

> It is fallacious to state that aboriginal woman has been regarded
> generally by her menfolk as a chattel or as an inferior person; in
> many separate native communities there is no case of woman's
> subjection as a class and no stress on her inferiority. On the con-
> trary, she has always maintained herself in what could be de-
> scribed as equality with the men—economically, sexually and
> even ceremonially.[16]

They describe woman's alleged equality with man:

> Because of her sex-specific activities the woman at times shows a tendency to more open subordination; she is prepared to leave the initiative in action and in behavior to men, to seek their advice and to follow their recommendations. But this is mainly a matter of convention . . .
>
> The natural tendency of man is to play the more dominant part in the business of living and maintaining himself and his family. He is freer to act without encumbrance of menstruation, pregnancy, children, etc. That is, biologically he is better fitted to be the hunter, the fighter, and the dancer; and consequently these pursuits have, through the evolution of his social structure, developed institutions and behavior relevant to his physical and mental make-up.[17]

This allegation of absolute equality, however, is taken to the point of absurdity. We are told the following about female Australian aborigines:

> It is apparently her role to play the less aggressive part in social and marital life—her attitude toward men and her emotional composition act as a complement to those of men. She panders, consciously or unconsciously, to the dominant and aggressive strain in man; she likes to feel, as women do in our own society, the physical force and apparent strength of man. This approach is particularly evident in sexual activities. For example, in an incident mentioned above, 'nali:ndali received a beating from her husband. This is not a case of brutal maltreatment by the husband: a woman can, if she wishes, return the blows; nor does she particularly enjoy a beating, and usually it will produce in her sullenness and antagonism. But at the same time she expects such treatment if her behavior has been such as to warrant it. On the other hand, unjustified beatings and arguments will lead to bitter and resentful thoughts and actions.[18]

This account is reminiscent of the common barroom story which claims that women become even more affectionate once they experience man's superior physical strength.

Another example of questionable research comes from the Austrian priest Martin Gusinde. Gusinde, one of the few scholars who were able to do studies among these sub-Arctic tribes, lived among the Selk'nam, who existed at the Stone Age level and today are nearly extinct. Gusinde described the relationship of the sexes as being perfectly equal. The young people seek out their own marriage partners and the husband is just as economically dependent on his wife as she is on him. In addition, there are common initiation rites for young people. Father Gusinde gives a glimpse of the young Selk'nam male's image of his future wife.

> I answered the question: What qualities does the love-sick Selk'-nam lad prefer in the loved one of his choice? She should present a balanced, fully developed body and pleasant facial features; the lighter her skin color, the more desirable she is. Versatile and skillful at work, she should give the impression of being clean in body and clothing. In the way of spiritual attributes, he desires in her soft, quiet reserve submitting meekly and completely; quarrels and sullen sensitivity would be foreign to her.
>
> The woman must remain closely united with her husband at all times and perform any services he wishes without questioning. She should be happiest in their own hut, and should bring many beautiful children into the world, nurturing them with a mother's tender care. This is the most desirable wife. Nothing does more for the husband than to have his wife praised far and wide and to be envied for possessing such a treasure.[19]

Gusinde does give actual indications of sexual equality, for the young woman can choose her marriage partner. However, it is a strange kind of equality Gusinde is defining.

Many ethnologists believed that an inferior position of woman was not necessarily implied in bride purchases or many other practices. The majority of ethnologists still take this position, such as the respected British scholar E. E. Evans-Pritchard:

> We observe, for example, that in some [primitive] societies women crawl in the presence of their men or that people never eat in the presence of the other sex; but if we were to take these as signs, as we would be inclined to do, of abject female subservience or of a relationship of extreme reserve, or even of hostility between the sexes, we would draw entirely wrong conclusions.[20]

That crawling is a gesture of submission must go uncontested. Taking meals separately, however, must be assessed according to who gets to eat first, and who gets how much. In many societies different food taboos exist for both men and women. In societies without these taboos, the woman receives only the man's leftovers, and one can rightfully speak of her inferior position.

Eskimo tribes, which have neither social classes nor private property, are often cited by European intellectuals as proof that people are peaceable by nature and that war is a result of spurious social developments. Many travelers, missionaries, and researchers of the nineteenth century reported that a number of Eskimo tribes were free in their sexual relationships, and that wife trading was a frequent practice. Although the information, reportage, and various larger surveys are ample, there was practically no investigation of what significance and function wife trading had. In 1970 ethnologist Lawrence Hennigh considered the history of this custom and came to the conclusion that Eskimo wife trading created social alliances between two men. He wrote:

> The system seems casual to an outsider at first. An acquaintance dropped in for a visit, there was a period of ordinary conversation, then the guest said, "I think your wife is rather pretty." The host had the option of replying either, "I think your wife is pretty also," or "I agree, my wife is pretty." In the first case a trading agreement had been reached; in the second the visitor had been politely refused. The response of the wife is not known for sure. Informants say that she would have nothing to do with the other fellow at first, "but she always gave in at last." Ceremonial reluctance was common however for true marriages also, and it is not clear how much of this feminine hesitancy was spontaneous and how much was custom.[21]

It is not clear from the reports whether the woman was asked in advance. One incident that Hennigh reports implies that she was more or less forced to obey her husband.

> In Barrow a whale captain and his harpooner decided to exchange wives just before the whaling season. When the captain's wife protested vigorously, she was told that if she didn't cooperate they would not get any whales that year. When they didn't get any whales anyway she was furious.[22]

This anecdote was passed down only because, in the Eskimo view, the conduct of the woman was comical. Wife trading between men who worked together was self-evident. According to Hennigh, the most important reason for wife trading was to establish allies in remote settlements for their children. The children who were born after the wife trading were *katuks,* half brothers and sisters, and were obliged to offer each other mutual protection from enemies.

> Wives could not be traded between declared enemies. Warfare was common and women were sometimes captured but, if raped, they were killed soon after to prevent the creation of half sibling relations.[23]

Thus, wife trading among the Australians and Alaskan Eskimos served the same purpose: to form an alliance between men and to

reduce acts of hostility. Since the Eskimos knew the connection between coitus, procreation, and pregnancy, their intention goes beyond
the goal of the Australians. From wife trading, if possible, the next
generation was to arise, assuring the alliance. The Australian and
Eskimo societies used married women as instruments to serve male
alliances and status politics.

Five factors responsible for domination in a classless society
without political leadership will be familiar from the examples
cited.

1. Disposition rights to the woman through her relatives.

2. Presence of a male solidarity structure with exclusive title to
explanation and preservation of world order by means of ceremonies
(initiation rites and secret knowledge of myths).

3. Disposition rights to the sexuality of the married woman for the
husband's use as well as for the use of strangers (marital sexual duty
for the woman, wife trading, or wife lending).

4. Rape.

5. Male polygamy without the consent of the wife.

The last three factors are special extensions of the rights involved
in the first. These forms of male domination are identical with the
forms of domination which we know from hierarchically organized
societies that produce economic surpluses and are able to support such
specialists as chieftains, artisans, medicine men, and priests. In such
societies the woman is not only a valuable source of labor but at the
same time satisfies sexual needs and produces children to safeguard
or extend a man's welfare and sphere of influence.

These examples support the theories of such feminists as Kate
Millett and Shulamith Firestone, who advance a theory of domination that goes beyond the economic perspective of the theory of
historical materialism.[24] For example, if we compare the development of productivity in the societies of the Australian aborigines,
the Fuegians (as described by Martin Gusinde) and the bush people, then we cannot explain why in only one society young people
are free to choose a marriage partner. Nor can we explain why the
young female of the bushmen receives special attention from her
family during her first menstruation, while the Australians' rite basically focuses on the young men. Or why Australians and Eskimos
regard rape as male sport, while among the bush people rape is
unknown.[25]

Anyone dealing with the problem of the origin of female oppression must immediately reject the hypothesis advanced by Marxist and
Christian scholars that, without exception, social equality of man and
woman exists in classless societies. Hypotheses of the fundamental
object status of women in classless societies, propounded by Claude
Lévi-Strauss in his celebrated basic work *The Elementary Structures
of Kinship*[26] must also be challenged.

According to Lévi-Strauss, a fundamental characteristic of

human societies is the exchange of women. In order to understand this, one must know Lévi-Strauss's theory of the rise of the incest taboo. The incest taboo is the foundation of the social order. It is based on the ability of the human mind to produce order and rules to play by. According to Lévi-Strauss, there is no genetic aversion to incest, but the avoidance of incest affords a human group advantages by forming alliances between two groups which trade their women. Human beings who, according to Marx, make their own history lay the groundwork for their conquest of nature when they draw up the rules of exogamy: only women of an outside group are suitable marriage partners. The simplest rule of exchange between two groups consists in marrying a cousin on one's mother's side.

> The prohibition of incest is less of a rule prohibiting marriage with the mother, sister, or daughter, than a rule obliging the mother, sister, or daughter to be given to others. It is the supreme rule of the gift. . . .[27]

Lévi-Strauss seems to view the incest taboo—and thus the command to marry only members of an alien group—exclusively from the male point of view. He never mentions where men acquired these rights with which they exchange wives, or what skills or means they employed to exercise these rights. The premise of his famous theory on the formation of kinship structures is the basic accessibility of the female members of a society. Do women really possess a biologically determined, genetically set willingness to be the commodity of male society?

Lévi-Strauss was greatly influenced by his teacher, the ethnologist Marcel Mauss, who in his famous *"Essai sur le don"* described exchange transactions in primitive societies. Mauss regarded the "gift" as a total social phenomenon, an idea which Lévi-Strauss expanded on.

According to Lévi-Strauss, women are valuable because they guarantee the gratification of men's extensive need through their labor, their sexuality, and their ability to reproduce. Of course, this still doesn't explain why they are just another barterable commodity, like a lump of salt or a forged spearhead or a honeycomb. Nonetheless, he concedes one distinction; that women, because they are a "natural stimulant," are men's most precious possession, and their trading remains a staple. Lévi-Strauss could not have exposed the sexist character of his theory any more effectively. He implies that men are born dealers in women, and that it is quite unimportant whether those men stimulate the traded women.

Lévi-Strauss adds that women are a commodity for which the demand always exceeds the supply. In addition, he claims that men possess a natural tendency toward polygamy.

Social and biological observation combine to suggest that, in man, these [polygamous] tendencies are natural and universal, and that only limitations born of the environment and culture are responsible for their suppression.[28]

Naturally, Lévi-Strauss acknowledges this "natural and universal" tendency only in the male, and does not mention that in primate groups the females are generally markedly polygamous and promiscuous and, when in heat, constantly present themselves to any approaching male. Nor does he speak of the natural tendency toward polygamy of women of human societies. Since he considers needs of the human society from only a man's point of view, he says:

Consequently, to our eyes, monogamy is not a positive institution, but merely incorporates the limit of polygamy in societies where, for highly varied reasons, economic and sexual competition reaches an acute form.[29]

Lévi-Strauss expressly denies that, in the exchange relationship between two groups, the woman can be the subject. This appears to result from his contention that men possess all political and social authority in all societies. As he views the exchange of women as the basic commodity transfer in a society, he suppresses what actually comprises an entire playing board of strategies possible in the domination of one marital union between two members of different groups. To list only a few:

1. Bride and groom are able to choose each other freely. In his *History of Human Marriage* Edward Westermarck cites a great number of examples from all parts of the world where marriage is a free decision of both parties concerned.[30]

2. The bride settles on a groom who must accept this decision; reported by Father Wilhelm Schmidt from Indonesia.[31]

3. The groom negotiates with the consent of the bride with her parents, or he negotiates without her consent.

4. Either only the father or only the mother seeks a groom for their daughter or a bride for their son, and negotiates without her or his consent.

5. The father of the bride and the father of the bridegroom negotiate by themselves. In many societies it is the father's sister who seeks the bride for her nephew; in other cases it is a grandmother or the uncle on the mother's side. If neither the groom's group nor the bride's group is able to negotiate, a king or a chieftain reserves the right to rule over the marriage.[32]

What is it that actually distinguishes this exchange of women— whose worth is expressed in money or cattle—from slave trading? The bride price and its mutation, in a cattle-tending society, for example, are certainly established as the precursors of the capitalist money market. The impulse to polygamy is obviously not only biological but derives also from a socially formulated drive to possess. For, according to Lévi-Strauss,

> . . . the desire to possess is not an instinct, and is never based (or very rarely) on an objective relationship between the subject and the object. What gives the object its value is the "relation to the other *person.*" Only food has any intrinsic value for someone who is starving. But few objects afford a constant interest at all times and in all circumstances. "What is so desperately desired may be wanted only because someone else has it." An important object assumes "great value . . . if another person begins to take an interest in it."
>
> The desire to possess "is essentially a *social* response." And this response should be "understood in terms of power—or, rather, of *powerlessness.* I want to own it because if I do not it may not be there when I need it . . . If another has it, he may keep it for ever." Hence, there is no contradiction between property and community, between monopoly and sharing, between the *arbitrary* and *arbitration.* All these terms designate the various modalities of one tendency, or of one primitive need, the need for security.[33]

Sometimes he explains the exchange of women in terms of the market economy (scarcity of goods, supply and demand) and sometimes in terms of a neutralizing reciprocity. Lévi-Strauss further contradicts himself. Either the woman is "one of the objects of exchange" or "the feelings of the young woman are considered"; both are not admissible at the same time, for one cannot speak of a commodity, of an object of exchange, and at the same time furnish it with a potentially decisive influence on the fulfillment of the transaction. In fact, a variety of possible options between the right of self-determination for groom and bride and the control over both or one of the two by members of their families exist and not simply for males. While Lévi-Strauss attributes the tension in a society primarily to the perpetual scarcity of women (the most precious commodity), he neglects to say that in all societies in which there is marriage of son or daughter without their consent or despite their explicit reluctance, there is constant internal tension. In the majority of primitive societies these are resolved through a high divorce rate. In others, in which only the male can request a divorce, such as the Islamic or the early Chinese and Japanese societies, there are a great number of female suicides.

After nearly five hundred pages Lévi-Strauss finally arrives at a remarkable observation:

> . . . each woman preserves a particular value arising from her talent, before and after marriage, for taking her part in a duet. In

contrast to words, which have wholly become signs, woman has remained at once a sign and a value. This explains why the relations between the sexes have preserved that affective richness, ardour and mystery which doubtless originally permeated the entire universe of human communications.

How this affective richness and the ardor of love can be explained in the exchange he describes remains a mystery that Lévi-Strauss invented but did not solve.

8/Justifications of Sexist Power

We do not want to show how people think in myths, but how myths think in people, without people becoming conscious of them.

—*Claude Lévi-Strauss*

Jomo Kenyatta, the first president of Kenya, who studied anthropology in London with Bronislaw Malinowski, told of a Kikuyu myth about the allegedly terrible reign of women in hoary antiquity. The historical background of this myth probably constitutes a transformation of the clan system from matrilinear to patrilinear succession; in addition, however, it provides information on why men now rule women: In earlier times the Kikuyu women held a superior position in society. They were cruel warriors, dominated the men, and practiced polyandry. Since women were terribly jealous, many men were condemned to death for adultery and minor offenses. Men felt they were treated unfairly and planned a revolt against women's absolute rule. The women, however, were physically stronger than the men and better warriors. So the men decided to rebel when the majority of women, especially their leaders, were pregnant. On a selected day the men seduced the female leaders and the majority of their followers. Within six months the women were practically immobilized as a result of pregnancy; men then took over the leadership of the society. They immediately prohibited polyandry and established polygamy.[1]

This myth is supposed to legitimize the exercise of male power in the Kikuyu society. It vindicates sexist structures by blaming all methods of male domination on women, who, in ancient times, invented them. Sexual infidelity in the woman is no longer tolerated in Kikuyu society, because women allegedly used the same methods against unfaithful men as the men today use against them. The men broke down the women's resistance by making them immobile and dependent.

Another myth, which says that primitive women took the sexual initiative and were punished for it, derives from the East Eve in Dahomey. The myth is told by Hermann Baumann.

> Soon after God Mawu had created man and woman, he set them far apart. They could hear each other, but not see, for they had eyes, but no ability to see. They also had legs, but they were not able to walk with them. They had to move along by rolling . . . Mawu observed them. The man wanted to go to the woman, but he was afraid of making noise by rolling through the dried leaves and rousing God's attention. One day the woman caught a toad, roasted it on a spit, and devoured it greedily. The poison squirted in her face and she was able to see. Her first wish was to get to the man. She moistened the dried leaves, went to the man, and told him how she had learned to see. The man also wanted to see and rolled forward, but forgot to moisten the foliage and God heard the crackling sound. He cursed the woman: in the future she would have to wait for the man to come; she was no longer allowed to seek the man out.[2]

This myth too contains an explanation of power establishing why women are condemned to be sexually passive, why they are never permitted to seize the initiative. It was their own fault, for they broke a commandment from God.

Among the Indian tribes in Tierra del Fuego, the Yamana and the Selk'nam, there exists a myth that tells of women's rule and the initiation into the men's association. Besides the purely male initiations, the Yamana hold a mixed initiation ceremony in which young women and men participate together. Father Martin Gusinde extolled the partnership of man and woman, the democratic and cooperative coexistence of these peoples. He maintained that the myth of the Fuegians is descended from tribes residing farther north. However, this explanation appears inadequate, for if the marriages of the Fuegians were really so equal they wouldn't have needed to adopt the following myth demanding the solidarity of men and the subjugation of women.

> In primitive times, women possessed complete power over men; men were submissive and obedient, performed housework, and could not participate in decision-making. The women, led by Mrs. Moon, devised a plan to keep men submissive forever. They disguised themselves so that the men thought they were all-powerful and strange creatures. One day, Mrs. Moon's husband, Sun, overheard some women discussing their tricks and man's gullibility. Recognizing the scheme, he enlightened the other men, who then planned a revolt, killing nearly all the women. The men then disguised themselves, just as their wives had, to frighten their future spouses into submission. Thus, men usurped power through these spirit roles of woman's deceitful plan.[3]

The American ethnologist Joan Bamberger tried, with a number of other women ethnologists, to examine the roots of male domination in primitive societies. She cites a number of examples from South American societies in which the motives of conquest or subjugation of women are linked with the robbery of trumpets, flutes, and masks.[4] A variation of the myth among the Mundurucu says that women possessed flutes and spent so much time playing them that they neglected their husbands and their households. Because women possessed flutes, they also controlled the government. Men had to gather firewood, fetch water, and prepare the bread. Once men stole the flutes, they gained the dominant role. Among the Cubeo there is a cult hero named Kuwei, who conquered women, just as Heracles did. He stole the trumpets from the women and gave them to the men. Bamberger believes that these myths give men's dominance an ideological base.[5]

Women of African, Melanesian, and Australian tribes also invented religious rituals and masks. Hermann Baumann wrote:

> Another Cubeo myth tells that Kashashi, the legendary wife of the king Samba-Mikepe, invented the Shene Malua and the Mokenga masks. She put a Kalebasse with cut face on her head to frighten her disobedient child. But her husband was afraid that the boy might acquire a fear of women; he forbade women to wear masks and founded the Babende, a men's society which had an initiation rite and masks. Among the Nupe we also encounter the same theme; women possessed masks before the men, which perhaps represents a serious indication—accepted by the school of cultural history—of a close connection between mother right and mask . . .[6]

An important quality of the explanation advanced in this myth is its "ahistorical" content. The myth is used as political propaganda. Only when patriarchy is absolute does it fail to consider that a different state of affairs preceded it. It explains its claim to govern as divine and timeless, and spends little energy explaining its origin from a condition of previous powerlessness.

A dominion, however, which has to reckon with female counterweight tends to legitimize its existence in terms of the contrast between past and present. This is the case in many primitive societies where women control food production. The purpose of this dialectical process is to paint such a terrifying "picture" of the opposite world that all agree never to permit such a thing. The initiation rites of Papuan peoples also depict this. Women first possessed omnipotence, youth, strength, and health. Instead of flutes or masks, though, it was powerful snake grease that men stole from them. In Australia, mainly in the north, myths state that women were the original inventors and custodians of all religious ceremonies and sacred rituals that are now exclusively men's. These myths state, however, that women are happy with their submissive role.

The Berndts noted that women do not produce their own version of these myths, though they still regard these sacred ceremonies as their property, commenting, "They are doing it for us," or "It's my dreams the men are acting out."[7]

Lévi-Strauss first became well known outside ethnological science through the structuralist analysis he developed of the conceptual world and myth of South American Indians. His method is based on the assumption that myths, like sociological structures, are products of permanent and unconscious human attempts to discover order and rules in the chaos of the world around them. Myths of a people reflect the need to express unconscious logical contradictions of the culture. Differences in marriage rules and kinship order among neighboring tribes always give rise to a new combination of structural elements of the myth. For Lévi-Strauss, the unconscious is not a site of displaced guilt feelings, as for Sigmund Freud; he analyzes only the logical-formal elements of a myth and pits the opposition pairs it contains against one another. Only in this way, says Lévi-Strauss, are myths understandable.[8] Thus, Lévi-Strauss shows little interest in discovering who tells a myth and against whom it is directed.

In the myths he analyzes, "male/female" constantly emerges as a fundamental opposition pair, but he fails to note not only that the theme of the myth is sexual hierarchy but also that the myth represents an instrument of the doctrine of masculinity and the forced solidarity of adolescent boys against their mothers and sisters. Thus, the story of the rise and dissemination of a myth and its unconscious logical structure is therefore distinguished from its function in a society. Contrary to the myths already described, the message of this myth is that female subordination came about through a mistake or the woman's breaking the taboo.

Let us consider the most important domination myth in the Western Christian sphere, the myth of the Fall. The snake—and various types of lizards—personifies eternal youth, immortality, fertility. The snake possesses eternal youth because it can exchange its old skin for a new one. In the myth of the Old Testament, it partakes of divine knowledge of immortality. Although Eve is made out of Adam (in a patrilinear society the man must head the genealogical tree), it is she who tries to possess divine knowledge. There are two trees in Paradise: one whose fruit represents divine power (the tree of eternal life), and the other, whose fruit induces sexuality. Eve, who dared to reach for divine power, broke God's commandment, thus legitimizing man's domination over her. "Thy desire shall be to thy husband, and he shall rule over thee."

Adam is also punished, "because thou hast hearkened unto the voice of thy wife . . ."

A husband who allows his wife initiative must eternally atone.

The myth of the Fall and the expulsion from Paradise was an instrument of the absolute power of patriarchal Western civilization. It represented woman's permanent inferiority; without this myth the European witch trials, for example, are unimaginable. If myth and religion, as superstructural phenomena, were solely products of an economic base, then the effect of this Biblical myth would be incomprehensible. The myth descended from the Semitic herding culture, passing through very different social and economic conditions, and has been adjusted to show that the domination of man over woman in the family is God's will. Simplicity, as well as ambiguity, which always supplies new excuses for oppression, seems to be an essential characteristic for the social function of a myth.

Even the seventeenth- and eighteenth-century theorists on law, beginning with Hugo Grotius and Samuel von Pufendorf, deduce the husband's power and paternal authority directly from the divine will.[9] The Catholic Church, of course, holds to this subordination as a God-given state. This kind of thinking has legal repercussions: the five-year struggle over the marriage law of West Germany is incomprehensible without the history of divine male authority. Interestingly, a statement by Pius XII on the "emancipation of the woman" offers an instructive example of a new trend which proclaims that female subjugation was, in fact, woman's loftiest state:

> The social emancipation supposedly releases the woman from the narrow circle of domestic duties and cares for children and family, in order to make her free for her inborn inclinations so that she can devote herself to other professions and posts, even those of public life.
>
> But this is no true liberation of the woman; it does not contain the reasonable and appropriate freedom the lofty mission of the Christian woman and wife demands. It is rather a corruption of the feminine experience, and of the mother's dignity, a subversion of the whole family order, so that the husband of the wife, the children of the mother, the whole family and household are always robbed of a vigilant custodian and guardian. This false freedom and unnatural equality with man will bring about its own corruption of woman, for once she descends from the summit and the throne, to which the Gospel elevated her within the family, she will soon (perhaps not so much in outer appearances, but indeed in reality) be forced back to her earlier slave status and, as in heathendom, become a mere tool of man.[10]

Since the time of the Enlightenment, scientific theory has taken the place of myth. Now the vindication of sexist rule appears in philosophical, belle-lettristic, or scientific garb. The myth of the Kikuyus, which Jomo Kenyatta tells, reproaches women for unjust and arbitrary acts when they governed. Friedrich Georg Wilhelm Hegel claimed in *The Philosophy of Right:*

> If women are at the head of the government, the state is in danger, for they act not in accord with the requirements of the general public, but in accord with random inclination and opinion.[11]

These ideas are still argued today in one form or another. For instance, a number of psychological tests are still in use to investigate whether males have a greater sense of justice than females. A Darwinist view of women as evolutionarily inferior because of the lesser weight of the female brain may have long since been discredited. Indeed the scientific myth of the inferiority of women has given rise to many theories and conjectures which seem grotesque in retrospect. But this should not blind us to the way in which other conceptions have arisen which operate in the same way, a point we shall return to later.

Part Three
Women without a Platform

9/The Fathers of
Socialism

And meanwhile I sit there going to pieces...
—*Jenny Marx*

*Poor Louise, she went from the frying pan
into the fire. But then, with us women it's
always a question of frying pan or fire,
and it's hard to say which is worse. At
best our situation is critical.*

—*Eleanor Marx to her sister Laura on the marriage
of Louise Kautsky*

The virtue Karl Marx cherished most highly in women was "frailty"; the virtue he ranked highest in men was "strength."[1] Can such a man really have been eager to see women's emancipation?

Marx commented very little on female oppression, and his treatment of the relationships between the sexes was superficial contrasted to the care and rigor he applied to other areas of his universal range of subject matter, or to his extensive excerpts on natural science, history, and economics. Evidently he was reluctant—or not in the position—to deal in equal depth with the many dimensions of the woman question. Perhaps the subject challenged his whole way of life and the relative importance of his scientific and revolutionary activity. (He may have wanted to avoid a subject so close to home, one that could not be dealt with from the distance of the revolutionary scholar.)

The opposition of male "strength" to female "frailty" implies that Marx regarded the characteristics of the sexes in terms of dialectics and sophistries; he did not describe what a synthesis of these sex roles would look like. He reeled off phrases on a higher form of sexual union, without elucidating what he specifically meant by this. Or he used sophistries such as "The relationship of man to woman is the immediately natural, necessary relationship of human to human." It is not only natural, but in his opinion "the most natural." This relationship should show "to what extent the human being has become a natural being, to what extent his human nature has turned him into nature." He severs what it means to be human from what it means to be natural in a false opposition. The relationship is necessary and natural only if it serves in procreation. Otherwise there is no immediate and necessary relationship of man and woman.

In France, the writer George Sand fought against the Code Napoléon, which legitimized even physical violence against the wife. A husband who caught his wife at adultery and killed her went unpunished. As a supporter of the socialist ideas of St.-Simon, George Sand was the first woman in Europe who addressed both social conditions and women's rights in her journalistic and literary work.

Marx, on the other hand, never directly criticized woman's legal incapacitation, which John Stuart Mill, in 1869, characterized as nothing but bondage legally sanctioned.

The July revolution in France had brought a relatively free press but no improvement in the legal status of woman. Though divorce was permitted by the Code Napoléon, it was prohibited again as of 1816. In England wives had no legal rights and husbands could carry out punishment. It was a well-known saying that over every bed of an English husband hung a whip. Inasmuch as Marx wanted to advance the proletarian revolution, it is remarkable that he did not immediately capitalize on strikes and demonstrations by women workers for equal pay.

Not only did Marx and Engels not develop the matter of women's rights further, their thinking was far behind that of many contemporaries. The English journalist Harriet Martineau's classical work *Society in America* (1837) was, alongside Tocqueville's *Democracy in America,* the most informative text available on the functioning of democratic principles in American society by a European in the nineteenth century. She dealt equally with women's rights, the race problem, and class struggle. She believed that the emancipation of each class would occur only through the efforts of the class's individuals. Women had to act. The American Declaration of Independence would lead to the independence only of America's male population.[2] Her view of the female's spurious education, which "would encourage her weakness and penalize her strength," is of course diametrically opposed to Marx's ideal of woman. George Sand and the half-deaf Harriet Martineau, who, by means of an iron will, earned her living as a journalist, were characteristic of the women and men who fought for social progress. For women, the questions of emancipation and social conditions are of equal value, whereas for men this relationship is incidental.

In 1848, history was—for Marx and Engels—the history of class struggle. It is revealing to compare the *Communist Manifesto,* which Marx and Engels wrote that year in London, with the female declaration of independence, delivered that same year in Seneca Falls, New York, by one hundred women. The Declaration of Sentiments was a feminist manifesto that struck a completely different note from the beseeching pleas and appeals of German women; men must accept women as human beings. The American women saw the relationships between the sexes as a clear-cut power struggle.

> The history of mankind is a history of repeated injuries and usurpations on the part of man toward woman, having in direct object the establishment of an absolute tyranny over her.
>
> He has never permitted her to exercise her inalienable right to the elective franchise. He has compelled her to submit to laws in the formation of which she had no voice. . . . He has made her, if married, in the eye of the law, civilly dead.
>
> He has taken from her all right in property, even to the wages she earns . . .
>
> He has endeavored, in every way that he could, to destroy her confidence in her own powers, to lessen her self-respect, and to make her willing to lead an . . . abject life.[3]

These excerpts show that the radical American women already realized the drastic character of sexual domination, an empire that emanated from the misery of economic exploitation.

Even as a young man, Marx neglected to explore the definition of sexual relationships in Hegel's writings. More important for judging the position of Marx on women's liberation, however, is his major attack on the leading French socialist, Pierre Proudhon, in "Das Elend der Philosophie" (1846–47). Proudhon's pathological hatred of women, his petit bourgeois notions of the family, his negative view of women's work (which he believed robbed men)—attributes that were later important in determining the position of the French members of the Internationale—obviously left the young Marx cold, although the French St.-Simonists' protest against Proudhon could not have escaped him.[4]

The *Communist Manifesto,* too, touched upon women's rights only indirectly and accused the men of the bourgeoisie of finding their chief pleasure in "seducing each other's wives."

The American communes, which attempted economic and sexual equality, caught the interest of Marx and Engels, but by 1848 the second generation of early socialists were scoffed at as reactionaries and sectarians for holding to "the old views of the masters contrary to the further historical development of the proletariat."

If Marx and Engels were more farsighted in their analysis of capitalism than the founders and members of the American socialist communes, their negative judgment of these social experiments was nonetheless unjustified. The early socialists, mostly religious men such as Charles Fourier, analyzed human misery differently than

Marx. At the center of their thought was the immediate restoration of human happiness. According to them, one could, through a new communal society, persuade others of the advantages and opportunities for happiness in such a society.

The concept of feminism is attributed to Charles Fourier.[5] The so-called North American phalanx was the most progressive of the Fourieristic communes, giving women the right to speak in public assemblies, to vote, to receive the same wages for their work as the men, and to freely choose any profession. In other American communes housework was divided between men and women.

For Robert Owen, the early British socialist, the equality of men and women was the most important basis of his commune, New Harmony. Boys and girls were educated in the same manner and received the same professional training. "A new phase of existence" was aspired to.[6]

Owen's son, Robert Dale Owen, was a member of Indiana's state government and reformed its marriage law concerning divorce and the right of a woman to manage her property and wages herself to the woman's advantage.[7] A comparison of Marx and Engels with Robert Dale Owen is important in terms of the subject of contraception, which was never discussed in Marx's and Engels's writings. From 1828 to 1832, the American movement for birth control was initiated by Robert Dale Owen, together with Dr. Charles Knowlton.[8] In 1830 Robert Owen's book *Moral Physiology* was published, and seventy-five thousand copies were sold in America and England. Owen recommended mainly coitus interruptus. The male sacrifice involved would be insignificant compared with its advantages. A multitude of case studies were presented in his book to demonstrate the effects of this method, and Owen believed men would practice it.

In 1876 Charles Bradlaugh and Annie Besant, both members of the English Free Thought movement, began a birth-control campaign, reprinting Dr. Knowlton's *Fruits of Philosophy*. They were arrested, and their case went to Central Criminal Court and passed through all the appellate courts up to the Lord Chancellor, before they were acquitted. The number of brochures disseminated between 1876 and 1891 is estimated at two million.[9] Charles Bradlaugh and Karl Marx knew each other. Marx's supporters, and his wife and daughter, attended Bradlaugh's lectures. Yet, by the time Bradlaugh and Besant began the campaign for contraception, Marx had become his opponent.

At the end of the eighteenth century, the British political economist Thomas Robert Malthus had propounded a law of population which posited that food production could not keep up with the population increase.[10] Malthus used this law to reject any government subsidy for the poor, as this would only lead to further population increase. This brutal theory was also directed against the first English socialists. However, the Malthusian formula that was rejected by

Marx, as well as by other socialists, did not lead them to more concrete solutions. Although Marx was aware of England's population doubling within half a century, for example, population increase was insufficiently considered in his theory.

Charles Fourier was more perspicacious, rejecting the Malthusian inferences, of course, but more clearly realizing the problem of permanent population explosion. He also included in his considerations a condemnation of fertility for depreciating the quality of life and women's opportunities for happiness. Fourier wrote that at some point the human possibilities for colonization and expansion would end.

> What then, when the whole globe is so inhabited that for the rest there remains nothing left to colonize? One replied—that the Earth was not yet overpopulated and at least three hundred more years would pass before this point came. This is a mistake, for the world will already be overpopulated after 150 years. In any case, after 150 or 300 years the question will be pressing and still not solved if we stick to present-day views and methods.[11]

Fourier applied one of his imaginative preventive formulas to the calamity: a complicated theory to save women from continually having children.

Engels, on the other hand, simply believed that a socialist society would care for all children equally, for those born in and out of wedlock.

> This removes all anxiety about the "consequences," which today is the most essential social—moral as well as economic—factor that prevents a girl from giving herself completely to the man she loves.[12]

The phrase "a girl from giving herself completely" designates not the complete fulfillment of female wishes in socialism but rather the fulfillment of male dreams. Nearly continuous pregnancy, regardless of whether or not a society assumes responsibility for child care, was probably never the female wish.

If Marx had taken his wife's right to self-realization as seriously as he took his own, he would have been forced to come to terms with this problem. In the first years of their marriage, Jenny Marx was condemned to bear one child after another, and, in such poverty, these children had little chance of survival. On April 8, 1857, Marx wrote to Engels:

> My wife has at last been delivered. The child, however, was not fit to live and died forthwith. This, for her, was no misfortune. However, partly on account of immediately associated conditions that

have made a terrible impression on my imagination, and partly because of conditions that brought about this result, the reminiscence is very painful. It is not possible in a letter to go into such a matter.[13]

In 1851, on the birth of the Marxes' daughter Franziska, who lived only a short time, Marx wrote to Engels: "My wife was delivered of a girl, unfortunately, and not a *garçon."* [14]

Male grandchildren, on the other hand, he greeted with "Vivat, little citizen of the world. *Il faut peupler le monde des garçons."* In 1881, not exactly tactfully, he writes to his daughter on the birth of her child that he always preferred the male sex.[15]

Jenny Marx was uncritical of her husband; their family roles were bourgeois in concept. The learned paterfamilias, Marx, is opposed by an internal matriarchy. All biographies of Marx mention the domestic rule of both women, his wife Jenny Marx and their housekeeper Helene Demuth, whose plans Marx followed meekly as a lamb. The correspondence with Engels also shows the total male inability to share personal feelings and to communicate inner problems. They both kept up to date with current events, articles, and intrigues; they reported on their health and their finances, and politely, at the end of his letters, Engels sent his compliments to Frau Marx.

Engels also kept sexuality, emotion, and intellect distinctly separated in his life—as did Goethe and Heinrich Heine. Engels's companion, the working-class woman Lizzie Burns, could neither read nor write. There is no indication that he had liberated his beloved from many years of illiteracy.

Marx's three daughters were victims of sexism. If one of his sons had lived, Marx would probably have tried to educate him. In a time when universities, one after another, were becoming accessible to women in a number of European countries (France, 1863; Italy and Belgium, 1876), Marx never thought of giving his daughters a practical professional or academic education. A systematic education would have enabled them to understand better and further expand the whole theoretical foundation that their father laid for the revolution.

Marx and Engels deny a power relationship between the proletarian husband and his wife, for the male worker possesses no private property that would make it in his interest to rule over the wife's reproduction capability, as was the case of the bourgeois husband. Men and women of the proletarian class were just as free to marry as they were to divorce. In the few instances where Marx makes special mention of women, it is always to say that the cheaper women's and children's work supplant that of the man:

The less skill and demonstration of strength the handicraft demands, and the more modern industry develops, the more the work of men is displaced by that of women and children. Sex and age differences no longer have any social validity for the working class. They are only instruments of labor who, according to age and sex, have different earnings.[16]

Marx never breaks through the male perception pattern. Only from the man's perspective can women's work be a question of displacing the man. The fact that men took away women's jobs or that women were rarely given positions of importance is never clarified by Marx. Moreover, a major share of these women—widowed, single, or abandoned mothers—had to support their children by themselves. Unlike under bourgeois marriage, the children remained with the abandoned mother. In the proletarian family, children were an economic burden of no use to the husband. The whole of early capitalist society was confidently based on the fact that the proletarian mother did not simply leave her children to their fate; that she did not, so easily as the husband, resign herself to drinking; that in a situation of unlimited exploitation, in which many fathers simply walked away, she preserved her social instincts.

Marx and Engels did not discuss the temperance movement, organized mostly by women, although proletarian alcoholism hindered the organizing of the working class. Instead, they tried to create from the male proletarian an innocent angel: "The proletarian is propertyless; his relationship to wife and children has nothing more in common with the bourgeois family relationship . . ."[17]

Forty years later Engels says:

And now that large-scale industry has taken the wife out of the home and into the labor market and the factory, and often made her the bread-winner, no basis for any kind of male supremacy is left in the proletarian household—except, perhaps, for something of the brutality towards women that has spread since the introduction of monogamy.[18]

A small blot on proletarian marriage is conceded, but just as quickly dismissed. Engels leaves the question of the cause of proletarian male brutality unanswered. In the good proletarian sexual relationship

the eternal attendants of monogamy, hetaerism and adultery, play an almost vanishing part . . .

In short, proletarian marriage is monogamous in the etymological sense of the word, but not in the historical sense.[19]

It remains a puzzle how the man who in his youth had written *Condition of the Working Class in England* (in 1844) arrived at such glowing assurances. He must have known that the unbearable exploitation of the worker didn't create ideal, good-natured, egalitarian family life, that class antagonism hit the proletarian hardest.

In *Capital* Karl Marx discusses only superficially the economic situation of women. He mentions a newspaper report on the death of a milliner who was employed in a highly respectable London dressmaking establishment that catered to the court. During the busy season she had to work 26 1/2 hours without a break. Elsewhere he quotes at length from the reports of the British factory inspector.

> What is the feeling among the working miners as to the employment of women? "I think they generally condemn it." The mineworkers questioned are also against the employment of widows underground. The work is dirty, physically much too strenuous for women. Many of the girls lift ten tons a day.[20]
>
> "Do you think the women employed about the collieries are less moral than the women employed in the factories?"
>
> "The percentage of bad ones may be a little more . . . than with the girls in the factories."[21]

Marx does not grow indignant over the moralizing of the male workers who here confuse sexual morality and economics, but at certain points joins in their lament. Marx makes his most important statement on working women in *Capital.*

> However terrible, however repulsive, the break-up of the old family system within the organism of capitalist society may seem, nonetheless, large-scale industry, by assigning to women and to young persons and children of both sexes, a decisive role in the socially organised process of production, and a role which has to be fulfilled outside the home, is building the new economic foundation for a higher form of the family and of the relations between the sexes.[22]

The removal of private property, the abolition of the production process in its "naturally brutal form," turns the cooperation of the sexes in production into "the source of human development." The official doctrine of the socialist states today rests on this Marx quotation. Marx and Engels evidently realized that women's labor was unavoidable, and they did not oppose it as did the Lassalleans in Germany. Nevertheless, the remarkable fact remains that Marx and Engels, who critically followed every phase of development of the labor movement, did not resist the treatment of women's work by the labor movement and, above all, by the Internationale. In 1866, the German division of the International Workers' Association, founded in London in 1864, published a paper rejecting women's work, which Marx and Engels did not comment on:

Bring about a situation in which every adult man can take a wife and start a family whose existence is assured through work, and then there will be no more of these poor creatures who, in their isolation, become the victims of despair, sin against themselves and nature, and put a blot on "civilization" by their prostitution and their trade in living human flesh . . . The rightful work of women and mothers is in the home and family, caring for, supervising, and providing the first education for the children, which, it is true, presupposes that the women and children themselves receive an adequate training. Alongside the solemn duties of the man and father in public life and the family, the woman and mother should stand for the cosiness and poetry of domestic life, bring grace and beauty to social relations, and be an ennobling influence in the increase of humanity's enjoyment of life.[23]

The first German socialist to consider women's rights seriously was August Bebel. In Leipzig, during the early eighteen-sixties, he was acquainted with Luise Otto-Peters. Margit Twellmann, historian of the early German women's movement, believes that one of the things that stimulated Bebel to write *Woman under Socialism* was this contact. The book has had, to the present day, over 160 editions and has been translated into most world languages. Bebel's book—together with Engels's (which appeared some years later)—forms the keystone of the socialist stand on the woman question. Bebel's intentions toward women were exceptionally benign. When the book appeared, he was sitting in jail, considered by many to be a martyr. For many women, it appeared to be the Gospel, and it was a text that was accessible to them—in contrast to the difficult works of Marx.

With Bebel's publication, the socialist movement had in hand a weapon previously missing in the women's movement, which had been stagnating everywhere. Its publication also meant a modified stand on the organizing of women workers, who until then had organized as women's trade unions or women's federations cooperatively affiliated with the men's trade unions.

The persuasive power that emanated from Bebel's book was founded on the great effort and seriousness of the author. Bebel was the first male writer who in popular form attested to women's predominance in prehistoric times. (Bachofen and Morgan were then unknown.) Bebel demonstrated that their lack of rights and destiny were historically determined and could only be explained if women's oppression was placed within the context of the entire social and economic development of humankind. This emplacement within a general explanation of the world distinguishes Bebel's book from John Stuart Mill's *On the Subjugation of Women,* which, granted, offered a more differentiated psychology of male-female relationships, but not the striking overview of past and future that Bebel's work contained.

Since Karl Marx had concerned himself little with women's rights, the theories of Bebel and Engels were attempts to fill the gap in the Marxist view of the human being and, further, to make the connections between the rise of private property, the family structure, and the role of the woman. In the process Bebel and Engels offered a typical example of the way in which women can become stopgaps of political, sociological, or philosophical theories. "The woman and the workingman have, since old, had this in common—oppression."[24] This statement was supposed to form a political alliance between female and male workers and to place women's rights within the more general question of human rights. Bebel, however, is continuing the theory of Marx and Engels; workers are defined in terms of their position in production and their origin, both characteristics of a class. The source of workers' oppression lies in the capitalistic system. Because many women are workers, it would be sufficient to say that working women and men are oppressed. However, Bebel will not make this statement. By pitting woman and worker against each other, he conveys the idea that the amount of oppression is the same for women and male workers. In addition he suggests—continuing the theses of Marx and Engels—that, together, women and male workers possess only one single oppressor: the capitalist.

If the Marxist model would concede that the female sub-proletariat could come to think of itself as a class, or the entire female sex could form one class, then a third force would be set into play that would explode the whole model of society. For the antagonism, the mechanism of revolutionary transformation, arises only from economic development which separates rich and poor. Consequently, there is no room for one further economic contradiction, i.e., that between men and women, and from the outset, other non-economic contradictions eliminate the model as a driving force of social events.

On the very first page Bebel established the following difference between man and woman:

> However much in common woman may be shown to have with the workingman, woman was the first human being to come into bondage: she was a slave before the male slave existed.[25]

Thus, being a slave implies economic opposition to the ruling class. Accordingly, the formation of class consciousness in women and the class struggle against men would be possible. For: "All social dependence and oppression is rooted in the *economic dependence* of the oppressed upon the oppressor."

What was the woman then lacking in her historical development in terms of class formation if this statement of Bebel's is correct? Within the socialist model, the problem of women's oppression and liberation cannot be solved without contradictions, unless womanhood is regarded as the first class-creating element, and the most oppressed portion of the system, exposed to twofold oppression, as woman and as female worker.

For Engels the association of the class and the woman question raises even more complicated problems:

> The first class opposition that appears in history coincides with the development of the antagonism between man and woman in monogamous marriage, and the first class oppression coincides with that of the female sex by the male.[26]

While Bebel describes the woman as the first to enter into bondage, Engels says the oppression of the woman occurs parallel with the formation of the first class difference; female oppression and slavery appear at the same time in history. However, neither Bebel nor Engels discusses whether (or not) women offered resistance or whether they considered their own interests the same as those of enslaved men. The interest that Marx and Engels, in their long historical studies, brought to bear on the understanding of emancipation movements, revolutions, and uprisings, the belief that all history was the result of class struggles, was missing. They offered no exploration of the women's movements or the participation of women in class struggles.

In order to critically analyze the doctrine of Karl Marx from a feminist point of view, one must distinguish between two closely allied areas: on the one hand, the economic and, on the other hand, the sociological, with its class theory.

The purpose of a feminist criticism of Karl Marx and his successors cannot consist of a rejection of the basic characteristics of his economic theories and the description of the conditions of production in capitalism, even if many of them are in need of revision today. On the contrary: women, in their capacity as female workers, were just as much subjugated by the laws of capitalism that Marx discerned.

However, Marx developed a sociological pattern that plainly acknowledged the conditions of production as that which constituted the division of society into classes. In such an explanatory model, the oppression of one sex by the other has no independent existence. This led, unfortunately, to the view that women's inequality derived exclusively from the existence of social classes.

10/Feminism and Socialism

If every woman legally has a tyrant, the tyranny that men experience from their own kind leaves me cold. One a tyrant for the other.

—Hedwig Dohm

In the working class, the bearer of an extremely hopeful future, change sets in most abruptly, and so it is also up to change to bring a favorable solution to the woman question, which is a necessary component of the labor question. Therefore, quite apart from the consideration of natural differences resulting from the sexual relationship, it has the pleasant task of repealing the marital laws which still impede the woman from achieving social and political equality with the man.

—Commentary on the Erfurt platform, 1891

I f only I were a man, I repeated over and over. At that time I did not yet know that, even as a girl, I could accomplish something in the socialist movement or in political life. I never heard or read about women in meetings, and the appeals in my newspaper were always addressed only to the male workers.[1]

So writes an anonymous author. From childhood she was forced to work ten or more hours a day. By chance a Social Democratic newspaper fell into her hands and she bought it regularly from then on. Its contents were a revelation to her, and she tried to convey what she had read to the other women in the factory. However, for a long time she could not relate to the newspaper's politics:

> I still had no notion of the woman question. There was nothing in the paper about it . . . I first became aware that Social Democrats fought for women's equality when I happened to read the platform of the Social Democratic Party congress. However, I still did not know how women themselves could work together on Party undertakings.[2]

When she went to her second meeting, long after she had purchased her first Social Democratic newspaper, the speaker talked about class antagonisms.

> Everything inside me urged me to cry out: I know that too, I can tell about that also! But I ventured nothing, I didn't even have the courage to applaud; I considered it unfeminine. None of the speakers addressed themselves to the women, who it is true were present only very sporadically. But they spoke of only men's misfortune and men's misery. I found it painful that they did not talk about working class women, that they did not address themselves to women and call upon them to join the struggle.[3]

These accounts illustrate the value attributed to the situation of women in everyday life by male party comrades, Social Democratic editors, and labor functionaries. For socialist men class liberation was primarily a liberation of men; women's emancipation was a secondary promise of historical development. In the more than hundred-year history of the European workers' parties this has not changed.

In 1895 the German Social Democrat Johanna Loewenherz issued a pamphlet entitled "Wird die Sozial-demokratie den Frauen Wort halten?" Only the socialists could abolish "the curse of poverty" and "the tragedy of the sex."

> The woman's place is with this party, to which the future belongs. Firstly, to struggle together to bring about this future more rapidly; secondly, even now, to represent women's special interests: men's respect is won only through skill. Social Democrats always doubt the woman's ability. This distinguishes the evil intent of the Social Democrats from the evil intent of the capitalists, in whom it means greed, thirst for power, and cravings for Berlin nightclubs. If the Social Democrat's doubt in woman's ability is dispelled, he will joyfully acknowledge her equality.[4]

To the effect that the labor movement and the Socialist Party were the only forces of the future which would end women's oppression, and the oppression of others, it is odd that all the reassurances of women socialists inevitably incited complaints. This female lamentation over oppression and the men's lack of judgment in their own organization pockmarks the history of the Socialist Party, a monotonous racket on the road to the better future promised. Werner Thönnessen, who studied the influence of politics and literature of German Social Democracy on the women's movement in the period from 1863 to 1933, comes to the conclusion that "proletarian anti-feminism" was supported only when the party ventured into revisionist waters, as around the turn of the century or when, as in the twenties, it had been striving for more bourgeois, reformist goals.[5] However, this thesis can hardly be documented, for the hostility to women is not always connected to the theoretical orientation of the party. The Social Democratic women of the Left as well as the Right were discriminated against by the men of the respective group to which they belonged. This held true for even Rosa Luxemburg, who never directly came to terms with the question of women's rights—perhaps because unconsciously she feared the pain of such an analysis. Expressions such as "impudent mosquito" or "back-biting jerk" characterize the attitude of her male colleagues toward the deformed little woman who set out on male terrain and immediately entered into a vehement discussion of Marxist theory.[6] Even she, whose academic education was equal to that of the male intellectuals of the party's elite, came up against intense male criticism which could not be explained away solely as the initial battle of revisionism. Her activity as editor of the Leipzig workers' newspaper touched off a rebellion against her, and her appointment as editor-in-chief of the *Leipziger Volkszeitung* created similar difficulties; men did not want to grant her the same authority as they had her male predecessors.[7]

Insight into the discrimination against party women is also provided by Lily Braun, who, as the daughter of a general, was active chiefly in the bourgeois women's movement but then joined the Social Democratic Party. At a women's meeting it was objected that the socialist women's newspaper of the party, *Die Gleichheit,* which was run for over twenty years by Clara Zetkin, did not further the organization by an influx of women workers to the party. Lily Braun writes in her *roman à clef, Memoiren einer Sozialistin:*

> When I remarked that the general party press might at least remember to give the woman question, as an important instrument of our agitation, a good deal of coverage, everybody laughed. "Then you sure don't know our men," commented the fat Frau Wengs beside me. "They don't want to hear anything about us." "Most of 'em don't allow their wives to go to meetings or get joined

up with organizations. They're supposed to sit home and darn stockings," called out another . . .[8]

This tense relationship of the socialist women to the party press organs persisted. By the end of the twenties, 63 out of 120 Social Democratic newspapers in Germany had women's supplements, but only in isolated cases were these edited by women. The women's supplements were constantly criticized by women party members. Marie Juchacz, the leading SPD delegate in the Reichstag, called them "public garbage dumps," since contributions that women sent in were printed in the women's supplement where no men would read them.

The discrimination against women in the allocation of party functions was, just as much as today, a constant subject for discussion among socialist women. In 1895, Johanna Loewenherz complained about the lack of female delegates at the party congress. Lily Braun reports on a women's meeting in which all the disheartenment and the half capitulation of the female Social Democrats to their male party comrades was expressed:

"We have written equal rights for the sexes into the platform; we must first carry it out in our own party," I explained. "You'll get quite a brush-off from the men comrades with that!" said Martha Bartels. "With them, when anybody like us opens their mouth, it's still: 'Behave!' " "At home—and in the movement," said one other woman who had been in the party for years. "You know how we were treated last year," added fat Frau Wengs, "when we wanted to put just one single one of us in the general assemblies as a delegate to the party congress. 'That's what happens when you go out on a limb,' the confidantes told us." "So we must keep going back," I replied. "Yeah—in the end they'll do it for the beautiful eyes of Comrade Brandt," jeered Martha Bartels. Finally we decided to make one more attempt, and there was success at one of the party meetings, first of all, in carrying through my delegation to the party congress of the province of Brandenburg. The pleasure of the women comrades from this success was that of children beginning a new game: for a time all fighting was forgotten.[9]

This account provides insight into the helplessness of the women party members to assert themselves in the party machinery. It was all the more difficult since the central figure of the German women socialists, Clara Zetkin, rejected any gender struggle as "women's rightsish." Even modest attempts at the emancipation of party women were regarded by their male comrades as departures from the strategy of class struggle.

Since the days of the French Commune in 1870–71, the German Social Democratic Party had been the strongest in Europe and had assumed the ideological leadership role in the socialist movement. Clara Zetkin did not use this key role in order to carry on the struggle within the labor movement and claim for women workers, to the greatest extent possible, autonomy to act in the face of an already powerful hierarchy of male functionaries. She thus set the course for the socialist women's movement which till now has determined the direction of things and which has been partly to blame for the powerless, satellite-like quality of socialist women's organizations.

Clara Zetkin's reputation as the sole female theoretician of the woman's question is among the unscrutinized legends in the history of socialism. She adopted the completely familiar arguments of Marx, Engels, and Bebel. All she added was the irreconcilable battle stance toward the bourgeois women's movement. She mixed up the American and English radical feminists with conservative or denominational women's movement organizations. At times her writings give the impression that she regarded it as her life mission to pillory the bourgeois women's movement, the most dangerous of all reactionary forces:

> Together with capitalism, the bourgeois women's movement strides across the continents . . . dragging with it the allegiance of many millions . . . The classic expression of the counter-revolutionary nature of the bourgeois women's movement is the fascistic women's organizations in Italy, Poland, Germany, the United States, and other countries. In short, the bourgeois women's movement is a serious, dangerous power of the counter-revolution. With it there can be, there must be no compromise, no alliance; it must be defeated so that the proletarian world revolution may triumph.[10]

However, in the twenties, when she drew this demonic picture, her point was a moot one. The bourgeois women's movement was actually dead, and the sophisticated propaganda machinery with the tens of thousands of active staff existed neither in Europe nor in America. Nevertheless, Clara Zetkin made the radical feminists, women pacifists, and women Fascists out to be indistinguishable "forces of the counter-revolution." In 1889 this fight against feminism and supporters of women's rights was initiated by her, with the approval of European labor, in her famous report "Die Arbeiterinnen und die Frauenfrage der Gegenwart."

Werner Thönnessen writes:

> With Clara Zetkin's publication, socialist theory on women's emancipation is complete. The remaining work of Social Democracy consists, theoretically, in the further clarification of subordinate questions and, politically, in the transposition of Zetkin's

principles into agitation and organizational mobilization of women workers in industry. This task is mastered in the twenty-five years following, until the outbreak of the First World War, again under the controlling interest of Clara Zetkin.[11]

At the Gotha party congress of the SPD in 1896 Clara Zetkin delivered the key report on the woman question. Bebel may have tried in his writing to win the bourgeois women over to the socialist movement, but Clara Zetkin—herself of bourgeois origin—denied that the proletarian movement and the bourgeois movement had anything in common. The bourgeois women's movement exhausted itself waging a battle against the men of their own class. Zetkin believed, however, that: "Hand in hand with the man of her class the proletarian woman fights against the capitalist society."[12] The fact that Clara Zetkin came to the conclusion that working women and the women of the bourgeoisie had no common basis for their struggle was understandable in view of the prevailing practice at that time of the women's associations which, often enough through tactless philanthropism and moralizing condescension, had incurred the wrath of the women workers.[13] Still, the shortcomings of Marxist theory become apparent here: there were exact descriptions of the men's roles in the class struggle, but not of the women's roles.

The direct exploitation of woman by woman in the capitalist system took place outside the production process—in the household—and consisted of a feudal dependency which, in a time of speculation and brutal greed for profit through capitalist production, worsened. For even in impoverished bourgeois households it was a matter of status to have servants. Capitalist or bourgeois women exploited other women by hiring servants and acting like female slaveholders, demanding long work hours for small remuneration.

The gravest error in Clara Zetkin's analysis lay in the fact that she overlooked particular conditions. A strong organization of male workers could be formed only if a very much weaker organization of female workers was tolerated. Only by delegating housework and child-care responsibilities to women could the male worker—in the little time that remained after a twelve- or ten-hour work day—have any chance at all to develop his class organizations—trade unions, parties, and cooperative buying associations. This has not changed. In a class struggle such as the one Clara Zetkin had in mind—in which the question of unequal division of labor between the male worker and his wife, between son and daughter, was not discussed but was pushed aside—women always, and inevitably, attained only an extremely low level of organization.

Like Clara Zetkin, the daughters of Karl Marx, Eleanor Marx and Laura Lafargue, believed that socialist women and bourgeois women had nothing in common. Eleanor Marx enthusiastically greeted the resolutions of the Second International Socialist Labor Congress, which was held in Brussels in 1891. Emphatically the congress declared:

> A Socialist labor congress has absolutely nothing to do with the bourgeois movement of women's rights . . . The congress stresses the difference between the ordinary bourgeois peace league, which screams peace, peace, where there is no peace, and the economic peace party—the Socialist Party—that wants to remove the causes of war. With equal clarity the congress stresses the difference between, on the one hand, the party of women's rights women, who recognize no class struggle but only a struggle of the sexes—who, belonging to the propertied class, demand rights that are wrongs against their sisters from the working class; and, on the other hand, the true women's party—the Socialist Party—which gets to the bottom of the economic causes of today's unfavorable conditions for women workers and summons the women workers to fight together hand in hand with men of their class against the common enemy: the men and women of the capitalist class.[14]

However, there were other voices among the European socialists warning of the idea of the collapse of male workers' and women's liberation and registering their deliberations. Among these was the Swiss socialist Anton Dodel:

> The woman question is an essential part of the whole social question. On this subject all thinking humanitarians are of one and the same opinion. However, there are supporters of the aspiring, equitable order and new creation of social conditions, friends of the social revolution, who for their part, as we mention the question of women's rights, attach only subordinate significance to it, just as if it were automatically and directly understood that the question of women's rights will be solved at the same time as the labor question: in the narrower sense of the term and without any special effort—so to speak, only as an aside, a kind of secondary phenomenon, concomitant in the series of events of this world historical development. I believe that this interpretation just mentioned is a greater mistake, which can entail unwholesome delays and far-ranging complications afterward, which ought to be avoided.
>
> For the male worker of our day, despite all explanation in social questions, is still for the most part caught up in the error of the bourgeois men's world, according to which the woman actually signifies something weaker, less complete than the man. Thus it is conceivable that organized labor may fight for the total liberation of the male proletariat from the pressure of capitalism and deal this last deathblow without liberating women. Only then would it be obvious that one half of the human race had managed

to procure an existence worthy of humankind while the other half had had to struggle, only to come off the loser—moreover, under the curse of inequality with respect to rights. It is conceivable that the condition of society may be such that, where the man may be free—economically and morally free, and able to enjoy his life— his wife, his mother, his sister, and his daughter would remain as unfree as they are today.[15]

Similar to the thoughts of Dodel were those of the English socialist Edith Havelock-Ellis, who belonged to the circle of English social reformers which included Eleanor Marx and Olive Schreiner. Edith Havelock-Ellis, married to the sexual psychologist Havelock Ellis, found a large audience for her writings on pacifism, socialism, and marriage law. Her suggestions for a "marriage novitiate" and a motherhood tax for every man earned her the reputation among conservatives of being a revolutionary woman, while even her old friend Emmeline Pethick-Lawrence, Emmeline Pankhurst's sister-in-arms, considered her inexperienced in the woman question because she rejected the risk of violence in the struggle of the Suffragettes. But Edith Havelock-Ellis was far more realistic than Eleanor Marx, who would not admit the legitimacy of separate emancipation movements of women and men:

The labor problem and the question of women's rights are twin sisters. The male worker has awakened, and the woman has awakened, and both their problems are in many respects the same. Both of them must achieve freedom and, with it, equal opportunity. I should not like to go so far as Upton Sinclair, who says that the labor movement and women's movement should reach out their hands in order to truly win their rights together. They must each press for justice: not for their cause, but for the cause of the entire community. However, the men—at least the majority of them—are not independent enough to be trusted not to exploit the women for the designs of the working man.[16]

The first effects of Clara Zetkin's theory of proletarian women's liberation were already visible in German social democracy. It was precisely because she interpreted opposing interests of men and women within the party as having practically dissolved that she found such an eager reception in the party. In the general appeal for participation in the party congress of 1892, it was stressed to women that they could achieve their social liberation not in a battle of sex against sex —as the women of the bourgeoisie—but in the only way that led to the goal: through the struggle of class against class.

A woman's average day was so disconsolate that her feelings for socialism took the place of religiosity. Clara Zetkin constantly tried to heroize the women socialists' attitude to life. She made it clear to them that they would have to "annunciate the disinherited of the Gospel." According to Lily Braun, who was active in Berlin, the female functionaries, when they came home dead tired, were welcomed by their drunken husbands with blows or importunate tenderness. It was women like "fat little Frau Wengs" who after the party congress were chosen as confidantes for all of Germany. Lily Braun writes, "Once I visited fat little Frau Wengs; she was convalescing three days after the birth of her seventh child, and I found her once again behind the wash barrel." These women, Lily Braun says, "accomplished the utmost that they could accomplish; it was not their fault that it nevertheless was so little." But she criticized—not wholly without self-interest—the fact that such women as Frau Wengs were placed in the vanguard:

> Was it not a mockery of the women's movement that they who scarcely had time to read a newspaper, for whom the writing of a letter was an almost impossible task, should be placed in the vanguard.[17]

This comment illuminates the tension between the educated party women who mastered the jargon of scientific socialism and those whose liberation they demanded. Whether Clara Zetkin's pathetic tone of voice affected this first generation of female functionaries' attitude to life is questionable. She dismissed the struggle of the bourgeois women's movement for the right to university study as a "ladies' question" although she was among those first privileged to enjoy a better school education. In the twenties, the party paid dearly for her refusal to compromise with women of bourgeois origin who arrived at the larger social question only through their oppression as women. This becomes particularly apparent in the composition of the Reichstag in the Weimar Republic. Here the Social Democratic women were inflicted with a double inferiority complex: first, their schooling, which was usually inferior to that of the men of the party elite; second, they felt the lack of education they had in comparison with the women of the bourgeois parties.

Minna Cauer, who at the beginning of the nineties published the first magazine of the radical feminists, *Frauenbewegung,* took her stand in opposition to the women socialists:

> Surely the question of women's rights ... is above all an economic question: however, if it should be and become that which Bebel characterized as the liberation of humankind, then it must tackle not only this one aspect—that is, the economic—but it must be undertaken down the line: in government, law, economics, psychology, physiology, ethics, and religion.[18]

The question of women's rights, in her view, overlapped classes and parties. She was in favor of higher education for women.

In their memoirs, which they wrote in exile during the time of National Socialism, the two most committed women of the Left wing, Lida Gustava Heymann and Anita Augspurg, wrote of what kept them from joining the Social Democratic Party. Female Social Democrats had consciously rejected the women's movement as a bourgeois organization:

> What myopia! Had not decades of experiences in all countries shown that the multitude of Social Democratic men were in no way inclined to put into practice at home the equal opportunity laid down in the party platform? The Social Democratic German male, whenever he had the chance—in his family—exploited the woman for his personal ends, in the same way as bourgeois men. He was ruled by the same overbearing complex: he was always prepared to play the despot toward women and to reserve for the strong sex the better paid, very often less strenuous professions and leave to the weak sex, the arduous and poorly paid jobs as those Nature meant for women.[19]

The Social Democratic women, according to Heymann and Augspurg, were "controlled by male supremacy within the party."

What German Socialists like Marx, Engels, Bebel, or Georg Vollmar had accomplished through their writing was always acknowledged with gratitude by the radical women's movement. For radical women, "equality was the indispensable precondition," but had not been the goal. Full equal rights for the woman in civic life was only one phase, only a means and a way to reform "the formal and sterile system of the male state."

The resolutions of the conference of socialist women, a conference held in Munich in September 1902, show that these reservations against the Social Democratic Party were justified. There was a controversy in the European socialist movement prior to the conference over the expediency of the women's vote. Many members of the party feared a loss in votes through women's suffrage, for too many women were still bound to the church to vote for the socialists. Consequently, the Social Democratic women decided to limit the demand for woman suffrage to a rather gentle presentation. The text of the resolution reads:

> In the struggle that the proletariat is leading for the conquest of the universal, equal, secret, and direct suffrage in nation and community, the women's vote must be demanded, and in agitation, must essentially be retained and advocated emphatically. However, the demand can be placed in the foreground as one of the more crucial points in the action program of this struggle, only if by this means the expansion and safeguarding of the political rights of the working class are not imperiled.

From a feminist point of view, the splitting of female human rights into class interest and special women's interest is unacceptable and in effect discriminatory. This often recurring point shows how far removed in reality the Social Democratic women were from regarding themselves as the human norm.

Clara Zetkin charged the bourgeois women's movement with the sin of dilettantism. Yet the Left feminist wing of the bourgeois women kept trying to infringe upon the organization of women workers. Minna Cauer wrote:

> The greatest and most difficult task for women lies in familiarizing themselves with the question of the women workers, who can tolerate the slightest dilettantism even less than the general woman question.[20]

Clara Zetkin neglected the fact that women, for the first time, were developing their own forms of self-help.

Lida Gustava Heymann, daughter of a Hamburg patrician, had sworn "never to let [her] personal freedom be infringed upon by men, that is, insofar as this is at all possible under the given conditions in the male state . . ." After the death of her father, she used her economic independence to create relief agencies for women.

The women of the Left did not waste much time on a political theory of feminism: they jumped into the midst of politics, acquiring their knowledge from practice. In 1896 they supported the strike of women workers in the ready-made-garment industry; introduced a movement for seating accommodations for commercial employees; and from 1894 to 1898 petitioned for the abolition of servant regulations and demanded the appointment of female factory inspectors and police officers. In 1901 the first meeting with the woman leaders of the labor organizations took place. The Social Democrat Emma Ihrer reported before the radicals on the subject "The Next Goals of Protective Legislation."[21] She received the assurance of full support in her demands. The most well-known leader of the radicals, Anita Augspurg, protested against the male employers who kept women workers from exercising their right to free association. She referred to the bad example of the national government, which as an employer of post, railway, and other civil servants, made the right to free association illusory. The socialist Anna Blos writes of this period: "We know today that the bourgeois women mentioned, from their point of view, not only wanted to do good, but also achieved it."[22]

In the focus of the radical women's efforts, along with the organization of professionally active women, was school reform. The radical Left wing felt that the surrogate educations for women were practically worthless. School reform was not supposed to be a girls' imitation of the existing secondary school for boys but was based on the principle of coeducation.

From the very outset, the radical women's uncompromising battle for their sex and their interpretation that society's misery was the result of a totalitarian male state differentiated them from the moderate women's emancipation of their class and the planless accommodation politics of the Bund Deutscher Frauenvereine (Federation of German Women's Associations), which collected an iridescent political spectrum of opinion under one umbrella organization. Heymann described the relationship of the radical and conservative women's movement at the start of the century:

> The conservative woman, always emphasizing that women were a different breed, tried to create for women educational and vocational opportunities, in order to gradually make it possible, by way of social activity in the community, to develop a helping and supporting role in the existing male state. Naturally their tactics for this are always: "Caution! Don't offend anybody! One mustn't provoke men too much, because they're the ones who rule the nation; influential people must be well disposed toward us: we need them. In order to achieve partial results, one must always be prepared to compromise."
>
> The radical faction was something! . . . they disputed the idea that men should have the exclusive right to make decisions. In the fight for economic, social, and political equality, they saw no cause to view the differences of the female sex as a sign of its secondary importance or incompetence. To the radical women the norms and aims of the existing government, ruled one-sidedly by male intellect and on behalf of male interests, were no *noli me tangere*, to which they had been integrated and subordinated . . .[23]

The radicals created for themselves their own political federations. The first effort at such organization was the association Frauenwohl, which was founded in 1888 by Minna Cauer. Within a few years, local groups of this association arose in several cities.

All current political questions were debated by the Frauenwohl,

> whether it concerns customs, the fleet, the Poles, or the Alsace-Lorraine question . . . the employment of women doctors was demanded in schools, in health clinics, in the vice squad, in prison. From an awareness that rejected the penal code across the board, a complete transformation of the prison system was demanded. A special commission set up for this purpose dealt with this question in exhaustive detail. Prisoners were visited. Arrangements were made for the return of ex-convicts, appeals were drawn up to alleviate the lot of the prisoners, to replace the desolate lethargy of prisons with courses and continuing education.[24]

The radical feminist contributions to the autonomous women's movement around the turn of the century have remained almost completely unknown until recently because until now the history of the German women's movement has hardly been a subject worthy of historical research. Their demands and also their successes were ascribed chiefly to the conservative women's movement, although it constituted a constantly retarding force and for the most part even a reactionary phase. From the Left wing came the ideas and the initiatives: without it there may not have been a single suffrage association in Germany. The liaison and affiliation with the international organizations of the women's movement were sought out and sustained by the radicals. Nationwide demonstrations and petitions to change family law legislation for the German Civil Code, which went into effect in 1900; the fight against the criminalization of prostitution and against discrimination aimed at the out-of-wedlock child and the single mother; the initiative for large-scale maternity benefits and school reform—all these concepts and initiatives originated with the progressive portion of the women's movement. Most importantly they provided the discussion of paragraph 218 concerning legalized abortion, which began shortly after the turn of the century. The Social Democratic lawyer Gustav Radbruch, called the earliest champion of new abortion laws, opposed paragraph 218 with support from the women's movement. The first person to advocate the elimination of punishment for abortion, which at that time was five years in jail, was the Countess Gisela von Streitberg.[25] The debate on the criminal code reform and the change of abortion paragraphs 218 and 219 led to a heated controversy within the bourgeois camp of the women's movement. In 1908 the legal specialist Camilla Jellinek—in the General Assembly of the Federation of German Women's Associations, which was held in Breslau— took issue with the arguments of the female opponents of abolition of paragraph 218.

> In the destruction of budding life no protected interest is infringed upon, for the embryo is not a legal personality. But the threat of punishment is an unjustified infringement upon the opportunity to control one's own body, and upon the freedom of the personality.

Within the women's movement the primary opponents to a reform of the abortion laws were the spiritual leaders of the conservatives: Gertrud Bäumer, Helen Lange, and Marie Raschke. Helen Lange, the education reformer after whom a great many German secondary schools for girls are named, believed that childbearing was a woman's duty. Legalizing abortion would lead to a "numerical, physical, and moral weakening of the people," and by this means drive "the people one step further down the road to decline and degeneration." She even drew the ugly comparison that self-mutilation for the purpose of being suspended from compulsory military service was punishable according to German law; she also wanted to see this employed in the intervention of abortion. There was talk of "duty to race hygiene," and Gertrud Bäumer even charged that the suggestion of the repeal of paragraph 218 came from the group that was endeavoring "to liberate sexuality from responsibility." All the arguments in the debate underway in West Germany and other countries since 1968 on the legalization of free abortion already appeared in this report by Camilla Jellinek. And the conclusion she drew is just as relevant for the feminist movement of today: "On that score I have no doubt: if the men had to bear children—a male paragraph 218 would never have been created."[26]

It is not possible to establish exactly when the discussion of paragraph 218 began in the Social Democratic Party. It became an official point in the platform of the Independent Social Democratic Party, which during the war had separated from the socialist majority. In the Weimar period, however, drafts of legislation proposing to eliminate paragraph 218 were introduced into the Reichstag again and again by isolated groups of Social Democratic or, later, Communist delegates. After the Second World War the demand for free abortion crops up over a five-year period in the yearbooks of the Social Democratic Party.[27] Then it disappears for twenty years and does not again become a party demand of the Social Democrats in West Germany until the international abortion campaign of the new women's movement began.

This comparative presentation of the early socialist movement with the early women's movement shows how two political currents, both based on emancipation, on liberation from oppression, and on the conquest of human alienation, failed to unite their efforts. This was not completely the fault of the women's movement, but to a very considerable extent that of the SPD and their precursors. The early history of the socialist movement in Germany demonstrates in a purely exemplary fashion what fatal results a false theoretical goal can have. The erratic course set by Marx, Bebel, Engels, the women's leader Clara Zetkin, the empty eschatological promises to the women that capitalism's Judgment Day would come, resulted in the emergence of a party whose understanding of sex roles was basically the same as that of the bourgeoisie. For the party women there remained only one choice: making the views of the "fathers" of socialism into their own, as Clara Zetkin had done. Thus, they became active opponents of the autonomous women's movement, while, simultaneously, not being taken seriously by the party men. In the years when the socialist organizations were formed, women were up against a male elite which was already politically trained and intellectually dominant and which would not let them find a consciousness of their own. The Socialist Party, to a great extent, reinforced women's sense of inferiority. Women socialists did not struggle hand in hand with their male comrades, as Clara Zetkin believed, but rather were taken in hand by men.

11/War against the War

It was in us that Germany spoke, felt, willed; our personal soul merged into the soul of our people.

Death on the battlefield fits into the great chain of human striving and struggle. With it a generation will win prosperity. Out of the feeling that he alone, out of millions of others, has been chosen to give his very death the nobility of a purpose, the soldier, in all ages, has found it sweet and sublime to die for the Fatherland.

And deep in the soul women can sympathize. It is a mother's fundamental experience that life and strength must be sacrificed so that new life can bloom all the more beautifully.

—Gertrud Bäumer

If we begin to accept war as inevitable, then women might just as well give up life immediately, for under such conditions it is not worth the trouble of preserving the human race.

—Emmeline Pethick-Lawrence

Among women there has never been a militant international slogan such as "Workers of the world, unite!" The thought of forming an international force against the resistance in our own fatherland never occurred to women. In this sense they have never wanted or had an Internationale.[1]

This view of leading German emancipationist Gertrud Baumer reflected the feelings of the conservatives. In 1916 she wrote:

> "Heimatdienst" (Home Service) is, for women, the wartime translation of the term "women's movement". . . just as the war has stirred the will of our people, revealing its deepest essence, it also made it possible for the German women's movement, more clearly than it could have done in peace, to show what it wants to be: the National Women's Service.[2]

With the outbreak of World War I the women's movement and the socialist movement lost what could be called their historical innocence. Until then they had represented people without power or rights throughout the world; now they betrayed not only their principles but also the understandings that had arisen at the start of their organization: for the labor movement, that internationally organized capital was to be fought only by an international labor organization, and, for the women's movement, that women of all countries were oppressed by a patriarchal world civilization. Social Democrat Lily Braun provided one of the nastiest chauvinistic propaganda papers; she, who had fought long for woman's equality, now rejoiced: "With one blow all the particular women's rights demands, always culminating in equality with man, were gone . . ."[3]

In Braun's view, everything women had fought for suddenly acquired value, only within the context of war:

> And now: the women's movement! No area of our social life provides such clear, such classical proof of the cultural significance of the war. The women's movement was facing the danger of being bogged down. The war led it out of the natural spring of womanhood to torrents of fresh waters . . .[4]

The National Women's Service, organized by the bourgeois women's movement, employed—and patronized—women workers in war service. Women workers, together with aides of the Women's Service, sang:

> *In service to the Fatherland,*
> *the woman busily moves her hand;*
> *there is cooking, nursing, mending;*
> *as war leaves many wounds for tending.*

This makes us lasses active too,
and if our deeds achieved are few,
for love's labor here we sit,
soldiers' stockings we will knit![*5]

The First World War's chauvinistic delirium over the fatherland divided the socialist parties and the women's movement. In England, Emmeline Pankhurst and her daughter Christabel became patriots overnight; they no longer demanded the vote but gave recruiting speeches and lectures on the German peril. For this outburst of feelings for England, those suffragists in prison were rewarded with amnesty. Pankhurst, who had been one of the first women to enter the Labour Party, gradually moved right, politically. On behalf of the English government, she traveled on a secret mission to Russia and the United States; she publicly reprimanded her daughter Sylvia, a socialist feminist and advocate of pacifism who worked in the East End of London, organizing welfare centers, kindergartens, restaurants that sold food at cost, and a small business that manufactured toys on a cooperative basis.[6]

Feminist pacifism has unfortunately been bypassed by general historical research, though pacifists everywhere played instrumental roles. In America, women of the national suffrage organizations nearly worked harder on the food supply and the Red Cross than they did on their declared political goal, the woman's vote. Carrie Chapman Catt, a declared opponent of the war, who was elected president of the National American Woman Suffrage Association in 1915, had to urge women to continue fighting for the vote. NAWSA, the largest American suffrage organization, financed and founded its own war hospital in France and employed its own women doctors.[7]

Women everywhere expressed their opposition to the war, to a world full of frenzy and rising patriotic feelings that found expression in killing. During the balloting on the U.S. Declaration of War, Jeanette Rankin, the only woman Senator, added the only vote of opposition to a fervent majority of war backers. In the German Reich, the Social Democratic endorsement of war credits divided the party. Clara Zetkin, Rosa Luxemburg, and Luise Zietz remained embittered opponents of the war. Zetkin demonstrated her moral courage and her political stature when, in 1914, she began printing provocative antiwar articles in *Die Gleichheit*. Altercation with the party leadership over her position led to her suspension as editor-in-chief. Leading women

---

*The German text reads:

> Zum Dienst für liebe Vaterland rührt fleissig sich die Frauenhand;
> es wird gekocht, genäht, gepflegt, weil Kriegszeit viele Wunden schlägt.
> Das macht uns Mädel auch mobil, und leisten wir auch nicht so viel,
> zur Liebesarbeit sind wir hier, Soldatenstrümpfe stricken wir!

socialists did not agree with the politics of the Social Democrats in the Reichstag, and as a result of the removal of class conflicts, almost all prominent Social Democratic women eventually went to prison for their loyalty to internationalism, and later joined the Independent Social Democratic Party (Unabhängige Sozialdemokratische Partei or USPD).[8]

The formation of a woman's peace party was the brain child of two European women who had entered the United States in order to mobilize the American suffrage organizations against the war: the Hungarian journalist Rosika Schwimmer and Emmeline Pethick-Lawrence.[9] At the international women's congress in Berlin in 1904, which concluded with the founding of the International Woman Suffrage Alliance, Schwimmer met Carrie Chapman Catt. Schwimmer worked in the Hungarian woman suffrage movement and in 1913 organized the International Woman Suffrage Congress in Budapest. The following year she worked in London as international press secretary of the International Woman Suffrage Alliance, and was a correspondent for several large European newspapers. One frequently quoted anecdote from her life is that of a breakfast she had with Chancellor of the Exchequer Lloyd George on July 9, 1914. She warned him that the incident of Sarajevo would certainly cause a war with Serbia if something was not done immediately, and that such a war would have inestimable consequences for all of Europe. This anecdote comes from the war memoirs of Lloyd George, who reports that Rosika Schwimmer was the only person who at the time realized the imminent danger of war.

Immediately after the outbreak of fighting, she tried to organize an antiwar movement, driven by the conviction and fear that a war waged to its end would only result in a peace treaty that would embody new causes for future conflict. The primary element in her plan was the hope of intervention by the neutral powers: the United States, Switzerland, the Netherlands, Sweden, Denmark, and Spain. Other points of the program provided for the establishment of a world parliament, a world court, and international non-military sanctions. By August 1914, women from Great Britain, Germany, France, Russia, Austria, Italy, Switzerland, Denmark, Sweden, Norway, and Holland had already signed a petition stating this goal. Their suggestions for peace were immediately translated into many languages and disseminated throughout the world by women's organizations. Rosika Schwimmer presented this petition signed by one million women from thirteen countries to President Woodrow Wilson and enlisted American women in the international women's pacifist movement.

Just as spectacular was Emmeline Pethick-Lawrence of Britain; her pacifism associated feminist involvement with the ideas of the Union of Democratic Control, an organization that English liberals and socialists supported in order to assure a permanent peace at the end of the war. The program they advocated was not so emphatically addressed to an immediate end to war, as was Rosika Schwimmer's, but contained a whole catalogue of demands to ensure a constructive peace, above all disarmament and international controls on the production of arms and their export. Women of Europe, according to Pethick-Lawrence, bore no responsibility for the decline of the West: on the contrary, male governments had arrogantly rejected all women's warnings and denied them the vote. Now it was time for men to vacate the judge's bench and let women take over. "A new peace that expresses the birth of a new spirit" must be brought about by women.

The most important encounter in the United States for these European champions of women's rights was a meeting in Chicago with social reformer Jane Addams. Addams had made her first public appearance for the peace movement in 1899, when she took part in the anti-imperialist agitation against United States annexation of the Philippines. As a pacifist, she believed that peace and anti-imperialism belong together. Another source for her conviction of the possibility of peaceful coexistence was her work in the poor districts of Chicago. In her writings Jane Addams created a new concept of pacifism that had nothing to do with dovish good conduct or a passive will to peace; she no longer focused only on the avoidance of war but also on the active, enduring fight for a new value system, which was to replace celebrated military virtues. Addams demanded a moral equivalent for war and a patriotism that would encompass the whole world. Although she was active in the American women's movement before the outbreak of the world war, she had worked primarily in a pacifist alliance supported by both men and women. Through her encounter with Rosika Schwimmer and Emmeline Pethick-Lawrence she realized it was necessary for women to form their own peace organization.

On January 10, 1915, the Woman's Peace Party was founded in Washington. The platform contained eleven points, the most important of which were: calling a conference of neutral nations to bring about a prompt peace, limitation of arms and nationalization of weapons production, organized opposition to militarism in one's own country, democratic control of foreign policy, humanization of the government through the extension of voting rights to women, establishment of an international police force to control rival armies and navies, and the removal of economic causes for war. The program for a constructive peace, which was also passed, contained detailed stipulations and demands for security, and a future peace policy. A "Concert of Nations" was to take the place of the old foreign policy; this new concept featured equal importance of powers and self-determination rights of the inhabitants of a territory over their autonomy or the annexation of a different nation.

Although a number of the other peace organizations had produced similar demands, the program of the Woman's Peace Party was the most comprehensive to date, and it paved the way for President Wilson's later international program. At the conference, women were not sparing in their criticism of established pacifists. They complained that the greatest pacifists on military disarmament had only lulled them to sleep. They also objected that the pacifist movement had not acted promptly at the start of the war. The war was, in the words of Carrie Chapman Catt, incompatible with the interests and ideals of women as feminists and humanists. The International Woman Suffrage Alliance, with Catt as president, was invited to Berlin in June 1915, for the world congress for woman suffrage. But in September 1914 the Federation of German Women's Associations, the largest German women's organization, canceled its invitation to the international alliance; only the feminist Lida Gustava Heymann was cooperative. She had written and disseminated an appeal to the women of Europe to protest against the war and to convene an international women's conference immediately in a neutral country. In February 1915 a preliminary meeting had taken place in Amsterdam in which four German women participated. An international women's congress later that year, in The Hague, resulted.

> The purpose of the congress was threefold: to present a protest of women against the war and its human slaughter; to proclaim the demand of women's political equality; and to try to bring about an end to the war.[10]

The four German representatives at this preconference must have suffered a severe disappointment after their return when the Federation of German Women's Associations not only refused to participate but regarded any promoting of the congress as an infraction upon the solidarity of the German women's movement, "inconsistent with any responsible position or activity within the Federation of German Women's Associations" and "incompatible with the patriotic character and the national duty of the German women's movement."[11]

There were conflicts with authorities in several other countries as well.

> The English government caused women great difficulties. One hundred and eighty delegates were registered, but were refused permission to leave the country. A storm of indignation went up. As a result of an interpellation in the Lower House, the Home Secretary, Mr. McKenna, selected 24 out of the 180 women and "graciously gave them permission" to participate in the congress. But the Admiralty (that is, Mr. Winston Churchill) decreed otherwise; a few days before the congress and through its duration, shipping between Holland and England was suspended.[12]

However, the conference was held, from April 28 to May 1, 1915, with participation from all important countries. The American delegates came on a Dutch-American steamer sporting a flag which, in big blue letters, bore the word PEACE. From the warring powers forty-three delegates took part—twenty-eight from Germany, nine from Hungary, and six from Austria. The American historian Marie Louise Degen, who in 1939 wrote *The History of the Women's Peace Party,* reported that the German delegates were subject to severe repression from German authorities. In The Hague, 1,136 delegates gathered from twelve nations to protest the war and to discuss immediate measures that could be carried out in particular countries. The most ample and affectionate greetings came from the conference of socialist women who had met in Bern in 1915—twenty-five delegates from Germany, England, France, Holland, Italy, Poland, Russia, and Switzerland. They formed two deputy committees, which, in roughly five weeks, visited European statesmen of fourteen countries. Mockery, scorn, caricature, and biting irony were the reactions of the international press. When the *Lusitania* was sunk by the German navy, Jane Addams and her peace committee in Berlin visited German Foreign Minister Gottlieb von Jagow and Chancellor of the Reich Theobald von Bethmann-Hollweg. Jane Addams wrote of this encounter:

[The Chancellor] said he had never heard a German say that he wanted England crushed. I said I had never heard an Englishman say that he wanted Germany crushed, only that he wanted German militarism crushed. He said that this was a distinction but not a difference. The army of Germany is a part of the empire, and he went on speaking as they do, in the half mystical way that is so difficult for us to understand. It is as if their feelings for the army are like those of a church for its processionals.[13]

The great tour made to the warring powers, as well as to the neutral states of northern Europe and to the Vatican, had visible effects. Four hundred meetings held in Sweden on one day put the government under pressure. Women gathered so much information on tour that they believed their plan of a peace initiative of the neutral states, such as Sweden or Holland, could be realized, provided that all participants could save face in the process. In America, though, Jane Addams's mission was appraised in a letter by presidential adviser Colonel Edward House as a collection of astonishing misinformation on Europe. Four days after her return, a mass meeting of three thousand people took place in Carnegie Hall, New York; thousands had to be turned away. Jane Addams reported on the Hague women's conference and their visits to the different statesmen. The high point of her speech was the complaint that this was "a war of old men." Young men who had been at the front had reported that this bloody war of bayonets and trench fighting was endured only by numbing oneself with drugs. The English took rum, the French absinthe, and the Germans knocked themselves out by inhaling ether. Before America's entry into the war, women's associations and sympathizers from all parts of the United States sent twelve telegrams to President Wilson to pressure him into calling a conference of the neutral powers. Anita Augspurg and Lida Gustava Heymann formed a "Women's Commission for Lasting Peace" in Germany and, as a result, were watched closely by the police. House searches took place, their mail was censored, they were no longer allowed to travel in neutral countries; in particular states of the German empire women agitators were deported or taken into protective custody. According to Heymann, women's associations whose leaders were suspect were not allowed to hold meetings, or even gather in private houses. Resolutions which were sent to the Chancellor of the Reich in May 1917, urging him to end the war and to consent to peace without annexation, were censored by the press. Women were often able to avoid even angrier repression only by cleverly insisting that they had founded no organization but only worked together on a casual basis.[14]

The conviction that the majority of women were against the war was broken only by the martial war cry of the conservative women's movement:

> It alienated many pacifists that the organized women's movement in Germany, with the exception of the extreme left wing . . . had failed in the decisive moments. One must not forget, though, that the German bourgeois women's movement . . . amounts to only a small percentage of all women. These bourgeois women were sociopolitically brilliant, but in regard to foreign policy, with a few exceptions, they were totally unoriented when the world war broke out.[15]

Women in some countries clearly demonstrated how much they disapproved of the military. In Australia there was a referendum during the war on the introduction of compulsory military service. Because a large number of franchised males were serving as volunteers with the Allies, the women, eligible to vote since 1902, cast the deciding ballots: military conscription was rejected. The referendum was repeated again in 1917, with the same results.[16] While the women's peace movement in the German Reich was suppressed to an unprecedented degree, almost all large American women's organizations maintained special peace committees. In January 1917 Jane Addams noted that in twenty-seven countries, including Japan and China, there were "women's committees for lasting peace." Dutchwoman Aletta Jacobs headed these organizations and, despite press censorship, kept up communications among women. At the start of the war in Great Britain, Edith Havelock-Ellis fought for the participation of women in the government.

> The day when women find their place alongside men in the government as well as in the administering of external affairs of their nation will also be the day when war is declared dead as a means

of settling conflicts among men. Neither blare of trumpets nor the waving of flags will lure women into the insanity of reckless devastation of life or cover up the deliberate deaths with any other name than that of "murder," whether it means the slaughter of many or of one single individual.[17]

The armistice agreement had just been signed when the American peace party, led by Jane Addams, again made banner headlines. On November 15, 1918, the major American daily papers carried on their front page an appeal from three German women to Jane Addams and the wife of President Wilson to use their influence to alleviate the tough conditions of the armistice. Due to government censorship, the telegram had been intercepted, and Jane Addams knew of it only through the newspapers; its authors were the feminist activists Alice Salomon, Gertrud Baer, and Anita Augspurg, whose country was threatened with "total starvation" by the conditions of the armistice.[18]

By 1918 the war experience had become the catalyst for a large part of women's activities. The International Woman Suffrage Alliance called for universal disarmament. In May 1919 the founders of the Women's International League for Peace and Freedom, begun during the war in The Hague, gathered in Zürich. Suspicious that the Versailles Treaty contained stipulations that would make future wars inevitable, the League delegates met with statesmen who had gathered in Versailles, though with little result. The demands of the League were radical. Although the English delegates, for example, had received exit permits only on the condition that they not participate in socialist activities, the following principles of the League were approved: total disarmament (land, sea, and air), free world trade, a world economic plan, national ratification of treaties only by a freely elected national representation, and complete freedom of travel and of exchange of information and opinions through all states.[19]

The Women's International League for Peace and Freedom would continue its antiwar agitation under difficult conditions. When the conference on the reduction and limitation of arms finally convened in Geneva in 1932, the peace league had collected six million signatures on a disarmament petition to be presented to the conference participants.[20] The goals were universal and total disarmament under international controls, and struggle against Fascism. In August 1934, one year after Hitler's takeover, an international women's congress, held in Paris, formed a permanent international women's committee to fight against Fascism.[21] Augspurg and Heymann, who had organized the German section of the Women's International League for Peace and Freedom, eventually built up over eighty organizations in Germany. Meetings of the pacifists in Munich in the 1920's were repeatedly disrupted by bands of Hitler supporters, who threatened and injured members with brass knuckles and rubber truncheons. After one such encounter, eight or nine women met with the Bavarian Minister of the Interior to request the expulsion of Hitler from Bavaria, on the grounds that he did not possess German citizenship.

"A foreigner?" repeated Schweyer, adding, "well, you can't really say that. He was born across from the inn near the Bavarian border to Braunau." "That objection is pretty shaky," the women said. "If a Communist from Braunau had incited the masses the way Hitler has, he would have been expelled from Bavaria long ago." Driven further and further into a corner, Schweyer shrugged his shoulders and fell silent. We told him that the day would come when he would remember our demand and be sorry not to have met it.[22]

Lida Gustava Heymann traced the defeat of the Hitler Putsch of 1923 to the Bavarian regional diet member Ellen Ammann, who made certain that the endangered persons left Munich by car and that national guard troops were ordered from Würzburg to Munich. Moreover, Ellen Ammann sent the pacifists a message saying they should leave Munich as quickly as possible. Neither feminist lived to see the end of the war.

A number of the demands of the Women's International League for Peace and Freedom were later taken up by the politicians. The founding of the League of Nations and the United Nations stemmed, in part, from the thinking of the pacifist women's organizations. Behind it was a foregone conclusion that women, because of their biological capacity to produce life, have a more immediate interest than men in the settlement of conflict by peaceful means. Women, the feminist pacifists argued, possess no interests whatever in economics, politics, or prestige which they could satisfy in war. At the same time, they saw it was impossible to safeguard peace by aggressive acts through the mobilization of masses of female voters to which the politicians would react sensitively. The political strategy that they followed was focused on the goal of eliminating points of conflict in international and national politics. In 1917, the pacifist Lida Gustava Heymann went so far as to declare: "A Europe with woman suffrage would not fall victim to world war." This quote shows both the illusion and the idealism of feminist pacifism. After World War II the struggle between female pacifism and chauvinism continued. It became increasingly clear that women's actions were influencing political decisions in West Germany, for example. When Adenauer made his solitary resolution on the rearmament of West Germany, German women fought, though unsuccessfully, the formation of an army. Women resisted the German Treaty and entry into the European defense community. Less than 20 percent of German women were then in favor of rearmament.[23]

In order to demolish this inner resistance within the major Bundestag debates on German rearmament during 1952–53, female deputies were appointed as speakers in order to influence women voters. Yet, these deputies spoke on behalf of the conservative majority and voiced the propaganda of rearmament. It was a lost chance of parliamentarian self-representation, even more deplorable because it was the only time in the history of the Bundestag that women politicians had been allowed to express themselves on a major national question.

12/The Collapse of the First Women's Movement

No sooner had women attained political equality, than they joined the men's parties, walking in the yoke of party discipline as submissively as they had been accustomed to doing under the guardianship of the man.

—Rosa Mayreder

In November 1918, when woman suffrage was proclaimed in Germany, a new era of humankind was to begin. Hedwig Dohm had prophesied: "We may be sure that after a few generations the franchise and political responsibility will have effected a revolution in women's minds and a clarification of women's character."

The German philosopher Max Scheler expected a revolution of the conservative values as "perpetual braking power," women would stop the "hurtling carriage of civilization and culture." He was already asking himself: "How would the political equality of women affect the relationship of the papacy to the state or the king in Italy? How would it affect the relationship of France to the chair in Rome?"[1]

On one point, a point which the socialists were also apprehensive about, Scheler turned out to be right: the women's vote was universally conservative and Christian.

The second women's movement, which began in the nineteen-sixties, blamed the fetishistic demand for woman suffrage for the fact that, from the moment the vote became a political reality, the larger question of women's rights increasingly disappeared from discussion. However, "Votes for Women" had become an all-encompassing formula only in the Anglo-Saxon countries.

Edith Havelock-Ellis, opposed to the strategy of the suffragists, assessed the value of suffrage as follows:

> The vote is urgently needed, because it is one point of the great circle of justice, but it will never and can never be this circle itself. It is one of the means by which a woman can perceive herself as a whole and not as an accessory. What is shocking about today's woman is that neither her body nor her time nor her individuality really belongs to her.[2]

The common denominator of the women's movement was a prophecy of better things to come, a prophecy that foundered in the course of political life. The gist of the promise was that women would fundamentally change the political atmosphere, that through their influence politics would lose its brutal quality, party egoism would be subdued, and the well-being of all would be better kept in account. Typical of these optimistic expectations, interwoven with specific demands, was a passage from a book by Rheta Childe Dorr, *What Eight Million Women Want,* published in 1910:

> I dream of a community in which men and women divide up the work of government and administration according to their special skills and natural capacities. The distribution of labor between them occurs according to natural and not traditional criteria. No one is paid according to their sex, but according to their work. The city will be like an enormous, well ordered, comfortable, and healthy household . . .The rule of men is based on power, on violence. All that is vile, all that is base, all that is egotistical is a form of violence. Even poverty is a form of violence. Women will not tolerate violence.[3]

In the name of eight million women members of the International Woman Suffrage Alliance, Dorr projected her maternal utopia as a large pampered household. Anything but a radical, she was a typical representative of the American women's club, interested in accomplishing practical changes and bringing order to the world, and she offered a harmonic answer to the needs of all.

However, beneath the promise of global health lay a whole spectrum of demands for reform. Maternity benefits and school reforms, disarmament, equal rights for out-of-wedlock children, decriminalization of prostitution and abortion, reasonable working hours, equal rights in marriage, the right to work, fair pay, elimination of the double standard—all political goals the international women suffrage organizations had been striving for. Why was so little of this realized? Why did women founder as soon as they entered parliament?

American women had suffered great disappointment over the

fact that, immediately after the end of the war, Congress did not adopt suffrage for women. When, with women's help, slavery was abolished, black men received the vote. Women's embitterment increased when they had to look on as, in many cases, the votes of these black men and other immigrant minorities, illiterates, were bought by the party and by private business to block the women's vote, a vote which might have forced the downfall of entire industries, such as the distillery business. Thousands of voters, unfamiliar with America's constitution or legislative process, were persuaded to believe that the striking of the word "man" in the election law would mean that *only* women could vote.[4]

After World War I, the American movement started one last, and successful, campaign. Carrie Chapman Catt, in particular, felt it was a disgrace that the United States, boasting equality, was not the first but the twenty-seventh nation to grant suffrage to women. German women got the vote within a few days after the armistice.[5] Quite a number of countries did not grant women suffrage until 1945. There were also curious interim solutions. In Belgium and Canada, after 1918, only widows and mothers of war casualties received the vote, and in El Salvador and Great Britain the voting age for women was set higher than for men. In France the fight for women's votes lasted until 1945, although the popular front government under Léon Blum appointed a woman minister.

The very first steps into politics were a fiasco for women. Until then there had been only men's parties, save for the Socialist Party; it never occurred to the women's organizations, with their abundance of members, to transform their apparatus, their entire network of local organizations, into women's parties. They thought that entry into established parties would bring them the yearned-for gain in political prestige. Therefore, they devitalized their own tested and effective campaign organizations and degraded them to insignificant associations in the pre-parliamentary arena instead of establishing them as independent political forces. Membership in these parties meant the destruction of the self-confidence and identity acquired from long campaigns. In their organizations they had been leaders; now, in the name of woman suffrage, they again became slaves, at best show horses and façades for a male party elite. There was an imperturbability with which women conducted their downfall as an independent political force.

The historian J. Stanley Lemons, in his book *The Woman Citizen: Social Feminism in the 1920s,* describes the situation of women who entered male-controlled parties:

All over the country women loyal to their party and intelligent toward their party duties as well as voters' rights have been peremptorily discharged, without reference, from posts they eagerly accepted expecting an opportunity for services.[6]

Nevertheless, Carrie Chapman Catt insisted that women remain in the parties and continue the struggle. Others, such as Winifred Starr Dobyns, the first president of the Republican Women's Committee of Illinois, soon gave up trying to reform the party from the inside because "once in the party, we are under [men's] control. Our publicity value is lost."

One political observer, Frank Kent, declared it was an undeniable fact that in each city in the country, and in each nation, the woman's right to vote increased the power of the political machinery and of the political bosses. The party machines received women's votes by employing all female relatives of male party members in election campaigns and, with their support, won women's votes for male candidates.[7] The Democratic Party nominated Harriet Mills, an extraordinarily well-qualified candidate, who was defeated by a mediocre party functionary because she received no support at all after her nomination by the party apparatus. Consequently, women's organizations considered forming a women's lobby that would elect only women, but Carrie Chapman Catt did not support this move. In 1920 the Democratic Party doubled its national delegation so that it took one female and one male member from each state, but in each case it was the male party member who had to nominate the woman.[8] Another woman candidate, N. Martin, finally came to the conclusion, after several unsuccessful campaigns in 1925, that the advice of woman suffrage leaders was totally wrong.

> There is no doubt that Mrs. Carrie Chapman Catt sounded the doom of feminism for many years to come when she urged the newly enfranchised women to humbly "train for citizenship," to join the men's parties; "to work with the party of your choice" . . .[9]

Martin urged women to support only female candidates and not to cooperate with the large parties; not until half of the lawmakers were women could one speak of equality. Mrs. O. H. P. Belmont, president of the National Woman's Party, went even further. This party arose from the radical wing of the American women's movement, founded by Alice Paul, and had received a great deal of publicity by adopting the methods of the suffragists. The National Woman's Party accepted only women, liberating them from the humiliation of belonging to the old political parties. "I do not wish to see any woman in the Senate as a Republican or a Democrat."[10]

The one-time suffrage militants did not succeed in re-forming the parties, though in the twenties and thirties they conducted successful campaigns for the removal of corrupt politicians from office in especially flagrant cases.

It is interesting to note just how female members of government attained their positions. In 1931, one of the more well-known women senators, Hattie Ophelia Caraway of Arkansas, who held office almost fifteen years, first entered politics after her husband's death. She had never identified with suffrage, but, by 1943, became co-sponsor of the Equal Rights Amendment (ERA) and was the first woman in Congress to support this law.[11] Caraway, however, was not typical of women in politics. By 1970, sixty-seven women had been elected to the House of Representatives and ten to the Senate. Until 1949, almost all female members of Congress were widows appointed as the successor to their husband after his death. After 1950, women were more often elected directly. By 1963, thirty-six women had been appointed, and thirty-four members of Congress had been elected. Usually the widows remained in Congress only through t   f the legislative term. Of the ten women who entered the Se   a period of almost fifty years, seven were "upgraded in r   three won their seat by their own efforts, and two of those women were widows who had won re-election.[12]

Great Britain certainly offers the most astounding example of the decline of the women's movement. In 1912, the feminist movement, organized primarily in the suffragist organization's Woman's Social and Political Union (WSPU), possessed a "war chest" of roughly $240,000 and had an annual budget of nearly $170,000. On June 21, 1908—in order to underscore their demand and with the support of thirty special trains from all parts of the country—they brought 250,000 people to Hyde Park, an unprecedented number of demonstrators. Only nine days later, when Prime Minister Herbert Asquith still reacted noncommittally to the demand for suffrage, the WSPU gathered 100,000 people in an illegal demonstration on Parliament Square. The police called up an army of 5,000 policemen, including 50 on horseback, and nevertheless required more than four hours to gain control of the situation.

Of course, all British parties—not just the Labour Party—had grown smart enough to secure the collaboration of a few militant women, even before woman suffrage was adopted. Käthe Schirmacher wrote in 1912:

All political parties in England possessed an auxiliary troupe of trained, eager women ready to make sacrifices, without these parties having done—or having thought of doing—even the slightest bit for woman suffrage. This devotion without any wages, signifying political immaturity, Mrs. Pethick-Lawrence calls "the sin of self-sacrifice."[13]

After 1918 this "sin of self-sacrifice" in England, as well as in America and Germany, became the prevailing tendency among women: the once powerful movement of suffragists, the only movement in Europe that fused women together into a kind of class with laborers, office and shop workers, as well as aristocrats, gradually dried up.

Only with the legal reform law of 1935 were married women released "from the trinity of children, the mentally disturbed, and married women" and classed as persons legally of age.

In the German Reich, after the proclamation of woman suffrage in November 1918, many women of the bourgeois suffrage movement did not know where to turn politically. Dorothee von Velsen, who took over the presidency of the Universal German Women's Federation from Helene Lange, describes in her memoirs how she suddenly faced the decision of whether to join a party. A woman colleague called her up and demanded her support for the elections.

> "But for which party?" I asked, bewildered. "There is only one," the colleague answered, "Gertrud Bäumer, Dr. Lüders, Alice Salomon—we're all members of the Democratic Party."[14]

Prominent female opponents of suffrage were elected immediately to the most important seats in the National Assembly. The president of the German Evangelical Women's League, Paula Müller-Otfried—who withdrew from the Federation of German Women's Associations on account of its demand for suffrage—let herself be nominated by the strongest opponents of woman suffrage, the Deutsch-Nationalen Volkspartei (German National People's Party).[15]

Regine Deutsch assessed the conduct and collaboration of thirty-seven women elected to the National Assembly in her book *Die politische Tat der Frau,* published in 1920. She wrote:

> Without the majority of German women having wanted it—indeed, against the wishes and will of a portion of them—the revolution of 1918 gave women the right to vote. Resistance to the vote came largely from the right-oriented women's associations.[16]

The hidden reason for the nomination of women candidates by suffrage opponents was first and foremost the thought that the devil was best exorcised by Beelzebub. It is amusing that not only the Protestant women in the German Reich but also German emigrants rejected the franchise.

In South Australia, which had adopted universal suffrage in 1894, German immigrants had founded large settlements; pastors inveighed with a special intensity against granting the vote to women.

> The woman's vote has been imposed upon us. We Germans have not sought it. However, now that the law exists, we would be playing the fool if we did not make use of it. We therefore urgently demand all German women to have their names regis-

tered and vote in the next election. In the end it will be possible, with the help of these women, to repeal this useless law. If it is not possible, then at least we can oppose its unwholesome results.[17]

Bavaria's first republican premier, socialist Kurt Eisner, proclaimed universal suffrage for all citizens. Women's assemblies were held in Hamburg and Munich, and allegiance was sworn to the republic. Lida Gustava Heymann and Anita Augspurg visited Eisner, whose revolutionary integrity and humane socialism inspired their confidence. Eisner respected the decision of the two feminists never to become members of a political party. Nevertheless, he asked for their collaboration. During the few months that the Eisner council regime lasted, women agitated freely and helped plan an education commission. Anita Augspurg became a member of the revolutionary Central Workers' Council's provisional parliament. Augspurg and others were especially interested in marriage and education rights and in the economic position of the woman in the new state:

Among some farmwomen, the interest appeared so lively that they joined with the speakers to plod along through the high snow in the next village. They helped, carrying knapsacks, passing out flyers, going from house to house with the bell, gathering women to a meeting.[18]

Catholic clerics spoke out against the candidacy of Anita Augspurg for the regional diet elections. They "babbled on about the menacing peril of free love, free marriage, and of the illegitimate child." Augspurg was defeated. Elections for the German National Assembly were set for January 1919.

Having argued all along that it was not the women's mission to be taken in tow by men's political parties, we wanted to assure women of representation in parliament by female delegates proportionate to their numbers. We proposed the idea of a women's ticket and calculated the chances of all women joining together. Our calculations were wrong . . .[19]

Kurt Eisner ran for the Independent Social Democratic Party.* He demanded that a woman candidate be placed second on the ticket;

---

*Translator's Note: Joris de Bres, in translating Werner Thönnessen's *The Emancipation of Women: The Rise and Decline of the Women's Movement in German Social Democracy 1863–1933*, offers the following explanation (on p. 81):

The Independent Social Democratic Party (USPD) began as an opposition group within the Social Democratic Reichstag caucus and voted against the war credits in December 1915. They were subsequently expelled from the Party and with the support-

Lida Gustava Heymann was chosen. Deeply suspicious of the Prussian response, she wrote after the elections:

> The old Reichstag and the new National Assembly have an ac-
> cursedly similar appearance. Many of the old delegates from the
> mercifully departed Reichstag are back again. As incredible as it
> may seem, they have had themselves nominated by their old party
> under a new name, and have been re-elected by German men
> . . . and, even more incredible, by women.[20]

On the other hand, Regine Deutsch lauded the great political success of the German women, compared to what was happening in other
countries:

> Nevertheless, German women could proudly say that nowhere in
> the world, after women first voted and ran for office, was there
> such a large number of female representatives entering parlia-
> ment. Women abroad, who followed the sudden change in the
> status of women in Germany with interest, expressed their aston-
> ishment; to them thirty-seven female delegates seemed like an
> unprecedented success. In England's lower house there is only one
> woman.[21]

Most delegates had difficulty in viewing women as colleagues;
some expected female representatives to take the political stance of a
madonna:

> The woman's franchise has articulated the thoughts of the medie-
> val scholars, elevating those thoughts to the nation's inspiration,
> "that in a woman there was a mastery in service, a pride in humil-
> ity, a power in obedience," and the German people will soon be-
> come aware of the powerful weapon the Creator gave to women
> in the form of their hearts.[22]

But from the outset women of all political factions—except those
of the Independent Social Democratic Party—were not prepared to
demand full equality with men in parliament. Gertrud Bäumer, superior counselor in the Interior Ministry, was the first to express this
view in the National Assembly:

ers formed a new Party, the USPD, in 1917. The old Party came to be referred to as the
Majority Socialists. The issue that caused the Party split—the war credits—cut across
many more significant differences within the Party, and many diverse figures such as
Bernstein, Kautsky and Zetkin found themselves together in the ranks of the USPD.
Little, apart from this one issue, separated the two Parties, but they failed to reunite
until 1922. By then, the real differences within the pre-war SPD had assumed tangible
form in the opposition between the KPD (the Communist Party) and the Social Democrats.

I'm not one of those people whose ambition is to be appointed by the National Assembly as an adviser on military questions or the like; I see the task of women not in absolutely equal participation in all things but I believe that the vote must lead to a special employment of womanpower—internally and also externally—in the areas in which her special responsibilities lie.[23]

The cult of the female creature and her mystical conception that the people were more than the individual, the vindication of war as idealism prepared to stake its life on something larger than individual concerns ("Germany must live, even if we must die"), led to sympathies with the National Socialists. In 1932, shortly before Hitler took power, Bäumer expressed her deepest regrets that the very party that had developed so much feeling for the people—the National Socialists—was so hostile to female civil rights, as if this hostility did not have its roots in the conception of motherhood that she herself had emphatically advocated.

It is almost tragic that the party which, whatever you think of it, in the very vague diffuseness of its goals upholds the character of the people's movement out of instinct and feeling . . . has developed so one-sidedly in the reactionary male spirit. There are certain indications that a new position on the status of the female citizen will develop.

Gertrud Bäumer was proclaiming Hitler's race theologies: no sexual self-determination for the woman, no aspiring to individual erotic happiness, only for the elevation and "renovation of the race" was the woman obliged to make her child-bearing capacity available. Her conception of government was oriented in a medieval parliament of estates. In the "various circles of life which in their representatives—the farmers and artisans, the clerks and the banker—comprise the common destiny, that of the mother must not be excluded.[24] In articulating such views she must have completely disregarded the fact that she was not a mother, thus, according to her own thinking, she was no true representative of women in parliament. Equally contradictory in her thinking was the fact that, while she denied a married woman and mother with small children the right to leave her children alone, she placed herself, as if a mother, side by side with farmer and banker.

The women who were elected to the constituent assembly had from the start programmed the failure of any attempt at emancipation during the Weimar Republic. They used woman suffrage to explain to men of the National Assembly that they wished to claim no other rights. Only the Independent Social Democrats proposed: "All stipulations that curtail the legal position of the woman in the area of civil rights are to be abolished."

Since women could not be drafted, many male representatives to the National Assembly felt that the sexes could not possibly be regarded as legally equal. Constitutional motions on equal status for out-of-wedlock (and in-wedlock) children, which Luise Zietz fought for, were rejected, because male politicians of the Center and Right-wing parties believed: "sexual liaisons to be sinful and reprehensible, and we wish to turn against the modern trend making this sexual liaison permissible and equal to marriage."[25]

Men felt that fallen women could become Catholic nuns to liberate themselves from their sexual defilement through long-term inner atonement.

> We have the cloisters of the Good Shepherds who attend to these mothers with tender loving care as they can be trained only by the most noble of women. We want these mothers to work their way up again, as, to use an image, the water lily rises up out of the slime to the light and there in purity unfolds in the sun.[26]

In 1919 Luise Zietz sponsored a bill in the National Assembly to abolish discriminatory taxation of married women but was voted down. Women's wages were lumped in with the income of the husband, and the total income was taxed. This ruling was still in effect in West Germany until the end of the fifties.

Evaluating the work of the female delegates in the National Assembly, Regine Deutsch adds a careful criticism:

> No doubt the fact that women are also representatives of female voters, who comprise the major share of all voters, is self-evident. Indeed, one may say: A portion of the female voters have expected more from the policies of their delegates. The consistent women's rights champions, who hoped all their demands would be met by the women in parliament, point out that Denmark, whose national assembly included a far smaller number of women in the first session, had achieved a reform of the marriage law.[27]

During the Weimar Republic (1919–1933), the number of women delegates in the Reichstag dropped. This occurred in almost all industrial countries with woman suffrage and a parliamentary system. In 1926 Anita Augspurg and Lida Gustava Heymann tried once again to appeal to the women's unity. They printed an appeal in their magazine *Die Frau im Staat.*

> It is not a question of oppressing or supporting any party: in this amalgamation of all women, party interest is not paramount. Party strength ought to be taken into account, but it is most important to increase female influence through the number of female

delegates in all parliaments and municipal authorities and to give these female delegates of all persuasions opportunity to enter parliament not by the grace of the party but through women's own strength . . .[28]

Since 1919 the two had proposed a women's ticket of all women candidates of all parties as well as unaffiliated women. Anita Augspurg had devised a formula whereby the number of women candidates would be fixed according to the estimate of the parties' last election statistics. In 1931 their idea was finally abandoned.

At a meeting in Göttingen, in 1930, the Federation of Women's Associations debated the possibilities of a women's ticket and the establishment of a women's party. A pilot commission was set up; but achieved no results.[29] By this time, women were firmly entrenched in the male political parties. The woman's vote had become a double-edged weapon in the fight for women's liberation. Almost all women politicians docilely subordinated the women's interests to party goals. Those conservative women representatives who were least prepared to influence the legislative process in favor of emancipatory goals were the ones who succeeded in the Reichstag. The Left wing of the women's movement either devoted itself to the struggle for pacifist goals or resigned. Unfortunately, the Left-wing women socialists lost their chief activist, Luise Zietz, who died in 1922. Stagnation set in among female Social Democrats: shortly after 1918, women had represented 26.8 percent of party membership, an all-time high, which, by 1923, dropped to 10.3 percent. Only during the years 1926 to 1931 would the figure slowly double again.[30]

Because the nomination of the candidates was a party privilege that precluded publicity or visibility, discrimination against women candidates was inevitable from the start. On the Social Democratic ticket in 1920 a quarter of the members were women, but only one woman had a chance at the nomination.

It was, so to speak, a concession that was made to the old party demand. Many competent women had to step aside in order to make way for a man. Nowhere were women nominated in accord with the number of women voters. The apportionment of women was often a question of power, and women are the weaker.[31]

In the formal sense, the victory of the suffrage movement today has been a practically complete one; a document from the United Nations Conference on the International Woman's Year reports only nine countries that grant women no political rights. Seven are Arab: Bahrain, Kuwait, Oman, Qatar, Saudi Arabia, United Arab Emirate, and Yemen. In addition, women have no rights in six states within the Federal Republic of Nigeria, or in Liechtenstein.[32]

Although there is no comprehensive overview on women in political functions, a great deal of individual data show that the trend is on the decline.

In many countries, even in the West, parties are loosely defined organizations whose memberships are not divided according to sex. Only the Scandinavian countries have national legislatures with female membership over 10 percent. Finland, which introduced the franchise in 1906, has seen an increase in the number of female representatives from 9.5 to 21.5 percent. Finnish and Norwegian parties average about 25 percent women. In Denmark female membership of the Social Democrats is approximately 40 percent.

Many African, Asian, and South American nations have granted women political rights after winning national independence. For these nations, woman suffrage became a kind of status symbol, a sign of progress in the first years after their independence. However, many countries in Asia, Africa, and Latin America were quickly transformed into military dictatorships, where civil rights of any kind meant little. Among developing countries in which a legislature exists, the constitution of the newly created state of Bangladesh exemplifies the perversion of political rights: its constitution guarantees fifteen seats for women, but these women are elected not by female voters but by the three hundred male members of parliament.[33]

Thus, it was not the woman's franchise *per se,* but a women's vote without political power, without systematic goals that turned women into political eunuchs. Only the "refusal to be a servant of the church, of the state, of the society, of the husband, of the family, etc., only this, not the ballot, will liberate women." This was the prophecy of American anarchist Emma Goldman when she spoke out vehemently against the promising future American women associated with the vote.[34]

Part Four
Sex and Economics

13/The Division of Labor between the Sexes

Human beings are the only species of animal in which the woman is supported by the man, hence, the only one in which sexual relations are simultaneously economic relations.

—*Charlotte Perkins-Gilman*

"The whole of so-called world history," according to Marx's famous definition, "is nothing but the production of human beings by human labor."

Marxist thought, like conservative thinking, assumes within the family a spontaneous, natural division of labor between the sexes; biological differences become grounds for the division of labor: "Within a family, just as in a tribe, arises a natural division of labor from sex and age differences, on purely physiological grounds . . ." In *Capital* Marx describes the industry of a self-sufficient farm family:

> The different jobs that these products generate—cattle breeding, spinning, weaving, tailoring, etc.—are social functions which possess their own natural division of labor. Sex and age differences, changing with the change of seasons like the natural conditions of labor, govern their division among the family and the working hours of the individual members of the family.

From his description, one can deduce that the division of labor and working hours between the sexes, because natural, is consequently fair.

Claude Lévi-Strauss regards the sex-specific division of labor as a series of taboos. Each society assigns certain tasks to one sex while barring them for another. These taboos create a dependence among individuals, and make the lives of the unmarried adults in primitive societies difficult. Hence, the sexual division of labor is the most effective means of promoting group living and the small family. George Peter Murdock wrote:

> Through concentration and practice each partner acquires special skill at his particular tasks. Complementary parts can be learned for an activity requiring joint effort. If two tasks must be performed at the same time but in different places, both may be undertaken and the products shared. The labors of each partner provide insurance to the other. The man, perhaps, returns from a day of hunting, chilled, unsuccessful, and with his clothing soiled and torn, to find warmth before a fire which he could not have maintained, to eat food gathered and cooked by the woman instead of going hungry, and to receive fresh garments for the morrow, prepared, mended, or laundered by her hands. Or perhaps the woman has found no vegetable food, or lacks clay for pottery or skins for making clothes, obtainable only at a distance from the dwelling, which she cannot leave because her children require care; the man in his ramblings after game can readily supply her wants. Moreover, if either is injured or ill, the other can nurse him back to health. These and similar rewarding experiences, repeated daily, would suffice of themselves to cement the union. When the powerful reinforcement of sex is added, the partnership of man and woman becomes inevitable.[1]

These are the arguments which, according to Murdock, the sexual division of labor in every known society has produced. He regards it as unnecessary

> to invoke innate psychological differences to account for the division of labor by sex; the indisputable differences in reproductive functions suffice to lay out the broad lines of cleavage.[2]

This view, which is shared today by almost all ethnologists, is indeed so general that it hardly explains the differences in status and work of man and woman in primitive societies.

The most important justification for the specific division of labor of the sexes, accepted in ethnology, is the immobility of the woman: her duties of child care prevent her from venturing from camp. Yet, how accurate is this assumption?

In many societies women travel great distances in order to sell their products at a market; nursing mothers take their small children with them. The only universal male task is that of hunting, which often calls for days of absence from the campsite or village; women must raise the children. In primitive human societies the hunt is practically ruled out as a female group activity because over a period of several years the mother is the main source of nourishment for the infant and small child.

Only under special circumstances did women ever hunt, such as during the feudal society of Europe's Middle Ages, when wet nurses would care for the children of noblewomen. In primitive societies women borrow their husband's or brother's spear for a short hunting trip.[3]

In 166 societies that George Peter Murdock studied, hunting was an exclusively male activity. In only thirteen societies did women occasionally hunt alone or with their husbands.[4] In an even more comprehensive comparison of data including 741 societies, Erika Bourguignon and Lenora S. Greenbaum, two American researchers, arrived at the same finding: that hunting is almost without exception a male activity.[5] Men usually manufacture weapons and smelt and treat metals, while in only one society is the mining of ore the female's job.

Another explanation for the sexual division of labor claims that man performs the heavy physical labor and woman the less strenuous. Yet, while in over 90 percent of all societies woodcutting is a man's task, Murdock found that, in 70 percent of these societies, women also carry heavy loads. Building houses and erecting huts or rain shelters is exclusively a female task in thirty-six societies. Weaving baskets, mats, and cloth, making pottery, preserving meat and fish, making clothes, preparing drinks, alcohol, and narcotics, threshing grain, tattooing and hairdressing, searching for firewood, making and tending fires, cooking, gathering herbs, roots, and seeds, bearing water, and tending small livestock are predominantly women's jobs. For a large number of societies today, in fact, data exists on which activities are exclusively male or exclusively female and which are performed by both sexes. For the most part, however, we are left with an unanswered question as to the criteria in a society by which areas of activity devolve to one sex or the other. This is clear only in the case of males being assigned the hunt and weapons manufacture. One theory says that certain inventions produced by members of one sex lead to new activities that remain entrusted to this sex. Women, for example, invented arable farming. Thus, it would be explained, in some societies women alone perform almost all the field work. Yet a number of inventions, such as reed plaiting, pottery making, and fire making, were not made in any individual society; the technology spread into various societies.

Murdock writes: "New tasks, as they arise, are assigned to one sphere of activities or to the other, in accordance with convenience and precedent."[6] Murdock's description suggests that a harmonic process of adaptation exists in the division of work spheres between the sexes. According to Murdock and Lévi-Strauss, the division of labor is an arbitrary, random process. The majority of field researchers have made no systematic observations on this question. In addition, the relationship between work load, work value, and the rights of the marriage partner are seldom defined with any precision. Even in ethnological field studies, the measurement of time spent on activities and jobs is a much more reliable source of information than the assessment of income, results of labor, or prestige of the job.

Margaret Mead, a pioneer of American social anthropology, believed that women in primitive societies are superior to men because of their motherhood. Proceeding from biology and Freudian psychology, she tries to construct an apparent power balance of the sexes among primitive peoples. Women's childbearing capacity provides them with an immediate concern for life; therefore, according to Mead, men must have certain prerogatives or one must grant them compensation mechanisms. If men need heroic actions, then the women accept it as a matter of course and brightly tend to life's daily needs. Thus she describes the division of labor of the Iatmul, a head-hunting tribe in New Guinea:

> Here the women work fairly steadily but cheerfully, in groups, without any sense of being inordinately driven. They are responsible for the daily catch of fish, for the fish that is taken to the market, for gathering firewood and carrying water, for cooking, and for plaiting the great cylindrical mosquito-baskets . . . Men's work, however, is almost entirely episodic . . .

This uneven division of labor is described by Margaret Mead—and praised and justified—as the "ability of the Iatmul woman to work steadily at unexciting tasks, without boredom or serious disturbance in rhythm, and the disinclination of Iatmul men for any such tasks."[7]

By never examining the issue of an uneven work load and male conceptions of honor or female obedience, Mead gives the impression that the uneven burden of man and woman represents the natural self-realization of the sexes.

Phyllis Kaberry's 1952 study of the Nsaw in Cameroon uncovered the following: Men clear away trees and heavy shrubbery for new fields, and they help in the harvest. Their combined economic activity amounts to less than ten days a year. Women work in the fields while men remain in the village, drinking palm wine and telling stories. The Nsaw say of a bachelor that he "has to work almost as hard as a woman."[8] The American ethnologist Judith Brown, in an investigation of division of labor theory, comes to the conclusion that the financial obligations of the Nsaw husband toward his family were often ignored. They had to provide oil, salt, and if possible meat, and earn money for the bride price. In addition, they had to produce a multitude of social contacts for drinking bouts and hospitality. Nevertheless, Judith Brown completely overlooks the domination aspect of such a sex-specific division of labor, which is very reminiscent of that between an idle aristocratic class and the peasant population performing the heavy physical labor, as was common in Europe in the Middle Ages.[9] Even the leadership functions of the manager demand for their fulfillment a large measure of sociability, receptions, "business lunches," etc.

There are a number of classless societies in which women not only bring up the children and do the housework but are also responsible for almost the total production of the society. The Yanomamö in Venezuela and the Somali in East Africa burden women with the heaviest labor. The Somali once regarded their female children as capital and sold them as slaves in times of famine. Under threat of physical violence, women were forced by their husbands to perform all the hard and unpopular jobs. They were allowed to keep only sheep and goats. Somali men, on the other hand, regarded it as beneath their dignity to tend any animals but camels, cattle, and ponies, the most valuable economic property of their people.[10]

One informant from the Tsambigula tribe in New Guinea reports that little girls are warned to work:

> Don't forget, you are a girl. You are not allowed to play with other children. Boys may, but not girls. If you play now, you will never progress beyond it when you're grown up.

If in the evening the young men sing their love songs, mothers caution their daughters: "If you dance on the sweet potatoes, your future husband will not love you. Be strict with yourself. Then you will not find the work difficult when you get married." When a mother sees her daughter playing in the garden, she makes sure she is punished severely and beaten.[11]

The American ethnologist Charles Wagley became witness to a gang rape among the Tapirapé Indians in Brazil. A much too independent young woman who had refused to help in the preparation of the manioc (women's work) was given by her brother to the male members of the village to be raped.[12]

In societies in which the woman's work load is much larger than the man's, the man's activities are prestigious and are associated with his honor or with male domination in society. A man who dares to help his wife would be compromising himself in temporarily accepting her inferior status. The Swedish scholar Hilma Granqvist wrote:

> I met at the end of December 1926, in the mountains of Artas, Sheikha Shahin carrying a heavy iron plough on her head only a few weeks before her youngest son was to be born. She was with her husband Abd il-Salam, and they were both on their way to Bet Sahur, where he was going to plough and cultivate the Shepherds' Field for the owner. He was driving the ass laden with a sack of grain. Now Abd il-Salam was weak and old and his wife young and strong but even if he had been able to do it he could not have

carried the plough. Eastern custom does not allow a man to carry a burden, otherwise he will lose the respect of the others. The custom is a hard one, binding on both men and women, and does not allow either to overstep the limit set by society. As life is in the rural districts of Palestine the women must do heavy and strenuous work and they submit to it without complaining. The women would be the last to rebel against this order of things which cannot be helped.[13]

Similarly, Richard Antoun wrote of Arab women that they gather herbs and roots, raise chickens, sheep, and goats, cook the meals, and look after the children. They spend entire days in the woods gathering dry twigs or dung and straw, which they mix into flammable briquettes. The Arab farmer must choose between two tasks which are equally important for his honor. He must constantly supervise his wife and his daughters, since the slightest talk of violations of the virtue of female members of the family wounds his honor. On the other hand, he is not allowed to take part in the work of the women, for that would violate his male dignity.

In this conflict between male honor and male dignity, according to Antoun, male dignity triumphs. In the Palestinian village in which he was staying, for example, one of the village elders was criticized publicly in the Friday services. He had let his daughter go out to gather twigs in the woods, all alone. To accompany her would have brought him into conflict with his position as elder. An elder governs and commands the activities of his house; he does not take part in them. He was always ready to prepare coffee for a guest or a traveler. But he would not groan beneath a load of firewood on the public road.[14]

Similar to the slavish situation of the woman in the Middle East was that of the female population in the mountain tribes in the Caucasus.

In Daghestan, "it is derogatory for a man to carry anything less dignified than a gun." While the husband stands about and gossips at the local mosque or putters with his gun, the wife must slave from morn till night. The husband, of course, does the sowing, makes the hay, threshes, shears the sheep, builds houses; but these jobs are not sufficient to keep him busy all year round. The wife does most of the harvesting, and . . . "brings half of the grain on her shoulders, leaving the other half for the donkey." She has to cut the grass for the animals, care for the horses, cook, weave, milk the cows, mind the children, do the usual housework, set the cakes of cow-dung out to dry, clean the wool, spin, and fetch water. Even the small girls of the family must take part in all these tasks. Frequently one can see nine-to-ten-year-old girls carrying unbelievably heavy jugs of water, while boys as old as they, if not older, sit around and amuse themselves.

The male mountain dwellers of the North Caucasus, according to Louis Luzbetak, comprise a purely idle class; women carry loads of hay and wood great distances, up to 120 pounds at a time.

> The men prefer this sort of "domestic beast" because she can stand much more than a horse or an ox; the only difference between her and a domestic animal is that she eats bread while an animal is satisfied with hay. An ideal wife in the eyes of the Avars is one that is robust and, above all, very diligent.

In these tribes a man is never allowed to carry or fondle his child or to rock it to sleep. The Ossets would call a man a very insulting name —"Baba" (that is, old woman)—if he ever milked a cow or took care of the children. A father of the South Caucasian tribes may never carry his child in the presence of others or even say a friendly word to it. The only thing he can do in these tribes without losing face is to hold the child by the hand when it is old enough to run.[15]

In one study composed of two samples, one of 499 societies, the other of 249, the American social anthropologist Peggy R. Sanday attempted to examine whether there is a positive correlation between the number of women in production and their status. The measurements for female status were: (1) control over their own production; (2) demand for female products; (3) female participation in political activities in any form; (4) presence of female solidarity groups which represent female political or economic interests. Sanday did not find a positive correlation.

> In many societies it appears that women are employed as slave labor and have no control over what they produce. In other societies females work at low market value jobs while male labor power is expended on goods that have a high market value.

The African Azande, for example, show how a low female status can improve if the women possess a commodity to barter with. The woman's status changed when the Azande came into contact with the European colonial masters; the fruits of their field labor acquired a monetary value. The activities of the men—war and hunting—were devalued by the presence of the colonial rulers. Eventually, men took over the farming, curtailing the women's sphere of control. However, for the Ibo of East Nigeria, colonization worked in favor of the women. Though the Ibo women had made pots and traded and tended their farms, the men had controlled the greater share of their income and held the prestige activities of yam farming and slave trading. The mobility of the Ibo women at the markets was limited because of many war disputes. When these stopped as a result of European influence, the trading activity of the women increased. Eventually, the women raised a plant which eliminated the annual famine and acquired a high stable market value. Thus, it was increasingly difficult for husbands to keep their wives in a subordinate position.[16]

It is quite clear that every women's movement poses the question of origin and development of the sex-specific division of labor. Margaret Mead became world-famous through her book *Male and Female,* in which she portrayed the relativity of female- and male-defined activities in seven societies of New Guinea and the South Pacific. With this book, she introduced a large readership not only to her knowledge but also to the idea that there is no naturally determined sexual division of labor. If there were, then it would certainly be divided more sensibly and rationally between the two sexes. After the publication of Margaret Mead's much quoted study, the culturally dependent division of men's and women's jobs was often interpreted to mean that, in societies in which women perform work that males in our society perform, those women must accordingly have greater influence. The prestige of a job is not exclusively linked to the nature of the activity, however. In one society, for example, milking is considered the job of the man; in another it is women's work. Nevertheless, it is almost always true that work possesses greater prestige when done by a man. A comparison of men's and women's work between two or more societies can occur only if, in each of them, the prestige of the jobs of men and women is determined and the possibilities of deriving profit or of creating a power structure by means of this work are ascertained.

The extent to which the division of labor can deviate from that which is familiar to us is shown among the Tibetan nomads:

> Woman cannot deal with needle and thread. All needlework, including the woman's costume and her wedding dress, is men's work. This seems all the more peculiar as, among the feminine ornamental objects the nomad woman receives upon her marriage, is a symbolic (wooden) sewing cushion.

Among these Tibetan nomads there is another work-role reversal. The women weave the wool cloth and the tent squares out of yak hair; however, the spinning of the thread with the freely suspended spindle is predominantly men's work.[19]

In pre-industrial Europe, spinning was woman's work; weaving, on the other hand, was men's work. Nevertheless, the needle and spinning work of the Tibetan man does not mean that his wife performs the more prestigious and esteemed activity in this society.

Although the ethnological literature up to the present day yields very little information on why and under which influences certain activities are assigned to one or the other sphere, it can, however, be established that in many societies that still have no social classes and educate no specialists, the division of labor between the sexes already shows an unmistakable class character. The sexual division of labor is not purely spontaneous, as Karl Marx and many scholars after him assumed; it is dictated by male force. It also suggests that only the participation in power positions or the building of their own power structure will provide a means whereby women can overcome their social inferiority.

14/Heroic Deeds and Housework

You've sliced our bread
and cooked our coffee
and pushed the pots around
and mopped and sewn
and spun and made things
all with your hands.

You've covered the milk,
given us candy
and carried out the papers—
you've counted the shirts . . .
and peeled potatoes . . .
all with your hands.

—*Kurt Tucholsky*

For men must work
and women must weep.

—*Charles Kingsley*

In the beginning, as Goethe had Faust say, was the deed. In order to distinguish humans from animals, and to define their relationship to the environment, the planned act, the deed, was deemed a unique human achievement.[1] Even today there remains a curious gap—not only in the philosophical interpretation, but also in that of all the behavioral sciences—between the concepts of acting and working.

In pre-industrial society these concepts were substantially different. In essence, acting and doing expressed a male's domination or control over others: waging war, administering the law, running government, conducting scholarly studies, etc. Work, on the other hand, was the toilsome, physically strenuous activity of the peasant class, day laborers, and craft persons. Industrial society ended this semantic opposition between working and acting. Work has become the endeavor of all men; the class-determined differences in male work are expressed in such descriptions as "going to the salt mines" and "working your ass off" in the jargon of factory workers and in the action concept of work, what is considered the leading activity of males described as "dynamic activity" offering "the elation of decision-making" and similar qualities related to potency and competition. Against this background of worker's sweat and thrilling male competition, led by the managerial type threatened with circulation problems and heart attacks, the woman's housework appears idyllic, not comparable with either the drudgery of workers or the tough competition principle of employees aspiring toward executive posts.

To thinking oriented in male freedom and self-determination, the housewife's work involves no acting, but purely monotonous repetition, a series of gestures. José Ortega y Gasset asks:

> Or is it work perhaps that the mother caring for her children, the wife or the sister is doing? But what an incredible secret is inherent in this: no sooner is it done than it has vanished, leaving not a trace of an action or enterprise![2]

Because woman's work, in the minds of male essayists, evaporates into nothing, it becomes an "incredible secret." The woman, defined only by her relation to man, is an invisible service. For the essayist to admit her work is a matter of strenuous labor he would have to ask how meaningful and important this peculiar work is and at whose expense it's made possible.

> Man does battle with his body, crosses our planet as a daredevil explorer, piles stone upon stone to make a monument, writes books, lashes out at the air with his talk; and even when he is just reflecting, the collected calm of his muscles contains something so intrinsically active that it suggests the tension before a daring leap. The woman, on the other hand, does nothing, and when her hands move, it is more likely to be a gesture than an action.[3]

A woman has nothing of the "challenging quality that characterizes man's contribution." The "evaporation of any achievement is one of the most striking attributes of a lifetime profession that calls itself womanhood." Woman can work from morning to night, and her work will never lose its drone-like character, since everything she does in the house, in man's thinking, is nothing more than the activity of an automaton without imagination or creative purpose:

> No matter how tirelessly or selflessly active the woman may be, no matter how rich her work and "creativity within her sphere" . . . the productivity in the sense of this interdependence and,

simultaneously, independence of subject and object is not her strength.[4]

Thus, Georg Simmel believes that women are hard-working but limited, and men are creative, their work always serving as the basis of a spiritual project in which their intellect is objectified. When a woman produces something, she follows no creative plan of her own. Yet, the same activity, professionalized and turned into male handicraft, represents constructive activity and independent thought.

Always on the lookout for what is new and original, "men generally grow bored sooner than women." The work of the housewife is the voluntary accomplishment of an intellectually limited creature giving its best. Let us compare Simone de Beauvoir's presentation of the development of the female role (which she has set in an imaginary infancy of humankind) with the male stereotypes of female work:

> But in any case giving birth and suckling are not *activities,* they are natural functions; no project is involved; and that is why woman found in them no reason for a lofty affirmation of her existence—she submitted passively to her biologic fate. The domestic labors that fell to her lot because they were reconcilable with the cares of maternity imprisoned her in repetition and immanence; they were repeated from day to day in identical form, which was perpetuated almost without change from century to century; they produced nothing new.[5]

No one reading this would be able to tell that Simone de Beauvoir is trying here, with the help of male values—and, moreover, applying criteria of our own time—to describe the self-image of women who lived ten thousand years before us. What has confused her is precisely the same mythological aura of male importance that she intends to make the subject of her study.

Do women devote their time to giving birth and nursing while men spend their time on significant activity? Nursing is an activity, even though it is associated with a natural body function. A woman can relate to her body in a conscious and purposeful manner. She can determine the frequency and duration of the nursing, and she can also abstain from it. Nursing is an act of female productivity and not an unconscious animalistic function over which the woman exercises no free will. A man who takes a job with the highway department because he is in good physical condition and is strong and muscular is essentially acting no differently from a woman who hires out her services as a wet nurse.

In contrast to animal mothers, whose suckling period is determined by an innate behavior schedule of the animal mother and by natural growth, the human mother consciously takes the initiative of feeding the child. And the care of human infants requires planning and skill. It calls for an investment of time and attention. If an infant nurse in an obstetrics clinic feeds the newborn baby with the bottle, the difference between her job and that of the mother is to be realized only in the pay—and possibly in the fact that the professional mother, the infant nurse, does not have such an intense relationship with the baby.

In her book *The Second Sex* Simone de Beauvoir fell victim to the notion that men were the sole inventors of all tools and technology. She is trying to define the initial domination of the male in early society. However, she is heroizing his part in the development of civilization and submitting to the old idea that, because of pregnancy and the care of small children, women remained excluded from the development of culture by biological causes.

> Man's case was radically different; he furnished support for the group, not in the manner of worker bees by a simple vital process, through biological behavior, but by means of acts that transcended his animal nature. *Homo faber* has from the beginning of time been an inventor: the stick and the club with which he armed himself to knock down fruits and to slaughter animals became forthwith instruments for enlarging his grasp upon the world. He did not limit himself to bringing home the fish he caught in the sea: first he had to conquer the watery realm by means of the dugout canoe fashioned from a tree-trunk . . . In this activity he put his power to the test; he set up goals and opened up roads toward them; in brief, he found self-realization as an existent. To maintain, he created; he burst out of the present, he opened the future. This is the reason why fishing and hunting expeditions had a sacred character. Their successes were celebrated with festivals and triumphs, and therein man gave recognition to his human estate . . .

This existentialistically colored cult of man goes even further. Early man, it seems, had attained high points that woman never reached:

> [His] activity had another dimension that gave it supreme dignity: it was often dangerous. If blood were but a nourishing fluid, it would be valued no higher than milk; but the hunter was no butcher, for in the struggle against wild animals he ran grave risks. The warrior put his life in jeopardy to elevate the prestige of the horde, the clan to which he belonged. And in this he proved dramatically that life is not the supreme value for man, but on the contrary that it should be made to serve ends more important than itself. The worst curse that was laid upon woman was that she should be excluded from these warlike forays. For it is not in giving life but in risking life that man is raised above the animal;

that is why superiority has been accorded in humanity not to the sex that brings forth but to that which kills.

Here we have the key to the whole mystery. On the biological level a species is maintained only by creating itself anew; but this creation results only in repeating the same Life in more individuals. But man assures the repetition of Life while transcending Life through Existence; by this transcendence he creates values that deprive pure repetition of all value.[6]

In this passage de Beauvoir fell head over heels into the metaphysical whirlpool of existentialism. Existence turns into a privilege or a synonym for man. The man defines himself through action and struggle; the woman through childbearing and repetitious jobs. He risks his life; her life is biologically risked in childbirth. He kills animals not for his survival but to increase the standing of his tribe. Uncritically, de Beauvoir bestows upon certain male activities the halo of importance and heroism, destroying the chance of our arriving at any sort of equitable judgment of the work performance of the sexes formed in a historical light.

The labor power of woman was exploited not only in the production plant, the shop, and the factory but also by the husband. In earlier centuries, husbands were less squeamish about rating their wives according to their work productivity. Unabashedly thinking of his own profit, the eighteenth-century German writer Justus Möser emphasized the working qualities of a housewife. In his *Patriotischen Phantasien* a widower is seeking a new wife.

I want an upright Christian woman, of good heart and sound mind, suitable household company and vivacious but withdrawn creature; a diligent and hard-working housekeeper, a tidy and sensible cook and a vigilant gardener.

Making a contrast to the educated woman, he then describes the qualities of his deceased wife:

Heaven knows that I have never required it, but, unassisted, my blessed one got up every morning at five o'clock, and before the hour struck six, the whole house was put in order, each child was dressed and at work, the servants in their vocation, and in the wintertime, on many a morning, more yarn was often spun than is now produced in many households within an entire year. Breakfast was now taken casually; each one took his in hand and went on about his business. My table was laid at the proper time and crammed with good dishes indeed, which she herself had prepared: they were pure and simple in selection, but well cooked.

In sixteen years of marriage, she earned the dowry for four daughters, amounting to more "than the money that she received from me in all that time. So much had she won by diligence, order, and good housekeeping."[7] Thus, his wife earned him a chunk of money.

In an age when inequality has been declared illegal, men can no longer use such open language as that of Justus Möser's *paterfamilias.* Because housework is a job without remuneration, it must be camouflaged as much as possible. In the current-day jargon of family politics and in the language of social scientists, housework is upgraded; viewed in the light of linguistic psychology, there is a systematic attempt to substitute the word "work" with "domestic obligations" or "domestic assignments." This use of language is international. Even the International Labor Organization in Geneva uses the concept of the "familiar obligations of the woman" in its proposals, guidelines, and international agreements. With a new label, housework supposedly becomes the labor of love binding her to her family and to society. This so-called ethical achievement simply impedes many women from demanding remuneration for their work. So long as housework is propagandized as an obligation, the woman will be spared from honestly examining her own dependent, unpaid position in marriage and the household.

If production remains and is consumed within the family, it has, according to the Marxian definition, no commodity function.

> Not every product of labor is a commodity. If with the product of his labor a person covers his own needs or those of his family, he is only creating a product, an object, but not a commodity. Only the product of labor that proceeds through exchange (buying and selling) to consumption (use) becomes a commodity.[8]

This sentence would be correct if five words were omitted: "or those of his family." With this addition the Marxists have traditionally ignored the most aggravating problem in evaluating labor encountered by all existing societies with monetary intercourse, whether capitalist, non-capitalist, or mixed economies.

The negative appraisal of housework in Marxist theory arises from a concept of labor oriented to production by factory machine and that ascribes only a second-class rating to service tasks as labor. Today, housework consists predominantly of service and caretaking functions.

Friedrich Engels believed the position of the woman changed radically with workshop and factory production:

> The domestic labor of the woman . . . became . . . an unimportant extra . . . to emancipate woman and make her the equal of man is an impossibility as long as the woman is barred from

social productive labor and is restricted to private domestic labor.[9]

Engels's observation is more demagogical than analytical. Housework never disappeared; it was never an insignificant extra. It was always an organizing principle of life. What distinguished housework and child care from other work was that it possessed no concretely defined exchange value. In the dogma of Engels and Bebel, private housework should dissolve into public industry.

For millions of women the kitchen is one of the most strenuous, time-consuming, and extravagant facilities in which health and good humor are lost, and which is an object of daily anxiety, especially if, as in the majority of families, means are extremely meagre. The end of kitchen work will be a relief for countless numbers of women. The kitchen is a facility that is as backward and antiquated as the workshops of the small craftsmen; both mean the greatest inefficiency, a great waste of time, energy, heat, and lighting material, nutriments, etc.[10]

There are the electrically driven potato and fruit peelers, pit removers, sausage stuffers, grease strainers, meat choppers, meat roasters, baking devices, coffee and spice mills, bread-cutting devices, ice crushers, cork pullers, cork compressers, and a hundred other apparatuses and machines which will make it possible for a relatively small number of persons with moderate effort to prepare the food for hundreds of table guests. The same thing is true of washing and cleaning appliances.[11]

Who were all these imaginative machines supposed to serve, women or men? According to Bebel, the woman selects her vocation "to correspond with her wishes, inclinations, and natural abilities, and she works under conditions identical with man's." For the woman of the future is a superwoman. According to Bebel, she possesses an astounding versatility.

Even if engaged as a practical working-woman in some field or other, at other times of the day she may be educator, teacher, or nurse, at yet others she may exercise herself in art, or cultivate a branch of science, and at yet others may fill some administrative function. She joins in studies, enjoyments or social intercourse with either her sisters or with men.[12]

This ideal woman of the future produces like a man but retains typically female functions besides (educator, teacher, nurse), incidentally produces a work of art or becomes absorbed in scientific literature. She then indulges her erotic interests. The freedom of the woman is almost grotesque:

> Woman is free, and her children, if she has any, do not impair her freedom: they can only fill all the fuller the cup of her enjoyments and her pleasure in life. Nurses, teachers, female friends, the rising female generations—all are ready to help the mother when she needs help.[13]

This future projection shows the inconsistency of socialist theory when it comes to women's work. Bebel's utopia tries to suggest that traditional female work can be abolished neatly. In the care and education of children his visions become absurd. An infant or small child does not feed itself, does not dress itself, and does not wipe its own nose. The only conceivable alternative to child care is the day-care center. This possibility, of course, has its limits.

The young Marx wrote:

> In all preceding societies human beings were hunters, fishers, or herders or critics and had to remain so if they did not wish to lose the means to life—while in the communistic society, where people have no exclusive vocational area, but can educate themselves in any field they like, the society regulates the general production and thus even makes it possible for me to do one thing today and another tomorrow, to hunt in the morning, to fish in the afternoons, to tend cattle in the evening, after supper to criticize, just as I like; without being either hunter, fisher, herder or critic.[14]

This notion of Marx contains two wishes: first, the despecialization of human activity and, in contradiction, the utmost versatility of vocation for the multi-specialists. The regulation of production by society can at best mean an equitable redistribution of work, possibly also a saving of time. It cannot dismiss from this world the unpopular but necessary jobs, and it can never guarantee total individual freedom. It is almost unimaginable that a woman would have concocted this sort of free space. For in all preceding societies women were mothers, and their vocation—the care of children—demanded continuity. It is hardly conceivable that Marx would have come up with the idea that, in a Communist society, the mother should be a bit of a mother at breakfast, tend cattle in the evening, and do one thing today and the other tomorrow. Thus, socialist theory aroused false conceptions by suggesting that, with socialization of the means of production, division of labor was subject to unrestricted free choice.

If Marx, Engels, and Bebel had thought more seriously about the division of labor between the sexes, they would have envisaged a different division of labor. But because their androcentric perspective held fast, the unpaid and socially non-exchangeable services of women remain the common foundation of socialist and capitalist countries.

15/The Automation and Socialization of Housework

Who cleans the john, who picks the hair balls out of the sink?

—*Dolle Mina pamphlet, 1969*

In the *Komsomolskaya Pravda* (May 27, 1967) there was a piece by two Leningrad women readers intended as "an open letter to our husbands." The authors demanded that women be given jobs that were physically lighter but at the same time sufficiently paid. Instruction in home economics should be made compulsory not only for girls but for boys. In this way, the systematic alienation of men from housework would be prevented. This letter initiated a longer discussion in the paper over the division of housework in the Soviet family. The editors commented on the women's demand:

> One of the paradoxes consists in the fact that the man enjoyed more advantages from the mechanization of daily life than the woman. According to data from the Institute for Economy of the Siberian Division of the Academy of Sciences of the U.S.S.R., the woman uses on the average nineteen hours more a week for housework than the man.

Nevertheless, in the 1961 platform of the Communist Party of the Soviet Union, and at the Twenty-third Party Congress of the Soviet Communist Party in 1966, the old hopes were merely reiterated, that by mechanization and collectivization housework could be kept to such a minimum that it would no longer be a burden for the working woman.[1]

In the war of ideological systems the woman's advantage in terms of emancipation in the socialist countries plays an important role. However, the "double burden" in capitalist as well as in socialist systems is at best regarded as a regrettable but at times inevitable side effect of women working outside the home. With progressive technology the problem will solve itself someday. Until then the husband's negligible participation in housework will be regarded as a mere peccadillo. From this double work the entrepreneur, the husband, and the state profit from the free jobs performed after hours which are necessary to bring up and educate the next generation. In all countries the daily climax of patriarchal exploitation takes place after business hours. Meanwhile, empirical observation in the industrialized countries has shown that housework will not simply be abolished by automation or rationalization. The double burden is in fact not a question of an interlude, or an interval, that at some point will end.

In a multinational study (under the leadership of the Hungarian sociologist Alexander Szalai), in which the division of labor in profession and family was studied and compared in twelve countries, the situation of gainfully employed wives in capitalist and socialist countries was characterized by the fact that, on the average, they worked 5.7 hours for household and family on their days off. In all countries included in the study, the husbands undertook a very small portion of the housework. On working days gainfully employed women have 3.3 hours to devote to housework, while gainfully employed men contribute only 1 hour.

> It speaks for itself that among the many thousands of gainfully employed women included in the multinational survey sample of the time budgeting project, 10 percent would report no leisure time activities on a typical workday while almost all gainfully employed men had at least a little leisure. The exceptionally small amount of leisure time that gainfully employed women manage to have at their disposal and the work loads that housewives bear are two factors that are strongly responsible for the limited participation of women in public life, vocational training, and education.[2]

Comparisons that were undertaken in medium-sized cities of six countries between the housework of gainfully employed men and women showed that in a Czech city the husbands did scarcely a quarter of the housework of their wives, while in Poland, the United States, and France the men's portion in terms of time varied between 12, 13, and 17 percent.

Lowest was the amount of time during which husbands participated in housework in comparison to their gainfully employed wives in the city of Osnabrück, West Germany. Married women worked longer in their households in Osnabrück than in the three East European provincial cities covered in the survey. Hence, the time spent on housework seems to be independent of household machines, which in West Germany, for example, are available in greater quantities than in the cities in socialist countries. Reports from the Soviet

Union and from the United States contained alarming remarks that completely repudiate the old notion that the woman could be totally relieved of her burden by means of household technology.

In 1924, gainfully employed women in Moscow and Leningrad spent, all told, 4.47 hours per workday on housework; in 1959, 3.87 hours; and in 1965, 3.6 hours. The shortening of work hours in the forty-year span was also roughly more than an hour for gainfully employed women. However, child care and caretaking functions for other members of the family were not included in this study.[3]

In the United States, between 1952 and 1967–68, the household work expenditure of gainfully employed women rose from 3.8 to 4.5 hours. Although the American woman has all that August Bebel dreamed of at her disposal, she was not freed of housework. While time could be saved on many work operations, an increase in the amount of time was spent on shopping and repair work in the household, which is done by the majority of American women on a do-it-yourself basis.[4]

Shopping, which has increasingly become the task of housewives, has since the twenties taken up more and more time in America. Housewives spend nine hours a week shopping for the groceries for their family in supermarkets, whereas in 1920 this took no longer than two hours.

Full-time housewives in 1924 in the United States spent fifty-two hours a week on their housework; in 1970 they spent fifty-five hours on it. This is the finding of a comparison of twenty studies financed by the American government. Comparative studies were carried out in 1965–66 in Michigan. In these studies women had to keep a diary of their work activities at fifteen-minute intervals. The gainfully employed women, on the other hand, got by with twenty-six hours of housework a week. The author of this study, Joann Vanek, came to the conclusion that full-time housewives try to exceed their work quota because their job is socially undervalued.[5] However, this explanation does not allow for the fact that the gainfully employed woman who does her housework in the evenings has a more intensive job, which leads to even greater exhaustion. The gainfully employed woman takes care of her children only after work, while a large portion of the housewives' work is performed for the children.

Neglected in the studies quoted is the increase in service tasks that the housewife has to perform for her family as a result of the newly acquired leisure time of the other members of the family: shorter working hours for the husband, five-day weeks, and Saturday off from school for school-age children. The greater the amount of leisure time of the family members, the smaller the leisure time of the housewife. In many families she has to perform the usual housework on vacation, whether the vacation is spent in a trailer or a rented apartment.

In the aforementioned study of twelve countries by Alexander Szalai, it also appeared that gainfully employed men devoted only half as much time to the care of children as gainfully employed women.

Above all, in the basic tasks involved in the care of small children—feeding, bathing, dressing, etc.—the fathers scarcely took part at all. Reading aloud, entertainment, games, going for walks, and taking the children to school were the activities in which gainfully employed mothers and fathers participated equally.[6]

Sexism enters into the domestic life undisguised even when men are without gainful employment:

> Case studies on the families of twenty-four men unemployed during the depression show that men with more leisure time in which they could have taken care of the household work and the children, in fact did even less than in the time in which they had been employed full-time.[7]

Even at pension age, it is still the wife who cleans the apartment and tends to the household.

In cases of equal occupational work load—for example, in marriages in which both partners work as teachers—little has changed even among young married couples. A 1973 study of couples of married teachers in Rhineland-Palatinate by the sociologist Lothar Krecker shows:

> Especially striking is the sex-specific over-burdening of the woman in the cases where she practices the same profession as her husband. Of course, in instances where professions are different, with only half-day attendance or absence from home required for the woman teacher and with allegedly or truly lighter professional responsibilities, the more or less total assumption of housework by the woman in compensation can still be argued for and justified. When the work load outside the home is the same, this allowance can no longer be made. When the demands upon man and woman as a result of professional duties are the same, parity (I am deliberately applying the concept from the discussion on worker control to this situation) in the housework is probably the only equitable solution . . . Of women teachers whose husbands are also teachers, only 6 percent state that their husband does not help in the household. But his regular help with the housework is found in only 49 percent of the households.[8]

Helge Pross's study "Gleichberechtigung im Beruf," of 7,000 women, carried out simultaneously in EEC countries, reported:

> Now as before, there are certainly great numbers of husbands who refuse to offer any help. There is no help at all from the husbands of gainfully employed wives in households in

Italy	49 percent
Luxemburg	39 percent
West Germany	32 percent
France	31 percent
Belgium	26 percent
Holland	24 percent

The most exasperating pashas are Italians and Luxemburgers. At any rate, approximately one out of every three wives there can count on help from relations. The men in Holland and Belgium are especially cooperative. In Holland, 15 percent of the wives questioned said the husband attended to the household by himself. There is evidence that the average working woman in the Netherlands has a more comfortable life than her female colleague in the other member states of EEC: favorable and relatively short working hours, many kindergartens and preschools, and spouses who are ready to help. All the more remarkable, then, is the fact that precisely in Holland, so few women succeed professionally. In Belgium the woman works halfdays only if she does all the housework. If she has a full-time job, she is assisted at home by her spouse. The situation appears to be similar, if not quite so favorable, in France and in West Germany. Assisting husbands constitute a kind of an international of dishwashers and shoppers, and the wives, an international of cooks, washerwomen, scrubwomen, and nursemaids. That is, for the husbands, household work is an odd job, for the wives, it is the main occupation.[9]

Magdalena Sokolowska wrote about Eastern Europe in a similar vein:

> In Poland it is said that the women work in "two shifts." One of the shifts is occupational work; the other, housework. The fulfillment of this double duty brings with it a heavy burden, as shown by the medical studies carried out at the beginning of the fifties on the female manual workers employed in the textile industry of Lódz. The women unanimously stated that the site of most of their heavy labor was the home.[10]

The only country in the world in which husbands feel repercussions if they do not take part in the housework is the People's Republic of China. The criticism of male supremacy began during the Cultural Revolution. One-sided division of labor within marriage is officially denounced as neo-Confucianistic thinking. A husband whose wife files for divorce because he has neglected to share in the housework is called on the carpet and re-educated by the Party. The extent to which this practice has been initiated even in the countryside cannot be judged. However, from the propaganda of the People's Republic of China, equal participation of the husband in the housework has today become an official demand of the all-powerful Party and not simply a gentle appeal to the husbands' sense of chivalry and their equality-mindedness, as in other Eastern and Western countries.[11]

In a paper given at the world conference of the International Woman's Year in Mexico Szalai said:

> It should be sufficiently clear that—whatever hopes we may continue to place on the future development of labor-saving household technologies—these will bring no pat solution of the problem, at least not in the foreseeable future. The gap between the negligible participation of men in household duties and the burden that women bear in the household is much too great, and there is no technology in view that can diminish the work load of women in volume which would be necessary for a substantial improvement of their situation.[12]

16/Sexism in the Labor Market

There have been clerks, copyists, for centuries. Today, because these positions have multiplied a hundredfold, because there is a shortage of male labor, and because, for the most part, they cannot be highly compensated, these jobs are filled by women.

—Arnold Gehlen

After World War II the constituent assembly of West Germany, the Parliamentary Council, discussed in its Central Committee the question of equal pay for the two sexes. The Communist delegate Karl Renner demanded that the wording "equal pay for man and woman for the same work" be included in the Basic Law. All parties declared that equal pay should be incorporated in the equal rights article; all constitutional rights could be tested in courts and judges and legislation were to be bound by them. On December 3, 1948, the Social Democratic delegate Elisabeth Selbert explained:

> I want the equal rights of women to be a conclusive, binding right based on the constitution . . . I am thinking, for example, of the signing of many new wage scale contracts in the very near future.

Chairman Carlo Schmid summed up: "I can doubtless state here, as the general view of the Central Committee, that the clause on equal rights for men and women implies that men and women receive the same pay for the same work." Believing that Schmid's statement would be enforced, Selbert and other female politicians did not fight for a more specific equal rights law. As Selbert stated: "It is my opinion that the interpretation in the Parliamentary Council was so comprehensive and precise that it would not require renewed emphasis or a special challenge."[1]

Unfortunately, many wage scale contracts signed after the constitution went into effect on May 24, 1949, ignored Article 3. Moreover, female employees suffered wage cuts of 10 percent and higher. In the metal industry of Bavaria, wage differentials for women existed even in 1962, merely reduced from 27 percent to 20 percent.[2] Several labor courts rejected Article 3.

Even constitutions like that of Mexico, which was the first to contain an article on the constitutional right to equal pay for man and woman, have not created equality in wages. As early as 1908 a law was passed in Norway requiring equal pay—without notable success. Great Britain's Labour Party approved equal pay in 1947, but did not enforce this. The state budget would be too greatly burdened, and inflationary consequences would be unavoidable.[3] Moreover, the equal wage law has often been enforced in an extremely arbitrary fashion in different countries. In West Germany, for example, the equality clause of the Basic Law

> led to a heated struggle in German judicial administration and jurisprudence. The outcome is still an open question. One side claims the designation of equal wages as an immediately valid constitutional right, binding not only from the executive power, but also valid for all wage-scale and individual labor agreements. But the other side disputes the relevance of this and holds that Article 3 of the Basic Law obligates only the government to observe the equal pay policy and leaves the private sector untouched.[4]

The political platform of socialist countries incorporated equal pay for man and woman; yet the most capitalist country of the West, the United States, was far more progressive on this point than other Western countries. While the employers' organizations generally rejected the principle of equal pay on the grounds that the value of women's work would be less than that of men's work, the North American employers' associations made an exception. According to a 1944 study in New York State ninety-eight wage agreements contained seventy-three concrete wage equality clauses.[5]

This phenomenon apparently resulted from the relatively strong position of the American working woman during wartime. In 1955, when Congresswoman Edith Green introduced equal pay legislation into the House of Representatives, women's war efforts were long in the past and Green's motion was vetoed.[6]

In the very year the West German Basic Law became effective, both private employers and government continued their practice of discrimination. The Bavarian Ministry of Culture issued special injunctions to female teachers in order to force them back to school to teach. In a Bundestag debate of December 1, 1949, the KPD denounced the employers' practice of wage discrimination. Delegate Grete Thiele complained:

On the basis of unequal wages, employers try, in the wage negotiations, to implement percentage wage increases and not flat-rate increases. Through the percentage wage increases at this uneven wage level, the gap between the men's and women's wages grows wider and wider . . . It is immoral for some workers to be paid less than others because of sex or age.

A violent falling-off of debates over wage discrimination has been misconstrued by many German sociologists as proof of the success of women's emancipation. On this premise, sociologist Helmut Schelsky stated, in 1955, that there was no longer any exploitation of the woman in industrial work.

An equally prominent exponent of sociology, Arnold Gehlen, could state: "If after decades of practically equal educational opportunities there are still so few women in leading political and economic positions, then one must eventually seek the reasons for this in certain fundamental differences in the sexes."

Now, however, it is time to retire certain notions that at the time of the emancipation struggle made good sense, but are no longer plausible: the demand for proportionate involvement in politics, heavy industry, leadership in major organizations, or the constantly reiterated emphasis on a woman's right to the individual development of her personality and talents because she is as spiritually mature as man and of equal birth.[7]

In the history of West Germany, Article 3 of the Basic Law has remained a well-intended phrase that has failed to protect female workers from capricious payment. Even the unequivocal judgments of the national labor court only support the illusion that the woman employee could succeed in gaining her rights by legal recourse. With wage settlements came only detours of the constitutional rulings of the national labor court, through slight regroupings of wage categories.

Trade unions also contributed to the expansion and stabilization of the gap between male and female incomes. In 1962 the German Federation of Trade Unions apologized for accepting unequal wage groups:

To the trade unions this development was not agreeable, but they were forced to go along with this course because a different agreement with employers, and thus an eventual elimination of the considerable wage differences between men and women, would not have been reached.

No trade union, not even the strike-minded British trade unions, has ever considered the underpayment of women as grounds for a strike or other corrective measures. In Great Britain, for example, female wages in 1972 were still 59.3 percent of male wages.[8] The attitude toward female members is solicitous and patriarchal. Although it is generally understood that the common purpose of the industrial trade unions in West Germany is not only to fight for wages but also to advocate socio-political goals, the unions' views on work are as patriarchal as those of the Weimar Republic.

Whereas in 1963 the German woman industrial worker received 68.7 percent of the man's wages, nine years later she received only 2 percent more. Compared with other Western industrial countries, West Germany—the country with a high wage level comparable only to the United States and Sweden—fares very poorly. In Sweden the female hourly wage increased between 1963 and 1972 by 11.1 percent to 83.2 percent of the man's wages. In Denmark and Australia, for example, the rise in female wages was higher than in West Germany.[9] For decades futile efforts have been made to find criteria to equate the particular advantages of the female labor force, such as manual dexterity, with those of males (muscle-power). The International Labor Organization in Geneva has provided for equal pay for equal work. Whether it should be termed equal pay for equal work or equal pay for work of equal value is a question that representatives of both socialist and Western industrialized countries continue to dispute. In all countries for which comparable data are available, an immediate link can be seen between the dimensions of sex hierarchy and the payment of women. If in a highly industrialized country like Japan the women received in 1972 only 47.5 percent of the men's wages, while in Sweden women received 83.2 percent, then it can easily be seen that the value of a job has to do not with the criteria of the job but with the society's stamp of sexism and the male power structures associated with it.

If Christian conservative parties in Europe advance the concept of the meritocratic society, because rating individual performance is the only thing that keeps an economy competitive, then it can be stated that women, no matter what their occupational categories, have never been paid on the basis of their performance. For example, in April 1974 women in white-collar jobs in West Germany received only 63 percent of the male salaried employees' salary. In occupations in which women compete in the labor market, and comprise a minority, and in which payment is settled not through wage scale agreement but by private business labor contracts, salary discrimination exists. Inequality is further compounded by particular company regulations, company pensions, retirement money, vacation increments, Christmas bonuses, relocation payments, etc., which often one-sidedly favor the man.[10]

In West Germany, a woman rarely holds a high-level job in industry, insurance, or banking; the large firms, in particular, where the trade unions and works committees are better represented, offer apprenticeships in these areas only for male applicants. The trade unions support sex-specific, differential education for young women and men in commercial areas, and the women are automatically led into blind alleys: shorthand-typist, typing pool, receptionist.

In 1961, 84 percent of the female apprentices in West Germany were working in only twelve fields. In Great Britain, in May 1970, there were 112,000 male apprentices who were training to become skilled workers; the number of such female apprentices was only 110. Of the 7 percent of the young women who took up an apprenticeship in England, three-quarters of them had to limit themselves to the hairdressing trade. For a little less than half of all educated women in Canada in 1972–73, the target profession was shorthand-typist, a job in bookkeeping, or a similar pursuit.[11]

> What can explain the fact that wages so frequently drop, and certainly do not rise, if women break into a professional field in great numbers. Why have the wages in the so-called women's professions always been low? It appears that for no reason, in a society ruled by men, the work of women is classified as inferior.[12]

This quotation shows the total hopelessness with which the International Labor Organization, founded in 1919, still addresses the question complex of unequal pay. The answer must involve a theory of sexism. In the Soviet Union, for example, nearly 75 percent of the doctors are female. Because this has therefore become a women's profession, the negative effects of feminization of the profession have set in. The social prestige and also the payment of women doctors in the Soviet Union are totally out of proportion to the social influence and the income of the doctors in West Germany. The only alternative for preventing such developments lies in a control of vocational training through subsidies that no society to date has worked out. Only in Sweden is a first attempt underway to take steps in this direction.

Since 1945 the belief that in democratic countries which guarantee civil rights, the matter of equal rights could be attained through an unending demolition of prejudice has existed. Small steps were extolled, but it was seldom considered whether these small steps were not in themselves steps backward. In the United States, this painful realization came at the beginning of the new women's movement: the average earnings of women, which in 1960 had totaled 63.9 percent of the men's wages, had, by 1970, fallen to 59.4 percent. There had been no progress, only a deterioration. Equally alarming were the data for families in which the mother was the breadwinner. From 1959 to 1971 the number of these poor families rose from 23 to 40 percent. In 1971, approximately two-thirds of all adults who were among the poorest population were women. Of 15 million welfare recipients in 1975, 10 million were mothers and children.[13]

In a welcoming address to a Chicago women's conference on January 24, 1970, on the employment situation of women, the black politician Shirley Chisholm stated that sexism in wage discrimination exceeded even racial wage discrimination: "White working women earned less than black male workers, and naturally black working women earned least of all."[14]

In 1940 the number of gainfully employed women in the United States suddenly began to grow. Around 1900, 20 percent had been gainfully employed, the majority of them only before marriage. In 1940, 30 percent, and in 1970, 50 percent of the American women worked outside the home, half of them in the age group between thirty-five and fifty-nine. Since 1950 there was a rising trend among women whose children had reached school age to go back to work.

In 1970, American sociologist Dean D. Knudsen studied what the U.S. Department of Labor has always enthusiastically called a positive development for the female work force. Knudsen found great statistical distortions. The development and the status of man and woman in an occupation can be measured only in relative terms. Thus, the Labor Department stated in 1960 that, within ten years, the number of professionally qualified women had risen by roughly 41 percent. Knudsen writes: "The statistic is impressive until comparable figures for men are at hand: almost 4 1/2 million and a rise of 51 percent in ten years." He therefore selected the most frequently used yardsticks of class affiliation and status to determine: profession, income, and education. Result: The more the amount of female labor power in a professional group rose, the more the relative income of the women dwindled in the last twenty-five years. While the average salaries for teachers in grade and secondary schools rose, the number of female teachers dropped. Although there was an enormous increase in the number of women teachers—especially in the age group of twenty to twenty-four—the percentage increase for men from 1940 to 1966 was more than three times as high as that for women. The educational data that Knudsen compared with the occupational positions of men and women underscored the negative professional development for women in a period which constantly was lauded as an era of evolutionary rapprochement in achieving ideal equality. In questions of education, women were "in a worse situation than they had been in twenty-five years earlier." Knudsen concludes: "In the narrow correlation of profession and income with educational achievement it appears probable that the women will remain in an inferior position even into the next generation."[15]

From 1966 to 1973, the European Social Science Coordination Center in Vienna conducted a research project on conceptions of the world in the year 2000. Ten countries took part in this international comparison: Finland, Great Britain, Japan, Yugoslavia, India, the Netherlands, Norway, Poland, Spain, and Czechoslovakia. Sociologist Eva Bartova asked men and women in these countries: "Do you believe that in the year 2000 women in leading positions will be more common or less common than today?" And: "Do you hope that women will be more common or less common in leading positions?"

Eva Bartova wrote:

A different picture, more peculiar and contradictory, comes to light in the area of hopes. In all countries the hopes of the men for more women in leading positions were less frequent than their expectations.

Women generally showed a stronger desire for access to leading positions, while men could not identify with this female desire. Men from the two socialist countries—Poland and Czechoslovakia—most frequently expressed negative comments and least wished to see women in leading positions. Similarly negative were Japanese men. They feared that the employment of women would impinge on both their professional and private opportunities. Eva Bartova links the findings in Czechoslovakia with the degree of saturation of the labor market in which almost all women of working age—with the exception of mothers who have children at nursing age—are included.[16] In Poland the degree of gainful employment among women corresponds somewhat to that of West Germany (Poland in 1969: 30 percent). According to Magdalena Sokolowska:

Just as in other countries, the portion of women who fill leading positions does not correspond to the level of women's education ... For the great majority of women, this is unattainable, for in the fulfillment of domestic duties there still are no equal rights.[17]

In 1974 only 1.8 percent of the top executives in West Germany were women. The average income of a female manager was about one-third below that of her male colleague.[18] Such figures, especially Knudsen's findings, show that the publication of data on the improvement of female professional qualifications is misleading. If at the same time the professional qualifications of the men are strongly improved, then the women do not have a greater, but rather a smaller, chance of finding a good position. Their advanced education may not weigh as heavily as it should. The practice of apprenticeships and vocational counseling leads female graduates in the Western world into a professional impasse. This results from the fact that the distribution of vocational opportunities is still left to the "free play of natural forces" without regulatory government intervention. The situation seems to be getting worse, not better.

Part Five
Biology and Ideology

17/Biology and Genetics

The Y chromosome is really a sad affair.

—*Ashley Montagu*

The history of male domination is bound to biologistic theories. Over thousands of years and across cultural borders the message has been the same. Occasionally a famous doctor such as Rudolf Virchow will announce that the essence of woman is derived from her ovaries; sometimes it is stated that the woman resembles the lower races because she is allegedly more inclined to flat feet.[1] Those are details; the fundamental idea of female inferiority is always the same.

A particularly influential study on genetically conditioned sex differentiation was published in 1889 by the Scottish biologist Patrick Geddes. In this book, *The Evolution of Sex,* contemporary knowledge of the reproduction process was combined with Geddes's notions of the social position of women, to give the impression that science had finally found a tenable foundation for sexual characteristics. The male sperm cells, according to Geddes, showed a tendency to squander energy, and female passivity came from the complementary tendency to store up nutritive substance. The entire evolution from the lowest organisms up to human life supposedly depended on these male and female qualities. Male and female sex roles were separate, even in the lowest forms of life, and no women's movement in the world could change this. Only by re-creating "the whole of evolution once again on a new basis" could differences between the sexes be eliminated. His famous thesis on the irrevocability of male-female relationships, which was quoted everywhere, reads: "What was decided among the prehistoric Protozoa cannot be annulled by an act of Parliament."[2]

The fervor with which phrenological measurements were made in the last century in order to establish the inferiority of both women and blacks by measuring the circumference of the skull and the weight of the brain, is echoed today by intelligence testing. A world-famous Russian scholar of human genetics, Theodosius Dobzhansky, believes that children inherit their intelligence from their fathers only.[3]

His accompanying tables of a study of British children correlate the intelligence quotients of the children exclusively with those of the fathers, a perfect example of sexist perspective in intelligence research.

Every conversion of the findings of human biology and genetic research into value concepts must inevitably end in racism or sexism of one or the other variety. Biologism is the application of findings that are always only provisional and abstract to the inborn qualities of human beings in a political context, misusing them as a weapon in power struggles.

In *The Banquet of Xanthippe* (1950), which appeared under the pseudonym of Delphica, a scientific lecture is quoted which, in the view of the female author, is a characteristic example of the way in which "the poison of the theses of inferiority infiltrates the female consciousness." Because the man has a smaller Y chromosome, while the woman has a double X chromosome, "the man is incomplete, thus he is the seeker, the creative one, while the woman, in her completion, rests, having no part in that which is creative."

Delphica comments on this statement:

> I probably need not emphasize that, in the reverse case, if fewer chromosomes had been counted in the female cell, man would still have a higher value: from his wealth and his affluence, creativity would once again be his and the unfinished woman, without any hesitation, would be declared second-rate.[4]

Even researchers who support women in their struggle and wish to furnish them with scientific arguments succumb to the temptation of biologism. The American anthropologist Ashley Montagu, in his book *The Natural Superiority of Women,* explains the superiority of the woman by a genetic deficiency of the man. A feminist stand, however, can never be justified genetically, and the categories of inferiority and superiority are in themselves expressions of sexist positions.

Since the discovery of sex chromosomes, genetic research explored their evolution as autosomes, and with the subsequent type of specialization, namely the size differences of the sex chromosomes. The discovery that the X chromosome is among the largest chromosomes and the Y chromosome is one of the smallest, by the researchers J. H. Tijo and T. T. Puck, in 1958, unleashed grave doubt about the biology of man. For not only is the female egg 85,000 times larger than the spermatozoon, but the Y chromosome, compared to the X chromosome, is also a mini-chromosome.[5] Because the female organism has a second X chromosome, its genetic information is almost twice as large as that of the male.

Human geneticists believe the following factors are responsible for the evolutionary development of sex chromosomes. Among mammals, the chromosome of the gametes is homologous in each pair of autosomes. This makes possible the recombination of the chromosome segments only in meiosis. In two X chromosomes this exchange is also possible. In the heterogametic sex, however, the sex-determining information must be isolated; X must be effectively separated from Y, for otherwise the specialization as sex chromosome would be canceled out through their recombination and the exchange of information. Because in the reduction of one of the sex chromosomes in the heterogametic sex (XY combination), some genetic information is omitted, the only genes that can be assembled or left in the Y chromosome are those which guarantee the organism's capability for life. Even in view of this established fact, the female homogametic sex would still have an advantage in genetic information because it has two X chromosomes. There must also be a balancing mechanism. This balance was summarized in 1961 by the English geneticist Mary Lyon: In a purely random fashion, one of the two X chromosomes is inactivated in the course of the early female embryonal development. It appears that the authors who attribute a redeeming or curative function to woman on account of her "more complete" biology—always with honorable motives—have failed to notice the inactivation of one of the two X chromosomes. For instance, Ashley Montagu wrote:

> It is as if in the evolution of sex a fragment of an X chromosome was broken off and took with it some rather pitiable genes, and as a result was unable to stop the other chromosomes from expressing themselves in the form of the incomplete female, the creature that we call the male!
>
> This "Just So Story" makes man into a kind of stunted woman, a creature that is not as biologically well equipped as the woman because it has only one single chromosome.[6]

The biological advantages which women have, however, do not consist in the double X information but in the fact that chromosome segments with defects are replaceable by ones without. This possibility for genetic correction does not exist in the male; he may have defects in both the Y and the X chromosomes. Those associated with the Y chromosome appear only in the man and are statistically easy to calculate.

> The fact that the man is provided with one Y chromosome appears to bring him more disadvantages than if he had no Y chromosome at all; for while the Y chromosome carries few genes of any value, at times it also contains some which—to put it mildly—bring bad luck. Up to the present at least four developmental flaws are traceable to genes which occur only in the Y chromosome and thus are transferrable only from the father to the sons. These are a scabby type of skin (ichthyosis hystrix gravior), thick hair growth in the ear (hypertrichosis), non-painful severe damage to the hands and

feet (keratoma dissipatum) and a fin formation between the toes which consists of a connecting skin between the second and third toe.[7]

Among women, defects occur significantly less often from the genetic information of the X chromosome. For example, it is highly unlikely that a woman will receive a mutant gene from both her mother and her father that is responsible for hemophilia. It is also known that color blindness and a lack of color vision appears much more frequently in men. To date, approximately thirty-five genetically linked diseases associated with the sex chromosomes have been found. They occur almost only among men (sensory aphasia, stuttering [according to Ashley Montagu], etc.).

The higher life expectancy of women became author Esther Vilar's argument against the women's movement, in order to chastise women's dronelike idleness. Walter Steigner, the director of "Der Deutschen Welle" (The German Wave), introduced the International Women's Year on his radio station with a comment condemning any further improvements in the plight of women. His reason: women already had a higher life expectancy and a lower pension age than men.

And even Ashley Montagu, the man who wrote the first plea for the genetic superiority of the woman, attacks the women's movement on account of its alleged hostility to children.

> Some women in the movement are evidently looking desperately for enemies, for even in view of the overwhelming evidence, they go on clinging to the idea that a day nursery can be every bit as good as a mother ... But there is no substitute for the truly loving mother, either biologically or in the surrogate. When a baby is born, a mother is born too.[8]

The woman possesses genetic advantages and a more stable biological constitution, according to Ashley Montagu, in order to fulfill herself completely in the mother role.

> Women could and should take up any occupation or any profession if they want to. But when they become mothers, they must recognize that they have taken up the most important of all occupations and professions put together, for what could be more important than the creation of a living human being.[9]

This argument strikes one as curious. For, in the first place, those who have not realized the importance of children's education are sitting in the patriarchal institutions, in the government and business bureaucracies as well as in the legislatures, and have not bothered to make the education of children into an appendage of the business and administrative processes. The feminist movement emerged as a defense community for the interests of women and children.

Even more contradictory is Ernest Borneman in his book on the history of the rise of patriarchy. After a practically sadistic evaluation of the female sex chromosomes, he demands the liquidation of the female functions and organs—pregnancy, menstruation, and breasts should be abolished so that the social motherliness of the woman can take effect.[10] Why—of all the genetic advantages that she possesses—the female body in its biological repertoire must first be totally accommodated to that of the man remains obscure.

Every direct effect of genetic information on behavior, on aptitude, and on intelligence and imagination—concepts on which there is no agreement—is not only inadmissible speculation but, in terms of the thinking of molecular biology, basically false. There are no genes that produce intelligence. The study of molecular biology, as currently pursued, is not interested in the connection between genes and intelligence. It asks: what is the appearance of the immediate gene product? This is by now a trivial statement. First, genetic information is responsible—perhaps even exclusively responsible—for the synthesis of certain products, such as proteins in complex or less complex structures. These proteins are the building material with which the organism, in its ontogenesis—that is, its individual development—creates characteristic features. In part it is proteins that appear as constant distinguishing features on the body surface: muscle proteins, skin protein, blood-group substance, etc., or proteins play a role in the assembling and functioning of the organism, or intervene in a metabolic process in a quite specific area in order to initiate a further step in development.

The development of the central nervous system, which controls the development of the brain and essential portions of what we call intelligence, is not dependent primarily upon original genetic information but can be influenced secondarily. Female or male hormones could have effects on the formation of the central nervous system, for they already begin to function in the first weeks after conception. At any rate, whether or not this is the case, whether or not these secondary influences really play a role, are purely hypothetical questions. It is more than questionable whether the quality of intelligence, in its complexity, ever can be analyzed so scrupulously that the biological inheritance and its possible influences on the differences between the sexes can be precisely described. The chemistry and physics of thought and sensitivity and their connection with the subject elude description. Only the defects of intelligence are describable and can be statistically grasped.

18/Man as Helmsman
of Evolution

*The penis of the male undergoes a
dramatic modification with sexual
arousal. From a limp, flaccid condition it
expands, stiffens and erects by means of
intensive vasocongestion. Its normal,
average length of nine and a half
centimeters is increased by seven to eight
centimeters. The diameter is also
considerably increased, giving the species
the largest erect penis of any living
primate.*

—Desmond Morris

The male is the favorite animal of the physical anthropologists.
Whether in technical publications or in population descriptions, the
illustrations portray male figures. Man—even regarded semiotically—
is the symbol for "human being." The purpose of the following comparison is to elucidate the way in which any anatomical fact can be
explained and interpreted through apparently logical arguments as
an advantage, sometimes on equally convincing grounds as a disadvantage.

Ashley Montagu wrote:

The woman is in many respects a more highly fetalized type than
the man . . .
The promise of development of the human child is more completely realized in the woman than in the man.[1]

His chain of reasoning is the following: in comparison to the large
primates (gorilla, chimpanzee, orangutan), the skull of the adult
human bears a much closer resemblance to that of the fetus. This
also holds true for other characteristics such as hair growth, head
size, and nose formation. The human being is a more strongly "fet-

alized" living creature than the ape. In addition, the head forms of the baby anthropoid ape are more similar to human forms than those of adult apes. Ashley Montagu thus concluded that similarity to a fetus is a criterion for higher development. He found that women show more similarity to fetal forms, thus were more highly developed.

Arthur Schopenhauer came to the exact opposite conclusion:

> Women are suited to be nurses and educators by virtue of the fact that they themselves are childish and shortsighted—in a word, big children all their life: a kind of intermediate stage between the child and the man, who is the actual human being.[2]

One could produce multiple examples of opposite conclusions drawn from the same biological data. The Darwinists also wrote of woman's lower stage of development. At the conference of German anthropologists held in Breslau in 1884, Paul Albrecht gave a lecture on the greater bestiality of females in anatomical respects. "Data proves that the female sex is clearly the more hirsute—that is, the sex closer to our wild ancestors." The fact that women were less often bald, the "more powerful development of the inner incisors," and different dorsal vertebra forms would offer substantiation.[3]

Philosopher Georg Simmel professed as early as 1919:

> If one actually accepts that the development of human beings came to a halt at an earlier stage with its female than with its male branch, it is a completely arbitrary contention; that it achieves its completion only with the advance to the male stage . . . Now naturally, everyone is free to value one stage more highly than the other—although a value comparison between species of creatures of which each wants to be judged exclusively according to its own ideal and who possess no common denominator that is at all certain, always has something awkward about it.[4]

The difference in physical strength of the two sexes has for thousands of years been regarded as the most important criterion for the inferiority of the woman, mentioned by even Aristotle and Thomas Aquinas. The difference in strength seems to have developed when the prehominids began living on the ground and the males assumed the tasks of defense. There are, for example, enormous differences in body size and strength between a male baboon and a female baboon, in an ape species that does not live in the protection of the treetops. The earliest human skeleton findings, however, disprove this view. In Australopithecus, a pygmylike, erect type whose hands and feet were human, there existed, "obviously, in comparison to the large anthropoid apes, a relatively less significant sexual dimorphism, that is, difference in size and strength of the sexes."[5]

Though within human populations there is an enormous span of variation in size and strength between the sexes, the average shows a constant sex difference. The Semang, a small Negrito tribe on the Malayan Peninsula, show almost the same size differences between men and women as exist among Europeans.

> The degree of variation for men amounts to 138–175.0 cm and for women 131.0–156.8 cm . . . The female sex is 10–12 cm smaller than the male, on the average 10.8 cm . . .[6]

The Australian aborigines, who are like Central Europeans in stature and body size, show similar sex differences in size; however, both sexes possess less subcutaneous fat.

After achieving physical maturity, the average white American man is approximately 10 percent larger than the average white American woman and possesses a volume of muscle twice as great.[7] Insofar as comparative data is available, men are at least 30 percent stronger than women. The stronger development of the male muscle tissue is influenced by the hormone androgen; the greater fat development of the female body (about 25 percent body fat as compared to 15 percent body fat in the male) is equally dependent on hormones. Moreover, men possess a larger cardiopulmonary capacity and thus the possibility of absorbing greater quantities of oxygen. In relation to their body size, women have a smaller heart, smaller lungs, and a lower total metabolism. However, their energy consumption is more economical than that of men.[8]

Differences in achievement between male and female athletes are less than they were earlier assumed to be and do not correspond to the difference in strength. Comparing records set by men and women shows that the fastest man in the 400-meter free-style swim in the 1924 Olympics was 16 percent faster than the fastest woman; in 1948 it was merely 11.6 percent faster, and in 1972 only 7.3 percent faster.[9] The difference between the world records in the 100-meter dash has been reduced from 1.3 to .9 seconds in a quarter of a century.

Nevertheless, all these figures give an incomplete picture of the performance ability of the female body. In many sports, as in many areas of life, what matters most is not maximum strength but endurance. The records for the crossing of the English Channel are held by women, and it is no longer utopian to believe that, if women were admitted into such disciplines as the marathon race and the 50-kilometer walk, they would have a good chance of winning.

It is the tyranny of the male definitions of their body that prevent women from developing their own physical self-confidence. How have male and female physical differences developed with the humanization of the ape?

The observations of primates in their natural habitat are still meager; the secondary literature and the interpretations of primate behavior, however, are so comprehensive that they assume to have

discovered an unrejectable scientific basis for bourgeois sexual morality, for the housewives' marriage, and for the division of power in state
and society. The image conveyed by various best sellers of this type,
read around the world, closes the gap between the Biblical idea of
creation and evolution theory by means of new patriarchal myths.

Behavioral scientists and zoologists satisfy their readers by suggesting that nature was the only force that worked rationally and was
directed toward a marvelous finale. Under the pretext of observing the
human being as a zoological species among other species, they develop the same androcentric perspective as the church fathers: creation and evolution both lead to man.

The English primatologist Desmond Morris was not content to
confirm the phenomenal virility of the "naked ape" as the primate
with the longest phallus and the strongest sexual desire. If in the myth
of the Old Testament the female body was created out of the rib of the
man, then from Morris, with the help of the ideas of evolution theory,
comes a streamlined product, beautiful in form, which developed
breasts and buttocks because it seemed so sexy to Stone Age men. As
a result of the new upright walk, the position in coitus also changed,
becoming frontal.

Morris writes:

> Because our females have rather a heavy suckling burden and
> because the breasts are so obviously a part of the feeding appa-
> ratus, we have automatically assumed that their protruding,
> rounded shape must also be part and parcel of the same parental
> activity. But it now looks as though this assumption has been
> wrong and that, for our species, breast design is primarily sexual
> rather than maternal in function.[10]

However, after infants were still going hungry in nineteenth- and
twentieth-century Europe, during and as a result of the two world
wars, because their mothers had too little milk or came down with
mastitis, this explanation of the evolution and purpose of the female
breast and its superfluity in the nourishment of the human infant
seems rather remarkable.

The concept of sexual natural selection comes from Charles Darwin and is an important part of his theory of evolution. He believed
that women and men choose sexual partners on the basis of physical
attributes. That Darwin's basic ideas of selection, mutation, and descent were correct is undisputed today—yet, when authors more than
a hundred years after Darwin regard the male and his pleasure as the
sole force shaping the female body, absurdity results.

Morris believed breasts and fat deposits of the female body are
formed by male natural selection. He did not, of course, realize that
subcutaneous fat and breast and buttock padding form a very effective
layer of insulation in the female ape. In the male, a similar insulation

results from hair on the chest. It is also conceivable that these fat deposits of the female were "permanent reserves" which offered her chances for survival. The form of the female buttocks is determined by the different pelvic formation underlying them and the muscle tissue, while the breast consists of fatty tissue,[11] though Morris disregards this difference. That in today's Western societies men like breasts and bottoms may be a result of this female body development, but not its cause. In a great number of societies breasts are not regarded as especially erotic stimuli or release for male sexual feeling.

The present-day sex ratio in primitive societies with a technology and way of life corresponding to that of the Middle and Early Stone Ages yields a shortage of women. There are no unmarried women, but often unmarried men, who are, for the most part, the scorn of the community.[12] Sexual natural selection by elimination contests could therefore have been effective only among men. It is interesting that the surplus of men appears to be limited to the Paleolithic Age; the Mesolithic findings show near-parity. A breakdown by probable age of death shows a clear surplus of women in the age group twenty-one to thirty years old (fifty-two women to thirty-five men); in other words, in the Early and Middle Stone Ages, women probably died earlier than men.[13]

Hence, it is more probable that the shortage of women worked as a selective factor affecting the morphology of the male body, for each woman whose children remained alive contributed to the pool of genes and to the transmission of heredity information, while presumably some men produced no offspring.

The evolutionary pressure upon the characteristic features of the female body consisted of several selecting trends that assured the survival chances of our society: walking and development of a larger brain. In the depictions of many authors this complex selection pressure on the entire species turns into an initiative steered by the man or by the child, to which the female body in its development had to be subjugated.

> Thus, they learned to speak and to think, to plan and produce complicated tools, and the brain of the children also became larger . . . A brief glance backward will show us that, with the increase of the brain, the female was placed in an especially difficult situation. The skull of a child had to be large enough to accommodate the enlarged brain, but at the same time small enough to pass through the birth canal of the mother. One might think that it would have been simplest for the female to develop a larger birth canal. However, they were not able to do so. The characteristics necessary for the bipedal walk made an enlargement of the birth canal, beyond a certain limit, physically impossible.
>
> So the adjustments took place not in the maternal organisms but in the child . . .[14]

In reality, however, the woman had to bear the main consequences of the adjustment to the upright walk. In their positioning and arrangement, the intestines and uterus, as a result of the upright walk, are spatially much more limited than in other primates. This limitation in the pelvic space produced a formation of uterus and placenta unlike that found in any other female mammal. The great enlargement of the uterus in the course of pregnancy, its contraction during and reduction after birth, require a construction that is unique. The muscles of the uterine wall run in a spiral formation so that the organ can enlarge without passive stretching, or sharp growth, but exclusively by material displacements of the muscles, which result in a thinning of its wall. The intense nourishment of the human fetus by the highly differentiated placenta occurs in the smallest possible space, essentially a burden to the mother.[15] In terms of the history of evolution, it is important for the uterus to have taken this shape before the human being walked in an absolutely erect fashion.

For no other mammal female is it so perilous to give birth. The human child has a much greater weight at birth than infants of other primates. The weight of the brain is the reason for this. Birth lasts longer than among other primates, which can, in part, be traced to the upright walk. It would be wrong to say that the evolution of the reproductive organs in the human female has been imperfect or not optimal; it may be, rather, that her development is the best "emergency solution."

Except in optimal nursing conditions almost 100 percent of all women who carry their first child to full term are injured in the delivery. Even if extreme care is exercised it can happen that birth traumas cause injury to the genital structure.

So wrote American sex researcher Mary Jane Sherfey, who traces a major share of women's frigidity to genital injuries in birth, of which women themselves are not often aware.[16] The zoologist Joachim Illies wrote:

Every birth brings the mother's life into immediate danger; in the Middle Ages the mother usually died in the seventh to eighth birth, at the latest, while of five children only one survived.[17]

As late as 1930, the general director of the Indian public health service estimated that one-tenth of all Indian women were dying as a result of pregnancy. In the eighteenth and nineteenth centuries nearly one-third of the mothers in the infirmaries died in childbed fever shortly after birth. In the overcrowded hospital wards the danger of infection was even greater than under the primitive hygienic conditions in deliveries performed at home.[18]

The fact that death and mortal danger play a role in the consciousness of the pregnant woman appears in a poll of five hundred women who, on their arrival in an American maternity home shortly before confinement, almost all admitted that the thought of death had occurred to them.[19] The extremely high mother and child mortality, in other words, were probably the most effective factors in the evolution of the female body.

For the zoologists the most significant difference of the human being, in comparison to the ape, has been established: "Clearly, the naked ape is the sexiest primate alive."[20]

Other primate females are only sexual when not pregnant and not nursing. Their readiness to copulate, triggered by endocrinological impulse, is linked to season, climate, and the state of being.

> Human females behave quite differently. Potentially they are ready to conceive at almost any time. They are able to copulate during almost their entire monthly cycle and the whole year. What brought about this change? What advantage is connected with it?

The primate researcher Irven DeVore has a noteworthy answer to this:

> If the human mothers, like the ape mothers, had to renounce sexual intercourse during the dependency period of the children, the interruption of her sexual activity would have lasted years and would have led to the weakening or disruption of the relationships that males and females make with each other. However, as surely was the case, if a mother had already been able to have sexual contact again soon after the birth, this danger would have been avoided.[21]

The logic of these arguments is by no means enlightening. Male and female in other primate groups remain together without lasting sexual relations. So the author sees as the actual basis for the development of human sexual conduct a new kind of need in man.

> Perhaps this change was also an adjustment to a new psychological situation, which arose with the fact that the men became hunters. Although sexuality is a pleasant activity, it also exerts a very disruptive influence in aggressive animals that live together in groups. Obviously apes and humans solve this problem without further ado so long as they are living in their natural habitat. The hunt, however, probably made the human males more aggressive, so that they became excited by sexual competition, which among us, their offspring, is certainly the case, of course. Especially for hunters every struggle for sex could be extraordinarily wearing because squabbling and ill will had severely impaired their abil-

ity and desire to work together hunting. However, if their females were constantly ready to conceive, the strife necessarily became less.[22]

Accordingly, female sexuality today is a result of the fact that men became hunters.

Even if one accepts this conceptual model, the explanation remains misleading, suggesting that the woman's more frequent preparedness to conceive would have developed in order to reduce the aggression in a group of men. The more intensely and frequently the females are prepared for sexual intercourse, the more rivalries one would expect among the men. Also, the hunt can hardly have been the determining factor for the prolonged sexual responsiveness of the woman. Because this contradiction is somehow known to the authors, they acknowledge the next step in human development: "Besides, if every grown male had a female for himself, the possibilities of demoralizing power struggles over sex would immediately be considerably decreased."[23] But for Desmond Morris, too, it is imperative that the woman

is already prepared to mate again during nursing—otherwise, of course, in view of the long dependence of the children upon her, the situation would be nothing short of catastrophic.

Because the idea of longer sexual abstinence is obviously horrifying to Morris, the "pair-bond" must have developed.

The females had to stay put and mind the babies while the males went hunting ... The males had to be sure that their females were going to be faithful to them when they left them alone to go hunting. So the females had to develop a pairing tendency.[24]

This chain of reasoning is bewildering, as is frequently the case with Morris. If all the men went hunting, however, they could be absolutely certain of their women's fidelity, without the development of the "pair-bond."

Why, indeed, he asks himself, did Mother Nature lock this natural bolt (hymen) of the voluptuous maiden?

By making the first copulation attempt difficult and even painful, the hymen ensures that it will not be indulged in lightly. Clearly, during the adolescent phase, there is going to be a period of sexual experimentation, of "playing the field" in search of a suitable partner. Young males at this time will have no good reason for stopping short of full copulation. If a pair-bond does not form they have not committed themselves in any way and can move on until they find a suitable mate. But if young females were to go so far

without pair-formation, they might very well find themselves
pregnant and heading straight towards a parental situation with
no partner to accompany them. By putting a partial brake on this
trend in the female, the hymen demands that she shall have already developed a deep emotional involvement before taking the
final step, an involvement strong enough to take the initial physical discomfort in its stride.[25]

Here the quintessence of the modern bourgeois marriage, which of
course may be preceded by a bit of premarital intercourse, becomes
highly stylized into the principle of evolution.

Marriage is a universal human institution, but it is a thoroughly
synthetic, consciously directed form of co-existence. In the majority of
societies "love" has not been a prerequisite to marriage. But even for
scientists who do not describe the evolution of human beings as a sort
of big cake-baking game played by nature, the history of the evolution
of human sexuality is oriented toward the harmony of the nuclear
family.

Ann Roe and Lawrence Z. Freedman, both internationally recognized scholars in the area of evolution theory, wrote:

> Certain revolutionary changes have worked out so that sexuality
> became a fundamental factor in the total psychic development of
> the human being and its significance extended beyond that of
> reproduction. The human being is by preference a sexual animal.
> Perhaps what is most important is the permanence of the sexual
> drive in the man as well as in the woman. Among mammals only
> the human is free of the limitation of cyclical sexual drives ... It
> appears possible that this permanent sexual drive is an essential
> factor throughout for the constancy of the male-female relation-
> ship which, together with the required dependency of the human
> child, result in the known unity of the nuclear family.[26]

There is no way to reconstruct the particular course of development of sexuality into a model free of contradictions, given our contemporary knowledge of the sexual behavior of humans and the other
primates. The data available has been collected almost exclusively
from Western countries in the twentieth century. For the most part,
the observation of sexual behavior styles and the physiology of anthropoid apes have been made in captivity, in the laboratory, or in the
zoo.

Thus far, proof that other primate females also experience feelings similar to orgasm consists of only a few studies, the findings of
which are still too fragmentary for publication.[27] We know equally
little about the exact extent to which we depend upon hormonal influence. One further problem is to what degree the sexual drive is fixed
genetically and to what degree it is influenced by nutrition, by ecology,

or by circumstances (for example, war). Because all these factors are unsettled, the latitude for ideology-laden scientific interpretations is especially large. The adaptive advantages of development are considered unilaterally through the eyes of men.

The majority of evolution theorists who concentrate on sexuality and praise the year-round sexual responsiveness of the woman as advantageous overlook in their interpretation the fact that the largest difference in sexual behavior in terms of that of other primates exists in man. A male chimpanzee, for example, becomes sexually active only if this behavior is biologically induced by the condition of the female chimpanzee.

The researcher Jane van Lawick-Goodall graphically describes a scene in the reservation on the Gombe River. A young chimpanzee female, whose tumefaction from being in heat had already subsided, tried a few more times to present herself to the male but got no response. However,

> The fact remains that the female chimpanzees have developed in such a way that they are able to mate with the male only ten days a month, assuming that they are neither pregnant nor nursing— which for older females means that under circumstances lasting a period of up to five years they must abstain from any sexual activity.[28]

However, how can one speak of "abstaining" if a nursing chimpanzee *has* no sexual needs?

The permanently sexual animal who copulates even without the slightest sexual excitement or biological readiness on the part of his female partner—indeed, even against her physical resistance—is the human male. His modes of behavior are the great biological exception in comparison with other mammal males. And in the majority of societies and states the "sexiest ape" has codified his outsized permanently sexual demand into the marriage laws. Copulation is compulsory for the wife. Perhaps the lack of restraint and the self-determination of the male drive is related to walking erect. The female sex organ is more concealed in this way. Not even swelling during the period of heat, that striking optical signal in which edema-like structures arise around the vaginal tract, exists in human females as a visual trigger.

Sherfey, a colleague of the sex researcher Alfred Kinsey, tried in her own work to draw the evolution line from the sexuality of the female subhuman primates to sexual reaction of the woman. She sees the heat swelling of the primates transformed in the latter to the hormonally controlled premenstrual syndrome, which begins in the middle of the cycle and produces large collections of water in the body, primarily in the uterus and in the entire pelvic areas of the woman. But even she has no satisfying explanation for the total absence of estrus of the subhuman primates during the nursing period. She believes that the ovulation during the nursing period and the menstrual cycle that resumes with this is "not an especially adaptive phenomenon, but rather a purely random by-product" of the female sexual development and traces it back to the "enormously increased hormone spill-over . . . which is prepared for pregnancy in the reproduction tract and the entire rest of the body."[29]

In 1934 an American scholar studied the resumption of the period in 2,885 women. In 34 percent menstruation returned two months after birth. After six months 70 percent had one period. In a different study it was found that between 42 and 63 percent of the nursing women who were already menstruating regularly again had their first cycles without ovulation.

A mother whose own state of nutrition leaves much to be desired and who is nursing fully, without the child receiving supplementary food, has, in the opinion of one American woman expert, the best chance of not becoming pregnant again immediately.[30]

The male sex drive unleashed by signals from the female partner and the cycle resuming soon after the birth are the two factors mainly responsible for the biological tragedy of the woman. She can at any time, against her will—even in a physically weakened condition—be made pregnant.

The "pair-bond" for her means her life is constantly in mortal danger by births quickly following one after the other. Yet the monthly ability of the woman to conceive, which renders possible constant sexual attacks by the man, is celebrated by the majority of zoologists as an evolutionary advantage for our species. But in the history of human reproduction freedom "from the limitations of cyclical sexual drive" resulted in enormous wear and tear on the mother's body.

In the history of the evolution of human reproduction the unequal participation of the two sexes has led not only to a fundamental social injustice but also to a lasting psychic conflict for women, which cannot be compared to the experience of any other primate females. Of course, the relative freedom of genetically fixed modes of behavior, the possibilities for self-determination which are established in human beings, exist for the woman as for the man, but in regard to the reproductive function of her body she has remained biologically a prisoner.

Shulamith Firestone called pregnancy a deformation of the woman for the benefit of the species. This wording, however, does not get to the heart of the female dilemma, which lies in the fact that women have no free choice over whether or not they become pregnant. A woman who wants a child lives in compliance with her biological condition if she becomes pregnant; a woman who is pregnant against her wish lives at war with her body. The fetus is a foreign body whose growth consummates inside her without her being able to do anything about it on her own strength and from her own will. Her biological function produces in her ego a disastrous defeat. No man is subject to this stress situation between body and consciousness.

Only in societies that grant women sexual freedoms and in which out-of-wedlock children are integrated without social stigma is this fundamental conflict of woman alleviated. There, in each case, motherhood brings social recognition, even if it is not wanted.

Almost all primitive races impose taboos which forbid sexual intercourse with the marriage partner for at least a month, but usually for one to four years after a birth.[31] It is more than probable that such rules, in the interest of the health of mother and child and the survival of the group, were enforced primarily by women.

At the beginning of this century, the Englishwoman Katherine Routledge discovered that the average number of births of the mothers of the Akikuyu was less than four. However, she was even more astonished when she found out that infant mortality was only 84 out of 1,000 births, compared with 138 out of 1,000 births in England.[32]

Members of many primitive peoples, in their first contacts with whites, were shocked when they heard that European mothers bore more than ten children.

> Because the infancy period stretches out over several years, the sexual separation of the couple is an extraordinarily long-lasting one. That is certainly a very remarkable trait which no doubt must be understood as a half unconscious measure of primitive hygiene.

Among the Bactrians, the Medians, and the Persians, the same punishment was established for sleeping together during confinement and the nursing period "as for coitus in the menstruation: 200 lashes or the payment of 200 desems was the punishment for those who sinned against the prohibition."[33]

In many social groups parents are separated during childbirth. Johann Frick describes one Chinese society:

> Many an energetic mother-in-law goes to bed at night with her daughter-in-law . . . to prevent the possible insistence of the son . . . It is more dangerous when . . . space is limited . . . the man may demand marital intercourse . . . According to the statements of a midwife who knows the suffering of the majority of women, sleeping together within the first month is always very painful for the woman and very dangerous. Many contract chronic illnesses or even fatal illness.

Nonetheless, many men still had intercourse with their wives which resulted in another pregnancy in less than a year.[34]

Societies in which the women have to refrain from sexual intercourse longer than one year after the birth are, in the view of the American scholar J.W.M. Whiting, characterized by the intake of little protein and by polygamy. That polygamy is causally connected with postpartum prohibition, however, is not quite likely in societies in which extramarital intercourse is socially tolerated. Under Western influence, with the pressure of missionaries and mission schools, this long postpartum taboo, which protected mother and child in many parts of the world, was given up.

Long-term prohibition of sexual intercourse after the birth: such a regulation existed in none of the so-called high cultures. In Judeo-Christian and in Islamic cultural circles, either only shortly after the birth or after a four-to-six-week abstinence period, women had to submit to sexual intercourse again. For the most part, she sank to the status of a mere childbearing machine. When Christian concepts of evolution were renounced after Darwin, some found an even worse justification for childbed death. Werner Sombart, a famous German political economist and social Darwinist, wrote:

All that we know from experience about the necessary preconditions for the normal physiological development of the race is that within the scope of such a development there is no place for the humanity of the woman. Rather, the interests of the species demand no more and no less than that, between the age of twenty and forty, at regular intervals of twelve months each, the woman is willing to subject herself to pregnancy and remains in a position to do so. With this minimum of achievement the genius of the species cannot be belittled.[35]

19/Psychoanalysis and Zoology

*Clearly, the opponents of the modern
women's movement see in motherhood the
guarantee of the rights of the child.
Hence, their hostile attitude toward the
subversive women of the emancipation,
who, it seems, are planning nothing less
than a new spiritual Massacre of the
Innocents.*

—Hedwig Dohm

*There is nothing else in her relationship
to the child, before or after its birth, for
this most typical of all relationships
reaches down so deep into the human
depths.*

—Georg Simmel

With Freud's developmental psychology and all the excitement
it created in the science, the last phase in the social deprivation of the
power of the woman began. The upbringing of the small child—a
female monopoly on experience and knowledge—fell under the sur-
veillance and control of men, who were able to legitimize this intervention by their scientific interest.

The woman's experience of herself and her unaffected approach
to the child were confronted by unproven theories on the lifelong
negative consequences of these mother-child relationships, creating a
powerful source of guilt feelings and new possibilities for the black-
mail of women.

The scientific observations of the small child seem like a caricature of relationships of patriarchal majesty. The therapist and father
sits with notebook poised nearby when his wife changes the child's

diaper, waiting until she shows him the cleansed infant for examination and he describes in detail "her" (not by any chance "his") feelings in caring for the baby. The following quote from Erik H. Erikson, for example, cannot be understood in any other way:

> The waking infant sends a message to its mother and unleashes in her a whole repertoire of feeling-controlled relations in words and acts. She nourishes him, addresses him with a warm or anxious voice, and begins to act, by establishing the possible sources of displeasure with all the senses—seeing, feeling, smelling. Then she begins to remedy its needs through the necessary services, once again tucking him in and putting him to bed, preparing his food, picking him up, etc. When one observes this for several days ... it becomes clear that this daily happening proceeds in a highly formulaic fashion: the mother seems to feel obliged to repeat a sequence of acts which arouse in the child predictable reactions which in turn encourage her to continue in this manner.[1]

The situation is absurd: men, who are not prepared to share the work associated with infant and child care, select early childhood behavior as the subject of their research. In other words, babies are interesting to men as objects of research but not as objects of paternal care or fatherly "services performed." If one reads the Erikson quote more precisely, one finds all the primeval male clichés on maternal instinct. Maternal behavior is exclusively "feeling-oriented," so to speak; at the animal stage—through feeling, smelling, seeing—the woman begins to sense the sources of the infant's discomfort. Her intelligence apparently does not function within the confines of motherhood. It is an element of much male ignorance to believe that the smell of dirty diapers arouses "great desire" in mothers.

Even before male scientists, under the influence of psychoanalysis, set about formulating instructions for the care of small children, women at the beginning of the nineteenth century had lost an important area of practice to the scientific development of gynecology and obstetrics. The innovations in this area came from men who, on the one hand, had access to anatomical knowledge, and who, on the other, could fall back on ancient knowledge handed down by midwives. The political upshot of this withdrawal of jurisdiction over obstetrics is the organized resistance of the gynecologists to the right to control one's own body and their refusal to discontinue pregnancy which, until now, was carried out in all countries only in the face of prevailing opposition from the medical profession.

The majority of women today no longer acquire their opinions on childhood education from the oral tradition of their own mothers and grandmothers, but from paperbacks and parent magazines that compete with each other to publish the latest mythical views of the child psychologists. As a result, hardly a woman manages to escape the prefabricated perspective and observation mode of a particular school claiming to be scientific, even if her own observations rebel and suggest different conclusions to her.

Thus, Freud and his contemporaries were not at all interested in seeking an empirical investigation of the behavior of infants. Their way of life was much too patriarchal to permit even a temporary systematic observation of infants and small children. Freud's developmental psychology was the result of hypotheses which he obtained mainly from the analysis and interpretation of life stories of adults. Because the father first becomes an influential factor of the child's development in the oedipal situation, Freud maintains, each person originally knows only two objects of love, "himself and the woman who cares for him."

The first analyst to focus her critical view on the observation of children was Freud's youngest daughter, Anna. She wrote:

> The succession of libidinous phases of development (oral, anal, phallic), the particular fact of Oedipus and castration complex, the regular occurrence of amnesia of the early childhood: all of these discoveries were,without exception, the result of the analysis of adults. The central point of analytic interest was by no means direct activity with the child but inferences of childhood experiences, which could be made in the adult's analysis.

Despite the strong influence of psychoanalytic research on the child-rearing habits of parents, Anna Freud, at the end of her life, does not appear to be very happy with their pedagogical prospects.

> A retrospective view of the first half century of psychoanalytical teaching on child rearing leaves no doubt as to its unfinished and contradictory character ... For the pedagogical world it remained disappointing that the new psychoanalytic education was not more complete than the theory underlying it, with which it had to keep abreast: it was fragmentary, unsystematic, and involved in constant change.

She then sums up the disillusioning balance:

> By and large, psychoanalytic pedagogy remained behind the task it had set for itself in the beginning. The children who had grown up under the new regime might in many respects be different from the children of earlier generations. But they are no freer of anxiety or conflicts and for that reason no less subject to neurotic and other psychic disturbances.[2]

Anna Freud does not mention the chief negative consequences of her father's theory—namely, the idealization of motherhood among the masses of the American and European middle classes; Freud believed the infant comes into the world as a bundle of instincts and, subjected to the mother's omnipotence, becomes a passive product of the satisfactions and frustrations it experiences through this relationship. Of course, Freud saw the behavior of the mother as being determined, not by her inferior, dependent position in the society or by economic circumstances, but by the development of her own oedipal situation. If she was lucky and the newborn baby was a boy, she could fully satisfy her ancient wish to transform the "stolen" paternal penis into a male baby.

The image of the infant in Freudian analysis and that of the mother resemble each other: in their relations to each other both are described one-dimensionally. Anyone who regards the infant as oral and subject to instincts thus defines the woman complementarily as the child's object of lust who is responsible to society for every suspension of lust. Erikson, who coined the concept "original trust," wrote:

> The oral phase also forms the origins of the basic feelings of trust and evil in the child, which through its entire life remains a source of original anxiety and original hope.[3]

Erikson imputes to infant and mother in nursing the same emotional one-dimensionality:

> In this space of time the child lives and loves through and with its mouth, and the mother lives and loves through and with her breasts.[4]

Even facts of nature—the inequality of individual physical requirements such as, for example, the lack of adequate milk, unfit nipples, physical weakness in the infant—are the fault of the woman. The image drawn by pediatricians oriented in depth psychology, by gynecologists, and also by zoologists and ethnologists of the relationship between mother and child is evidence of the belief that nature works in terms of the "ideal," constituting a prestabilized harmony that the non-nursing woman, with her egotistical motives, is deliberately trying to disturb.

In the entire literature of depth psychology, bottle feeding—which is the predominant method of infant nutrition in the twentieth century—is scarcely recorded or, if so, only negatively. For in psychoanalytic theory it is the mother's breast that is ascribed quasi-demonic qualities (as the introjected evil object).

The second stage of orality, teething, provides the basis for sadistic and aggressive instincts. The child has an impulse to bite and injure the mother's nipples. The mother reacts by frustrating this "cannibalistic" impulse of the child. As many mothers today do not nurse and as the biting on the bottle nipple is not answered by a frustrating reaction from the mother, the phenomenon of aggression, according to the logic of the Freudians, falls flat.

However, because, contrary to its claims, depth psychology possesses no natural scientific basis, its authors are repeatedly able to draw up new cause-and-effect models, for they are not forced to verify these statistically. No one would deny that the early mother-child relationships are influential factors in forming personality; only the problem of determining which influences have which effects remains to be clarified.

One of the chief advocates of this new mother-child biology is the German zoologist Bernhard Hassenstein. For him, zoology, behavioral research, and psychology have entered into a "fruitful dialogue." The purpose of this dialogue is not difficult to guess: to produce new instructions for conduct of the mother.

> In bottle babies the relationship between the volume drunk and effort required to suck or number of swallows depends on the size of the opening in the nipple. If, on account of an opening made too large or widened, the drinking goes faster than the corresponding rate in breast feeding, the relationship between two components of the central nervous impulse reduction (satiation, appeasement) is detrimentally altered.

For Hassenstein, one mother making too large an opening in a nipple amounts to an argument against bottle feeding in general.

> Today no one can yet say exactly what this chronic increase of drives does somatically and for later psychic development. But one suspicion grows stronger and stronger: that oral addictions and depression are to be feared as late results of early childhood oral frustrations.

What no one can say, Hassenstein says clearly enough. For him there is a

> spontaneous regulation of the nutrition to the young organism within the infant-mother system . . . In humans, as in animals, mother and infant form a self-controlling system which guarantees the wholesome nourishment of the infant.[5]

Now to what extent are these comments on ideal natural systems really true?

A 1959 study by an American author, who is in no way a propagandist for bottle feeding, paints a sober picture. F. E. Hytten analyzed several hundred samples which he gathered from mothers in the act of nursing over a period of twenty-four hours. One-third, he found, either produced quantities of milk inadequate for the needs of the infant or the quality was not suitable, or both. Three months after the birth, the majority of mothers felt exceptionally tired. Only 2 out of 106 women whose own mothers supported the household had no difficulties with the nursing. Two-thirds of them gave up breast-feeding.[6]

Moreover, in nursing, as in allegedly painless birth, a false image of primitive peoples is repeatedly drawn. Women who live closer to nature should have no difficulties in producing milk. However, C. S. Ford, an American sex researcher, on the basis of the existence of countless methods to improve the flow of milk, concluded that these women have exactly the same problems as women of the industrialized world. Just "don't expect every child to survive in a state of rosy health; many of their babies simply die."[7] Children who, even after the first year of life, must still live only by the breast are for the most part undernourished.

Once there was a philosophically based movement of this sort, supposed to lead oblivious women back to their natural duties: an ideology that seamlessly linked the contention of the natural freedom of man with the establishment of the natural imprisonment of woman, as do the writings of Jean Jacques Rousseau, setting all of Europe in a "mania for simplicity." One of his disciples, the German poet Jean Paul, scolded and warned his female contemporaries about: all the frivolous women who would rather waste time on the lover and father than nurse the helpless infant son at the breast.

All back-to-nature movements, as well as those of Christian theologians, contend that natural law is basic to the need to find steadfast, unchangeable order in the world. For this kind of thinking, the relationship between mother and child is a solid reference point for the eternity of nature. The natural, biological part of the mother-child relationship that is independent of will (pregnancy and milk formation) soothes the anxieties of males wishing to dwell on something absolutely good, useful, and unchangeable in human existence. The relative, being in the process of change, and the abundance of all individual differences in nature are for them a horrendous idea. The faster the social change and technical progress, the greater men's need for the eternal natural, which gives them ground beneath their feet. Thus, the principle of relativity—that all biological functions and all substitutes (for example, bottle feeding) can at the same time have advantages and disadvantages that are dependent upon the situation, the culture, and the persons—is unbearable.

For a twentieth-century European mother, who has the possibility of sterilizing bottles and using milk preparations, this nourishment not only entails less risk, because she spares herself and the baby from complications through breast nursing, but under certain conditions is even healthier for the baby. There was, for example, a high concentration of DDT found in mother's milk some time ago.

In addition, nursing requires an exceptional mental harmony in the mother, which is not often found in the nuclear family, in which she singlehandedly must care for the household and possibly other small children. Any psychological burden or agitation can make the flow of milk dry up. On the other hand, in developing tropical countries, where milk preparations and infant nutrients are expensive import articles and possibilities for sterilization are scarcely known, the improper use of prepared baby food can have perilous consequences. Cases of this kind have recently been reported from developing countries.

In other words, anyone arguing for or against nursing should base this argument not on "natural duty," but on economic conditions and the latitude for conduct determined by them.

Further, there are women in our society who wish to go through the more intimate physical relationship of nursing. But women must consistently defend themselves against unthinking patriarchal norms that prescribe breast nursing as the only behavior for true motherhood, condemning everything else as ethically less valuable.

If Rousseau's "nursing obligation" was understood by some aristocratic and bourgeois women of the early nineteenth century as a moral demand which women of progressive circles for a time pursued, the depth psychologists and behavioral scientists repeatedly assert the natural scientific character of their demands. At the beginning of the fifties, the mother's twenty-four-hour-a-day indispensability for early childhood education turned to dogma.

Thus, the class-bound women's roles reversed themselves in a remarkable fashion. First, it was the bourgeois women who were supposed to develop into heavy-duty machines for the production of indulgent mother love. This is also true for nursing: according to one English study from 1963 there were in America and England a far greater percentage of women from higher income brackets than lower nursing their babies.[8] In earlier times, women of the bourgeoisie entrusted their child to a wet nurse or a nursemaid. The absence of the woman worker from her child was socially tolerated—for one thing, she was needed as cheap labor, and for another, the intensive and exclusive mother-child care helped the bourgeoisie to feel an ethical superiority toward the proletarian parents, who sacrifice their relationship to the child to "a standard of living." This surfaces time and again among conservatives in questions of family politics.

While the National Socialist ideology of "nursing capability" was equated with "the will to nurse," the Freudians imparted to the woman guilt feelings of a gentler nature, appealing to her conscience in the name of a humanistic psychology. The most recent example from books produced in West Germany is seen in a 1976 study by Franz Renggli, the student of Swiss zoologist Adolf Portmann.

In connection with nutrition it must further be emphasized that, even in the last century, the majority of mothers nourished their children at the breast. Today, on the other hand, they are for the most part nursed only in the hospital or not at all ... Thus the last possible physical contact, namely the contact during the feeding situation, is withdrawn from the child.[9]

The author, born in 1942, conjures up a horrific vision of abandoned babies which one would rather ascribe to a hermit, far from any family life, than to a young man of today. Normally, babies today, unlike many babies in the nineteenth century, bathe daily in warm water set at body temperature, are dried in preheated soft terrycloth towels, creamed, oiled, and powdered. Because of the possibilities of modern technology and the invention of the disposable diaper, a child is diapered and cleaned more often than was ever possible for European mothers of past centuries. All these acts, in the opinion of the author, seem to be carried out by invisible hands. In his ideological reality, "the last possible physical contact . . . [is] withdrawn."

However, in his analysis of mother-child relationships, Renggli goes even a step beyond this portrayal of the individual results of motherliness denied. Daringly, he outlines the following culture theory—based on an intercultural comparison between three societies which he knows only secondhand through ethnographic reports:

All high cultures distinguish themselves in their treatment of children by the fact that, most of the time, the child lies on a sleeping place separated from its mother ... The banishment of the small child to a certain sleeping place necessarily results in a disturbed mother-child relationship, and this kind of child treatment formed an essential moment in the growth and development of the high cultures. Even more precisely put: the early separation of the children from the mother and the anxieties generated by this in the small child gave an, or even *the,* essential impetus to the formation of a high culture.[10]

He sees our own culture as being characterized by the tendency "toward natural scientific logic and abstract mathematical thought," a phenomenon that for him originates in the changes in the care of small children that have occurred since the Middle Ages.

Thus, all known changes in the technique of child care since the Middle Ages up to the present time in the last analysis have only one common goal: achieving the ever earlier separation, the ever more consistent alienation, between mother and child.[11]

According to him, the determinism of history, the goal of the ultimate mother-child separation, is determined by unconscious forces:

However, with increasing separation of mother and child in the period from the Middle Ages up to the present, child murder and exposure became more and more strongly prohibited, forbidden and finally penalized. Is there perhaps a connection between the two tendencies of development? I should like to formulate it somewhat drastically: the greater the desire to abolish infanticide in our culture, the greater the rejection tendencies and indeed the ever greater separation of mother and child. And vice versa: the more the child was rejected, the more guilt feelings developed that had to express themselves in the punishment of the infanticide— a vicious circle at the expense of the child![12]

He wanders the deep paths of the unconscious, however, not only in reinterpreting certain negative attitudes of society (for example those of landlords toward tenants with small children) into death wishes of European mothers; he also imputes to the Ifaluk mothers in Polynesia an infinite hatred of the child:

> In connection with the nursing the following detail was pointed out. The mother handles the head of the child with quite special care: first she supports it with a stiff towel, later with her hand, and indeed, she looks out for it up to the point when the child can crawl. However, she practices this support not only in the feeding situation but whenever she takes the child in her arms, and, as she does, so do all the care or contact persons on Ifaluk. Obviously, it is feared that the child could break its neck if it is not handled carefully. According to the psychoanalytic view a fear is interpreted in the majority of cases as a repulsed wish; that is, here again the latent death wish of the Ifaluk appears, and quite particularly of the mother toward her child.[13]

It takes an oversized dose of fantasy from depth psychology and less empirical acquaintance with the book's subject—the small child —to conclude as a matter of course that, from the type of head support of the baby common everywhere in the first months, the mother secretly wants the baby to break its neck.

Freudian-oriented anthropologists, as early as the thirties, turned the practice of nursing into the single basic cause explaining the development of the individual and, even more speculative, as the factor responsible for the character traits of whole cultures. One of the chief advocates of this view was Margaret Mead, who in her first works accepted the Freudian mother model without reservation. In *Male and Female* she describes the way in which the different temperaments of the Papuan tribes of New Guinea and other South Sea societies develop from the attitude of the mother to nursing. Even the temperament differences between girls and boys goes back to the behavior of the mother toward nursing:

> His mother smiles, the easy flirtatious or also aggressive embrace of her arms, the special passivity with which she gives him her

breast, tell him that he must find out who he is; that he is manly and not womanly. Thus immediately at the very beginning of his life it becomes an effort to the boy, the imposed endeavor to greater self-differentiation while the girl is urged to a relaxed acceptance of her self.

She does not say which societies this special observation relates to —it probably concerns a hypothetical description of ideal maternal behavior.

The attitude of the mother in nursing provides Mead with the model for an ideal upbringing specific to sex.

The way it was for them: the mother-child situation creates a complete continuity in which the girls learn to be and the boys, the fact that they must act.

This is nothing other than the acceptance of the Freudian patterns of activity and passivity, the eternal opposition of "being" and "acting," the noncommital chitchat, which, together with exotic-sounding data on primitive peoples, procured so many readers for the entire trend of anthropology and ethnology inspired by depth psychology.

Let us, for example, like Arno Plack, read Mead's findings, incorporated in his plea to change social morality:

The fact that the Mundugamor women lay their infants in hard, raw backbaskets (in which they miss any physical warmth or touching), and they often are left hungry quite a long time, is probably the main reason for the aggressive character of this Papuan tribe ... Their later, and very lively sexual life appears to the Mundugamor themselves as a constant overcompensation for the truly harsh treatment in early childhood. There the predominant character trait must remain aggressivity.[14]

The cause-effect chain is alarmingly one-dimensional: hardness, roughness, and nursing frustration result in aggressiveness and active sexuality later in life. It is no longer asked whether perhaps other tribes are also aggressive and which scale of measurement and assessment Mead used to classify societies as especially aggressive and sexually active.

In a similar fashion Erik H. Erikson describes nursing behavior among the Sioux Indians. The Sioux women nurse their children for several years, as do the majority of primitive societies. In teething, the children bite the nipples open; the Sioux mothers have frustrated the children by striking their heads and tying them on the cradleboard, stopping their motor movement. This procedure, according to Erikson, provides the explanation for the aggressive culture of the Sioux and other peoples. The majority of mothers of primitive peoples nurse their children past teething and frustrate them. So that they can wean the child, mothers in other societies, for example, administer bitter-tasting drinks extracted from plants that are supposed to produce memory loss.

Although little girls experience nursing frustration in exactly the same way, Erikson feels it determines the entire conduct of the male Sioux individual:

> Obviously the boy directed all his feelings of frustration and rage on the hunt for game, for enemies, and for loose women ... it was regarded as perfectly "proper" for any boy to rape any girl he chanced upon outside the territory.[15]

The link between orality/frustration/aggressivity/rape is closed and inevitable. Is the courage that is required to hunt buffalo comparable with the courage and aggressiveness needed for the rape of a girl? Doesn't the last aggressive act function in quite a different social connection? What about the question of punishment? The depth psychologists haven't explored the power and rights relationships in a hunting tribe with any degree of precision.

Only a few scholars found themselves prepared to study the Freudian hypotheses; instead of immediately interpreting the cultural character of entire nations, they first examined the influence of nursing to see how the early nutrition practice can generally be recognized and traced in the bewildering diversity of social behavior modes.

Two Yale professors, I. L. Child and J. W. M. Whiting, were the first (in the early fifties) to begin such a methodically difficult but influential undertaking. They collected data on early childhood education in seventy-five societies.[16] According to Freud, frustrations in the individual development phases, which are designated by him as oral, anal, phallic, and oedipal, lead to anxiety-laden fixations later in life. Therefore, Child and Whiting proceeded on the assumption that these fixations would have to be reflected in the explanations of the causes and origins of diseases in primitive societies. Their study found a significant connection, in fact, between nursing practices and social anxieties. This result, however, did not relate to the duration of nursing (two and one-half years, on average) but to the type and style of weaning. An abrupt stop to nursing and harsh methods of weaning were associated with the explanation of diseases (virus in the food, poisoning, talking, cursing, etc.). Successive studies confirmed these findings. It was also proved that "deficient as well as excessive gratification" can affect the personality negatively. In a comparative study of "German Postwar Children," those who were nursed for either an extremely short or an extremely long time differed from other children in their greater insecurity.[17]

The most dangerous and, until today, politically most consequential weapon in the hands of the Freudians was the studies of small children by the Austrian psychotherapist René A. Spitz. He was the first analyst to suggest, and the first to undergo, a training analysis as part of the education of the therapist. In 1910–11 he was analyzed by Freud. His most frequently quoted research was done in the forties. He studied ninety-one foundling children in an orphanage, all of whom showed severe developmental injuries. A portion of the children died in the first year of life.[18] Spitz interpreted these phenomena as the result of the deprivation of a mother relationship.

British researcher John Bowlby confirmed Spitz's interpretation by a study he did in 1951 on behalf of the World Health Organization in Geneva and which was disseminated just as widely around the world as that by Spitz.[19] The interpretations of these two scientists formed the dubious scientific foundation of the post-Hitlerian mother cult.

Moreover, neither Spitz nor Bowlby seemed to realize that orphans and foundling children lack parents—mother *and* father. In terms of this interpretation, Spitz described the famous "grinning reaction" of the child, which appeared at around the age of three months, and he generalized some of his observations into the contention of the so-called eight-month anxiety. A separation from the mother, from this point on, would cause insurmountable damage to the emotional development, for at this point individual bonding of the child to the mother occurred.

Today a whole school of psychotherapists, human ethologists, and zoologists is convinced that there is a sensitive phase of the mother-child relationship, a type of imprinting that was first described by Konrad Lorenz in 1935. The ideal mother would be a woman who was at the disposal of the child all day and did not once leave the child alone to tend to her natural needs: this is a situation that has never existed in human evolution. The human mother always had to supply or acquire food, and therefore intermittently had to leave her baby with other women, young sisters and brothers, the father, even in societies in which the child normally is carried on the back or on the hip. It is also common for a mother to nurse the child of another woman. In Arab societies the mother who wishes to nurse a child belonging to others must first obtain the approval of her husband, for he is the legal owner of her milk.

Tersely, John Bowlby establishes the father's lack of jurisdiction in the rearing of the small child—in his report for the World Health Organization—with the observation that the father was "of no direct significance for the small child, but is of indirect value through his economic and emotional support of the mother."[20]

Not until 1965, though, in the process of reviewing scientific literature on the behavior of small children and on child rearing, did the American psychologist John Nash realize that in the technical literature "child-rearing practices" meant exclusively "rearing by the mother" and the use of the word "parents" "for many authors . . . meant mother." Thus, for example, the key word "father" was not even in the index of the *Manual of Child Psychology*, which was published in 1954—a standard work in the professional literature.[21]

The political consequences of the long-since-refuted studies by Spitz and Bowlby persist to the present day. They met their defeat in the concept and programs of family politics of the political parties of Western countries[22] in the worldwide acceptance of a three-phase theory of the life of the woman, which was supposed to consist of the sequence of premarital professional employment, motherhood, and—in the third period—the reintegration into the profession after fulfilling maternal obligations. A young woman and mother aspiring to a political career would be unthinkable. Not until the third phase of life was the woman supposed to switch to politics and enter a party. "When we get into politics, the varnish is already worn off," summed up the later cabinet minister Anne Brauksiepe of the Christian Democrats (CDU).

With the findings of Spitz behind them, the CDU was able to offer an excellent justification for its anti-kindergarten and anti-day-nursery politics. The last big political fight in which the dubious findings of Spitz were once again argued was triggered by the question of the Social Democratic day-mother program—a model attempt which was supposed to be carried out scientifically over several years. This scheme, from which only already gainfully employed mothers were supposed to profit, ran into the solid resistance of the pediatricians and the women of the Christian Democratic Party.

The results of systematically accurate investigation of Spitz's deprivation theory are still not given proper attention. Bonn psychologist Ursula Lehr summarized the findings of decades of international socialization research in this way:

> "Professional people" who are unilaterally oriented in psychoanalysis trace retardation phenomena in institution children back to the lack of love and security and the lack of maternal attention. As a result of this conviction—or also because of a myth of a "voice of the blood"—they are not at all interested in verifying the alleged cause-effect relationships. Yet systematic studies of the hospital problem conducted on several thousands of children have shown precisely that a number of other factors can be responsible for the damage done to institutionalized children.[23]

She quotes the American scholar L. Casler, who analyzed his own and foreign studies on this theme and came to this conclusion: "None of these studies shows compelling evidence that negative effects of the institutionalization are the results of a lack of a mother's loving care."[24]

"Practically all summary abstracts," according to Lehr,

> share the belief that the really damaging influence of staying in the home must be seen in the lack of sensory stimulation. At any

rate, it is worth considering here that through the attention of other people ("through social stimulation") many sensory impulses are conveyed. Seen in this way, social stimulation is undoubtedly necessary . . . The fact that the mother herself supplies this stimulation does not increase the value of such exciting impulses . . .[25]

Even close contact with the mother will not prevent deprivation if the child does not have adequately stimulating contacts from the environment.

The negative phenomena that Spitz found were the result of a deficient institutional situation. The institutionalized children he studied were also so different in their racial and social origin, in their early history, and in their state of health that an objective comparison of their development was not possible.

In socialist states, where especially intensive studies were made on the development of small children in day-care centers, there were initially a number of negative reports. However, favorable findings were ascertained in East Germany in model day nurseries in which the conditions were optimally adjusted to the above-described needs of the child.[26]

From the convincing results of the personality research labeled positivistic, we can conclude that the infant is not simply the affect-driven bundle of an oral human being which Freud once described. The infant lives—in trite terms—not only from the breast or the bottle, but from the diversity of sensual impressions which she or he receives from the environment. The formation of the person must always be understood as a total process, for the newborn has an abundance of environment-related impulses.

In the first week of life the tactile stimulations are most distinct, for at this time the skin is the essential organ for recording sensory stimuli. But visual impulses and excitements are also decisive from the outset. Even in the first days of life the baby can distinguish large forms; in the first weeks of life it can distinguish and follow objects and persons by their different forms and movements.[27]

Even the hygienically white children's beds, for example, are a negative factor in the visual and spiritual development of the child. Linguistic and acoustic stimuli play a significant role after only a few weeks. The Swiss child psychologist Jean Piaget proved that, at as early as four weeks, children react to sounds and begin to make sound imitations.[28] It is not a drawback for a child to be cared for by several persons. Yet the mother usually most influences the child's early environment. According to Freud, the small child relates to its environment purely in terms of affect, and learning is guided by the pleasure/no pleasure opposition. Yet, this theory can hardly explain the fact that children learn to run, although they are constantly frustrated by falling down.

Because the infant possesses no consciousness of itself, according to Freud, it does not distinguish the source of any of its pleasure feelings. The infant's sexuality is amorphous and not genitalized. However, there is no reason to believe that the infant has different erogenous zones from the adult. It cannot yet be established whether the newborn can also distinguish different kinds of pleasure: The crying infant is soothed by stroking its genitals. This tends to indicate that its erogenous zones are located in the same places as adults—that is, in all parts of the body that show a high concentration of nerve endings, including the mouth area. From the diary of Héroard, the teacher of Louis XIII, which Philippe Ariès uses as the main document of his *Centuries of Childhood,* it appears that the successor to the throne, when even one year old (before he entered the anal phase, according to Freudian theory), amused himself with his penis: "He roared with laughter when the nursemaid moved his cock back and forth with the tip of her finger." "Very droll," notes Héroard, "frolicsome; let's everybody kiss his cock."[29]

According to Freud, the ego functions first develop through the chronological passing and assimilating of particular stages of development. However, the screaming of the newborn is indicative of a primary will at a psychic center—an ego that is not conscious of itself. Perhaps it is best to describe it with what is designated in many primitive societies as "body soul." The sexuality does not create this ego, but the ego has this sexuality as one of its dimensions. A woman—no matter which point of view scientists take—must assume that her child possesses such an ego. She must assume the existence of such a personality center from the start, for only by this means does she escape the danger of misunderstanding the infant either as a part of her own body, as an extension of her person, or as a manipulable object on a non-human level.

Although depth psychology, on the other hand, asserts that a mother who binds a child to her too closely causes immeasurable psychic damages, its advocates sermonize a style of maternal conduct that is oriented on an animalistic model. The desire for a sense of oneness, for rising up into another person, for the coinciding of the interests of two individuals without contradiction, is a dangerous yearning that leads to reality denial, which is repeatedly reinforced through biologistic interpretations of the mother-child relationship.

One example of the way in which the symbiosis with the infant ends in a depressive loss experience for the mother is contained in a letter Karoline von Humboldt wrote to her husband in 1795:

Oh, hardly anything hurt me so deeply as when he is already taken for a big boy now and not for a baby anymore. The big boy will no longer be *mine,* the way the little one was. I will no longer—never, ever again—have what in this sense belongs to me the way this boy does. It is my best child—of that I am so certain—and I am not able, as childish as I feel too—not able to part from him without a thousand tears.[30]

Herein lies the psychic dilemma of women who are forced into a dyadic relationship as a result of society's concept of an "original we," in which the mother and child, who are destined to part, merge into a spiritual physical unity after the birth.

The consequence of overidentification by many women with their children—in whom they perceive the sole source of their life and self-esteem—is by no means rare. In female suicides, for example, this tendency to achieve the "original we" is frequently clear. Precisely mothers with a strong symbiotic child relationship tend to take their sons and daughters with them into death, for the ego of their child exists for them only as a part of their own ego. In so doing, many are probably even acting out of an overdeveloped sense of responsibility, for they justifiably distrust the social environment.

In opposition to this dangerous work of the ideology of motherhood, the important job of a feminist-oriented psychology would be to win back for the women all the jurisdictions they have lost in scientific schools oriented toward the alleged well-being of the child and never on the psychic health of the mother (although it is the most important precondition for the first).

From the end of the Second World War till the present day, a complex multitude of social psychological studies—already difficult to assess—has appeared dealing with consequences of the mother's gainful employment upon the development of the children. At best they arrived at the finding that it was not injurious. Not a soul researched the effects of the mother's having *no* gainful employment, or the consequences of their lack of social influence and their exclusion from social contacts. To investigate the deprivation of the mother from a great amount of social stimulation and its effects on the development of the children remains a priority goal for feminist research.

Part Six
Sexuality and Violence

20 / Sexuality, Violence, and the Double Standard

He beat me until I fell over, unconscious.
When I came to again, he was lying in
bed snoring.

—*Bild-Zeitung,* May 1976

He may be lame, he may be mad
He may beat her as he will:
All that worries Hanna Cash, my lad
Is—does she love him still?

—*Bertolt Brecht*

Who knows, in the end the entire modern women's movement may be nothing but a revolt against the vicious thrashing of women, and its aim may be none other than the emancipation of woman from the cane.[1]

One hundred years have passed since Hedwig Dohm turned against the husband's right to administer corporal punishment; yet her demand for women's emancipation from conjugal flogging is just as pressing today. The settlement of marital problems with male fists is so widespread a phenomenon that physical violence toward women must be regarded as a universal characteristic of human society. Only the social sanctions that condemn or penalize or specifically legalize the beating of women differ.

Among primitive peoples the woman usually has a better chance of escaping the physical attacks of her husband if she is a member of a society in which no bride price, or an insignificant one, is paid. In these cases she can easily go back to her family without endless conflicts between the families over the reimbursement of the gift. In these societies her father and her brothers are inclined to welcome her back. The priest Martin Gusinde, speaking of the moral code of the Indians of Tierra del Fuego, reported that the young man is discouraged from beating his wife. Women are scarce, and his father-in-law would intervene if he mistreated his wife.

Norbert Mylius investigated the marital relationships of the East African nomads and hunting tribes and came upon an "abundance of reports that told only of beating and injury to the woman." In some tribes the woman has the possibility of defending herself against fierce cruelty. Among the Masai, an extremely patriarchal herding tribe, it is common for the wife to receive "moderate thrashing." If she is beaten too often, she has the right to seek refuge in the house of a peer of her husband. The husband of the wife then stops the beatings because he fears the curse of his peers.[2]

In the South African Bantu tribes, among the Xhosa, Zulu, and Sotho, wife beating is also a part of tradition. The ethnologist Laura Longmore states that wife beating is still common, although some husbands, chiefly those who live in the cities, told her that they refrained from this custom for fear of legal reprisals. In her study on the sexual life of the Bantu women in urban areas around Johannesburg she reports:

> There could be no doubt about the fact that many women in the city were treated harshly by their husbands. The main reasons they were beaten were infidelity on the part of the wife; should a man discover that his wife is having relations with another man, he will surely beat her; on the other hand, if the man has relations with other women and the wife complains, she is also beaten because a husband has the right to pay court to other women; it appears that the custom of polygamy has hardly died out; cases of this kind occur frequently. Secondly, drunkenness: men come from the Mai-Mai beer hall or from other places where they get alcohol, and demand the unreasonable or complain when they come home; the moment the woman tries to say something, she is beaten and violently injured because she contradicted him.[3]

The Yanomamös, an Indian tribe on the Venezuelan border of Brazil, which today numbers some ten thousand members, beat even little girls. Brothers are allowed to beat their sisters, and the girls are restrained from hitting back. The Yanomamös live by their gardens, in which they cultivate bananas and sweet potatoes. The men occasionally go hunting. When the husband comes back from a hunting expedition, the woman must drop everything and prepare his meal for him. If she does not perform these tasks, her husband will hit her with his hand or a stick. A husband who flies into a rage because the meal is not finished shoots his wife in the buttocks with an arrow or burns her with the end of a hot piece of wood.[4]

Among the Caucasian tribes the woman was also regularly beaten without the possibility of taking refuge. Lesghian husbands were especially famous for their cruelty. In a 1951 study on the view of marriage and family in the Caucasus tribes, Louis J. Luzbetak writes:

> The Lesghians have a saying that goes: "There are two gods: Allah and the husband." A husband has the right to beat his wife at every justifiable occasion but not in public.

Omarov, a nineteenth-century author, reported what his own mother had to suffer and "how husbands mercilessly mistreated their wives and brothers, their sisters." Usually the whip was used for this; many husbands possessed two whips: one for his horse, another for his wife.[5]

In the Christian-Germanic societies of Europe, the right to beat one's wife was derived from God's commands. The minnesingers and troubadours made a fine distinction between their own wives and the ladies whom they honored and to whose service they pledged themselves. Hedwig Dohm quotes from the love poem of a troubadour: "Take care not to beat thy lady—remember, she is not thy wife and thou canst leave her when anything about her displeases thee."[6]

The French king Humbert IV, who had a predilection for the city of Villefranche, accorded it various privileges, in which among other things: "Every inhabitant of Villefranche has the right to beat his wife, provided that death does not ensue."[7]

In didactic narrative that the knight Geoffrey de la Tour de Landry employed in the education of his daughters, the consequences which obstinate women have to expect are presented:

> Here is an example to every good woman that she suffer and endure patiently, nor strive with her husband nor answer him before strangers, as did once a woman who did answer her husband before strangers with short words; and he smote her with his fist down to the earth; and with his foot he struck her in her visage and broke her nose, and all her life after she had her nose crooked, which so shent [spoiled] and disfigured her visage after, that she might not for shame show her face, it was so foul blemished. And this she had for her language that she was wont to say to her husband. And therefore the wife ought to suffer, and let the husband have the words, and to be master, for that is her duty.[8]

In Germanic village law, which was not supplanted by Roman law until gradually in the sixteenth century, the right to administer corporal punishment was a part of the guardianship (*"Munt"*) of the husband over the wife.

Peasant family law was common law recorded in *Weistümern*.*

---

*Judicial sentences serving as precedents in old Germanic law.

A *Weistum* ("wisdom") was a complex of norms established either by an independent peasant community through unilateral sanction of a nobleman or through usage by manor lords and village cooperative society. Its validity was limited locally and for the most part did not extend farther than a few village parishes. In different *Weistümern* standards were set to protect women against beating. In some parishes the husband who in beating his wife had injured her had to pay a ransom. A blow with the fist, however, was regarded as less serious than a blow with the flat of the hand. In different *Weistümern* in Austrian villages the slap was fined five times as much as the blow with the fist.

> A misdemeanor on the part of the woman was the basis of the right to corporal punishment. This husband's right to use corporal punishment, however—at least according to one of the *Weistum*—amounted to a duty to use corporal punishment. For if the husband did not beat his wife, he was subject to a fine, just as she was.[9]

From some *Weistümern* it appears that women who were strong enough to protect themselves against male cruelties or who wanted to defend their honor themselves even challenged men to duel. "Names come up for it only in Austrian and Swiss legal districts, and here and there the view is quite different," writes Hans Fehr, who in 1912 investigated the legal position of women and children in the *Weistümern* in detail for the first time. It was considered a disgrace for a man to be challenged by a woman.

> Cases were known in which the provocation as such was punished, and different *Weistümern*... set a double fine for a woman's challenge, because in equating [woman] with man lay an insult. If a man challenged a woman to a duel, according to some Austrian *Weistümern,* he paid "five pound pennies," half the sum that a woman had to pay if she challenged a man.[10]

In Switzerland the opposite viewpoint is represented. In the *Weistum* of Three Farms of the Abbey St. Gallen from the fifteenth century, the challenging wife is equated with a minor and paid a fine ten times less than the male who provoked her. In a different Swiss *Weistum,* the challenge of the woman to duel was permitted in the case of arson, death, or rape. If the woman challenged her own husband, according to Austrian village law, she had to pay only a small fine. In Austria the *Weistum* of Streithofen and Einsiedel permitted beating of "the more beautiful one, that is, the maid."

The husband who did not observe his right to apply corporal punishment or let himself be struck by a woman was threatened in many parishes with repercussions, or he was ridiculed. Taking apparent delight in such measures, Wilhelm Heinrich Riehl described one such lesson in punishment which was still practiced in the sixteenth century in the Wetterau parishes of Kirchgöns and Pohlgöns, "not to honor a principle, but no doubt to honor Nature."

> The men of the neighboring villages solemnly came in with an ass, upon which the woman was set, and she was driven around the town, "so that the men according to God's commandment should remain the masters and keep the upper hand." The husband who had put up with it is punished as well as the wife who commits the outrage and only by the donation of an *Ohm* [137.4 liters] of beer to the allied communities could the guilty married couple buy their way free from the punishment.[11]

In the seventeenth and eighteenth centuries, peasant family law was separate from common law. The husband's right to apply corporal punishment when his wife was disobedient now became codified into the law of married gentry. The scholar of law and vice chancellor of Bavaria, Baron Wiguläus Xaverius Aloysius Kreitmayr, who established Bavarian law, mentioned the husband's right to corporal punishment in his five-volume commentaries on Bavarian provincial law, published between 1757 and 1768:

> Our Codex instructs wives that they belong to their husband not only in domesticis, but also that they are to show fitting respect, and no less commonly—decent house and personal service should be rendered. The obedience, however, is the correlate of superior power. The right to corporal punishment with words as well as deeds is also an *effectus potestatis maritalis* and is founded partially in Jure divino itself, if the Swiss version is correct, according to which the words of the text are: *Vir dominabitur tui,* which in German goes, as much as he will torment you and carouse.

The husband's right to apply corporal punishment was grounded in European family law until the end of the nineteenth century. According to one English parliamentarian, the newspapers in England around the middle of the nineteenth century were full of reports on mistreated women.

> In the *Review Britannique* from March 1853 one read the following words of a deputy: "Before the assembled parliament I hear from a member that in England a husband may beat his wife to the point of mutilation for a damages fee of £5 sterling. This member, Mr. Fitzroy, observed that one couldn't read the newspaper without being gripped by horror, so numerous were the examples of cruel and brutal treatment which the weaker sex had to suffer from men whose brutality should make all Englishmen blush with shame. He mentioned a number of examples of shocking cruelties."[12]

The American author Thomas Higginson, who in *Common Sense about Women* advocated the political rights of women, wrote:

An English Member of Parliament said some years ago that the stupidest man had a clearer understanding of political questions than the cleverest woman. He neglected to go into what a state a people must find themselves in who for many years have had a woman as a ruler . . .
In many things [women] will learn slowly; but in regard to everything that immediately concerns them, they will from the outset know more than many wise men have learned since the beginning of the world. How long it has taken the peoples of the English tongue to only partially redress the injustices of the old law! In a single sitting, a women's parliament, however, would have abolished the assumed right of the man to punish his wife with a stick not thicker than his thumb . . .[13]

After the middle of the nineteenth century, when, under the influence of the first emancipation movement, complicated women characters were described, even by authors without feminist intentions, literary critics appealed to healthy male experience. A sound thrashing would be enough to bring these misled figures to the right path. Hedwig Dohm said:

Some years ago in one of our leading newspapers was a discussion of French books which originated with one of the most well known and most famous literary historians, a mild man and splendid husband whose private character is unimpeachable. In this discussion it was said relative to the Flaubert novel *Madame Bovary:* "If she [Mme Bovary] had found a man who knew how to calm her down and occasionally used the rod—when it was necessary—perhaps she wouldn't have become such a pest?" We repeat, this ardent recommendation of beating for the improvement of irresponsible women comes from a German man whose breeding is the most eminent of his age. Isn't it wonderful how far we've come?[14]

About this time August Strindberg wrote a story about an advocate of women's rights who finally, as a result of a brutal blow from her husband, is not only cured of her ideas but moreover becomes as affectionate and cuddling as a kitten.[15]
In the eighteen-seventies, when more and more women in England were demanding their rights, a lady-in-waiting to Queen Victoria reported that the Queen was eager to enlist all those who could speak or write

to join in checking this mad, wicked folly of "Woman's Rights" with all its attendant horrors on which her poor feeble sex is bent, forgetting every sense of womanly feeling and propriety. Lady Amberley ought to get a *"good whipping."*[16]

Lady Amberley was the refractory mother of a rebellious son: Bertrand Russell.

While corporal punishment disappeared from the family law of European countries around the turn of the century, it was introduced into legislation in Islamic countries, which were securing their national sovereignty. "In the Egyptian family law the right of the man to use corporal punishment on the wife is confirmed. The women's organizations opposed it without results."

In Egypt the religious law of the Koran, to which every Muslim can appeal, was specifically made by the state into a component of the marriage law. In the views of old and modern commentators, the following Koran verses are regarded as basic to the redress of marriage conflicts: "And if you fear that [any] women are rebelling then admonish them, shun them in the marriage bed and beat them."

In his dissertation "The Position of the Woman in Sunnite Islam" (1968), the Egyptian Muhammad Schamah names the Islamic authorities who endorse the retention of the corporal punishment law:

To this az-Zamabšari observed that the husband was not allowed to beat his wife so robustly that she suffered damage to her health, and that the beating should leave no traces on her body—otherwise the woman could bring charges against her husband in court. Although the Koran permits the corporal punishment of the woman, Muhammad viewed beating as awkward behavior of the husband.

Another Islamic scholar, Šaltūt, believed:

There are women upon whom no amount of exhortation works; they still avoid the marriage bed. For such women one kind of punishment (that is, beating) is permitted. The Koran listed this as a last means of education to which men are entitled, the last remedy that one can fall back on when necessary.[17]

The fact that the right to administer corporal punishment is excessively used by the father, brother, or husband is shown in a Jordanian saying that goes: "The breasts of the men have no milk: men have no mercy."[18]

The fact that the late Japanese Prime Minister Sato, who frequently boasted before journalists of having soundly beaten his wife, received the Nobel Peace Prize only shows how little objection there is to private violence. In a representative inquiry conducted by a West German research institute at the beginning of the seventies, the majority of those questioned believed that the mistreatment of animals should be condemned more strongly than the beating of wives.

In today's Western society, physical aggression toward women is covered up by an ideology of chivalry and special courtesy, in contrast to the open brutality in Islamic and Asiatic societies. The perpetrator cannot be characterized by membership in a certain social class, income, or education. In East Germany, during 1970–72, about 10 percent of the divorces were filed on the grounds of violence.[19]

English lawmakers were the first to deal with this subject, after the English feminist Erin Pizzey in 1971 set up the first house in London for battered women (Chiswick's Women's Aid).[20] In February 1975 the British House of Commons appointed a committee of inquiry which in twenty-three partially open hearings—the responsible minister and Permanent Secretary were present—questioned beaten wives, called witnesses, and reviewed reports on violence in marriage. The committee members had assumed there were 5,000 women among England's 680,000 wives (as of 1971) who each year were victims of constant severe physical injuries from their husbands. In their final report they said that 5,000 would be only the tip of the iceberg. Concerning the prejudices which had been brought to bear against the work of the commission, the report published July 30, 1975, contained this introductory remark:

> Some people, including those in high positions, still repress the thought of beaten women. Is it not the husband's right to beat her? Isn't it her fault? Should she not simply abandon him? Mightn't she even be glad to be beaten? Such people should not forget that a large percentage of all known murders occur within the family: for many people the home is a very violent place. At least some of those murdered were badly treated women who could not run away or escape in time.

The committee of inquiry recommended to the legislators that every English city or country area of over fifty thousand inhabitants should establish a family crisis center with twenty-four-hour service. Two of the cases cited in this report are quoted here:

> For example, a Mrs. X. made an anonymous verbal statement on the twelfth of March. She had been beaten regularly in a period of sixteen years before she left her husband. In her own words: "One time I had ten stitches, three stitches, five stitches, seven stitches, right where he hit me. A knife was stuck through my stomach; I was hit across the face with a poker; I had no teeth anymore because he knocked them all out; I have been burned with a red-hot poker; I have been sprayed with petroleum and stood there while he snapped lighted matches after me." These

attacks occurred not only when he was drunk but "at any time, early in the morning, late at night; in the middle of the night he dragged me out of bed and began to beat me—he did it in front of the children too. It never made any difference to him if the children were there. I have been to the police... I brought my husband to jail. He stabbed me ten times, and they locked him up over the weekend. He came out on Monday morning again. He was forced to be peaceful; that was all. On Tuesday he gave me the beating of my life."

Similarly, a Mrs. A. told us: "About four years ago my husband began to work as a business manager . . . In the beginning it was pretty good. I worked with him part of the time, and then he began to stay away for the night because he was either in his own bar drinking or he went off to a different pub so I had to finish up with the staff, the hotel, and the children by myself. This went on for two or three months, and then he began to stay away on the weekends, and I still stayed back to get finished with things. Usually he came in Friday night and gave me five pounds. This was the support for my four children, for me, and also for the food. On Sunday he usually drank from nine o'clock in the morning till sometimes two o'clock on Monday morning before he came home . . . One time I had a broken jawbone, a broken cheekbone, a broken nose, and three broken ribs. That time he was sober. Normally he was completely drunk and missed me more often than he hit me. The police were not very helpful. One time he threw me through the glass door between my living room and the little kitchen. The oven door was hanging open, and I hit my head on it. The policeman came in and said: 'Is everything all right?' I was lying there and couldn't move, and he said: 'We can't do anything—your husband is home.' "[21]

In 1975 there were twenty-nine centers established by English women's groups to care for battered wives. In other countries the assistance programs for mistreated women were still at the beginning stages.[22] The first reactions in public opinion to press reports were skeptical and, even among the politicians who were prepared to set aside resources for the support of women's houses, there was lack of understanding for these women. Why don't mistreated women run away, instead of letting themselves be beaten again and again? Out of forty-nine beaten wives questioned by the sociologist couple Dobasch, not a single one of them had filed for divorce.[23] The motive for maintaining the marital martyrdom consisted in the economic dependence of the wives. In order to move out of the family dwelling, they needed money so that they and their children could find new lodging. Because in the majority of cases the marriage and family law proceeds from the principle of guilt in the divorce, such behavior can easily be declared malicious abandonment by the wife. In so doing, she loses grounds for support.

The other means of pressure that the husband possesses are the children. The majority of battered wives face the anxiety-making situation of having no work or of finding a poorly paid job which they cannot exist on. All-day preschools or all-day schools are rarely available, and the threat of losing her children keeps her from seeking divorce. That beaten wives wait for years until they file for divorce is related to a continual process of intimidation, resignation, loss of self-esteem, and the fear that no one in society will help them.

A police officer from Glasgow stated before the committee of inquiry of the British Parliament that in their experience, maltreated women hardly ever know, for example, how to get an injunction against the husband to vacate the residence; it was uncommon in Glasgow to undertake such a step. When the police are called by neighbors, they seldom arrest the husband; the policemen regard physical injury of the wife as a private conflict. They are also afraid they will waste time making out unnecessary reports, for in many cases the wife withdraws the charge and gives no evidence against her husband.

At the end of the forties, when the Swedish ethnologist Hilma Granqvist did a study on child rearing in Jordan, she heard reports of a European woman who had come to Trans-Jordan to help seduced or raped girls. They did not understand her. "Fallen women?" they asked with surprise. "There are none. We don't let them live."[24]

In the Middle East a young woman who has a sexual relationship before marriage is murdered even today. In the majority of cases, however, the killer is released. But even imprisonment has no deterrent effect. A young woman who is seduced, regardless of whether she acted voluntarily or under compulsion, is a stigma to the entire family. The family is threatened with isolation if they do not apply the single traditionally prescribed remedy for sin: eradication of the dishonor. The young woman must die. In the summer of 1960 an American anthropologist in a Jordanian village witnessed the social pressure on the family of a disgraced young woman: the father finally killed his daughter before everyone's eyes. The young woman, for whom the bride price was already paid, had been carried off in a taxi by three young men, had gotten drunk, and had been sexually abused. The three men were arrested, and the young woman was brought home to her father. The relatives of the three men wanted to pay a ransom to the insulted family. However, they refused "to carry off" the young woman, to marry her to one of her seducers. This would have been the only possible way to save her life. The uncle of the young woman met with all the leading elders of the region in order to discuss the case and to ascertain their position. Two weeks after the arrest of the three men, on the morning of the sacrifice feast (a major Islamic holiday), the father brought his abused daughter to the house of the family of the three men accused. In front of this house he killed her with his dagger. Then he went to the police and turned himself in to the authorities. On hearing the news, the men from his village marched into town to burn down the shops that belonged to the relatives of the defendants, but found these already guarded by the police. Then they went to the police station and demanded to see the father of the young woman. When he was brought out on the balcony, he was greeted with cheers from the three hundred men of his village.[25]

Until the end of the last century, Christian Western society, whose sexual code had great similarities with that of the Islamic society, also reacted to premarital sexual relations with capital punishment; in the majority of cases, drowning or forced marriage was prescribed.

> In some areas of Thuringia, up to the sixteenth century, incontinence was dealt with in such a way that a fallen maid was immediately arrested, as was the perpetrator. Both were held until the wedding took place. If the happy bridegroom did not pronounce the "yes" loud and clear, then the parish beadle did it for him.[26]

To what extent capital punishment was really carried out on those who had pursued premarital sexual relations is difficult to determine. Punishment appears to have been customary in medieval England.

> The treatment of women varied somewhat from manor to manor, as did the relations between the lord and his servants and the customary tenants. The lord assumed the right to take a fine from girls who bore illegitimate children. Sometimes the clerk simply records that certain girls are charged with *lerewita*, the Anglo-Saxon word meaning the fine payable for fornication. Sometimes the clerk notes that a girl has borne an illegitimate child and records the amount of the fine she owes the lord. On one court-day at Chatteris in 1272 no fewer than eight girls were fined, most of them paying six pence, but one of them twelve pence. Several of these girls, among them one called Matilda the fool, were pardoned payment because of their poverty.[27]

In the German empire in the eighteenth century unmarried mothers were threatened with more severe punishment. They were exposed publicly and flogged. An engraving from the middle of the century, reproduced in Max Bauer's *Frauenspiegel*, shows one such scene. While one mother is lying on the floor with her child, another one stands chained to a stake: before her is a city official with a whip.

In Algeria, where women fought successfully for the nation's liberation, and where it was announced that Algerians would find their own way to socialism, and where the politically persecuted were given asylum, unwed mothers are put into prison immediately after the birth of an illegitimate child. English gynecologist Ian Young reported on such cases. In one the woman had been able to keep her pregnancy secret from her father. Nurses reported her to the local police. With the help of one nurse, she managed to escape from the clinic, where she had given birth to twins. Shortly thereafter, both children were found abandoned. The woman had not managed to escape very far; she was soon picked up by the police and brought to prison.

But in other ways, too, the clinic was more frequently misused for police purposes. The local gendarmerie publicly apprehended women on the street at will, even when they were veiled, and brought them to the clinic in order to check whether the women had had sexual intercourse or were pregnant. Widowed women seemed especially subject to this treatment.[28]

According to Susan Brownmiller's extensive study on the subject, rape is man's political concept used to dominate the woman. Because the human anatomy made violent sexual intercourse possible, this simple fact suffices for the development of "a male ideology of rape."

When men discovered that they could rape, they proceeded to do so.

From prehistoric times up to the present day, I believe, rape played a decisive role. It is nothing more or less than a conscious process of intimidation by which all men keep all women in a state of fear.[29]

In her documentation Susan Brownmiller scarcely makes any distinctions between the motives and the causal conditions that lead to rape. The rapes of women that are part of acts of war, the rape by a street criminal, the rape by the woman's own husband (which in Brownmiller's study hardly occurs), and the rape that is encouraged and legitimized in a culture by particular views must all be judged and fought differently.

Rape as an act of war has always been practiced by armies of the world, usually with the consent or toleration of their leader. It is part of a complex of actions in which the inhibitions against killing have already, systematically, been lost.

Rape within a marriage is rarely criminally prosecuted. With the marriage agreement the husband, in primitive and in civilized societies, has almost unlimited sexual rights to his wife's body, regardless of her own feelings and needs. Ian Young again tells how a young Algerian woman was mauled by her bridegroom a few days after the wedding. The sixteen-year-old woman, bathed in sweat and tormented by pain, was brought in by the wedding guests. Young writes:

She'd look just like a little girl, if it wasn't all so swollen and sore. Simply to be touched there with cotton wool makes her jump and squirm. It's a marriage injury—a torn hymen, a lacerated vagina —and blood's everywhere. The discarded wedding robe's steeped in it, it's dripping into the enamel bowl. As Dr. Kostov draws up his stool, a huge clot catches him by surprise. It springs from between the girl's legs, to send up a shower of red spots onto his coat and glasses.

The doctor wanted to keep the young woman in the hospital until the bleeding stopped. The husband tried to persuade him to release the bride again.

> "Put yourself in my position," says the husband. "What's left of a marriage when the bride has to stay in the hospital?" Besides, he says, he likes his young bride very much. And he winks, to the man in me . . . "Your wife needs gentle treatment," preaches the doctor to the husband. "If you bring her back again, I won't touch her." "Then I will take her to Algiers," answered the young husband.[30]

Laura Longmore learned, through interviews with Bantu women in the area around Johannesburg, that the most frequent cause of the beatings they received was refusing sexual intercourse. Even when they were very tired or felt sick, husbands persisted. Isaac Schapera wrote of a different African tribe:

> Women frequently complain of the manner in which a husband makes use of his rights. Many told me bitterly that however tired they were they received little consideration, and that if they refused or resisted they were usually beaten into submission. One, only recently married, said that if she had known what was before her she would rather have remained single, for then she could at least have chosen her own times for sexual intercourse, instead of having to yield to her husband every night. In a divorce case heard in the chief's court in 1929, the junior wife of a polygamist complained that her husband had been so excessive in his demands, forcing her even when she was completely exhausted by work, and thrashing her with a leather strap when she refused, that at last she had no alternative but to run away. The husband was found the innocent party because his wife had deserted him. It is seldom that such extreme forms of protest are adopted, but quarrels owing to a husband's failure to consider his wife's wishes are a commonplace feature of Kgatla married life. The men, however, take up the attitude that intercourse is a duty every woman owes to her husband, and that she must carry it out faithfully (hence the verdict in the case just mentioned). "These women can't stop us," I was told; "we have given *bogadi* for them, and so we are entitled to make use of their bodies."[31]

Bogadi is the bride price. Schapera observes that it is a common saying among the Kgatla women that "the men carry a piercing spear: they run it through you and then go their way."

Arbitrary rape in marriage, in which the woman must always

fulfill the sexual desires of the husband, was justified by the German philosopher Johann Gottlieb Fichte with an outrageous argument. The woman had no sex drive but only a love drive, which compels her to be a means to the goal of another: the husband. "In the uncorrupted woman no sex drive expresses itself and there dwells no sex drive, but only love; and this love is the natural drive of the woman to satisfy a man."[32] After this starry-eyed declaration, Fichte gets to the heart of the matter. He sees that the execution of a sex act under such circumstances must degrade the woman, for it denies her any sexual impulse of her own. He also invents a new drive, ascribing to her an inborn drive to masochistic self-divestment. By this means the erotic usufruct of the female body by the man and the silencing of the woman is explained as an act of high moral content.

> And because then, however, they must accordingly be devoted to a drive, this drive can be none other than that to satisfy the man. In this act she becomes the means for another's goal; because she could not be her own goal without giving up her goal, the dignity of reason.[33]

For two reasons the prosecution of rape is especially hopeless. One of them is the ineradicable male notion that the raped woman was really a willing partner. The police and officers of the court regard the victim as hysterical or especially prudish and believe that she arranged to have the culprit overtake her by violence. The second reason why the estimated number of unknown cases remains so high in rapes lies in the fact that the victim often receives no understanding or compassion from society, like that received by victims of other acts of violence; instead, she encounters a mixture of contempt and rejection. When the woman declares a violent sex act has been committed against her, she is hurting herself; she is obliterating her own human dignity. What perversions the establishment of a double standard is capable of producing was described by philosopher Georg Simmel, the husband of a woman's-rights champion. The man can never lose his honor except by his own way of acting.

> It is only his behavior that determines his honor. The raped woman, however, is dishonored by something in which she was purely passive. Even if afterward she kills the rapist—which is not characteristic of her as it would be of the man—her honor is not restored. This cannot happen through any action of her own, but only if she marries the man.[34]

By marrying the sexual aggressor and voluntarily submitting to the demands of his drive, her honor is restored. She now offers the man the possibility of practicing the same sexual act as before under the protection of the law—only, according to Simmel's logic, the world no longer considers her disgraced.

The raped woman, in other words, would be better off keeping the act secret. Then no one would know of her lost honor: she could even be reintegrated into Islamic societies.

The political scientist Rounac Jahan studied the treatment of Bangladesh women who were raped by Pakistani soldiers during the war. She wrote:

> The non-acceptance of raped women in Bangladesh is a good illustration of the operation of the "shame" mechanism. If a woman is raped and it can be kept a secret from her social circle, then she is acceptable. It is not raping *per se* but the *Samaj's* knowledge about it that brings disrepute to the family. In such a case of a woman's violation the family is more concerned about the loss of face than her physical and mental health. One organization, which worked with the war-affected women in Bangladesh, informed the author that it maintained strict secrecy about the cases of violated women, because their chances of social acceptance depended on it.[35]

The national committee for the rehabilitation of the Bangladesh women in Dacca received only 22,500 applications from raped women. The majority of the estimated 200,000 cases were not registered because the family wanted to keep the rape secret. What happened on Cyprus after the civil wars was similar.

A successful act of sexual intercourse is regarded by men in our culture as a sacred remedy for female discontent. Many men believe a woman's psychic problems or unusual behavior—for example, demand for emancipation—is only the desire for brutal coitus. Once she has had sex, her exaggerated ideas will dissolve of their own accord.

In our culture the man must appear as sexual conqueror. The more the woman refuses, the greater his fantasy. The man, who feels himself to be the leader and seducer, cannot imagine that the woman doesn't want to be seduced. To take her resistance seriously would be a grievous blow to his ego; this is why many rapists never realize that they have committed a rape. According to the studies of the Hamburg sex researcher Eberhard Schorsch, in a number of cases, even after the rape, the criminal tries to flirt with the victim:

> Thirteen percent of the perpetrators behave in such a way that suggests a genuine, all-out misjudgement of the situation: they want to follow the girl home, ask if it was good and try to make another date with the girl.[36]

The cult of violence against women is reflected not only in the statistics of the criminologists but also appears in the outlets that our society creates for its frustration. From 1967 to 1971, plots of programs that were televised in the evening and on Saturday morning were studied by a team of scientists in the United States. The analysis of the acts of violence that were shown indicated that women were substantially more often portrayed as victims of these acts. White women were the victims of aggressive actions in these TV programs almost twice as often as white men. If the characters shown were members of other races, the disproportion between female and male victims was even greater. The number of black women shown as victims of acts of violence was three times higher than the number of black men.[37] The social pecking order that emerges in such findings is an exact reflection of the power relationships between the sexes in which sexism and racism mutually exert influence. The collective unconscious, whose fantasies the writers or the directors are staging, demands the physical annihilation of the woman as an element of suspense, uniting love and death into the myth. Movies and television have only created a new medium for the violence and death wishes directed at women. The French director Alexandre Astruc once put it this way: "Film invented the close-up in order to let people see women die."[38]

21 / Clitoridectomy the Western Way

Worthis objected: "But don't you think it would be best if both partners were equal?" Whereupon Freud replied: "That is practically an impossibility. There must be inequality, and the superiority of the man is the lesser evil."

—*Erich Fromm*

"There are sufficient grounds for hate," psychoanalyst Margarete Mitscherlich wrote in her book on sexuality and woman's problems, *Müssen Wir Hassen?* "We should hate systems or persons who call barbarous acts good, who glorify senseless cruelty, and who humiliate and exploit helpless people."

Though psychoanalysis is not among the systems she describes, barbarous traits and humiliation have resulted from this theory, once thought to sexually liberate female patients. In the name of medical progress, Freud developed the perfect instrument for the oppression of female sexuality and psyche, the removal of sexual taboos with a compulsory new rule for women: vaginal orgasm.

This method, in which the promise of health is based on elements of ample patience as well as psychic tyranny, reveals the Jesuitic character of psychoanalysis. For more than half a century, in the name of a liberating therapy, female patients were tormented by being forced to repress their clitoral sensation, to renounce their ostensible desires to be masculine.

Especially in the United States, where Freud's ideas are general knowledge—above all in the middle class—"normal" women were expected to experience vaginal orgasm. According to Freud, a young girl, in the process of her oedipal conflict, was disappointed by her clitoris because it was no substitute for the penis. As a result, she stopped masturbating and, once older, shifted erotic sensation completely to her vagina. Freud labeled the clitoris as male and active and considered a normal woman's clitoris as an erogenous zone as superfluous as the appendix.

Women patients who described sensations in the clitoris but did not experience the vaginal orgasm were treated for frigidity. Vaginal orgasm was a woman's maturity test. Those who did not experience it had to question their femininity. Hamburg psychoanalyst Lili Fleck summarized Freud's ideas on female frigidity:

> Freud regarded one of the most frequent causes of frigidity to be the clinging to clitoral excitability and thus to phallic, active, male desires, which were focused on the mother in the pre-oedipal period. He believed that the disappointment in the lack of a penis could cause a female to renounce sexuality altogether. When through identification with an active mother she is given up as a love object, this could be inconsistent with the process which normally leads to feminine masochism, in which activity is directed inward and transformed into passivity. This could detract from erotic pleasure. An exaggerated secondary narcissism, which should serve as a defense against the masochism, could lead to the whole body, instead of the vagina, being genitalized, and the genital wound will not be accepted but the woman will cling to an imagined penis.

These women would then enter into embittered competition with men and use frigidity as a weapon by disappointing and castrating the man. Ferenczi spoke of "genital warfare."[2]

Psychoanalytic theory invariably finds women guilty for the failure of sexual intercourse: man's inadequate sexual technique is never discussed.

> Lorand (a French psychoanalyst) [writes Lili Fleck] advocated the view that vaginal sensations always have an oral character and thus frigidity always has a relationship to frustrations by the mother in the oral period. Hence, vagina and mouth are equated, and the destructive impulses are conveyed to the father's penis, symbol of his love, which only the mother possesses . . .
>
> According to M. Heimann, the basis of frigidity is a protection against the devouring tendency of the vagina, whose wishes are unconsciously confused with oral needs. The vagina, in his opinion, would like to incorporate the penis.

As in the animistic thinking of primitive society, in which every bush, tree, and animal possesses a spirit of its own, psychoanalytic thought transforms sexual organs into bearers of independent will.*

This rape of female self-experience by a closed psychological doctrine first drew to a close in 1966, when the research team of W. H.

---

*Though absurd, any notion was welcome in order not to give up the concept of masculine/feminine developed by psychoanalytic schools.

Masters and V. E. Johnson presented the findings of years of systematic research. They studied each individual phase of sexual excitation and physical reaction through electrophysiological measurements and color film documents, and established that the clitoris is "an organ unique in the human anatomy."

> It serves alone in the reception and transformation of sensory stimuli. Thus, the woman possesses an organ which in its physiological function is perfectly adapted to the resolution or heightening of sexual excitement. An organ of this sort does not appear in the man.[3]

The clitoris is the primary excitation zone of the woman, and without its sexual stimulation, no orgasm will occur. The possibility for direct stimulation lies in manipulating the clitoris. "The possibilities for indirect stimulation are more varied: manipulation of other erogenous zones, coitus, fantasy."

Indirect stimulation is possible by stroking the breast or by transmitting the vibrations of the vaginal walls to the clitoris. If the clitoris is stimulated indirectly, the result is clearly a delay in orgasm. Masters and Johnson also found that the clitoris is an organ homologous in its structure to the penis, but that its reaction time to sexual stimulation is of longer duration than that of the penis.

> Unfortunately the different roles, that earlier were ascribed to the clitoris in the sexual reaction of the woman, became basic considerations of male researchers, regardless of the subjective statements of the woman.[4]

There can hardly be more impressive proof of the all-encompassing domination of the man. For in our civilization, despite all the laws which represent a formal equality, woman cannot bear witness for herself; if she speaks of her sexual sensations, of the experience of her body, then she is not believed. Not before she has been made a guinea pig in experiments of natural science, in which her physiological processes are measured by apparatus and her own description of the sexual experience plays a secondary role in the evaluation, only then —in the name of the religion of objectivity—are these findings regarded as knowledge.

A pamphlet written by the American Anne Koedt, "The Myth of the Vaginal Orgasm," became of central significance for the international women's movement. One of her most important arguments, used by sex researchers, was that there was no excuse for the ignorance of the sexual capacity of the clitoris. Many doctors were aware that the vagina contains very few nerve endings.

The German sex researcher V. Undeutsch made accurate knowledge on female sexuality available as early as 1950, though without much result.

> In female sexuality there is a very essential qualitative transformation caused by the change in the leading "erogenous" zones. The awakening is centered primarily and quite naturally on the clitoris. This is the organ corresponding to the male member and, in terms of its development, histology and physiology, the predestined release zone of the orgasm. In contrast to the vagina it is furnished not only with an actual tumescent structure but also in ample degree with the specific nerve endings from which the pleasurable stimulation of the genital sphere proceeds. In the transition to normal sexual intercourse, however, a quite extraordinary adjustment must occur: the shift from the hitherto clitoral mode of release together with the development of a vaginal orgastic excitability. When one considers that the mucous membrane of the vagina has no specific kind of nerve endings and is generally a very poor receptor, one of the most extraordinary difficulties of this conversion becomes clear. No wonder not all women experience orgasm.[5]

Although the findings of Masters and Johnson necessitated an overhaul of the Freudian concept, the first reaction and cautious discussion of the subject in West Germany proceeded at an exceedingly slow pace, and with reservation. Not until 1969 did Lili Fleck write that Freud was mistaken, that "the clitoris remains the stronger source of excitation."
She asks timorously:

> Couldn't this mean that the active-aggressive efforts ascribed to the psychological equivalent of clitoral eroticism are unleashed not by the passive efforts of vaginal eroticism but are active and passive drive impulses gratified simultaneously?

The ill-fated concept of active and passive had to be adjusted to fit the changed findings, causing depth psychology to engage in the most complicated mental gymnastics within their deadlocked discriminatory terminology.
In 1972 Margarete Mitscherlich wrote of just how impossible it is, despite good intentions, for new views on female personality to permeate societal thinking given the prevailing trends of psychoanalysis,

> if in the future we continue equating clitoral excitement with the desire for male-phallic sexual activity. Are we not, on the contrary, *forced* to assume that clitoral excitation is a part of normally complete female sexuality, and that it can also be gratified by orgasm triggered by coitus?[6]

Forced? How has this Western style of clitoridectomy (removal of the clitoris) actually functioned, and what justifies the comparison with the African circumcision rituals?

In Germany, long before Freud, clitoridectomy was often performed, because it was believed that sexual union could not take place with a clitoris that was too large.

> To this impotency, however, which is affected from the parts themselves, is reckoned particularly when the clitoris is far too large, whereby the congress of the male and female person is indeed hindered. One can remedy this error by removing it.[7]

In Freud's age the removal of the clitoris was a part of psychiatric therapy. Toward the end of the nineteenth century, a London surgeon performed clitoridectomies on female patients as treatment for hysteria, in order to reduce their excessive sexual desires.[8]

While the surgical removal of the clitoris results in an inability for orgasm, the Freudian method of psychologically eliminating clitoral sensation achieves an effect that is comparable to the results of clitoridectomy.

Freud's notions of female sexuality affected the total conception of sexuality in all Western societies. That Freud exerted influence only on the thinking of the upper middle class is true only on superficial observation. Countless women simulated orgasm. The denial of the clitoris as the woman's central sexual organ goes beyond the true realm of anatomical or scientific error. It is a conspiracy against the spiritual autonomy of the woman, herself not able to realize her own body experiences within male definitions.

The war against the woman's genitals—whether it is an intellectual war or a surgical operation—is only one out of a great many of the symbolic acts which diminish the woman. Instead of the removal or denial of the clitoris, other symbolic operations can be performed. For example, one typical female castration is the disavowal of her mind, the symbolic amputation of her psychic and intellectual organs.

The clitoris symbolically stands for the independence of the woman, for her own will and her superiority in sexual potency. According to Freud, this organ had to disappear from the consciousness of mature women, just as if they had never possessed it; otherwise they are no longer controllable sexual objects but sexual subjects full of their own desires and impulses, full of curiosity.

After the sexual revolution of the sixties, a deluge of instructional publications surfaced in the Western industrial countries. However, anyone who believes that instruction on female sexuality has progressed should take a look at sex-education books for children.

Wo Komm ich eigentlich her? by German author Thaddäus Troll is intended for seven-year-old children.[9] "When you were just born, your mama's breasts were like a milk bar." A woman's body—in a carefree, pseudo-progressive style—is reified and compared with a thing for indulgence. Describing the penis, Troll says: "But the most important of what you see there is hanging between the man's legs. The woman doesn't have one of these." The organs of the woman are still as unassuming as in the time of Freud. "But what does the woman have between her legs? She has a little opening. It is called a vagina. You pronounce it like va-jai-na. It's really a pretty name, isn't it?"

No instruction book of this kind mentions the clitoris as the woman's primary sexual organ. "After a time the penis of the man gets stiff and hard and much larger than usual. It grows larger because right now it has something to do."

Before our eyes the penis decides and dominates the situation. Then the man lies on top of her "and puts his penis into her vagina." Who is lying on top and who is lying underneath, and who is doing what, is clarified. "The places where it tickles most are, in the man, the penis, and in the woman, the vagina."

Then the ejaculation is described: "They call it semen. And no blade of grass and no rose and no cherry tree—and no human being, either—can come into being without semen." And further: "And what these semen bring about . . . that is really quite astounding." Or Don Juan-like: "How could an egg resist such magnificent semen?"

For half a page the semen and its virtues are described: in one sentence the egg is mentioned: "The semen seeks one of the tiny eggs, which the woman produces each month within her."

After reading this, the child will have fixed in her or his mind the relationship between eggs and semen (in reality 1:85,000) and male and female sex organs, and the categories of active and passive, acting and being, important and unimportant, are also conveyed here.

This book is representative of many other books written after the "sexual revolution" whose message is still: Men give women pleasure. Men are active, women are passive. And men make babies, for whom the woman furnishes the receptacle.

22/Sexual
Domestication in the
Third World

---

*The God Amma of the Dogon, the
Invisible One and Creator who created all
of life, first created the Earth. It was his
wife. He slept by her. But this first act of
creation went wrong. The member of
Amma bumped against the woman's
member: her clitoris, the termite mound
that sticks up out of the Earth. Amma
ripped out the hill, circumcising the
woman, and the Earth became obedient to
her master. Out of the disorder of the first
creation came Yurugu, the desert fox.*

—*Creation myth of the Dogon in Mali*

In 1844 in Germany notes were published about a journey in the
Sudan, by a person who characterized himself as "author of the letters
of a deceased." The writer was the famous Prince Hermann von Pück-
ler-Muskau.

Some clandestine chapters of his book bear the heading "Not for
Ladies." So that none of his bourgeois and aristocratic women readers
would fall over in a faint, the print of this chapter was placed upside
down and the even more shocking facts were written not only in German (of course) but also in Greek letters, which were then rarely
mastered by women.

[Women] have the reputation of being amorous, but only for
money, for the hideous operation of being sewn up and re-opened,
like cutting off another part of the genitals completely, takes away

from them almost all natural feeling. There are women who have suffered the first operation ten times because it is quite common that the husband, when going off on a journey, tries to assure her fidelity by sewing up his better half . . .[1]

The surgical removal of the clitoris and labia, according to some reports, is alleged to have been practiced as long ago as in the Old Kingdom in Egypt. Supposedly, circumcised female mummies have been found. Though there is no textual evidence, there was, in Egypt, talk of "uncircumcised maidens."[2] Egyptian boys were not circumcised at birth but when they were older. The Greek travel writer Strabo reported about 25 B.C. that the circumcision of girls was common in Egypt.

The circumcision of the male foreskin is evidently an ancient practice: many scholars date its appearance from the Neolithic Age. This operation was performed worldwide, with the exception of Europe. In contrast to female circumcision, only a portion of the foreskin is removed, and it is a relatively uncomplicated and painless operation that is seldom unsuccessful. In addition, it has the positive hygienic consequence of preventing the formation of smegma.

The circumcision of the female genitalia appears almost exclusively in areas where male circumcision is practiced. It is useless to speculate on the history of this development. The origin of morals and rituals, their function and their maintenance over long periods of time, do not result from the same motives and causes. A rite portrays and expresses a great number of ambiguous motives and sensations in one symbolic action. The more dramatic, painful, and momentous this ritual is, the more it adheres to the individual's memory and guides behavior in the desired direction. Not all initiation rites that are supposed to demarcate the transition between child and adult status are painful. Most societies have only male initiation rites.

If one compares only the painfulness of the procedure that youths must all bear in initiations, then, on the average, girls are better off than boys. That the removal of the clitoris is extremely painful provides no general information on the differential treatment of the sexes. The external circumstances, for example the accompanying festivities, are frequently the same for the members of both sexes. The difference lies in the social purpose of the rite.

Initiation rites for boys, when they are very painful, always represent an individual achievement in which several expectations for the prospective adult male find their synthesis. Pride, masculinity, self-awareness, and superiority over women: these are the ego-strengthening emotions that he is supposed to experience and that are supposed to make him conscious of his male role. In addition, of course, subordination to the command of the elders is demanded.

The initiation rites for girls, on the other hand, were invented not to make her aware of herself but just the opposite: her will is to be broken, her independence curtailed. She is to be brought to absolute obedience. The female identity is produced by a reduction of the personality. As a reward for this resignation, fertility and the attention of the man are held out as incentives. Clitoridectomy is performed by the Egyptians, the Sudanese, and the Somalis, in Ethiopia, among the Mandingos and the majority of Bantu tribes in Central and West Africa, in Ghana, Nigeria, Zaire, Congo, Kenya, Sierra Leone, Upper Volta, Mali, Senegal, Mozambique, and in the Central African Republic. In Asia, the Mohammedans on the islands off Indonesia, several tribes in Pakistan, and Arabian nomads perform female circumcision. On some of the Moluccan Islands the operation takes place between the seventh and tenth year of life and is associated with a major festival. "Not infrequently death by hemorrhaging comes after the operation; however, the children are then happily praised, for then they will enter into Mohammed's seventh heaven."

In Latin America, some tribes in eastern Mexico, in Peru, and in the western part of Brazil practice female circumcision, using a stone knife.

In Ecuador, in the province Maynes live the Pano Indians whom the missionary Franz Xavier Veigel visited; he was told that they used to submit girls to circumcision; when he inquired as to the reasons for this custom, he was told that they considered circumcised women more capable and clever in fulfilling their natural duties.

A Christian sect in Russia in the nineteenth century, the Skoptsi, also removed the clitoris, occasionally mutilating the female breast as well.[3]

In most areas, clitoridectomy is performed by an old woman, although it is reported that in northwestern Zaire a male priest performs it. One careful assessment, not including the inhabitants of the urban centers, shows ten million circumcised women in Africa.

But even in the capital cities, female circumcision is still widespread. In Ougadougou, the capital city of Upper Volta, French doctors estimated the number of circumcised women at 40 percent. Circumcised girls were found even among Christians.[4]

All previous endeavors to set up an investigation commission in the World Health Organization (WHO) to ascertain just how widespread the phenomenon of clitoridectomy may be have till now encountered resistance. The most important campaign to document the practice of clitoridectomy, and to call worldwide attention to this cruel and dangerous mutilation of women's bodies, was begun in 1975 by the American Fran P. Hosken, who, as publisher of an international press service (the Women's International Network News), discusses with women's organizations and politicians all over the world information that might lead to more effective legal measures against clitoridectomy.[5]

The Danish ethnologist Henny Harald Hansen wrote, in an article published in 1973, that no references to or reports on clitoridectomy in Egypt and other Middle Eastern countries had been published by scholars in the past forty years. Even women ethnologists in the West, who would most likely be able to obtain information, do not mention it. Clitoridectomy, which is still performed in Egypt on practically all girls from eight to ten—regardless of whether they belong to the Islamic or Coptic religion—is a subject that field researchers publicly avoid because it is too sensitive. Two doctors in Cairo, Mahmoud Karim and Roshdi Ammar, conducted a study, published in 1965, on 331 circumcised women, and established that 30 percent of them have a circumcision of the first degree, 50 percent a circumcision of the second degree (where the greatest portion of the clitoris is removed), and 20 percent a circumcision of the third degree (where the clitoris and the labia minora are completely removed).

Hansen was familiar with this study. Having visited a number of family-planning clinics, he estimated that 100 percent of the women counseled there were circumcised. A young woman doctor informed him that, if a woman was expecting a female baby, she wanted to circumcise her herself. The reasons she gave for this were of a religious and aesthetic nature. The Islamic faith demands this operation, and the other reason was a cosmetic one: women wanted to remove "something disfiguring, hideous, and disgusting." Besides, a little girl would be protected from sexual stimulation in the clitoris, which could be produced by her own activity or by the movement of her clothes.[6]

In a French report, the following reasons are named for the preservation of this cruel practice:

> A woman giving birth would die if she had not had this operation, for the clitoris is a dangerous organ.
> The clitoris "causes impotence."
> A man risks his life when he has sexual intercourse with an uncircumcised woman.
> In addition, the virginity and fidelity of the woman are mentioned as justification for the operation. Others believe that a terrible fate awaits those who do not submit to the tradition of their forebears.[7]

There are several types of female circumcision. The first consists of the removal of the tip of the clitoris, a method that is advocated today by the majority of official Islamic authorities.

The second type consists in the total removal of the clitoris, together with the adjacent part of the labia minora. This procedure occurs most frequently, and it was common throughout Egypt before there was a law prohibiting it. In Sudan the third type of circumcision, infibulation, is gradually taking its place. It is the operation about which Prince Pückler wanted to inform German men.

Infibulation, next to the Australian circumcision, is the most cruel procedure. Not only are the clitoris and the labia minora completely cut away, but also at least two-thirds of the labia majora. Then the two sides of the vulva are sewn together with silk thread or catgut, leaving a small opening for the flow of urine and menstruation.

The Somalian ceremony of circumcision was described by the Frenchman Jacques Lantier in his book *La Cité magique en Afrique Noire* as a ceremony which equals the castration of an animal. With cruelty that is hard to imagine, the genitals of the little girl are adjusted to the society's ideal of feminine.

The circumcision is performed by the mother and her female relatives. The father of the young girl must remain standing outside the door as a symbolic guard. The young girl sits on a chair that is barely clean, and several women hold her in place. Then one of the old women separates the labia from each other and fastens them to the side with thorns in order to leave the clitoris fully exposed. With a kitchen knife she detaches the skin of the clitoris and then begins to cut it out. While one of women continually wipes the blood away, the mother digs with her finger under the cut clitoris in order to loosen the organ. The girl screams horribly, her pain completely unattended. When the mother has torn the clitoris out, she continues cutting down to the bone and removing the surrounding parts of the labia. Then she digs around with her finger in the bleeding wound. The other participants of the operation also feel the bleeding cavity in order to establish that all the tissue is removed. Because the little girl flounders wildly from pain, frequently the rectum is injured or the urethra is also cut.

Then, the second part of the torture: the mother completely cuts away the inner labia and scrapes away flesh and skin from the labia majora. The girl has already fainted several times and is revived with a powder. The neighbor women conscientiously examine the mother's work and spur her on.

Because sometimes, in frantic pain, the girl bites her tongue off, one woman carefully observes the child's mouth. When the tongue sticks out, she sprinkles pepper on it, which results in an immediate withdrawal of the tongue.

When the operation is over, the mother fastens the two sides of the vulva together with acacia thorns. Her main goal is to produce such a small opening that only the discharge of urine and menstrual blood is possible. The smaller the artificial opening, the greater the value of the woman.

When the operation is ended, the girl is bandaged from the knees to the waist, and in this condition she lies on a mat for approximately two weeks without moving while urine and excrement remain in her dressing.[8]

The most extensive medical study on the procedure of the operation and its results was conducted by Dr. Ahmed Abu-El-Futuh Shandall, who, from 1962 to 1966 during his work as a gynecologist in the largest Sudanese hospital in the capital city of Khartoum, studied 4,024 female patients and interviewed them systematically.[9]

Of the women studied only 204 were not circumcised; the great majority—that is, 3,013 women—were circumcised and infibulated. Of the daughters of these patients, 500 of school age were also studied, of whom half were circumcised and sewn up and the other half had only had the simple circumcision. These numbers give only an overview; outside the large cities, the situation is much worse.

The immediate results of the operation were difficult menstrual periods, urine retention, infections, injuries of the surrounding tissue, severe injuries of the clitoral artery necessitating immediate blood transfusions. One hundred and two patients remembered having fainted during the operation. Others reported severe nervous shock.

Since 1950, at least in the capital city, local anesthetics have been used by many midwives. Yet, in the interior of the country and among the poorer population of the capital city, the use of anesthesia or hygienic precautions is uncommon. Of 336 girls, 130 required catheterization; however, after removing the stitches, doctors had to sew them up again, because their mothers would have brought them to a midwife immediately in order to close the vulva again.

Because the urethra is frequently injured, part of the treatment consisted of implanting a plastic urethra. Some women patients could not hold urine. The most frequent consequence, however, was the chronic infection of the vagina or of the total pelvic area, painful, rampant pock formation, cysts and abscesses which require drainage.

As a result of the tiny opening, every act of sexual intercourse became a painful procedure. Of three hundred husbands whom the doctor questioned, ninety stated they believed that sexual intercourse brought great pain to their wives.

The study mentions one especially cruel case. A girl was married at the age of fourteen before she had her first menstrual period. One year later she entered the hospital because of constant pain. In the examination it was noticed, among other things, that her urethra was almost two fingers wide. Her husband had practiced sexual intercourse using her urethra, believing it was her vagina.

Circumcision has resulted in all possible forms of complication in childbirth. Shortly before birth, the stitches must be removed by the midwife, which involves new danger of injury. If the birth goes quickly, the head of the child might rip the seam. Subsequently, the vulva is sewn up again in order to create sexual pleasure for the husband.

Besides pain and permanent infection, infertility, miscarriage, and stillbirth are the most serious dangers. This is due, in part, to the fact that an African woman's social status and lifelong respect in the community depend on her fertility.

The Sudanese study also proves that the clitoris and its nerve tissue are primarily responsible for the female orgasm. The female patients, shy and reserved, replied to questions regarding sexual gratification only after several visits to the clinic. Their answers were studied in the course of the treatment. It appeared that a great number of women knew nothing of orgasm. Over 80 percent of those infibulated had never been sexually satisfied, as opposed to less than 7 percent among the uncircumcised women.

It is medically proven that a loss of the nerve centers need not be accompanied by total loss of orgasmic capability. Even paraplegics occasionally experience phantom orgasms. Even without physiological accompaniment of a nerve condition of excitation in the genital area, because of the brain activity in such cases, an orgasm may be possible now and then. There is no clear-cut medical explanation for this. At any rate, the fact that orgasm occasionally occurs among a portion of the female patients of the Khartoum hospital suggests an association with these phantom orgasms.

In Sierra Leone, twelve- to thirteen-year-old girls are circumcised in the presence of the entire tribe. A matron carries out the ceremony on the riverbank by a full moon. The clitoris is removed to reduce sexual pleasure and to diminish the danger that the girl might react to male seduction. Then a name is given to her. She is kept in a hut in total confinement until a man asks her father about marriage. The part of the clitoris that is cut off is buried behind a tree or in the riverbank.

In Kenya, Ethiopia, and Somalia, the retaining of the custom is justified by the belief that no man would be willing to marry a woman who was not circumcised.

President Jomo Kenyatta, a student of anthropology at the London School of Economics who in 1938 published a monograph on his people, the Kikuyu (the most influential and largest tribe in present-day Kenya), provided the best insight into the motives and meanings of the practice of clitoridectomy. He described the circumcision of young men and women as an indispensable part of the puberty rites of his people.

Scottish missionaries and British authorities had tried repeatedly to persuade the Kikuyus of the cruelty of the operation and its danger of infection in women. In 1930 the question came up in the British House of Commons, and an investigation was scheduled. During this discussion, an international conference in Geneva recommended that the circumcision of girls be regarded as a criminal act and legal penalties be imposed.

Kenyatta opposed this:

In the matrimonial relation, the *rite de passage* is the decisive factor. No proper Gikuyu would dream of marrying a girl who has not been circumcised. It is taboo for a Gikuyu man or a woman to have sexual relations with someone who has not undergone this operation. If it happens, a man or a woman must go through a ceremonial purification . . .

He explained that the clitoridectomy, like the Jewish circumcision, is the *"conditio sine qua non"* of the whole practice of tribal law, religion, and morality.

> It is important to establish the fact that the moral law of the tribe is held together by this custom, and that it symbolizes the union of the entire tribal organization.[10]

The discontinuation of female circumcision would produce the disintegration of the social order and "keep the Gikuyus from [preserving] their spirit of collectivity and national solidarity," which they had possessed since time immemorial.

The ceremony and carrying out of the rites are supposed to reinforce the sense of self in both sexes. They are consecrated in tribal history and religious thought, and great festivities accompany these rites. The children are the center of the event: they receive new clothes and a new status. The fundamental difference between the treatment of boys and girls, however, lies in the fact that, before the circumcision, the girl must confess whether she has ever had sexual intercourse or masturbated. While it is expected that boys have masturbated, for girls, it is evil.

> If a girl is seen by her mother even so much as touching that part of her body she is at once told that she is doing wrong. It may be said that this, among other reasons, is probably the motive for trimming the clitoris, to prevent girls from developing sexual feelings around that point.[11]

If the girl admits to masturbation before circumcision, the entire family must go through a purification ceremony before the operation.

The fact that this rite is actually a method for subjugating the woman and is also recognized as such—indeed, in the double sense, since women are subjugated and men are freed of competition anxieties—is proved by the myth of the Dogon of Mali quoted at the beginning of this chapter.

The clitoridectomy often occurs together with a virginity test. The ceremony of the Nandi, a Hamitic tribe in Kenya, is described by John S. Mbiti, a student of African religion, in his book *African Religions and Philosophy.* Long before the initiation, when the girl is about ten years old, she must sleep together with boys in a group house. This is compulsory; if the girl refuses, the boys are allowed to beat her without the intervention of the parents. This is supposed to show girls how they have to behave toward men and how they must check their sexual desires.

No sexual intercourse is allowed when boys and girls spend the night together. Later the girl is examined, and it is a great disgrace for the girl and her parents if it is found that she has lost her virginity.

In such cases girls are killed with the spear, while the virgins receive gifts of cows and sheep.

On the evening before the circumcision, the clitoris is tied together. Afterward a dance begins that lasts for hours. The boys tease the girls and call them cowards and chickens. These ritual insults are supposed to make the girls courageous during the operation.

Later in the night the clitoris of the girls is subjected to prickly nettles. The old women who conduct the ceremony deliberately sing loud so that no cries of pain can be heard.

The next morning the people come to the ceremony, but remain at a distance of some 150 meters. An old woman cuts away the swollen clitoris. When it is said of a girl that she was a coward and that she screamed, or that she is no longer a virgin, her parents and her brother are so ashamed that they threaten to kill themselves or the girl.

Then from six months to three years, those girls are confined: they must stay with an old woman who teaches them how to behave, how to bring up children, etc.[12]

The Nandi believe that when a girl is not circumcised, the clitoris grows and forms offshoots. Children from uncircumcised women are supposed to be abnormal.

Thus, the socialization goal of the Nandi is preparation for the great work load that the young woman will have to assume. No Nandi man may touch his child or have anything to do with it before the child is at least ten years old; women educate the children completely.

Another form of clitoridectomy is practiced by some Australian aborigines. The operation goes along with a ritual rape of the girl. The psychotherapist and anthropologist Géza Róheim portrays the operation in this way:[13] Shortly after the first menstrual period the prospective husband, together with some clan brothers, takes the girl into the bush. There they make an incision with a stone knife from the vagina to the clitoris and split the perineum. Afterward the little girl is submitted to sexual intercourse by all participating in the ceremony in an established sequence, with the exception of the prospective husband.

Several days later the man who conducted the operation goes to the camp of the girl. He picks her up and embraces her and commands her always to be true to her husband. Then he has sexual intercourse with her.

In other tribes, the operation is performed by the husband, who, immediately after the incision, while the wound is still bleeding, must have sexual intercourse with the girl. The explanation given for this is usually that childbirth is made easier by the operation.

Róheim quotes one myth according to which the significance of the ceremony is to make the women "still."

From the viewpoint of the aboriginal man there are only two kinds of women—the kind who fulfill his wishes and the kind who refuse: *alknarintja* and *nguanga*—"wild" and "peaceful."

(The term for "to rape," according to information from Róheim's female informants, is "to make peaceful.") "This ritual applies a shock treatment upon the undeveloped sexuality of the woman in order to break her resistance."

Another group of myths deals with women of whom one out of three has a long *"chelia"* (clitoris), as large as a *"para"* (penis). An old woman who was the chief of all women cut away the male-appearing genitalia with her stone knife. Afterward the women were "mara" (good) and without a penis; they have only a little one left.

Róheim found that the fantasies of the women in this society, in which rape is a likely possibility, reflect the constant anxiety and flight from a shadow spirit. These spirits are the doubles of the men.

> The Australian woman is always the loving daughter of her father, and her whole sexual and psychic life consists of reaction formations and sublimations that are based on the Oedipus complex . . .
>
> She is born, sees the father in the primeval scene and goes on to desire his penis. But she must deal with her introjected mother, and her whole life is a flight from her true wishes, first from incest with the father and then from incest with the son.

Róheim's interpretation of the female anxieties in this society never takes into account the fact that the young Australian woman has experienced rape shock, and her anxieties are therefore real. Róheim:

> We know very well that the female's acceptance of having no penis is the delicate point in the development of female sexuality. In order to reach the transition from girl to woman, from frigidity to object eroticism, from homosexuality to heterosexuality, the woman must be subjected to violence: be raped, subjugated, castrated.

Thus, Róheim believes, for the simple transfer of the conceptual model of his depth psychology to a primitive society, that rape is a necessity.

He sums up: "In general we can say that the women of Central Australia lead a happy life."

23/The Future of Reproduction

Let me then say it bluntly: pregnancy is barbaric.

—*Shulamith Firestone*

If you can go to the moon, you can also make it possible to have test-tube babies, if only there is enough social pressure. And this social pressure might very well arise, for in vitro *parenthood would be one of the most liberating opportunities we could have.*

—*M. L. Jane Abercrombie*

No female theorist demanded the repeal of the biological division of labor or of natural reproduction of the species more compellingly than Shulamith Firestone. She regarded the abolition of pregnancy as an important element of feminist politics.

> And exactly as at the end of a socialist revolution not only economic class privileges are abolished, but class differences themselves are repealed, so must the feminist revolution—in contrast to the first feminist movement—aim for the removal of not merely male privileges, but of the sex differences themselves: genital differences between the sexes would then no longer have any social significance ... The reproduction of the species by one sex alone for the benefit of both sexes would be replaced by artificial reproduction . . .[1]

Yet, Firestone drew a whole medley of false conclusions. The furthest from reality and the most fatal is that, in her view, one must not only abolish male privileges but must also remove the two essential female sex functions, pregnancy and birth.

Would the misogyny of our culture then finally be abolished? Would test-tube births automatically negate the importance of the mother and father?

Firestone believes the feminist revolution must take place directly before the revolution in reproduction. She does not say how we can transform present-day society, though.

> For exactly in the same way as the temporary dictatorship of the proletariat takes possession of the means of production, assuring the abolition of the economic classes, the takeover of the control of reproduction by the women will guarantee the destruction of the sex-specific class society ... Women must ... temporarily take control of the fertility of human beings, and of the new population biology as well as the social institutions that have to do with the birth and upbringing of children.²

Faith in science and revolutionary attitudes enter here into a rare and illusory liaison in the thinking of Firestone.

The sensational embryological experiments by Petrucci in Italy and Edwards in England, who have managed to fertilize a human egg *in vitro,* distract from the current research fields of the medical doctors. The biochemical processes which occur in the placenta and in the wall of the uterus during pregnancy are still largely unknown, despite all the speculation that now surrounds a new reproduction technology. One German scientist estimates that about fifty thousand researchers are working in this field. The Japanese, in particular, have invested a great deal of research on this subject. The goal is complete knowledge about pregnancy, so that a perfect artificial placenta can be created or the human one can be improved.

In today's patriarchal world culture, it is far more likely that this research will usher in the ultimate and irrevocable defeat of women rather than their liberation. A revealing quotation that appeared in a Chinese party newspaper shortly after the first embryological experiments explains: "When one can have children without their having to be born, working mothers would not be kept away from the workplace to give birth."

The sexless society as the goal of human development? This would make the dream of all totalitarian states come true: the direct, immediate domination and control of the human being from the fusion of the sex cells unto death.

Transferring biological reproduction to artificial organs would achieve nothing but the nationalization of offspring, meaning, of course, the transfer of decision-making and social control of reproduction to the hands of men. Parliamentary and people's democracies, as well as military dictatorships, which today constitute the majority of governments, are so far removed from a feminist attack or takeover that any politician can only smile at the view of Shulamith Firestone.

All male power monopolies, viewed historically, are dependent on female reproduction, but the economic, military, and cultural institutions, the national and supranational organizations that have developed from them, comprise extremely powerful factors in their own right. If in the foreseeable future reproduction could be detached from the female body, women would then have even less chance of controlling these. If the "eternal feminine" becomes only a chemical formula, this development need not necessarily lead to the "humanization" of the woman; more probably, it would result in a total loss of power, the complete unimportance of female existence.

This future threat is absolutely real. For although artificial reproduction would be an enormously expensive technique for preserving the species, it could provide a nation with the prestige and advantages that today possession of nuclear weapons yields. An interest in such possibilities for breeding, under conditions in which atomic, biological, or chemical weapons were used, could result in better chances of survival. A nation that stored the germ cells of its citizens in radiation-proof depots and years later had them successfully inseminated would derive important advantages from the availability of such a method.

Another equally powerful incentive in the development of artificial reproduction techniques is the gratification of scientific ambition. The researcher who realizes the chemists' dream of breeding a homunculus, independent of the female body, will have reached a goal that will guarantee him world fame and scientific recognition. The idea that scientific reproduction will become practicable at exactly the point in time when the "feminist revolution" has drawn tangibly near, or that the use of such methods can be prevented in advance, is completely improbable. These lines of reasoning by Shulamith Firestone lead feminism into a dangerous impasse at the end of which may be further devaluation of the role of women.

It is a question of immediate concern to women. Every new biological possibility in this area can be to their detriment, in view of their negligible participation in decision-making processes and the fact that their social position depends almost exclusively on their capacity for motherhood. In this light the latest progress in achieving motherhood by artificial means has to be regarded with reservation. Already in animal husbandry artificially fertilized eggs are implanted into nursing animals. Thus a superior cow mated with a prize bull can produce up to a hundred offspring annually, who are carried to term by other cows, the "wet nurses."[3] Transposed to humans, after overcoming the barriers of religious and ethical inhibitions, a "model couple" could produce about twelve offspring annually. In view of the almost total oppression of the women in the majority of societies, who can actually guarantee that this degradation of the woman to the status of an incubator will not soon become a reality?

The method that has been discussed most widely to this point is cloning. To "clone" is to manufacture a perfect genetic copy of an animal or person out of her/his/its body cells. For animal breeding, the development of such a technique is interesting because cloning could perpetuate especially successful breeding specimens. The American biologist Joshua Lederberg rapturously greeted the prospects of cloning in humans in an article which appeared in 1966 in the *Bulletin of Atomic Scientists,* under the title "Experimental Genetics and Human Evolution."

> If one has identified a superior individual—and presumably a genotype—why shouldn't one then copy it directly instead of risking everything, including sex determination, involved in the use of recombination?[4]

"In other words," commented science reporter Gerald Leach in *The Biocrats,* "if an Einstein or a Russell appears, why not assure more Einsteins and Russells?"[5]

What had already been successful in plants, the Oxford biologist J. B. Gurdon achieved for the first time in 1966 in an animal experiment. Gurdon transplanted the intestinal cell of a frog into an unfertilized frog egg whose chromosome set had been destroyed by X rays. The cell behaved exactly as if it were fertilized. The tadpoles which developed from this were genetically exact copies of the frog from which the intestinal cell was taken.[6]

If the technical prerequisites for this procedure were fulfilled in humans, a man would only have to persuade his wife to bear in her womb a genetic copy of him. Or if by that time reproduction technology has also succeeded in the area of the uterine surrogate, and the breeding *in vitro*—that is, a breeding totally outside the uterus—is possible, reproduction could take place independent of the woman for the first time. The new individual would be a genetic copy of the father.

However unrealistic this goal of reproduction biology may be at the moment, men's views associated with it are revealing.

Gordon Rattray Taylor, in *The Biological Time Bomb* wrote that cloned humans could more easily work in teams, for they could understand each other as well as identical twins.

> The ability to function on a team is especially important in such sports as mountain climbing, in certain military units—I am thinking of the guard patrol or of a bomber crew—and possibly also among deep sea divers . . . A group of astronauts who lived dispersed on a remote planet is a further example. It is evident that a great many interested people (from the outer space authorities to the manager of an ice hockey team) would want to promote this kind of biological research.[7]

Taylor quotes one of the most famous geneticists, J. B. S. Haldane, who has endorsed cloning in human beings.

What was striking to him was that many exceptional personalities had an unhappy childhood and that many are broken by this early childhood experience. Thus it would be advantageous for great geniuses to devote themselves from their fifty-fifth year of life on to the rearing of their offspring developed from their own cell culture. In this way one could best spare them the disappointment of their "fathers."[8]

The possibilities of artificial reproduction are not oriented in terms of the welfare of the public, but toward the interests and values of the male hierarchy of existence: sports, mountain climbing, military goals, male genius breeding, reproduction of great fathers, who with their great sons are supposed to enter into a new educational symbiosis. Mothers will still be used instrumentally as the ones who make their wombs available.

However, the prospect of cloning also contains one aspect that is interesting for the women's movement and that, as speculation, at any rate, concerns some American feminists. While the man needs either an artificial placenta in order to produce his genetic copy or a woman who is prepared to bear it in her body, a woman need only transplant one of her body cells into the egg cell in order to clone herself. Because each body cell also contains the sex chromosomes, sex determination would always be possible. Thus, cloning could allow women an effective method of controlling reproduction.

24/Female Genocide

*Better if a daughter is not born, or does
not remain alive. If she is born, then it is
better if under the earth, if the burial
banquet is combined with the birth.*

—Verse of the Uighur

*One sex might be favored in the selection.
This can lead to a distortion of the sex
ratio. A surplus of men would limit the
population growth, but possibly increase
the general level of aggression in the
society.*

—Anne McLaren

The notion that the sexes complement each other harmoniously and that the division of labor between them is natural is a premise of Western social research that is almost taken for granted. It makes phenomena of our past appear to us as ethnological or folklore curiosities rather than as components of behavior that could also gain influence in our present-day civilization. It deals with the custom of female infanticide and the question as to the causes of such behavior.

One of the first important ethnologists of the nineteenth century, the Scotsman John Ferguson MacLennan, regarded female infanticide among primitive peoples to be so widespread a phenomenon that he considered it the cause of exogamy. The surplus of men produced by the killing of female children would automatically lead to women or teenage girls of other tribes being robbed, adopted, or bought.

That newborn children are killed is a universal phenomenon of human society. There is evidence for it among primitive peoples of all continents, but also in the great historical civilizations. Among some peoples it is a reaction to a hostile environment and poor nutritional conditions. Mothers who are still nursing one child and bring another into the world kill the new baby because of a lack of milk for two children. The killing or exposure of the newborn is a question of the survival of the group and a compensation for inadequate techniques of contraception. Whatever the reasons we must not lose sight of the fact that, in the majority of societies that practice infanticide, the newborn females are exposed or killed more frequently than the boys and, in many societies, exclusively. Female genocide was practiced even by the rich.

Indeed, naturalization inscriptions as well as Delphic holy inscriptions indicate that, almost exclusively, well-to-do families, and above all, merchants, practiced female genocide.

It is a fact that child exposure and killing of newborns were common in pre-Christian Europe. These paternal acts of terror were justified by the harsh environment and interpreted as necessary, responsible population policy. That such acts repeatedly clarify marital dominance relationships has not been considered by historians. Each act of taking away or killing a newborn broke the mother's inner resistance. Moreover, the female infanticide deprived women of future help in their work and of a possible female ally in their daughter.

In many societies, the change in the sex ratio spread male homosexuality and bachelorhood.

The figures from Greece are informative. For centuries the Greeks lived in fear of overpopulation; in the third and second centuries Greek families had only one or two children. W. W. Tarn, an English historian of antiquity, wrote:

> Of some thousand families from Greece who received Milesian citizenship *c.* 228–220, details of 79, with their children, remain: these brought 118 sons and 28 daughters, many being minors; no natural causes can account for these proportions.[1]

Of fourth-century Athens a ratio is mentioned of 87 sons and 44 daughters out of 61 families; the disproportion of the sexes constantly increased.

The ideal family had one or two sons (in case one died in war). Occasionally the sex ratio in Greece shifted to 1:7 in favor of the male population. This does not even allow for the fact that a number of the sons might have emigrated so that in reality the misproportion might still have been larger.

> Of 600 families from Delphic inscriptions of the second century, just 1 percent reared 2 daughters; the Miletus evidence agrees, and throughout the whole mass of inscriptions, cases of sisters can almost be numbered on one's fingers . . .[2]

Not only historians but also the majority of ethnologists view female infanticide only as a measure of population policy and not as an expression of male power, arbitrariness, chance disposition, and jealousy. The adaptive value of this female genocide is stressed unilaterally. Researchers who point out the psychological character of female infanticide are rare.

One exception is the American Milton R. Freeman, who comes to

the conclusion that the systematic female infanticide among the Netsilik Eskimos had causes other than ecological.[3] A half-dozen prominent Eskimo scholars who have considered this phenomenon con-
tented themselves with the generalization that female infanticide
served to balance out the sex ratio; the number of male members of
the tribe was so decimated by accidents that this was a sensible measure. Some authors even cite the opinion that years of breast feeding
a girl reduces the probability of getting a son who will take care of the
parents in their old age. Freeman regards these as "hindsight rational-
izations."

> In short, my thesis is that, due to the mutually dependent and
> complementary work roles, it is necessary to point out explicitly
> the male dominance. The comments by Netsilik informants them-
> selves shed much light on the dominance of the man over the
> women.

He cites an incident from 1913 which occurred during the visit of
a Danish scientist. The latter had contact with a famous hunter with
three sons who consistently chose death for his nine daughters. When
he heard that a daughter had been born again, he was in the process
of spearfishing—one of the hunter's favorite activities—and had made
an ample catch. He went to the tent of his wife and this time permitted
his daughter to live. Freeman writes: "The father's frame of mind is
manifestly significant in the decision of the fate of the female child."
He mentions another case from 1918 in which the mother had wished
to raise the female child. She said: "I could do nothing; in those days
we were afraid of our husbands."
  Freeman concludes from his investigations that the father is jealous of the mother, who, in the daughter, is raising a helpmate and a
companion, while he has none.

> He bears no grudge against the newborn child, but he considers it
> necessary to assure his dominance over his wife once again: he
> may even think she played a trick on him.

Although Freeman manages to believe that the advantages of population politics are an unintentional side effect of female infanticide
among the Eskimos, like all supporters of functionalistic theories he
must define this custom as being adaptive "because it reduces the
tension within the decision-making unit of the Netsilik society,
namely the household." In other words, the Eskimo man can compensate for his inner tensions by killing his daughters and not hurt the
Eskimo mother. Because of her powerlessness in the society her pain
is not tension that threatens their life together.
  India demonstrates the fact that the systematic killing of female
children does not result from environmental stress but is rather the

consequence of an excessive male sense of honor. In the Punjab and in Kashmir at the beginning of this century there were castes and tribes in which not one single girl was left alive. A branch of the Sikhs, the Bedees, were known as *koree mar,* or daughter butchers, a tradition passed down for three thousand years. Among other castes, the Rajputs and the Chouhans, the custom is supposed to have existed "since time immemorial."

Three main reasons were cited for female infanticide. The Chouhans were afraid of the high costs of the dowry and festivities for a daughter's wedding. They were too proud to be able to submit to being the father- or son-in-law of anybody at all, and they viewed it as unfortunate to keep a daughter alive. "The last of these three reasons was the most deeply rooted."

In the 1840s, when the Rajah of Mynpoory kept his niece alive, she was probably the first female child who was born and brought up in the citadel of the Chouhans since its construction. Yet when her father and, shortly after, the Rajah, died, this deepened the conviction of the Chouhan community that their deaths were caused by the survival of the little girl.[4]

In Rajputana and in the Jumna in Etawah there was one additional reason. The caste spirit required that a daughter could be promised only to a man of the same or of higher rank. Yet this required so many presents that the fathers would have become beggars. The concept of male honor, according to a British major, presented the Rajputs with a choice of either "sacrificing the happiness of the father or the life of the daughter."

Among the Bedees there was a saying by their caste founder, Dhurm Chand: "If the Bedees remain true to their faith and refrain from lying and strong alcohol, Providence would bless them with male children exclusively."[5]

Midwives of the Bedees killed the child, either by strangling it or by laying it on the cold floor and exposing it to the wind. Or the newborn daughter was killed immediately after birth by stuffing her mouth full of cow dung, or drowning her in cow milk. In Gujarat baby girls were buried alive. Their bodies were laid in a ceramic vessel, the opening of which was covered with a doughy paste. A small pill of opium was given to the child, producing death after several hours. In many cases the mother was condemned to kill her daughter. She smeared her nipples with an opium salve, let the child suck, and waited until it died.

"Even among the mission Indians there exists the custom of killing female children at birth, especially if the couple already possesses several daughters," states a report on the present-day practice of the Waika Indians on the upper Orinoco.[6]

A passage from the *Koran* says: "If an Arab hears that a daughter has been born to him, the sorrow colors his face black; this news strikes him as such an outrageous evil that he shows himself before no one, and it is questionable whether he will keep the daughter born to him to his dishonor or whether he should bury her quickly in the earth."[7]

What is the point of these descriptions of a custom that has long since been conquered? Is anyone seriously willing to claim that in the last third of the twentieth century such practices are still possible?

The answer cannot be an unqualified no. Certainly, it is improbable that female genocide such as that among the higher Indian castes will reoccur in our century. On the other hand, the psychological constellations that made such developments possible are still implanted in our culture: women are the unwanted sex.

Following are several examples of ways in which the tendency of disparaging appraisal of a girl's birth can further survive.

The normal sex ratio of births is 100 girls' births to 105 or 106 boys' births. Because the mortality of the boys due to genetic deficiency was higher than that of the girls until a short time ago even in industrialized countries, the numerical ratio of the two sexes was balanced approximately at the time of sexual maturity; however, it shifted beginning in the twentieth year of life in favor of the woman, so that in all Western societies there is a surplus of women.

Because in the majority of countries the maternal and infant mortality rates have also decreased and women have a higher life expectancy than men, the proportion of women in the world population must be somewhat higher than that of men.

Actually, by the year 1985 the proportion of women is projected to drop from 49.91 percent to 49.78, which means that there will be about 21 million fewer women than men.[8]

The deficiency of women cannot be explained by the opposition of industrialized countries to underdeveloped countries, but there are clear-cut differences between developing countries with a superpatriarchal structure and those in which, due to the culture, fewer attitudes hostile to women exist.

Arabic and Islamic countries have the smallest proportion of women.

Egypt	49.54 percent
Lebanon	49.21 percent
Jordan	49.15 percent
Tunisia	48.95 percent
Syria	48.73 percent
Malaysia	48.17 percent
Libya	48 percent
Iran	46.92 percent
Kuwait	43.19 percent

The United Arab Emirates shows the lowest proportion of women in the population, 38.14 percent, which may mean one of two things: either the women are regarded as so insignificant that any census of their numbers is inadequate, or they are consciously decimated by negligent care of female newborns and by inadequate infant and maternal hygiene.

Some countries of South America (Colombia, Ecuador, Cuba, Panama, and Guatemala) and Africa (Central African Republic, Rhodesia, Equatorial Guinea) are also conspicuous for their small proportion of women. India offers an example in which it can be proved that tendencies hostile to women are the causes of regression.

According to Professor Ashish Bose of the Institute of Economic Growth, an organization responsible for demographic inquiry on the status of Indian women: in the year 1901, for every 1,000 men there were 972 women; in the year 1971 there were only 930 women. The infant mortality of girls was 148 out of every 1,000 births; that of boys only 132 out of every 1,000 births. These numbers, which contradict those of Western countries, in which the mortality of boys is far higher than that of girls, are proof that girls in India are given less attention than boys. Physicians believe that females are not nursed or fed as well as males and nearly half the Indian women eat their meals every day after their husbands, fathers, and sons—a custom that leads to great malnutrition of women in the poorer classes.[9]

Some years ago this tradition of the separation of the sexes and the privileged male caused a sensation when it became known that in Biafra, children starved to death first, then women, and last men. Similar reports came from eyewitnesses of the famine in the Sahel Zone.

Still, every shift in the sex ratio in favor of the male population increases the aggression level of a society, as geneticists and biologists have unanimously agreed.[10] Sex selection soon will have great consequences for population politics.

Sex selection would most likely alter infanticide. Some population scientists, statisticians and doctors, have done studies on this subject. In a 1941 study on married couples in the midwestern United States, twice as many men as women preferred a son for an only child.[11] A similar study, which the Gallup Institute conducted in 1947, also showed that men had a much stronger preference than women for a son as the oldest child. In a 1970 poll among unmarried college students, 90 percent of the males questioned and 78 percent of the females wanted a son if they could have only one child.

The same percentage of males who were not students also preferred sons: 70 percent of lower-class women, however, wished for a daughter.

Nor do other statistics brighten the picture: if the first-born was a boy, parents waited on the average three months longer before having the next child. After the birth of a girl, American mothers experienced significantly more emotional disturbances. Pregnant women dreamt twice as often of male babies as female.[12]

These results indicate that, if sex predetermination is possible, the husband will want a son.

Yet, there is a reluctance to practice sex selection; in one recent

American survey 46.7 percent were against it, 38.4 percent were for it.[13] Nevertheless, the inclination to determine the sex of the child could be decisively changed. With a simple technique of sex selection motivation to use the method would certainly increase. With a complicated method motivation for sex selection may not increase until after the birth of the first child.

The ideal is the two-child family, the first child a boy, the second a girl. In a one-child or a three-child family, the fact that male children are more often desired would yield a surplus of boys. (In three-child families, for every 100 girls born, 125 boys would be born.)

Sex selection would result in an overwhelming surplus of first-born males. What psychological and social consequences this could have for women has until now hardly been analyzed, although there are an enormous number of studies on the influence of the position in the sibling sequence and the development of only children. The factors of intellectual performance capability, creativity, and neuroticism, according to many studies, are higher in first-borns. Parents usually invest more, not only in the education of sons, but in that of the first-born.

Western scientists may tend to belittle the results of sex selection, but factors such as job development and overall future outlook definitely have an effect on it. Mothers who desire sons need not necessarily value sons more highly but perhaps only hope that they could hold their own better in a world stamped by brutal competition.

Even tensions between political camps could be decisive in producing sons, for soldiers are needed. All countries with a strong patriarchal tradition have to expect a surplus of sons in case the technique of sex selection is not too costly or too complicated. In a patriarchal industrial society like Japan, for example, the consequences are easy to guess. Governments in all overpopulated countries may have an interest in such methods only because a male birth surplus solves population problems in the long run. For all developing countries with imperialist tendencies and a strong patriarchal structure, the male surplus may be so alluring that governments would promote the introduction of chemical preparations for sex predetermination. The motivation of women to take such a remedy would probably be much higher than the motivation to practice contraception, for in all underdeveloped countries the status of the woman is based on how many sons she brings into the world. Still, the consequences of such a change in the sex ratio would not be absolutely positive for women giving birth. Perhaps if females were in demand, their chances to marry would increase, but certainly their chances for liberation would not.

Part Seven
Structures of Sexism

25/Dictated Roles

*The only way a man can be a man is if a
woman is a woman.*

—*Elizabeth Janeway*

One striking feature of psychological theories influential in the twentieth century—with the exception of Freud's depth psychology—is that they totally omit the sex question or isolate it as a special problem. This is no accident but the interest of research influenced by the times. In the first two decades of the twentieth century equal rights of the sexes became a political doctrine. Psychological theory devoted itself to the investigation of personality. Sexual differences in personality were explained with the prejudices still existing—especially as many studies stressed that the individual differences among members of a sex were larger than the general differences between the sexes.

The works of two well-known psychologists, Charlotte Bühler and Gordon W. Allport, exemplify the lack of understanding of the problem of the sexes. In their conceptions, strongly emphasizing the role of the individual as a self-propelled being, both outlined a practically sexless "philosophy of the person" and the self. Nowhere do efforts toward self-realization and autonomy or the high ranking of "the creative process," which Bühler[1] places at the center of her personality theory, shed light on the restrictive social conditions forming the female personality, nor is it shown how this limitation in turn affects the self.

Allport, one of the chief exponents of humanistic and personalistic psychology, devotes little attention to the effect of gender in personality formation. His masterwork, *Pattern and Growth in Personality,* includes only a few banal paragraphs on sex differences.

He mentions findings of empirical studies presenting clear proof of the strong inferiority feelings of women. Not only do more women students feel physically inferior (39 percent of the male students as opposed to 50 percent of the female students) and intellectually inferior (29 percent of the male students as opposed to 61 percent of the female students), but they are also more verbal about these inferiorities.[2] Yet, Allport does not conclude that the female and male ego are different in principle; rather, it seems that the female ego is a copy of the male, but impaired by a few social handicaps. In addition, he deals only peripherally with sexuality, pregnancy, and birth.

Allport writes of the anti-feminism of the leading spiritual heroes of the nineteenth century in *The Nature of Prejudice:*

> What is interesting about this anti-feminism is that it brings with it satisfaction and security in belonging to one's own sex. For Chesterfield and Schopenhauer the gulf between the sexes was a gulf between an acknowledged "we group" and a rejected group of strangers. But for many people this "battle of the sexes" is completely unreal and unprejudiced.
>
> Because women in Western countries have assumed roles that earlier were reserved for men, the anti-feminism of Chesterfield and Schopenhauer seems truly old-fashioned today.[3]

With that, Allport thrusts aside the problem of anti-feminism.

The theory of "social learning" provides the scientific explanation most accepted today for characterizing the behavior of the sexes. According to this theory, the sex role is one among many social roles learned through reward, reinforcement, criticism, discouragement, and punishment. If a boy appears "brave" and conceals his fear, he is praised; a girl is complimented for her outward appearance and her charm. Thus, notions of "correct" male and "correct" female behavior form.

Walter Mischel, one of the main advocates of this behaviorist-influenced school, describes the way in which this process works:

> According to the theory of social learning, the acquisition and performance of sex-imprinted behavior modes can be described by the same learning principle as that used to analyze every other aspect of individual behavior. In addition to differentiation, generalization and learning by observation, these principles include the pattern of positive and negative reinforcement and punishment in specific occasions, and the principles of direct and vicarious conditioning.[4]

It appears that the theory of social learning was not developed primarily to explain sex differences in behavior, attitudes, motivations, etc., but to explore sex role training. The theory of social learning, however, does not examine why all other social roles are determined by sex, nor explain how sex role attributes change, nor pinpoint who and what determine role traits (politics, economics, religion, etc.).

The second weakness of this theory is that it regards sexual conduct—hetero- as well as homosexual behavior—as being the result of conformity and adjustment to cultural role patterns learned through punishment and reward.

The theory of social learning is a part of a long Western tradition. The seventeenth-century English philosopher John Locke excited his contemporaries with the allegation that behavior and thought were results of associations and linkages which, through pleasure and pain, produce likes and dislikes in the individual.

In the twentieth century the American psychologist B. F. Skinner and the Soviet scientist Ivan Pavlov proceeded from the same basic concept. From the reaction pattern of stimulus and response, they developed personal behavior styles. However, that the punishment/reward pattern is the sole factor responsible for conditioning sex roles opposes many empirical findings. For example, Harvard Professor Lawrence Kohlberg has established that, even with positive reinforcement, stronger masculine or feminine behavior in children cannot be induced.[5] Since many psychic and social phenomena were not explained satisfactorily by the behaviorist view, scientists such as Kohlberg turned to a theory of cognitive stages. The foundations for this were created by the work of the Swiss child psychologist Jean Piaget, who investigated the mental development of children. He discovered not a linear learning process, the extension of a spiritual-mental repertoire, but methods of thinking and principles of organization fundamentally different from those of adults.

Piaget was interested in the development of language, logic, and behavior, and presupposed no sex-specific differences. It took practically forty years for his work to be recognized.

Kohlberg, who also further developed other aspects of the theory of cognitive stages, used its basic assumptions to explain the acquisition of gender identity and of role and value conceptions. The concept of cognition includes all the psychic functions that we describe as feeling, thinking, recognizing, judging, and perceiving.

Cognitive theory differs from learning theory in that it does not regard the intellect, the human organism, and the sense organs as autonomous in feeling and thinking, nor does it hold that the world of social and other influences passively shapes feeling and thinking exclusively. Rather, what we call reason and logic are the products of a complicated reciprocal influence of internal and external structures.

There are also neither inborn thinking structures (as the philosopher Immanuel Kant once believed, viewing the categories of space and time as inborn determinants of cognition), nor a purely passive imprinting by environment through stimuli and rewards or punishments. Intellect, the type and style of perception, and logic are products of the confrontation of organism and environment.

The emotional, "affective" development (behavior determined by emotional stimulations) and the intellectual development (thinking, judging, understanding) do not develop separately within the ego, but represent only "different perspectives" of this structure.

Under cognitive structure are the rules of processing information or associating experiences to understanding. Recognition (which is portrayed most clearly in thinking) means associating things or setting events in relation to each other . . .[6]

The second central basic assumption of cognitive theory states that every human organism proceeds through a sequence of irreversible cognitive stages. There are not strung-together forms of thought and cognition—that is, a constantly expanding repertoire—but transformations, all completely new forms of thought, to bring order and control into the perception process. Each stage has a logical structure of its own that is distinguished from those of the previous stages. This system of cognitive stages rests on a "hierarchy of differentiation and integration." Each higher stage is at the same time more differentiated and more integrated than the previous ones.

However, the previous stages are maintained. Although, according to Kohlberg, there is a preference to solve a problem at the highest stage, a child goes back to the next lower cognitive stage if it does not succeed. The other stages remain available for use in adequate situations.

The evolution of gender identity occurs between the second and fifth year of life. In an investigation by Kohlberg some two-thirds of a group of sixty children between thirty and forty-one months (average age three years) could correctly determine the sex of a doll shown to them. Other researchers also produced similar results. In a more recent study from 1975 it appeared that, in an experimental sample, at the age of two children could identify the sexes. The use of gender designations for themselves, however, was scarcely possible for two-year-olds. At the age of thirty months, though, 25 percent still classified gender wrongly.[7]

Among three-year-olds, only half the children could answer whether they would be mothers or fathers. The most important clues for the child in identifying gender are obviously clothes and hair style.

According to Kohlberg, somewhere in the early development of the child is an irreversible self-categorization of sex, the point of departure for all values that the child encounters: "As soon as the boy categorizes himself as being male, he will value positively the objects and acts that agree with his gender identity."[8] He underscores the deviation of his view from the theory of social learning.

> The syllogism of the theory of social learning goes: "I want rewards; I want to be rewarded for behaving like a boy; that is why I want to be a boy." Whereas cognitive theory proceeds from the following sequence: "I am a boy; that is why I would like to behave like a boy; therefore the opportunity of behaving like a boy (and being praised for it) is rewarding."[9]

The child's views of "male" and "female," Kohlberg believes, are not the result of direct learning of sex roles from the parents and siblings. Among middle- and lower-class children or among children from white and matriarchal black cultures there are only slight differences in the views on sex roles and their assessment. Scientists have also shown that these general, simple notions develop just as quickly and clearly in children with only one parent or even no parent models.

According to Kohlberg, in all countries studied thus far, men are viewed by children as being more active, powerful, and aggressive than women. Fathers are judged to be "fearless, instrumentally competent, more powerful, more punishing, more aggressive, and less thoughtful."

> Thus power and prestige appear to be an important attribute of the child's sex role stereotype; aggression and threatening behavior are one further important attribute, and a third is consideration and child care. With the recognition of child care as a female function, the general differentiation is made between mother home and father outside-the-home functions.[10]

These stereotype views develop in children:

> By the age of four or five children seem to be clearly conscious of the sex differences of the adults in size and body strength and ascribe great importance to them. Size and body strength are especially significant for two reasons: first, because the general concreteness of thought in small children induces them to define social and behavioral attributes concretely in physical terms. Social power, they believe, is the result of physical force (strength, aggressivity, skill, etc.), which moreover derives from physical size. Secondly, the first basic social distinction that children encounter is that of age/body size (babies, boys and girls, adults)— a distinction that precedes the one between sexes. Age concepts (time) are more difficult for the child than concepts of size and are assimilated later. Thus, size becomes a fundamental indicator for all important age-status differences, i.e., differences of strength, of knowledge or wisdom, of social power and of self-control.[11]

Kohlberg concludes:

> In other words, it appears probable that the child's stereotypes of male dominance or social power develop extensively from these physical stereotypes of size, of age, and of competence. The children are first—nearly unanimously—convinced that fathers are bigger and stronger than mothers; thus, they believe that they are more clever than mothers, and accordingly they think that they have more social power and are head of the family.[12]

Kohlberg had shown earlier that a more decisive step in development takes place between ages five and six. Children of four and five do not yet understand that money is received in exchange for work. They see the mother as the breadwinner of the family because she buys the groceries. Therefore, these children more seldom describe the father as the head of the family than six-year-old children, who would say: "He works and earns the money."[13]

On the other hand, we have the impression that the answers obtained from children between five and eight years old can be explained only by the fact that both sexes in this age phase assign the male role a higher value or more prestige.[14]

Until age five, boys and girls prefer and value their own sex, though this egocentric view diminishes later.

Certainly the stereotype of adult womanhood is inferior to the male one in terms of power and competence, but to a child, whichever the sex, it is superior nonetheless. The mother or the woman teacher will be considered more competent, as well as feminine in appearance, dress and behavior, than the little girl. Therefore the feminine stereotypes appeal to the wish of the girl for competence and power.[15]

If one examines Kohlberg's cognitive development closely, it seems to be a new version of Freud's theory of penis envy. Kohlberg acknowledges the universality of sex stereotype as inevitable, stemming not from male pride and female penis envy but from other physical dimensions: body size and strength.

Kohlberg thinks that much of a child's views on sex roles differ radically from those of adults, because there are "qualitative differences between the structure of the child's thought and that of the adults." This is a weakness in Kohlberg's theory, though, for if this were actually the case, then adults and children would have truly radically different views. They, of course, do not. Physical size may be transformed in the minds of children to "greater power." But the concept that he who brings in the money is more powerful is the judgment of both the child and the adult. As is the concept that men are instrumentally competent and less considerate, and that mothers take care of children.

Girls with mothers who are gainfully employed appear to have the same primarily domestic definition of the feminine-maternal role as girls whose mothers are not gainfully employed.[16]

This can also be a clear reality judgment on the part of the daughter —unless Kohlberg could prove that gainfully employed mothers are not primarily responsible for child care and domestic duties and children recognize this.

The fact that children have an immediate conception of society's power relationships, regardless of size, physical force, and aggressive behavior, emerges from a number of surveys of black children which were done in the United States after the Second World War. Black children almost always preferred the color white. When they were shown two dolls, one white and one black, the majority of black children chose the white doll. When they were asked which doll looked nice and pretty, and which looked nasty and bad, the majority chose the white doll as pretty and nice and the black one as nasty. Black children of age levels three to seven preferred white dolls.

The white children interviewed also preferred white dolls almost exclusively. Not until the end of the sixties did studies in isolated cities come to other conclusions. The majority of black children interviewed in one study carried out in Lincoln, Nebraska, chose a black doll. Authors Joseph Hraba and Geoffrey Grant concluded from this that the "Black is beautiful" movement had increased their pride in their own skin color, for recently in Lincoln a black civil rights campaign had taken place and self-aware black organizations had arisen.[17]

These results can be interpreted so that the selection and the higher assessment of the white dolls by black children reflect a power relationship that the children have perceived accurately, and that the fact of the development of a black counterforce (Black power, Black is beautiful) also influenced the value concepts and predilections of the black children.

Without intending to generalize from the following example, I would like to quote a conversation with a seven-year-old girl whose mother is single and working in a demanding profession. In addition, the girl had a woman schoolteacher: that is, two white role models, both of whom had a higher than average intellectual education.

"Who is smarter in your class, the boys or the girls?"

"The girls."

"Why?"

"Most girls get better grades than the boys. They pay attention more."

"How about yourself? Are you smarter than the boys in the class or are you not as smart?"

"Equal. I'm just as good as the boys."

"In your opinion, are adult men or adult women smarter?"

"Men!"

"Why?"

"Why? Because—why, that's obvious."

"How is it obvious to you?"

"I don't know!"

From the conversation quoted it appears that the girl began by making a reality judgment about her class: girls had better grades than boys. The self-esteem of the girl may have led to an overevaluation—she herself had only satisfactory grades. Apparently her judgment about men and women came not from her range of immediate experience, for her mother and teacher were both working in intellectual professions, but from a culture in which, from picture books to television programs, men are portrayed as being mentally superior.

Kohlberg's studies on the cognitive development of the child, however, have great merit. They set the frightful Oedipus drama, which Freud linked to the discovery of genital differences, in a completely different light. Even children enlightened by their parents only rarely use genital differences as main criteria for sex assignment. During the study, for example, some boys asked Kohlberg if they would still be boys if they had no penis.

> In the course of this study children between four and eight years old were asked if a picture of a girl could be a boy if she wanted to by playing boys' games or getting a boys' hair cut. Most of the four-year-olds said she could be a boy if she wanted to or if she wore a suitable haircut and clothes. At six to seven years most of the children were quite sure that a girl could not be a boy regardless of the changes in appearance and behavior.[18]

As an explanation for this change in the children's observation ability, Kohlberg quotes the findings of Piaget:

> The development of such conceptual constants were dealt with by Piaget as preservation of the qualities of physical objects under apparent changes. Piaget and his followers have demonstrated that children under six years of age do not think that physical objects retain an invariable mass, number, weight, length, etc. if the perceptual configurations in which the objects appear, vary.[19]

Piaget proves the shift in identity concept of a two-and-a-half-year-old child in one of his most well-known examples:

> When J. saw L. in a new bathing suit with a bathing cap, she asked: "What is the name of that child?" Her mother explained that it was a bathing suit but J. pointed at L. herself and said: "But what's her name?" (pointing at L.'s face) and repeated the question several times. As soon as L. had her dress on again, however, J. called out quite seriously: "It's Lucienne again," as if her sister had changed her identity by changing her dress.

According to Kohlberg, a majority of four-year-olds in one study thought that a picture of a cat could also be a dog if it wanted to be, or if its whiskers were cut off. Not until the age of six or seven did most of the children clearly assert that a cat would not change its identity despite apparent perceptual changes. Even children who recognize anatomical differences believed that a boy could also be a girl and vice versa if they really wanted to.

> Unfortunately, psychoanalysis was inclined to deal with the connotative and symbolic meanings of the sex differences as something unparalleled. The presence of common symbolic meanings of objects depends therefore not on the singular characteristics of the sex drives and their suppression, nor on inborn archetypes; common symbolic meanings exist as a result of the general disposition of people to concrete symbolic thinking.[20]

Cognitive theory can explain some obscure phenomena, claimed by psychoanalysis to be castration anxiety and penis envy, with fewer contradictions. If female children think they may grow a penis, it may be related to the fact that they are not yet convinced of physical constancy.

A multitude of myths from primitive peoples shows a similar ignorance about physical constancy. In the Australian myth that was supposed to justify the circumcision of the clitoris, there was talk of three male organs that women had possessed or that could form shoots. One African myth relates that women could remove their sex parts and tie them on like an apron.[21]

Children in every society have specific conceptual capacities at each age level. For example, a child taught repeatedly about the birth process may still claim that the stomach is cut open in birth. Among the Nuba, for example, common notions of birth from the armpits or copulation in the armpits exist.

The American sex researcher John Money has reported startling cases of the dependency of sex role and gender identity on education.[22]

Since 1950, children born with indefinite, hermaphroditic sex organs were counseled at Johns Hopkins Hospital in Baltimore, Maryland. The counseling took place in obvious cases shortly after birth. In some cases children who had already been assigned as girls or boys were reassigned more closely to the morphologic sex. Reassignment caused no adjustment problems for children up to eighteen months of age.

The fact that there is a biological basis for sex-linked behavior was proved just as convincingly in the studies of Eleanor Emmons Maccoby and Carol Nagy Jacklin. One boy born with normal genitals but who had undergone a penis amputation, by accident, at the age of seven months was raised by his parents as a girl, upon the counsel of scientists. Then, as a girl, she showed interests defined as "feminine" and, for example, wanted a doll in contrast to her brother. With other children she showed more energetic traits than did her girl playmates. Money explains the accomplishment of the sex role identity in this way:

Gender-identity differentiation resembles bilingual differentiation in the child who has two native languages. Bilingualism is
confusing for an infant if both languages are spoken to him inter-
changeably by all people in his linguistic environment. He is then
likely to be slower than unilingual children in mastering either
language. The child's bilingual learning is unconfused if clearly
delineated according to the principle of one person, one language,
and always the same language, exclusively. Thus a child may
delineate Chinese, say, as the language of exclusive communication with the persons at home, whereas English is the language of
persons in the neighborhood and school.

The same principle applies to the models of gender role from
whom a child establishes his or her own gender-identity differentiation. It is preferable if the irreducible elements of the male
gender role are exhibited by males, and of the female gender role
by females.[23]

The positively coded system is the one in which the individual
becomes truly proficient in all minor details. The negatively coded
system may never manifest itself throughout an entire lifetime.
There is always a possibility, however, that in senility, when inhibitions weaken, the old man or woman may show some traits, even
erotic traits, of opposite-sexed gender identity, unthinkable in earlier years.[24]

Provided that a child grows up to know that sex differences are
primarily defined by the reproductive capacity of the sex organs,
and to have a positive feeling of pride in his or her own genitalia
and then ultimate reproductive use, then it does not much matter
whether various child-care, domestic, and vocational activities
are or are not interchangeable between mother and father.[25]

At first glance Money appears to have come to grips with the
problem of roles. Yet while his observation and analysis are precise,
the solution to the puzzle is not. The problem is one of role definition.
For which are the "elementary aspects" of the female and male sex
role beyond the immediate sexual behavior that leads to coitus and
which children normally are not shown?

Money does not concern himself at all with the existing power
difference of the sexes: This becomes horrifyingly clear in the portrayal of the counseling and development of the little boy whose penis
had to be amputated due to an accident in circumcision. He was ope-
rated on, an artificial vagina was put in, and under the advisement of
the hospital he was brought up as a girl, in contrast to his twin brother.
Each particular in which the female gender identity of the child born
as a boy manifests itself is a picture-book example of the elements of
the female role that the women's movement attacks.

At first the mother dressed the "girl" in pink pants and little lace blouses, and afterward, always only in dresses. At about two years she definitely wanted dresses rather than long pants. At the same time, the mother of the patient confessed:

> What really surprises me is that she's so feminine. I've never seen a little girl who was so neat and clean . . . She is terribly glad to have her hair combed . . .

When the twins were one year and ten months old, the mother was already formulating precise plans for their education and future. They were supposed to go to college, but for the girl it was less important.

> When the twins were five years and nine months old, they had clearly different goals for the future. The mother reported: "My son always picked very masculine things, like fireman, policeman or such . . . She doesn't want to be any of those things, she wanted to be a doctor or teacher . . . But she never wanted to become anything like fireman or policeman, that sort of thing was never interesting to her."

The mother appeared worried that she had not yet managed to "behave more calm and ladylike."[26]

Now, of these acquired female or male qualities, what can in any sense be called "elementary"? In this case, even the information on the child's future role as a mother was a lie, for naturally, this boy-transformed-into-a-girl can never be a mother.

26/Voiceless Women

*It must be for me as it is for one who is
mute, who—counseled by the most intense
of emotions—wants to speak, and cannot,
cannot.*

—*Hedwig Dohm*

*Voicelessness is among the characteristics
of the lower animal forms and is an
unmistakable sign of an intensely
inhibited and limited, closely constricted,
oppressed, dull, feelingless, more plantlike
than animal-like life . . .*

—*Ludwig Feuerbach*

"**M**en and women are two nations on one soil."

This observation by a famous rabbi hits at the heart of the relationship of the sexes: alienation and power. Women's roles and men's roles are dialectically formed products of our consciousness: projections and distinctions of psychic and social differences, concepts in which we form our biological being as sexual creatures.

Nothing absolute can be established about the states "feminine" and "masculine." Even the "objective" psychological differences are only statistical and hardly immediate experience. The essential properties of the sexes remain fundamentally undiscernible.

Male and female temperaments as collective creations, designs of our fantasy, imaginative power, and anxiety, are random creations that develop within a confrontation for power. Present-day psychological theories on the formation of gender identity, however, overwhelmingly deny or ignore this.

The fact that sex roles are learned says nothing about the realization of their qualities or about the variability of masculine and feminine roles within human societies.

Symbols in each particular culture, and the identification of these symbols as male or female (linguistic symbols, gesture, hair style, dress, jewelry, makeup, gaze, voice, intonation) convey identity. I am female, I am male.

No human culture has ever limited the male or female role to purely biologically recognizable sexual functions, because masculinity and femininity are defined together and thus present the archetypal model of dialectic role development. Psychologists also do not differentiate by sex role and economic forms, between sex and religion or world outlook. The theory of social learning of sex roles cannot forecast changes in the understanding of this role or thus perhaps explain the rise of a women's movement because it does not specifically evaluate sex roles. Yet a central theme contained in the concept of gender identity is the question: who am I allowed to be according to the norms of a society, and who am I not?

A theory of the ego is identical with a theory of power. It must answer the questions: what claims am I making upon this world for myself. To what purposes am I structuring my life? Where are my bounds, and who limits me?

The self-establishment of the ego is something Jean Paul once wrote about:

> Early one morning, as a very young child, I was standing below the front door and looking left toward the woodshed when at once the inner apparition, I am an I, passed before me like a stroke of lightning from heaven, and ever since remained luminous: My ego had seen itself then for the first time, and for eternity.[1]

In this description we recognize that pure introspection is not possible. Jean Paul speaks of an "inner apparition," but at the same time he is looking toward the woodshed. The visual image that he receives of his ego (a stroke of lightning from heaven, which remains luminous) shows that this ego can be established not in isolation but only through sensory experience, by contact with the outer world.

The "self-categorization" (Kohlberg) of male or female shapes the ego. No other social feature approaches the importance of sexual identity. The certainty: I was female, I am female, I will remain female, guarantees the continuity of the self. This gender identity is a structural framework that can be combined with and expanded by other qualities. It is precisely these coordinations of self that are at stake: the collective power struggle of the sexes.

Identity formation is controlled through opposition by selective identifications. Identity gain and dialectics (self-differentiation) are thus only two aspects of the same process. Ego formation is an act in which the ego relates continually to the totality of all natural and social phenomena, to the immediate surroundings, dwelling, home, speech, group, nation, factory, job, etc.

Hegel wrote: "Ego is this inseparable nexus of the particular and general and the particular as general of all Nature and of the universal, of all Essence, of all Thought."[2]

Does this definition of the ego hold true for women, too, or are they among those of whom he says: "The slave does not know his essence, his infinity, his freedom; he does not know himself as essence."[3]

He describes the relation of ego and environment as follows:

> When I say "I," I put into this every particularity, the character, the natural, the knowledge, the age. "I" is quite empty, definitive, simple, but active in this simplicity. The many-colored painting of the world is before me: I stand facing it and in this position cancel out the opposite, making this substance into my own.[4]

The incorporation and appropriation of the outer world is the function of the ego.

> Because if I have the possibility of deciding to go here or there—that is, because I can choose—I have conditions, which one usually calls freedom. The choice that I have lies in the universality of the will: the fact that I can make this or that my own.
>
> The choice lies therefore in the uncertainty of the ego and in the certainty of the content.[5]

With the conditions of the choice the ego joins into a dialectic dependency on the selected content: "I am also equally dependent on this content, and this is the contradiction that lies in the conditions."[6]

Elsewhere Hegel speaks of the "infinite avarice of subjectivity, to collect and to consume everything in this simple source of pure ego." Ego and freedom are immediately identical.

Because the ego can be established only with respect to the outside world, however, it confiscates parts of nature and the world of things as its own. For Hegel, as "the mystic prophet of private property" (Marx), the ego proves itself through its freedom. Private property is the symbolic extension of the ego and the appropriation of the world within certain rules.

> Thus, property and freedom of the ego coincide. The fact that I can exercise external control amounts to a kind of ownership, and so does the special feature that I make something into my own out of natural needs, drives, and arbitrary action, which is the special interest of ownership.[7]

The ego as free will makes itself tangible in ownership. Hegel does not exclude the woman from property or inheritance, but family property is administered by the husband and father. In identifying ego with property, important for Hegel, what remains unspoken is that the husband is the manager of his wife's ego.

Not only in Hegel's writings is the definition of ego determined by power, control, and competence. No distinction is made in this concept of ego between purely symbolic arrangements and identifications (nation, speech, etc.) and an ownership relationship. One example of the way in which the ego of an individual serves as a link to the society and expresses the person's power through this relationship is the famous saying of Louis XIV: *"L'état, c'est moi!"* Almost identical with this absolutist arrogance is Adolf Hitler's: *"Ich bin Deutschland und Deutschland ist ich."* (I am Germany, and Germany is I.)

Anyone wanting to secure command over things requires command over definitions. Power relationships are expressed through signs. Hegel writes:

> Taking possession by designation is the most perfect method of all, for the other methods also have more or less the effect of designation in them . . . The idea of the sign is namely that the thing counts for not what it is but what it is supposed to mean.[8]

Justifications for women's inferiority, for what Kate Millett has described as an "extremely clever kind of inner colonization," do not lie in biology but have to do with our mental facilities and communication structures. Sexual and economic battles between the sexes are like propaganda wars: it's a question of concepts and symbols. Those who design the rules can force others to perform in a desired way. According to Ernst Cassirer, the human being lives

> in a symbolic universe . . . He does not face reality . . . Instead of dealing with the things themselves, the human being in a certain sense constantly talks to himself. He has gotten himself so mixed up in linguistic forms that he is not able to see or know anything beyond the intervention of this artistic medium.[9]

The differences between cultures, and also between the individuals within a culture, lie in the extent to which they involve the available symbols and thus all ranges of perception, of nature and society, in this dialectic of sexual roles. Theoretically, it is possible to classify any phenomenon as male or female. Everything can be dualized, and into each thing, in each action, in each difference, we can inject female or male qualities. In many societies everything is dualized, from the division of labor to the universe and each natural phenomenon.

In our form of economy all latent possibilities for dualization into male and female are inexorably exploited by advertising and production. Qualities considered male or female are associated with products which thereby acquire an aura specific to the sex.

A dominated people are not supposed to recognize who they are or can be. It is characteristic that Theodor Gottlieb von Hippel, the German author of the Enlightenment, in his writings favoring civil rights for women, posed as his first question: "Why shouldn't the women be allowed to say 'I'?" In some Caucasian tribes women were never allowed to speak to their husbands, and if a husband asked a woman something, she could only whisper the answer. An American anthropologist made the following observation of women in the Middle East: The informant from the village in which he was conducting his study, a young man, saw a young woman running down the street and cursed her father. Women should never go out of the house, and if they do, they should be quiet about it, never run, and always move so that their voices cannot be heard. When two older women called out something to each other across the street, the same young man thought: "I would not allow my wife to do such a thing. I would lock her up and silence her mouth with a stone."[10]

To know nothing about oneself is the plight of subjugated people.

Often, a behavior attributed to one sex may eventually be attributed to the opposite sex. For example, Claude Lévi-Strauss separates cold and hot societies, as he calls them, primitive and civilized cultures, with the development of writing. The invention of writing meant a new source of power in the development of patriarchy permitting men to exclude women. Reading and writing became more important when trade and bourgeois society expanded. In the course of the Christianization of the Germanic peoples, women and priests were the first to learn to read and write. The advantages and opportunities that were presented by the art of writing were not then recognized by men of the feudal class. It was regarded by them as unmanly to concern oneself with knowledge. A boy who learned reading and writing was at best fit for a vocation in the church. In one text from this period, a knight is exasperated that his wife is instructing their little son in the rudiments of life and writing.

Fluency in reading was generally expected of upper-class women. They were intermediaries for the priests and the church and made certain that noblemen and knights would be more conversant with Christian ideas. The city burghers and peasants placed less value on female education. Still, there were girls' schools publicly supported by the cities. In many towns, schools and Latin schools, as well, admitted girls.

Reading and writing became unfeminine arts, though. Friedrich Nietzsche ridiculed the woman who would sink so low as to be concerned with books. And when women were finally admitted to secondary schools in Germany, there were embittered confrontations over whether or not girls should be allowed to learn Latin. The American Katherine Anthony, in her 1915 book on feminism in Germany and Scandinavia, was amused at the attitude of the German *Gymnasium* teacher who was opposed to the idea that a girl could decline a Latin noun—as if Latin were a secondary male sex characteristic. Even in the tenth and eleventh centuries, men of the German nobility hadn't been opposed to their wives' knowledge of Latin.

Modes of expression can change, for example. A boy who cries, or a man who sheds tears, is regarded in Western societies as unmanly. However, 160 years ago men wrote about their tearful emotions without embarrassment:

> O my brother! We did not dream of such destinies. You know me, I am no stone, but also no undulant wave—my breast can break, but my eyes run over only when I see mighty men weep; I will tell you, I have wept hot tears over the transitoriness of the beautiful and over the futility of this age.[11]

Goethe, the poet of *Weltschmerz* who brought all of Europe to tears, writes in *Werther* how the hero frequently hid in a garden, for which "not a scientific gardener but a feeling heart had drawn the plan."

In the garden bower, he confesses, he has already wept many a tear. Elsewhere his beloved Lotte is standing admiring the heavens and absorbed in the view, and Werther "lost himself in the stream of sensations" at the sight of her. "I could not bear it, bent to her hand and kissed her under the most blissful tears."

When the carriage in which she is sitting passes by without her noticing him, a tear comes to his eye. " 'Lotte!' I called out, throwing myself in front of her, taking her hand and moistening it with a thousand tears."[12]

A man in love who continually sobbed in the presence of his woman friend would seem unspeakably ridiculous today. Masculinity and rivers of tears are mutually exclusive in the present-day male sex role, which characteristically conceals tenderness. Let us take a different literary example:

> Our souls had to approach each other that much more intensely, for they had been sealed off against the will. We faced each other, we two small rivers rolling from the mountains . . .

From our present-day view of the sex roles, this encounter of souls would have to be a matter of a love experience between man and woman. But in this text from *Hyperion,* by Friedrich Hölderlin, it is a friendship between men.

> Alabanda flew to me, embraced me, and his kisses entered my soul. Comrade! he cried, dear brother-in-arms! Oh, now I have a hundred arms!

Today we would see in this an explicitly homosexual scene of salutation. It is immaterial whether Hölderlin is expressing homosexual tendencies. Then, a novel full of men's kisses and embraces did not imply homosexuality.

We had gone together to the field, sat intimately embraced in the dusk of the evergreen laurel, and looked together into our Plato . . .

Hyperion meets the hero Alabanda, and he makes haste to ride toward him as fast as possible.

My horse flew to him like an arrow . . . "Good evening!" called the dear, robust fellow. He regarded me with a wild, tender gaze and with his strong fist pressed my own, the sense of which I perceived deep within . . . "Glorious!" I cried, "just look! In love you will never outdo me." We became increasingly passionate and joyful together.

Like a young Titan the wonderful stranger walked among the dwarf people, who in joyful awe of his beauty feasted their eyes on his stature and his strength, and on the glowingly tanned Roman head, as on forbidden fruit, reviving themselves with stolen glances.

In other countries—for example, in those of the Middle East and in Southeast Asia—it is not regarded as unmanly for men to walk hand in hand and have physical contact in public. This cultural difference in the conception of masculinity for example in Vietnam contributed to the fact that the American soldiers regarded South Vietnamese soldiers as effeminate because they strolled through the streets holding hands.

Attributional changes, however, do not automatically signify shifts in power. Ernst Moritz Arndt wrote:

Then that's all there is to it: [women] should obey us, which is right: For otherwise it will be an upside-down world. After all, we must be men, and be able to rule.[13]

Two hundred years ago, when the male role incorporated emotional outbursts, women were not supposed to show their feelings, but to work, as inconspicuously as possible. "Is she modest, simple, amiable, obedient; was she brought up to be silent, decent, God-fearing, diligent and cheerful?"[14]

Norms of male and female dress often shift. Ten years ago it was an official scandal for a woman to appear in the West German Bundestag in trousers. When a woman first appeared in trousers, in the nineteenth century, cartoonists and journalists saw this as an attack on male identity.

The way women try to dissolve a cognitive dissonance between what they want to be and what they are can be shown in the following statement by Eleanor Marx:

When I turned six years old, for my birthday Mohr gave me my first novel—the immortal *Peter Simple.* This first was followed by a whole series of Marryat and Cooper. My father read all these books with me and talked over their content with his little daughter. And the little girl—inspired by Marryat's seafarers' tales—explained that she too wanted to become a "post captain" (whatever that may mean), and asked her father if it wouldn't work "to dress as a boy" and to be recruited on a warship.

Indian Prime Minister Indira Gandhi once said: "Up to the present day [I have] never felt like a woman." She always imagined herself rather as "a hard-working man."[15] From this statement it seems that she could cope with the contradiction between the power of her office and her female physique, which in India is the bearer of impurity and inferiority, only by declaring herself mentally and socially masculine.

Jan Morris, English author, and father of five children, has lived for several years as a woman. After decades of inner resistance to his unsurmountable wish to be female, he underwent several sex-change operations. In a flashback to a mountain expedition in the Himalayas which he made as a young man with a trim, thoroughly trained body, the author tries to contrast the experiences of having a female and a male body:

> He is the master. He feels that anything is possible to him and that his relative position to events will always remain the same. He does not have to wonder what his form will be tomorrow, for it will be the same as it is today. His mind, like his body, is tuned to the job, and will not splutter or falter. It is this feeling of unfluctuating control, I think, that women cannot share, and it springs of course not from the intellect or the personality, nor even so much from upbringing, but specifically from the body. The male body may be ungenerous, even uncreative in the deepest kind, but when it is working properly, it is a marvelous thing to inhabit. I admit it in retrospect more than I did at the time, and I look back to those moments of supreme male fitness as one remembers champagne or a morning swim. Nothing could beat me, I knew for sure; and nothing did.[16]

Years later, now a woman, Morris reflects on the experience of her "new" body:

> Psychologically I was distinctly less forceful. A neurotic condition common among women is called penis envy, its victims supposing that there is inherent to the very fact of the male organs some potent energy of the spirit. There is something to this fancy. It is not merely the loss of androgens that has made me more retiring, more ready to be led, more passive: the removal of the organs

themselves has contributed, for there was to the presence of the penis something positive, thrusting, and muscular. My body then was made to push and initiate, it is made now to yield and accept, and the outside change has had its inner consequences.[17]

Morris's self-portrait seems like an ideal experimental situation for the demonstration of hallucinatory interplay between being and consciousness. Even after the operation Morris did not acquire a new body with fundamentally new possibilities of experience. Morris traces this new physical experience only in part to hormonal change; the amputation of penis and testicles suggests loss of muscle power, physical tension, and initiative.

The myth of male strength and of female weakness is indestructible.

The following statement by American tennis star Billie Jean King is still a rarity:

I came into this world with the physical and, to a certain degree, mental ability to hit a tennis ball with precision and impact. That's all . . . On my best days I have this fantastic, absolutely unconscious sense of invincibility.[18]

When women also experience their bodies as being strong, durable, supple—feelings Morris attributed only to a thoroughly trained young man—this experience immediately calls into question their object status.

Can men and women make known their physical experiences without becoming the victims of hallucinatory modes of vision marked by centuries of male literary tradition? The female body is an invisible object: there are few authentic literary testimonies to it. Menstruation and pregnancy have been partially detached from taboo and turned into literature only with the rise of the feminist movement.

In German postwar literature, heroes engaged their sex organs in fantastic nationwide action for the conquest of the German past. This connection between male ego and organ can also be found in earlier literary epochs in other symbolic disguises: of feeling, of intellect, or of sexuality. The symbol always signifies power and totality.

The phallic symbol became an important descriptive tool in stressing the hero's ability to act. Gunter Grass symbolized in the penis of his hero Walter Matern, in the novel *Dog Years,* the connection between masculinity and German history. Matern wants to take revenge on former pals who had won him over to National Socialist thinking shortly before the war. After the end of the war he travels through the different German zones, paying visits to his former comrades.

Hedwig Dohm described the attempted escape of the widow of a government attorney. As an aging woman with grown daughters, she went into a kind of ecstasy of self-experience and, ill at ease with herself, posed increasingly heretical questions:

> They had put my nature in chains. Now I am let loose, and I wander around in the strange, new world and would perhaps cause mischief, but there is already a new chain: age. To live for others, this ought to be the right way, the true way to be. If it were so, and everyone lived for the other, then others would also have to live for me; it would be much simpler, if all people lived just for themselves.

Then she reflects.

> But I was always satisfied. "I"? But I was no "I" at all. Agnes Schmidt! A name! A hand, a foot, a belly! No soul, no brain. I have lived a life in which I was not present. I was a mechanism, which foreign powers set into motion.

For the first time in her life she acts on her own desires "in order to set free the little housewife soul." She goes to Capri and falls in love with a young man who suspects nothing of her feelings.

> I often have the uncanny feeling that I no longer know if I am and who I am. Then I may say to myself the name Agnes Schmidt, out of anxiety that I could forget it. But I *want* to forget it. Agnes Schmidt and I: What do we have in common?[19]

This heady process of self-discovery is the alienation process from what she and others have seen as the widow Agnes Schmidt. She does indeed manage to find herself, but now her consciousness stands diametrically opposed to reality; after her return from Capri she is brought to a sanitarium where she dies a happy old woman who has taken a look at her self.

A 1972 poem by Robin Morgan, one of the most militant American feminists, contains almost the same longing for the undiscovered "I":

> *because to admit to suffering, is to begin*
> *the creation of freedom.*

Sorrow is matched by a will to fight:

> *I want a women's revolution like a lover.*
> *I lust for it, I want so much this freedom . . .*
> *To even glimpse what I might have been and never never*
> *will become, had I not had to "waste my life" fighting*
> *for what my lack of freedom keeps me from glimpsing . . .*[20]

27/The Genitals
of Speech

*The usage of the concept of gender in
words is as old as Adam and Eve.*

—Franz Bücheler

One area in which we can quite clearly see the duplication of
the analogies male and female and their projective character is in the
theories of the linguists. For over two thousand years, there has been
an unresolved question: whether word endings of nouns and pronouns,
as well as articles, are an extension of the qualities regarded as male
or female. Many Indo-Germanic languages, for example, contain
male, female, and neuter parts of speech. Some contain only two
classes, as in French, and in others, such as English, the distinction of
the article or adjective has been dropped while that of the pronouns
(he, she, it) has been retained.

The quarrel over this question began among the ancient Greek
philosophers and grammarians. Aristotle, for example, regarded the
ending of a word as a criterion of classification. He contrasted "the
male, as it moves and acts" to the "female, as it suffers." This view
was then opposed by some philological theorists who pointed out
that natural and grammatical gender did not agree; the ends of the
words were only a morphological element. On the other hand, the
Sophists, including most notably Protagoras, tried to correct language according to natural sex divisions. To use the same word for a
male and a female creature was, according to their view, an erratic
development. However, their endeavors to change grammatical gender were ridiculed by contemporaries, and especially by the comic
poet Aristophanes.

Sometimes elements of both views—which are actually contradictory—are found woven together in one message. One of the leading
Alexandrian grammarians, men who from the third to the first centuries B.C. systematized the study of Greek grammar and thus laid the
whole foundation for scientific grammar, said: "The fact that grammar does not differentiate between the sexes is not in accord with the
truth."

The Scholastic grammarians of the Middle Ages as well as the humanists also justify the linguistic class separation into masculine and feminine through the Aristotelian tradition. A quote from an anonymous *Grammatica Speculativa* reads: "The masculine gender is the manner of recognizing a thing from the type of action, as *man, stone.** The feminine gender is the manner of recognizing a thing from the type of endurance, as *rock,† woman.*"

The Italian philosopher and social utopian Tommaso Campanella wrote in his *Philosophia Rationalis* (1638) of the opposition pair acting/enduring: "Just as acting *(agens)* is masculine, endurance *(patiens)* and the matter (from which something is built: *materia*) is feminine." God and fire are masculine, but earth and water are feminine, "because out of the one is reflected action *(actio),* out of the other endurance *(passio).*"

In 1925, P. Royen wrote the most comprehensive work on this subject. He summarized the theories of the Scholastics and humanists:

All these regard the gender of the noun as something founded in reality: either as an active masculine principle, or as a passive feminine one.[1]

In 1747, the Frenchman Abbé Girard had seen in gender "a relationship to the sex." The Englishman Harris clearly continued this sexist tradition when in 1751 he wrote in his *Hermes:*

Much has been regarded as masculine: That in which the attributives of the active influences and of information struck the eye; or which according to their nature were active, strong, and efficacious—and this without distinction of good or evil; that which was laudable or very notably outstanding. Whereas the feminine, on the other hand, were: those distinguished by the attributes of receiving, of containing, of giving birth and bringing forth, or those by their nature more enduring than active; or which were uncommonly beautiful and kindly; or those which refer to more feminine than masculine errors.[2]

Johann Gottfried Herder, in his "Essay on the Origin of the Language," awarded a prize by the Berlin Academy in 1772, went so far as to state: "Poetry and the creation of gender in language are also interests of humanity, and the genitals of speech, as it were, the means of their reproduction."[3]

The Germanist Jakob Grimm provided the most informative theory of gender in language. In 1831 he wrote: "Grammatical gender is a usage or transferral, albeit already advanced, in the earliest states of the language, of the natural gender to each and every noun."[4]

*Latin: *lapis,* the small, movable stone, for example, as a projectile.
†Latin: *petra,* post-Classical from the Greek, the rock, the unmovable stone.

He felt that the neuter is also related to sex, for the origin of the neuter gender was to be sought "in the concept of fetus or children of living creatures. The original meaning of neuter appears to be the undeveloped state of sex, not just an indication of sexlessness."

Wilhelm von Humboldt explained the category of masculine and feminine in terms of the "imaginative faculty" of the language, and Jakob Grimm's conception was similar. "Grammatical gender is accordingly an extension of the natural one to each and every object, which originated in the fantasy of the human language."[5]

Thus, noun gender was not the result of true personification but the outcome of naïve fantasy. The human imagination sees things as masculine, feminine, or embryonal.

What is revealing in Jakob Grimm's grammatical theory is the description of the criteria for the masculine and feminine grammatic gender:

> The masculine seems the earlier, larger, firmer, more inflexible, swift, active, mobile, productive; the feminine the later, smaller, smoother, the more still, suffering, receptive; the neuter, the begotten, the affected, materialistic, general, undeveloped, collective, the dull, lifeless.

In the neuter lies "the concept of the common, the despicable."

The grammarians of the nineteenth century discovered that all languages do not have natural and grammatical gender. The Chinese and the Altaic languages—Turkish, Mongolian, and Tungusic, for example—have no gender; the African Bantu languages divide nouns into eight or more classes, of which only a few have a gender distinction. In many of these languages the categories animate/inanimate, for example, are contrasted with each other.

The German philologist and Egyptologist Karl Richard Lepsius, who studied African languages and their grouping systems, believed that the opposition of human being and nature determined the classifications of the Bantu peoples in Africa. Lepsius also believed that the man had command over the language, especially in the Semitic and Hamitic languages. "Because man shapes the language, the distinction of gender proceeds from the exclusion of the feminine . . ."[6]

Because gender distinctions do exist in a number of African languages, for example Hausa and Hottentot, as well as in several Australian languages, Lepsius thought these were based on:

> The distinction and separation of the sexes and their prevailing moral order and opposition in marriage . . .
>   The spirit of the people was faithfully reflected in the language . . .[7]

The French grammarian Lucien Adam extended the gender theory to an ethno-psychological explanation of the different classification systems. He contended that the classifications developed through the opposition of strength and weakness. Creatures with more vitality became masculine; those with less vitality became feminine. The diversity of this life force was expressed in Caribbean languages; men and male animals and a small number of inanimate things fell into one category, and females and the majority of inanimate things into another. Among the Iroquois and the Chiquito, according to Adam, men and gods belong to one class. The next class includes all else: women, animals, and things.[8]

In 1910, the German linguist Carl Meinhof, using the African language Fulani, developed the contrast of the concept of man and woman even more strongly. The Fulani have a fourfold classification: persons, things, large, and small. Thus, large animals are frequently treated as persons, and small people, meaning socially unimportant women and children, as things, wrote Meinhof.

While the grammarians searched for a plausible explanation for the phenomenon of grammatical gender, the phenomenon itself became part of an ideological war against women's emancipation. For example, German author Theodor Gottlieb Hippel, at the end of the eighteenth century, was an early advocate of the education of, and improved civil rights for, women. Nevertheless, he also believed that reason and femininity were mutually exclusive, because the German word for reason has a masculine article.

> Reason! But beware! When you women take it into your little mouths. This word is—by your venerable Grace's leave—*generis masculini,* or if thou willst have it in German: *Es hat Haar um den Mund* [It has hair about the mouth].

The conservative Wilhelm Heinrich Riehl argued that "the state [was] of the masculine gender." And to the question "Where does that leave the women?" he answered: "They should remain in the family, for even the article of their gender clearly exhibits the predominant signature of femininity."[9]

Just as puzzling as grammatical gender are the different women's and men's languages spoken concurrently within one tribe. In Carib, after their rites of passage, young men scrupulously avoid the women's language, and use only the men's language. A number of theories have been developed to explain this phenomenon, but what psychic, social, religious, or other motives preserved this language separation has still not been explained. One thesis regards the sharp separation of the work spheres as a cause for the differentiation between men's and women's expressions.[10] Another theory is based on the hypothesis that the Carib women were kidnapped, thus their linguistic origins are different.

James George Frazer, the famous British ethnologist and student of myths, believed that in many marital liaisons between two tribes with different languages each sex retained its own language, but that only one of the two languages was used as a means of communication between them. Frazer mentioned as an example a city in Paraguay where the women understand Guarani exclusively, while the men always speak Spanish to each other and use Guarani only in conversations with their wives. In the women's language of the Mbayas in Paraguay, however, only isolated inflectional forms are supposed to differ from the men's language.

Other scholars deny that the abduction marriages and purchase marriages of other tribes have played a major role in the development of women's languages. Religious conceptions and the separation of the economic spheres may be viewed as decisive in the formation of women's languages.

In some tribes, men's and women's languages differ only by a letter at the beginning or in the middle of a word. In some cases the women's language seems to possess more resonant forms, which are valued for being older; in other tribes the men's language may be more resonant.

In Yana, the word forms in the women's language are shorter than those of the men's language. Among the Caribs and Australian tribes, men had a secret language, functioning mainly as war language, from which women and boys were excluded.

In many cases, where close contacts with another language occur —among emigrants, for example—it is usually the women with their negligible outside contacts who still speak the old languages in family circles, while the men are often bilingual. This was true of the Jews and the Gypsies.

In some Eskimo languages women spoke different ending sounds from men, though today, this no longer is true.[11]

Royen and the Dutch linguist Christianus Cornelius Uhlenbeck explain men's and women's languages mainly by men's fear of being infected by the weakness of women. "One can very well imagine that men's fear of being infected by the weakness of women is even greater if the women belong to a subjugated tribe.[12] If men speak women's language, it is done as a deception or trick.

The language usage of men and women differs, however, even in modern languages, for example in words designating sexual things. In Rumanian, men's sexual terminology is generally Latin, that which women use of Slavic origin.[13] Rumanian is a Romance language which for centuries coexisted with Slavic, the language of the Church; hence, Slavic words filtered into Rumanian. With the rise of a national sense of self-worth, Slavic words were perceived as less good, as alien elements, while pure Rumanian were regarded as superior. Thus, there arises an "elevated language" and a "people's language," the latter referring to the women's.

Analogous examples are presented by the countries whose elite uses a foreign language because it is considered superior to their own. This applies to the use of Latin in the Europe of the Middle Ages, as well as the role of Chinese in medieval Japan.

In the tenth and eleventh centuries, Japanese women of the upper classes were allowed to engage in literary activity. Students of Japanese literature believe that, over a period of a hundred years, almost every Japanese author of significance was a woman. The most well-known woman writer is Lady Murasaki Shikibu, author of the world-famous *Tale of Genji.* Court ladies and daughters of the aristocracy enjoyed more freedom in this period than at other times in Japanese history.

How was it that women wrote Japan's first literary masterworks? The solution to this puzzle is simple: this literature has been regarded as great only in relatively recent times. To contemporary men of letters, literary women formed a subculture with far less prestige than the official male poetry had.

Men who had literary aspirations persisted in the use of the Chinese language, then considered elegant, dignified, and prestigious —"the language of scholars, priests, and officials, occupying a role analogous to that of Latin in the West." But women, unburdened by psychological pressures of the sociopolitical hierarchy, "were free to make the fullest possible use of the *Kana* phonetic script, which allowed them to record the native Japanese language, the language that was actually spoken, in a direct, simple fashion that was impossible either in pure Chinese or in the hybrid Sino-Japanese known as *kambun.*"[14]

Sexual oppositions and divisions were often made in important plants and animals, both in primitive tribes and in ancient languages. In Holland and parts of Belgium, for example, different sex designations were used for hemp. In Tahiti various traits distinguish the sex of plants and of animals. The Malaysian tribes, the Maori of New Zealand, and the North American Indians all have complex systems of nomenclature for the sexual designation of flora.

The most sex-specific languages are Semitic, Arabic, and Hebraic; all nouns are masculine or feminine, the related adjectives must agree in gender, and, in addition, the verb must bear the gender of the subject. Moreover, pronouns are also either male or female. If someone says, "I love you," there are four possible ways of expressing this sentence, depending on whether a man loves a woman, a woman loves a man, a man loves another man, or a woman loves another woman.[15]

Linguistic taboos exist among the American Indians; women cannot use words that designate male commodities such as weapons. In some cases the woman will use a woman's word for men's things, and men will use a special male word for female things (for example, cooking utensils). Among the Hopi Indians men and women use different expressions for "Thank you very much." Similarly, the Portuguese also distinguish between the male and female way of saying "thank you." The Mazateco Indians in Mexico have a secret whistle language, in which the length of the whistled syllable corresponds to the word.

Only men are allowed to use this language; women imitating men acquire a bad reputation.[16]

In many languages even the word "I" is divided up into one female and one male expression. In Japanese, which otherwise has no grammatical gender, there is a general word for "I" *(watakushi),* but women who wanted to be especially feminine often said *watashi.* A third word for "I" *(boku)* was reserved for men of the warrior caste, the Samurai. The Chinese language, otherwise genderless, also has a female form of "I."[17]

Father Wilhelm Schmidt divides those languages with sex-specific categories of masculine, feminine, and neuter into four subspecies:

> 1. Those in which this difference appears only in personal (or demonstrative) pronouns; 2. Those in which it also appears in nouns, but refers only to persons (or animals); 3. Those in which a great number of or all inanimate things are divided into one of the two classes; 4. Those in which, in addition to the masculine and feminine classes, a third, neuter group exists.[18]

Schmidt points out that, often, sex differences are not specified in language when one person addresses another, but only when speaking of a third person.

In the Papuan languages, as in the Semitic languages, there is an excessive division into masculine, feminine, and neuter. The Monumbo in New Guinea divide personal and demonstrative pronouns as well as nouns, adjectives, numerals, and verbs into masculine, feminine, juvenile, neuter, and one additional class difficult to explain. The inhabitants of Bougainville in the South Seas have created not only a masculine and feminine class but also numerous other categories for large and small quadrupeds, birds, fish, trees, fruits, and tools.

In 1953, Herbert Seidler, in his *Algemeiner Stilistik,* tried to build on the theory of Jakob Grimm, who had implied that grammatical gender is an extension of natural gender in language. Seidler writes:

> Gender formation stems from a sentimental outlook on the world; it grows out of our human character, to which gender division is fundamental. What we experience as active, giving, large suggests male features; what we experience as passive, receiving, small suggests female traits.

Other scholars, most notably the Hungarian István Fodor,[19] no longer trace grammatical gender to natural gender, but to mechanisms within the language—an interchange of syntactic and morphological factors. This theory refuses to regard the natural sex or value differences (high and low) as the origin of grammatical gender.

For the substance of the thought is not transferrable to the structure of the language. Word forms are purely morphological phenomena which must be completely neutral in terms of contents and valuations; otherwise language, a system with specific rules, would quickly disintegrate.

John Money regards the different English third-person pronouns (he, she, it) as an important prerequisite for the formation of sexual identity, and this in a language which as a rule only has one gender article (the) in contrast to the three German articles or the two French.

That the agreement of natural and grammatical gender is psychologically important is evident in Indo-Germanic languages: the woman is frequently referred to in the neuter, a sign of degradation. The neuterization of the woman is always negative in the German language and used to deprecate. The neuter gender is still applied to the female child; however, there is a tendency in German to use the neuter word "girl" *(das Mädchen)* not only for the young, but for the grown woman. Even the customary sequence in which we enumerate the gender article implies something about the value assigned to each article *(der, die, das)*—masculine, feminine, neuter.

The way in which personal pronouns are used to degrade women is clear in the Indian Havik caste. If the husband of a woman has died, the woman is defeminized and only referred to as "it." The most frequent expression for a widow is *"hani,"* which means "the animal."[20] In Konkani, an Indian dialect, the neuter is used to describe females before puberty and females of lower rank.[21] It's interesting to note that Sigmund Freud described the lowest, most undeveloped and undifferentiated stage of each person as "it."

The importance of the linguistic forms for masculine and feminine in the unconscious are evident in the following example: During a West German panel discussion at the Year of the Woman conference in 1975, a cabinet minister and a secretary of state objected vehemently and emotionally to the feminization of their titles. The justification that one of them gave was that she carries out a function and this has nothing to do with her as a person. Therefore, her title would have to remain *Staatssekretär,* and not be changed to *Staatssekretärin.* The unspoken fear underlying such a rejection is that the feminization of a title would possibly depreciate the worth of the job.

In languages with grammatical gender, the male pronoun must be used for groups including both sexes. In French, for example, the third person plural of the personal pronoun is either the masculine form *ils* or the feminine *elles.* However, when the third person plural stands for a mixed-sex group, the masculine form *ils* is always used. This holds true for Italian, Spanish, and Portuguese; if a protest march of five hundred women and one man occurs, the masculine form must be used.[22]

In Arabic the most frequent word for "child" is *walad* (plural: *ulad*). This word for "child" is also the word for "boy." In other words, the question "How many children do you have?" can also be "How many boys (sons) do you have?" In the translation of Arabic texts it is not easy to decide when the word *walad* stands for "child" and when it stands for "boy."[23]

Another example is the concept of "people." The term "people" or "public meeting," for example, referred to political institutions in Greek city-states, although women were excluded from them. Semantically, that is, "people" stands for "man."

Again, this is similar to the concept "youth." The meaning of "youth" is in an uncertain degree linked with the concept of young men rather than with that of young women. Anyone, for example, who followed reports on the rising unemployment among youth found these substantiated by examples of male unemployment.

> So far as the individual is concerned, each is in any event the son of his time . . . Whoever expresses the will of his time, tells it to contemporaries and carries it out, is the great man of his time.[24]

This famous Hegel quotation shows that the concept of the individual is also thought to be purely masculine.

Schiller's *Hymnus an die Freude (Hymn to Joy)* says: "All human beings are brothers, where Thy soft wing lingers." According to this, all human beings are obviously men, for only they are brothers.

On the history of emancipation struggles the black American Eldridge Cleaver wrote: "We want to be human beings. We want to be human, or the world will be burnt to the ground on account of our trying."[25]

To be a human being is the political status most desirable to all oppressed. For it is a part of the rulers' psychological colonization strategies to destroy the self-esteem of those overcome by denying them human status.

Even at the beginning of this century the political economist Werner Sombart equated the human existence of women with the decline of the culture:

> Yes, I'd like to say that even any reflection on these things is an indication of decadence. The proof of the accuracy of this view is the fate of all previous cultures that have perished precisely because their women became human beings . . .[26]

Hedwig Dohm's famous statement was: "Human rights have no gender."

28/The Dialectic of Man and Woman

Conception is none other than this, that the opposed, the abstract ideas become one.

—*Georg Wilhelm Friedrich Hegel*

Tao produced Oneness. Oneness produced duality. Duality evolved into trinity, and trinity evolved into the ten thousand things.[1]

Throughout history, societies have created a precarious coitus of opposites. This concept of duality became the basis for philosophies, and, in addition, a basis for a division between man and woman. The above axiom from Lao-tzu tells, in the Chinese Taoist school of thought, how the multitude of things evolves from the unseparated unity. In the Egyptian hieroglyphic language, the word "everything" is formed from "the being and the not being." The concept "three" was equated by the Egyptians with "many."

The creation of the world was described by the Egyptians as the emergence of duality out of unity. Pre-existence is characterized by still undivided unity. The Egyptian words used to identify the primeval period are "before two things existed in this country." The essence of existence is duality in the form of a pair of opposites complementing each other. Although allusions to the end of creation are rare, the suspension of duality prophesies the end of the world. The undifferentiated original beings Atum and Osiris, the rulers of the dead, are separated by millions of years and will again be united.[2]

Chinese philosophy uses the principle of *yin* and *yang* to explain the phenomena of the universe. The *yang* is the male principle; the *yin* the female. The *yang* corresponds to Heaven, the *yin,* to Earth. From their marriage follows the transformation of all things, as does the semen between man and wife. The Middle Kingdom, China, is the point where Heaven and Earth touch. The appendix to the *I Ching* says the male principle is immeasurable—all things are indebted to it for their beginning. It contains the Heaven; its work is the transformation through which each thing receives its proper nature, which corresponds to its destiny. Consummation is the female principle. All things are indebted to it for their birth, and it obediently accepts the influences of the Heaven.

Before Heaven and Earth formed, an amorphous state existed which became an empty expanse, producing the cosmos. This caused a primeval fluid state, and that which was clear and bright in it formed itself into Heaven. That which was difficult, slimy, and muddled formed Earth. The unification of the clear and bright went rapidly, while the coagulation of the heavy and turbid was particularly difficult, so that Heaven was formed before Earth. The essence of Heaven and Earth formed the *yin* and the *yang,* and the united essence of *yin* and *yang* gave birth to the four seasons. The dispersed essences of the four seasons formed the myriad things. The hot force of the *yang* produced the fire, and the essence of the fire formed the sun; the cold force of the *yin* produced the water, and the essence of the water formed the moon. From the excess forces, by refinement, were formed the stars and planets.

Two principles which established the universe are used to explain the relationship between men and women. Appendix I of the *I Ching* says:

> When Heaven and Earth have intercourse with one another, all things have free development. When superior and inferior are in communication with one another, they are possessed by the same aim . . . Although the *yin* has its beauties, it keeps them under restraint in its service of the King, and does not claim success for itself.[3]

The gigantic creation of the universe and its preservation serve as a metaphysical interpretation to describe the relationship between man and woman. The sublimity of Heaven is contrasted to the baseness of Earth, just as the honored and the underling social position identifies the relationship of men and women. If the female principle thrusts itself forward, it becomes confused. In Chinese, earth, water, cloud, moon, winter, autumn are feminine, that is, heavy, coarse, impure, dark, yielding, contracting, cold, moist, square, and passive. In Polynesian conceptions of creation, the higher power, the male principle—light, life, and day—is contrasted to the lower, common, and profane, the female principle—darkness, night, and death.[4]

The Chinese frequently combine opposed adjectives and verbs. The combination of "little/big" means "size," of "light/heavy" "balance." The combination of "endure/fade" means "existence."[5] This dialectical formation, which is especially well developed in Chinese, is used in all parts of the world to regard the sexes, in their essence and qualities, as something sharply separated and antagonistic, possessing no identical qualities or faculties. The opposition Heaven/

Earth was reversed in the Egyptian culture; a heaven goddess and earth god existed, dividing the two spheres.

In Indonesia, in Ambon, for example, there was one creation myth in which the male heaven was close to the female earth. While the Chinese designated the color black as the female principle and the color white as the male principle, the reverse is true in Indonesian thinking.[6]

In Romance languages the sun takes the male article and the moon the female; in Germanic languages the opposite occurs. What is significant here is not the substance of the opposites but their evaluation (inferior, superlative, positive, negative).

Diffused throughout the world is right/left symbolism. Right is masculine and left is feminine. Only the Chinese regard right as feminine and left as masculine.[7]

The division of right and left, man and woman, existed even in the Early Stone Age. "In the late Tisa culture it was the prevailing custom that men were buried lying on the right side, women on the left side."[8]

The Kogi Indians of the Sierra Nevada believe that the permanence of the principle of the good, which they equate with the right side and the proper direction, is determined by the simultaneous existence of an evil principle, which is identified with the left side. The good can exist only because the evil principle is active. The main problem of human life, in the view of the Kogi, consists in bringing these two opposites into balance and sustaining their balance as complementary forces. The fundamental concept is *yuluka,* a term which can be translated by "to be in agreement" or "to be the same." The creative and destructive energies must be in balance.[9]

In one creation myth from Hawaii the human being is made out of the clay of all the world's directions. The right side was made out of the clay of the north and east; the left out of the clay of the south and west. Thus, Polynesian thought always equates the east with the right, and right always with man, light, and life. Left, on the other hand, is associated with the west and means the feminine, darkness, and death. Among the Maoris of New Zealand the right side of man is linked to the east. It possessed *mana,* force of life. The left side was the weak side, called the "place of the old woman." In Egypt the King was compared with the right eye and the sun; the Queen with the left eye and the moon. Among the Be-Tammaribe in North Dahomey, the right side of the house is masculine; the left side is feminine. Family altars stand on the right side. In the grave the man lies on the right and the woman on the left side.[10] This right/left division is found assigned to cardinal points on the compass, to seasons, and to colors in religions and rites throughout the world. In Europe the right/left division was an element of the Greek precepts on procreation. Above all, Hippocratic medicine used the right/left theory together with the opposition pair of hot and cold: boys develop in the warm, right part of the uterus; girls in the cold, left side.

Hermann Baumann points out that European popular belief used the analogy of right and left to determine the sex of an expected baby. Thus, in Iceland, and among the South African Sotho, the development of a girl's right breast indicates that her first child will be a boy. A woman must lie on the right side if she wants a boy.

Almost universally, the left hand was unclean and profane. This right/left symbolism and its positive/negative evaluation still continues; right embodies law and order; left corresponds, politically, to those negligible in power, those associated with the negative, trying to bring the world of order (the right and proper) into disorder.

In a 1972 study on sexual oppositions in a Hindu pantheon, Lawrence Babb found that a number of the local goddesses in the Chattisgarh region in Madhya Pradesh are always portrayed as the active force in world phenomena. The local goddesses are feared as being the ones who cause the pox, fever, and cholera. As the pox is a disease of the hot season, the conceptions of this disease are associated with the theme of heat. Because the chief manifestation of the goddesses' strength is the fever of the patients, the horrible goddess must be cooled. A multitude of precautionary measures must be taken against heat or heating. For example, no oil may be heated in her presence, otherwise the goddess will become even more mischievous. The entire hot season is dominated by the goddess cult.

The most evil form of female divinity is the goddess Kali, who, wrapped in a tigerskin with a garland of skulls, fills heaven with her roar. Her only emotion is wrath: black, blood-curdling wrath. Lawrence Babb thinks that in temple portraits of the goddess and a god, the goddess stands behind her husband in a subservient pose. This is true, for example, in the pair of gods Shiva and Parvati. But when the goddess is depicted in a temple in one of her terrible disguises, no male god is at her side. In some temples, Shiva is transformed into the goddess's bodyguard, subordinated, no longer portrayed as her husband. His characteristics are absorbed by her. In these transformations the dual conception of the divinity is associated with the opposition of male and female. If the feminine dominates the masculine, the couple is terrible; when the male dominates the female, the couple is kind and mild.[11]

Among the Zuñi Indians the first human being was named "He-She," or container of the cosmos. This man-woman transformed itself into the sun and generated two seeds, impregnating the great water. Thereupon arose the all-encompassing Father Heaven and the four-quartered Mother Earth. The earth-mother contains all creation in her womb. In the Zuñi cult religious life is dominated by a systematic opposition between the cult of the rain gods in the summer and the animal gods in the winter.[12]

Similarly, the Khasi in Central Assam have a creator-divinity which takes the definite article of the masculine as well as that of the feminine. The female aspect is linked to the obtaining and retaining of things; the male with the creating itself.[13]

Occasionally it is argued that the multitude of androgynous or bisexual god concepts show fewer traits discriminating against women than a monotheistic god figure with patriarchal qualities, such as the Jewish god Yahweh or the Christian God. Hermann Baumann makes this point in his work *Das doppelte Geschlecht.* He thinks that the sharp sex antagonism was neutralized into the bisexual creation deities. This is true only to a limited extent; the bisexual qualities that an androgynous god figure supports are not fused into an indistinguishable unity. Androgyny is also a synthetic, logical figure that is formed out of the combination of two conceptual qualities and jurisdictions previously strictly separated. This unity of the duality usually appears as being associated with the compulsion for harmony itself. The female part of the combined divinity stands in the same logical relation to the male part as otherwise in the dualistic systems. That is, the female aspect of a bisexually conceptualized divinity is frequently the negative or passive part.

Taoistic philosophers tried to resolve the complicated problem of the unity of opposites by claiming that *yin* and *yang* are one: still, it can be said that they are separate. In the Tao psychology every human being is made out of two principles whose fusion means birth, whose fission means death.

At the beginning of many creation myths is the archetypal egg out of which a pair of world parents emerged. Still, the question remains: where does the egg come from? Or in the beginning a pair of twins is created from whom all things and all oppositions ensue.

The unsolvable puzzle of the origin of things, their differences and their relations to one another, the question as to their original cause cannot be answered without producing a new contradiction. How did the one come into the world, how did the two essentially different things grow out of the one, different in that they are not identical, belonging together nevertheless?

Claude Lévi-Strauss interprets the oedipal myth and its variations as one answer to the ancient Greek conception of the beginning: that an autochthon, the first human, grew independently out of the earth like a plant.

A myth of the Mbowamb-Papua, which Hermann Baumann quotes, says that women descended from girls who had no sex parts, were neuter, and practiced only masturbation. A man met a bird who, by trickery, enticed him into affixing sexual parts to the women. However, one woman remained neuter. In an important tribal festival, the Kor-Nganap, the men try to assimilate this neuter, supernatural power of the women.[14] This myth expresses the idea that like can emerge out of like: namely, a woman out of a woman. If the reproduction proceeds symmetrically, a man would also be able to give birth to a man. As in this Papuan myth, almost every cosmogony begins with a monocausal act of creation. Not until a second generation does the genesis follow from the dialectic model.

As in the Chinese philosophy of the Tao, the one and the undivided, there exists the concept of the spirit in the Western world. Hegel writes:

> Mind attains its actuality only by creating a dualism within itself, by submitting itself to physical needs and the chain of these external necessities, and so imposing on itself this barrier and this finitude.[15]

The Hegelian system of thought arises out of a constant repetition of the act of creation. The consciousness proceeds unchecked in a process of begetting and engendering ideas. In this arises with each new idea and each mental move a simultaneous contradiction to itself, which leads to its uniting with itself again in a third stage. The synthesis thus contains the previous stages of the concept and at the same time leads out of itself, till a new process of division completes itself.

If we consider the Hegelian system of dialectics more closely, it then manifests itself as a giant spiritual fertility cult in which the opposites endlessly copulate. The colossal effort underlying his conceptual system functions as forced impregnation. For, of course, to him, it is not enough to define one concept in contrast to another and to use it as a provisional model for describing reality; the dialectic is real for him, the things immanent, "the inherent spirit of the content."

Hegel generates concepts only to cancel them out immediately in a new act of procreation. The perpetual fission of the consciousness and of the ideas by which new births are supposed to emerge seems to be patterned after the natural duality of the sexes, who in the moment of the sexual act become a unity.

As Hegel wrote:

> For that which is to be united must previously be separated; the force of the procreation, like the spirit, is that much greater, the greater the opposites also are, from which it is restored.[16]

The concept of cancellation, or nullification (which in Hegel and in Marx is crucial), functions as a description of an organism created, in the ideal case, by a few seconds of unconscious fusion and self-oblivion of man and woman. In this moment it can simultaneously come outside itself and exist until self-deterioration, which in the Hegelian rhythm of concept formation leads immediately back to the return of consciousness.

What is startling in Hegel is the totality of this principle in the application to human behavior.

Through Nature this relationship of passion is perfectly objective, the one in the form of indifference, the other, of particularity; this highly organized polarity in the fullest individuality of each pole is the highest unity that Nature can bring forth.[17]

The "highest organic polarity as the highest unity," yet the male sex as the universal, the female as the particular, subjective, which cannot stand for the universal—this is Hegel's concept of the different essences of man and woman, with their different final destinations.

The will has been doubled, divided. It is definite: it is character. The one character is this tension, the power of the opposition of being . . . is the lying open, the proceeding straight forward, the driving forth and being driven.[18]

This characterization of the male instinct, which proceeds straight ahead and drives forth, is contrasted to the other, which is "the evil, in-itself-being, the underground." He describes these two kinds of instincts, of which the one is active, the other receptive. The female being is thus "like a cape offered to the bull, which he runs toward and, missing it, is hit." He describes the divided extremes in this way:

The man has desire, instinct; the female instinct is the contrary, only an object of the drive, to stimulate, to arouse instinct and to let him satisfy himself.[19]

The female is the "knowing in itself" and the male is "the knowing as activity to the outside."

The movement of knowledge is thus within the inner self . . . Indeed [man and woman] approach each other with uncertainty and hesitation, yet with confidence, for each one immediately perceives himself in the other . . . reversal lies in the fact that each one perceives itself in the other, cancels itself out . . . gives up its independence.[20]

The nullification of the particular person within another is characterized by ecstatic thoughts of fusion and wishes for self-obliteration. "This recognition is love."

On the temporal level the unification flows into a state of equilibrium without desire; on the organic level it results in the child.

The synthesis of the sexual opposites is realized in the child.

The parents see their unity as a reality . . . and it is born out of their visible identity and center; the actual reasonableness of Nature, in which the difference of the sexes is completely annihilated, and both are in absolute unity.[21]

This idealistic self-gratification through words is a pretext for the cancellation and "annihilation of sex difference," for the process of biological reproduction is divided asymmetrically between the sexes. The child is not born out of both, but out of the mother, and even from the outset it is a sexual being.

The man, Hegel believed, is the "powerful and active one," the woman is the passive and subjective. The man possesses two lives. He has

> his actual substantive life in the state, in learning, and so forth, as well as in labour and struggle with the external world and with himself so that it is only out of his redemption that he fights his way to self-subsistent unity with himself.[22]

The woman, on the other hand, has only one life; her definition lies in the family.

According to Hegel, women are equals of men only in their relationship as sisters to brothers. Only as a sister does the woman lose her status as an object. As brother and sister, man and woman exist in a pure ethical relationship.

> . . . the moment of individual selfhood, recognizing and being recognized, can here assert its right, because it is bound up with the balance and equilibrium resulting from their being of the same blood, and from their being related in a way that involves no mutual desire.

However, the woman as wife is only a sexual creature and cannot be the subject of the desire. In her sexuality she cannot relate to herself. On the other hand, the man is the subject and a free agent.

> And since he possesses, as a citizen, the self-conscious power belonging to universal life, the life of the social whole, he thereby acquires the rights of desire, and keeps himself at the same time in detachment from it.[23]

Hegel writes: "Women may have insight, taste, grace, but not ideals." They are eccentric, moody, desultory, prisoners of their inner life, for they consist only of an inner body, whereas the man represents the outside surrounding and rules her.

The higher destination of woman exists in regard to man. In one letter to his bride, twenty years younger than he, Hegel wrote of the expectations he attached to their union. She should be "the reconciliator of my true soul with the kind and sort that I—too frequently—am, against reality and for it."[24]

The cumbersome, oddly rhythmical language of Hegel—the driving forth and returning unto itself, the thoughts of frenzied fusion, the creating and annihilation of the created in a rising and falling flow of language, the ejaculation of self in ideas—makes Hegel's prose a thoroughly eroticized performance. "Love is the simultaneous generation and disintegration of contradiction."[25]

The generation of the conceptual universe is the erotic liquefaction of oneself: thinking is an act of copulation. The ego is the phallus which, in imperialistic trauma of expansion, must touch all things and signs of things in order to ascertain itself. Each act of gratification passes into its opposite. And because thinking is analogous to the sexual act, it is a quality of the man; perceiving is a quality of the woman. Sons become the "heads" (phalli) of new families, the daughters become "women."

The subjugation of the woman has its foundation, not *per se* in the dualization of the forces constituting the universe, but in their hierarchization. Only when the dualism of male/female is unilaterally allocated values in accord with the pattern of positive/negative, good/bad, or high/low does such a system become an ideology of oppression.

In any case, the oppression and powerlessness of the woman are grounded primarily and most profoundly in these dialectically conceived acts of creation, as found in Chinese philosophy, in the myths of many primitive peoples, and in European philosophy—especially in Hegel. Proceeding from the difference of the sex organs and the differential functions in reproduction, an image of animate and inanimate nature is developed in which, on the one hand, the positive, on the other hand, the negative traits and qualities are conceptually separated from each other.

Even when Hegel talks specifically about the reciprocity of the male/female relationship—of the one who must acknowledge herself or himself in the other—it always remains a phallic monologue allowing no reciprocity to arise, for he feels the woman exists only within the sphere conceptually dictated to her: the family. He is the macrocosm and she the microworld.

The emancipation of the woman will be attainable only if she succeeds in liberating herself from the brutality of this dialectic, which locks her into the conceptuality of the negative.

29/The Vaginal Death Threat

*Who hurled me into the world's sorrow,
who set me into dire gloom?*

*The mentally gifted person shall perceive
himself as being immortal—and love as a
cause of death.*

—From scriptures of the Gnostic

In *Sexual Politics,* Kate Millett takes Henry Miller and Norman Mailer to task for their descriptions of coitus as an act of violence. Mailer's hero, having just murdered his wife, sleeps with his German maid, and in the sexual act fantasizes that her vagina and her uterus are a graveyard "full of cold gasses from the womb." Elsewhere he calls her vagina a warehouse. According to Kate Millett, the hero meditates (after changing to anal intercourse) that "the empty womb," that "graveyard . . . gambled a flower and lost."[1]

In Georg Büchner's drama *Danton's Death,* the hero says to his wife: "Julie, I love you like the grave." When Julie is startled, he continues:

> People say there is rest in the grave, and the grave and rest are one. If this is so, I am lying in your lap and already under the earth. You sweet grave, your lips are deathknells, your voice is my death toll, your breast my gravemound, and your heart my coffin.[2]

The Kiwai-Papua of New Guinea regard female sex organs as the source of all witchcraft: "The female sex organs are as dangerous as an open grave."[3]

Among the Maori of New Zealand, the vagina is *Te whare o aitu,* the house of the dead.[4] In their anthropogeny, the hero, when he poses the question of immortality, is strangled by the female organ.

Oswald Spengler writes: "With the knowledge of life, which remained alien to the animals, the knowledge of death has grown to be the power that rules human consciousness."[5]

The "eternal hatred of the sexes, born out of fear of the world" (Spengler) is produced by the conceptual unity of birth and death. In the mythic imagination, the place of death coincides with the place of procreation.

The mental unity birth/death forms the background for the majority of women's anxieties, long congealed into myth. Because these two concepts must be considered simultaneously, woman is viewed as the creature at rest in herself, with the "less definite unity of perception" (Hegel), while man perceives himself as the one torn to pieces. Because the woman is responsible for birth, she is also responsible for death; in her exist the collapse of the basic opposites life/death.

In a paper advocating woman's self-determination of her own body, the German writer Hans Henny Jahnn nevertheless expresses anxieties about female sex organs:

> The woman has learned that her reproductive organs are a convenient entry point for disease. A powerful system of particle carriers coated with the finest mucous membranes awaits the fertilization process. It admits cells willing to be both destructive and constructive. The miracles of life and decay lie alongside one another. Their fire spreads with consuming rapidity.[6]

In philosophical and mythological thought the conquest of death, and thus, of woman, depicts itself as a permanent logical problem. In Schopenhauer, for example, if one wants to fight against death, one must also struggle against life.

Sexual intercourse, creating new life, is equated with a crime.

> Yet now the act through which the will affirms itself, and the human being develops, is an action of which everyone is intensely ashamed, which they therefore carefully conceal, indeed, with which they are stricken with fright as if they had been caught in a crime.

The crime is that, with life, new death is brought into the world. In Schopenhauer the will to live is embodied in the sexual organs, and the negation of life and death is an affair of the brain. "The genitals are the actual center of will and therefore the opposite pole of the brain, i.e., the representatives of knowledge . . ."[7]

Let us compare Schopenhauer's theory of death and woman as representative of death with that of the Mbom in Cameroon. The Mbom believe only women can be evil sorcerers. Their evil power is located in sexual secretions and in the pelvic area. The magical powers of man, on the other hand, reside in the head.[8]

The notion that man conquers death by the mind is the foundation of the Christian religion and of Buddhism. The immaculate conception implies that, because God in begetting his son has not had contact with death, his son can suspend death. In Buddhism, at the end of life is nothing, in which life and death are negated.

A new possibility opens up for the celibate: escaping the act of procreation and thus breaking the chain life/death. In this lies the possibility of supremacy. Others are condemned to produce life. Thus, each sex act, in the view of the Catholic Church, must be addressed to procreating new life. All collective sexual anxieties are anxieties of death.

The Kogi Indians in the Sierra Nevada have developed a cosmogonic concept which clearly symbolizes the unity of life and death in the reproductive faculties of the woman. The world and human beings were created by the mother of the universe. She had nine daughters, and each of them represented a particular quality of the fertile earth —for example, black earth, red earth, clayish earth, sandy earth, etc. These fertile soils also constitute many layers within the cosmic world and represent a scale of values. People live on the fifth earth, the black earth, which is in the middle of the world. The cosmic world is regarded as the uterus of the universe mother, in which humanity lives. Even the earth and each cult house, each house, and every grave is a uterus. The caves and crevices and reefs of the earth symbolize the orifices of the mother's body. The roofs of the cult houses represent the sexual organ of the mother, doors that lead to higher levels, while the burial rites return the dead to the uterus. The priests lift the corpse high nine times in order to indicate that the dead return through the nine months of gestation. The tomb itself again represents the cosmos.[9]

The anxiety of woman is an existential anxiety, that of the one existing confronting nothingness. For this reason, the worst insult to a male Arab is an insinuation concerning his mother's genitals. In Spain it is a great affront if one asks a man directly about the health of his mother.

In Arab villages in the Middle East, men are never allowed to mention the names of women in public. Even after marriage, a woman is spoken of only as the daughter of so-and-so. Because head and genitals represent each other symbolically, the woman is never allowed to let her hair (considered the crown of her beauty) go uncovered in the presence of her husband. In Islam there are six states of impurity, of which three relate to men (seminal discharge, the sexual act, and death), while an additional three (birth, afterbirth bleeding, and menstruation) are female states of impurity. Performing ablutions after each act of sexual intercourse is a duty for Muslims. Each contact with impurity is in symbolic thought a question of life and death. The purification rite staves off the immediate danger of death.

Merely mentioning the name of one's wife can, according to Arab thinking, bring bad luck to the whole family. Hilma Granqvist cites the following case from a Jordanian village. The name of a married Bedouin woman sounded similar to the expression for "Good morning." This phonetic similarity caused the family's cattle to be stolen; members of the husband's family, forced to repeat her name each morning, were constantly risking mortal danger.[10]

The women's language of the South African Zulu (Ukuteak-wapapzi) forbids women to pronounce the name of the King, of their father-in-law, and of the brothers of the father-in-law. Of the royal family, a German scholar in 1880 wrote:

> They always have to invent words and syllables, and make changes according to circumstances. If the name contained a Z, then the water, usually *amanzi,* would be recast into *amandavi,* and so forth. Any woman who was alleged to violate this custom would be condemned to death by a priest of witchcraft.[11]

Hermann Baumann amassed a great deal of information on sex antagonism, bisexuality, and bisexual conceptions. Among other things, he describes the analogous actions which women perform when their men are in danger. The Ewe women in West Africa back their warring husbands by staging mock battles at home in men's clothes. In the mock battles of the Agni, women insult the enemies of their husbands with obscene expressions. This ritual is supposed to help the fighting men by attracting the death threat of the enemy. The women paint themselves white, and carry sticks which are marked like rifles. During this ceremony the women are regarded as being transformed into men. They assume the names of their absent husbands, brothers, and sons.[12]

Hedwig Kenner reports that in Lycia, in the region of Asia Minor, which Bachofen once assumed to be the birthplace of matriarchy, men put on women's dress during mourning periods. The symbolic thinking is clear: women are in less mortal danger than men because they are simultaneously the source of life. Therefore, men who practice mimicry are protected from dangerous, death-dealing influences.[13]

The connection between women and death is reflected in the sex change of the Greek soothsayer Tiresias, as he is portrayed in the *Metamorphosis* of Ovid. Tiresias comes upon a copulating pair of snakes and injures one of the snakes. Thereupon he is transformed into a woman. After he has spent seven years as a woman, he again encounters a pair of snakes mating. Once more he injures one of the snakes and is consequently changed back into a man.[14]

The transformation of sex is both a transition into the realm of the dead and a rebirth. Because the woman embodies life as well as death, her touch can have a rejuvenating and life-giving quality—just as it can bring death.

Women in the grasslands of the Cameroon, for example, have a significant role in the most important annual ceremony. Young girls of the chieftain's clan must draw his holy water. This spring water renews the strength and life of the chief. A similar rite was performed in Madagascar: virgins bathed in a pool in order to renew the lives of the King and Queen.

In the German Middle Ages there was a custom concerning the life- and strength-giving qualities of virgin blood. In order to win tournaments and to become invulnerable, the knight was supposed to tie under his right arm, on the bare skin, a piece of the chemise of a virgin who was menstruating for the first time.[15]

Among the Haviks, widows are suspected of being witches and death sorceresses. Supposedly they obtain their deadly poison from a lizard which they call Godinaga. Because lizards, snakes, and spiders, all of which shed their skins, are symbols of life and death, the connection here is unmistakable. When a husband dies before his wife, it is her fault; there are strict purity taboos regarding food, and since a Havik would never accept food or drink from a member of a lower caste, he could be poisoned only by women of his own caste. The widow is under suspicion, because of this association with the death of her husband. She must shave her head, may no longer wear jewelry, and must wear a dress that shows her degraded status. In spite of all her humiliation, she is regarded as dangerous.

A 1969 survey by the American anthropologist Edward B. Harper showed that even the educated Haviks believed that such women could poison other people. They believed widows used poison to ensure that, in their next incarnation, they would have many sons and would die before their husbands.[16] A widow must destroy at least one life per year or she herself will die.

The most important suspicion associated with the notion that the woman is the origin of life and death is expressed in the idea that she can be accused of death sorcery. In New Guinea, the war of the sexes occurs in endless insinuations. The most frequent is that women invoke death. If a man is warned that his wife is a death sorceress, there are various methods of determining the truth of this allegation. He cooks a piece of pork, paints it red, sharpens a point on a stick, and bores through the meat. In the night he creeps to the veranda of his wife's house and places the piece of meat near the entryway. If she is a death sorceress, her spirit picks it up and brings it to her. The next morning she has a red mouth from the meat she ate. She is then dragged out of her hut and hanged.

Among the Ndika, the parents of a dead child kill a pig on the morning after the funeral. All the women of the village are invited to eat it. If one of the women vomits, she is suspected of having killed the child by death sorcery. Long ago she would have been killed by the spear and thrown into the river. Today she is only ordered to renounce the magic.[17]

Lawrence Kohlberg has dealt with the different cognitive stages that children go through until puberty. Cross-cultural comparisons show that in an irreversible sequence, for example, children grasp the origin and cause of dreams. First, children realize that others cannot see their dream, that it takes place within and has no material substance. In the last phase of this sequence they comprehend that dreams are caused not by God or other higher authorities but by the thinking process of the ego. Kohlberg established that the Atayal in Formosa also go through this sequence, but that in puberty and in adult years return to an earlier cognitive stage. The adolescents learn that dreams are caused by spirits, and in the dream the souls abandon the bodies, live in other places and have experiences there.[18] Not even cognitive theory can say why the Atayal return to an earlier cognitive stage in explaining the phenomenon of dreams.

In death sorcery a similar regression to childish levels of reality judgments seems to exist. The death wish, frequently together with a magic formula, is sufficient to cause death. Papuan women are convinced that they can perform magic. They give their pigs fodder over which they pronounce magic formulas. Among the Vandeke in New Guinea, for example, one woman confessed, in answer to the district officer on a charge of death sorcery: "The *kumo* is in my head, and he looks like a little girl. It is not 'I' who the people want to kill; it is the spirit the people want to kill."[19]

The Nupe in Nigeria believe in the dual soul, the shadow and a living soul. It is only the shadow soul of certain women that roams about while the bodies lie sleeping, and the living soul steals the other.[20]

As is the case among the Brahman caste of the Haviks, there are also men among the Nupe who can perform magic. Among the Haviks the sorcerers aid the witches' victims. Among the Nupe, the men possess a good magical power that helps fight witches.[21]

Among the Nyamwezi in East Africa, each woman, alternately, prepares the meals for the whole village. Men eat either in the men's square or the men's hall. The women who bring the food are not allowed to enter the men's circle. They put the pots down in front of the hall, and the young men carry them inside. If misfortune or illness overcomes a family, women are held responsible. They are suspected of being witches and of secretly mixing poisonous substances in the foods.[22]

Among the Sandawe, the woman must hide while the man eats. Casting glances and speaking names are some of the ways women can bring death or danger.

The Kenyan scholar of religion John S. Mbiti writes:

The majority of African peoples have mythological explanations for why death first came into the world. The human being has in the meantime accepted death as part of the natural life rhythm; and yet, paradoxically, it is believed that each person's death has external reasons which make it natural as well as also unnatural. The people must find and attribute immediate causes of death. By far the most common reason, they believe, is magic—that is, sorcery and witchcraft. This is found in every African society, with gradual differences in emphasis, and often someone is guilty—by the use of these methods—of having caused the death of another person.[23]

The toll this anxiety can take on women becomes especially clear in the example of the Chinese in Tsinhai, who obeyed ruthlessly strict menstruation taboos and developed cruel visions of the punishment of female taboo breakers. The following report summarizes a paper by Johann Frick that appeared in 1952 in the journal *Anthropos.*

Socio-religious impurity *(tsang)* accompanies every female through her entire life. The tragedy reaches its high point when maternity leads to death. Death in childbirth is punished with blood hell, the most agonizing fate in the Beyond.

While the usual dirt and impurity of everyday life concern, and in a certain sense degrade, only parts of the human body, the *tsang* of the female essence implies an insult to the gods. The concise expression translates as "to offend heaven and earth." Even the girl is subject to the *tsang* from the first moment of her life. According to popular belief, the pure sun at the birth of a little boy sees the room of the childbirth under blood and the mother submerged in blood up to her neck. In the birth of the girl the mother is so plunged in blood that her hair is dripping with it. Beyond the room of birth, the blood is overflowing the yard. After the birth of a boy the mother's confinement lasts, according to rule, thirty days; the birth of a girl requires forty days, because girls are more impure than boys.

The woman must be careful not to let a drop of monthly blood fall to the earth, for she will offend the earth spirit, a very severe offense. She must tie her pants to her ankles. A drop of blood results after death in the punishment of blood hell.

Females are not allowed to sit on the thresholds of entrances, for every door is regarded as a "mouth of the house" through which the gods enter and exit. During menstruation, the woman has to refrain from carrying water. Impurity would insult the "dragon king," to whom wells and flowing water are sacred.

Riding games are very popular among the children. In playing, however, care is taken so that a girl never sits on a boy. If this ever happens, the girl will immediately be warned, or even punished, for this is impure. On the other hand, boys may pretend the girls are horses.

Each mother makes it clear to her daughter never to stand on men's shoes or to step over them. If a woman steps over a man's trousers or, after washing, hangs the clothes out to dry and lets them fall to the ground, she brings him bad luck. In all cases where the well-being of the man is encroached upon, they say the *tsang* of the woman has attacked him.

The blood hell is a "gigantic vat filled with blood and filth; so large that it takes 840,000 days to cross it and 120 kinds of torture find application there." It is only a women's hell. The blood hell has a special position in the Buddhist system of hells. The hells are not last stops of culpable lives, but only thoroughfares; the final destination of the living creature is the Nirvana. There is no dualistic goal of existence for good and evil, as there is in Christianity.

In the original Buddhism there were only eight hells, but now there are roughly eighty-four thousand.

Northern Buddhism has the same conception of the Western paradise. In this Western heaven there are only completely perfected people with ethereal, immortal bodies. Thus, the pole of eternal salvation stands opposed to a pole of eternal agony. The original, sole, final destination of Buddhism, Nirvana, is divided into two diametrically opposed goals: heaven—hell.

In the pure heaven there are no women, in the blood hell only women. In the pure country the living creatures can voluntarily be incarnate again; in the blood hell they must wait until someone is redeemed.

The woman dead in childbirth who awaits such a fate will be brought out of the house in disgrace and buried in dishonored ground. The normal respects for the dead are not paid; she has changed into a dangerous, loathsome demon.

The soul of the woman who died in childbirth lies "pressed against the ground": a heavy stone weighs upon her neck. Some believed that the soul was chained to the stone. She moans, indeed cries out in agony. Where her eyes are anxiously staring, she sees only blood. What she eats are clots of blood; what she drinks is bloody fluid . . . evil-smelling vaginal blood and amniotic fluid. The soul cannot move in the terrible agony which it endures.

Pregnant women must remain inside the birth room for a week. It is regarded as a serious outrage if, in the first days after the delivery, she wants to sun herself outside or even appear in sunlight. It is thought that this crime could bring about an eclipse, an extraordinary and fear-inspiring event. If the woman must go outside to relieve herself, she goes at night or when the sky is cloudy. The breaking of this rule can result in severe punishment: in addition, she cannot be reincarnated as a person, but only as an inferior animal—for example, a donkey.

Women lament about themselves: "Our sex is so impure." Religious doctrine nourishes this wistfulness with the justification that a common woman attains a higher reincarnation only if, in an earlier existence, she gave life to a little boy. This also gives her the right to return in her next life as a human being.[24]

During the witch craze in Europe, women—especially those living alone—were held responsible for death, disease, impotence, and infertility. W. G. Soldan and Henriette Heppe, German historians and pioneers in researching the witch trials, believed that in the century after its invention by Gutenberg the art of book printing served mainly to reproduce the most famous work on witches, the *Hexenhammer (Malleus maleficarum)* by Kramer and Sprenger. The history of the witch persecution in Europe has sexual, economic, and political factors underlying it that are much too complex (they vary from city to city, from one region to another) to be traced to one single complex of causes— for example, the hostility of the Church to sexuality. The American historian Erik Midelfort, who published one of the most detailed studies on the witch trials in southwestern Germany, comes to the conclusion that the democratic changes in Europe and the changed social structure were one component of the social climate that led to the mass persecution and extermination of inconvenient persons, mainly women. Not until the fifteenth or sixteenth century did the characteristic European marriage model develop:

> For the first time in all of Western history, so it appears, the ages of the man at the first marriage rose to twenty-five or even thirty, while the female marriage age went up from twenty-three to twenty-seven. The proportion of those remaining single probably rose from approximately five to fifteen or even twenty percent.

In southwestern Germany, as in the rest of Western Europe, the sixteenth century appears to have brought a profound change in the family model. In a society in which, by this time, 20 percent of all women remained single, identity problems and role conflicts resulted. In addition to the unmarried women were the widows, who often amounted to 10 to 20 percent of the tax-paying population. Since the patriarchal family was regarded as the basis of the society, "the growing number of unmarried women appeared to be a rebellious element in the society, especially if after the death of their fathers they liberated themselves completely from all patriarchal control."

Since even in Catholic countries nunneries were diminishing, there were few institutions that accepted lone women. "Unmarried women were especially subject to attack until the society had learned to adjust to the new family relations."

Soldan and Heppe wrote of women who had endured torture without confessing and were condemned to live under the supervision of their family throughout their life. Midelfort writes:

> In some cases the courts even appear to have acknowledged that the problem was connected to the dangerous woman with her obligationless, rootless, uncontrolled way of life. In 1571 the court in Korb, a few miles up the river from Rotenburg, released Agatha, the widow of Hans Bader von Bildechingen, on the condition that she swore to live peacefully and discreetly . . . day and night in the household of her son-in-law. The subordination under male command would help to solve the problem.[25]

Witch persecution, the initial victims of which were chiefly old women and widows, later extended itself to men, children, and the rich. Not until the stereotype of the old, lone woman was broken—and the persecution hit those with influence—did resistance against the Inquisition form.

The population growth that led to a depletion of productive forces before the Thirty Years' War, war and crises in economics, provisions and supplies, the ruthless exploitation in the countryside of serfs (who often usurped the widow's land when her husband died), plus epidemics, crop failures and famine: this is the background against which the witch tortures should be viewed. It was rumored that women invoked particular weather. If a miscarriage or stillbirth occurred, or if a woman died in childbirth, the midwife was held responsible.

Because women are responsible for death and life, they are also the cause of disease. Because they are the fertile sex, they are responsible for infertility. Droughts and catastrophes from bad weather are their doing.

In 1975 in the north of Nigeria the emirs began to trace the drought to the immorality of single women. They declared Jihad, the holy war of the Mohammedans, against prostitution. The drought catastrophe in the Sahel Zone was traced to the immorality of single women and to prostitution. In the city of Minna unmarried women were given one week to find a husband. Those separated from their husband were summoned to return immediately; otherwise they would be threatened with banishment. In the university city of Zaria, Emir Alhadshi Mohammadu Aminu summoned all the single women to his palace and gave them a lecture on Islamic morality. He accused them of being responsible for the drought, Allah's punishment for unchastity and whoredom. Young girls living on their own were supposed to return to their parents' houses immediately. Landlords in several north Nigerian cities were ordered to give notice to single women renting lodgings. In Maiduguri, in the northeast of the country, women's apartments were attacked. Claiming that the women were prostitutes, the crowds took everything that was not nailed down.

All contradictions of existence, all bad luck, all crimes have been traced to women's existence. What consequences this projection of the mother as unique cause and source of evil may have emerges, for example, in the ineradicable popular belief that it was German women who brought Hitler to power and evil mothers who led their sons to ruin in the Third Reich.

As a result, women tend to reproach themselves. The American psychiatrist M. J. Field found a strong tendency among the women of Ghana to accuse themselves of witchcraft. They frequently blamed themselves for having killed their children. The majority of these women lived with the sense of failure.

30/Symmetrical Relationships

---

*They called themselves "Oha Ndi Nyiom,"
which evidently has an abstract meaning
and can be taken as "woman of the
world" or "womanhood," and their
behavior on this occasion (namely, the
destruction of a courthouse) certainly
indicated that they believed they were
possessed by the spirit of womanhood and
therefore were invulnerable.*

—*Sylvia Leith-Ross, on the Aba uprising of the
Ibo women*

"Oppression always produces a state of war," writes Simone de Beauvoir. The first European women's movement in the nineteenth century failed because it regarded as its goal the entry into institutions of male power. It was a strategy of self-extermination. But Europe and North America were not the only continents on which strategies for the destruction of male rule were developed.

Hierarchical conceptions of the relationships of the sexes derive from male rule. However, there are relationships based not only on complementarity in which the man is assigned the main role and the woman the complementary role, but also on a hovering balance of the forces. We can distinguish two relationships: an antagonistic power division, in which men and women jealously guard their jurisdictions, limiting each other's power, and an approximately symmetrical relationship, in which, in the male as well as in the female sphere, parallel jurisdictions and power structures exist, and in which the female sphere is organized not only emotionally but also politically.

Ideological weapons that men use against women can be turned around and used as a collective means of self-affirmation against men. Women can use their alleged magical powers propagandistically in order to extort justice and to build a spiritual counterforce. American anthropologist Nancy McDowell discovered, after studying the kinship system in a Papuan village, that women often have an extraordinarily dominant status. The sharing of all food provisions is obligatory among relatives; if a woman believes that a male member of her family distributed meat unfairly to her, she will conduct a certain ritual to prevent his success in hunting.[1]

Also among the Kiwai-Papua, women lie naked, with their legs spread out, next to the door through which their husband leaves in the dawn to go hunting. By so doing, the woman attracts the game. The husband, in appreciation, offers her and her relatives a generous share of the game.[2]

Using love magic, women try to defend themselves from male dominance, especially in societies in which they suffer most intensely under the sexual double standard. A complicated ritual of love magic, for example, is performed by the Kabyle women in Algeria.[3] In Latin America, Brazil, and the Caribbean, women frequently hold spiritualistic sessions. The Umbanda cult, a spiritualistic religion associated with possession by spirits and exorcism, contains cultic elements of the African, native Indian religions, and Catholicism. Umbanda is only one of several syncretistic religions in Brazil and has its supporters mainly in the upper lower class and upper middle class. In the smaller cities the religious hierarchy of the Umbanda cult is made up primarily of women who function almost exclusively as mediums. Most male clients come to free themselves from female love magic. The American ethnologist Esther J. Pressel was present at one of these sessions. The client was a Brazilian of Italian descent who ran a small enterprise. During the past year his business had been doing badly and he believed that an evil *exu* spirit was destroying his luck. In the session the female mediums called upon their male *exu* spirits. The medium who had taken over the main task transformed her face as well as her expressions and manner of speaking into male behavior. Her inner male spirit *(marimbondo)* first requested a cigar and a glass of strong liquor, then suddenly explained that the client's problems were connected with his ex-lover. The insulted fiancée had paid an evil spirit to keep his business from being successful. The client confirmed that he had broken off the engagement and that his troubles had begun with that. Then the *marimbondo* sent the client and other men present to urinate. After breaking off the engagement, the client had been incapable of having sexual relations with women. Some months after this session, he confirmed that both his business and his relations with women had improved.

In 1934, the English scientist A. B. Deacon found an especially fascinating example of antagonistic equilibrium between the sexes. Men and women of Malekula perform sacred ceremonies which effectively protect them from the opposite sex. The male sacred objects and holy powers are called *ileo;* the female ones *igah.* Each village is divided into two, the male and the female. The women live in women's houses, the men in the men's house; the sexes seldom see each other. Only married men are permitted nocturnal visits to the women's hut. Women may not come into contact with sacred objects from the male half of the village. On the other hand, men must avoid everything that could paralyze their own holy forces. If a man saw women in their secret ceremonies, even for a moment, he would "become like a child" and lose his rank in the male secret society. Even those objects women touch during their rituals are dangerous and taboo for men. Deacon writes: "The relationship between *igah* and *ileo* is approximately that of the relationship between positive and negative electric charges."[4]

As early as the Middle Ages, Arab travelers reported on successful women's strikes in West Africa. The Arab traveling merchant Ibn Batouta, who in 1352 visited the Sudan, tells that the palace women during his stay in the capital city of Mandin went on strike, refusing to perform their domestic duties. The wild protest was directed against the injustice of the sovereign Mansa Shuleyman, who had committed an offense against his first wife. Among the Fulbe in the eastern part of West Africa there were frequent mass attacks by women against men who had harmed their wives.[5]

The Ibo women in southern Nigeria possessed their own political institutions, a kind of self-government which protected their special economic and sexual interests. They practiced extremely effective boycott and strike methods, astounding because the Ibo are a patrilinear and patrilocal people. In each village there was a women's society, which most significantly functioned as an organization of women traders to promote and regulate woman's primary activity—trade. The women's assembly *(mikiri)* discussed price increases and rules on trips to market and established fines for those who broke the rules. Because women could not fight for their rights individually, they fought collectively and often succeeded.

When they had grievances they first turned to the village elders. If their demands were ignored, women then took the matter into their own hands. One especially effective tactic consisted in having a "sit-in," besieging a man. They gathered in front of his hut and sang and danced until late into the night if necessary. In their songs they item-ized all their grievances against him, taunted him, and frequently called his manhood into question. While singing, they pounded on his hut with the mortars they ordinarily used to mash yams. Occasionally they demolished his home or pelted it with mud. A man who had mistreated or beaten his wife would be besieged until he promised to obey their laws. The women's styles of action were regarded by the community as legitimate and no man would have dared to intervene.

When they rose against men as a group, women mainly used the method of the strike. An English scientist reports a case in which men had ignored repeated demands from women to bring order to the roads leading to market. Women refused to cook for their husbands until the streets were in order. To carry out this strike effectively, all women had to cooperate. Another researcher reports of a case in which the women of an Ibo village swore to help any woman who killed a cow or other animal men had let graze in their fields.

The women's societies also acted effectively to assure their sexual freedom. In one such case, the men were embittered because their wives had open relations with their lovers. They met and decided upon a measure to force each woman to give up her lover and deliver a goat to her husband as penance. The women, though, held a secret meeting. Several days later they marched as a unit into the neighboring village and took only their babies with them. The men held out for a day and a half; then they begged the women to come back. They gave them a goat and apologized.

British colonial rule ignored the political institutions of the Ibo women and, through its autocratic decisions, brought confusion to the entire system of female self-rule and power equalization between the economic interests of women and men. In 1929, women rose up against the native chieftains and their British appointed courts of law. This war lasted about a month, and involved two million women. The war had begun in 1925, when the British government began taxing the Ibo heavily. When women learned that they would be taxed for various household items and small livestock, they protested. After gaining a quick victory, they fought to free themselves from British governmental interference. They marched for a native administration and demanded the discharge of the chieftains. The British officers panicked at the sight of the crowds, numbering in the thousands. The women burned the government buildings and in some cases freed prisoners. In two clashes with the English troops, more than fifty women were killed and others injured.[6] In addition, they also demanded the abolition of male taxation. During the entire uprising the Ibo men were completely passive. Never before had they seen anything like this: never had the women thrown sand at their own chiefs and the white men, and attacked them with sticks. Women who hesitated to join in were pressured by the rebelling women. Eyewitnesses noted that on their march women constantly repeated that they were prepared to die. Although the uprising was defeated at the end of December, the British had to send additional troops.

Ten years later, the Englishwoman Sylvia Leith-Ross was not able to discover anything about the precise motivating factors or the political contacts of the women.[7] Evidently, women tried to make themselves immune to the British bullets by rituals and secret ceremonies. In some cases the harassed British officers had promised that the women would have seats in the law courts. In 1933, when major reforms were passed, women were occasionally admitted to the native government. By building an administration which assumed numerous functions of the village assemblies, the British destroyed many of the original political institutions which women had set up to exercise control in certain spheres.

The main reason for the limited freedom that the Ibo women attained in a male-organized society was their economic role as tradeswomen and farmers. The powerful communication network that they controlled in this patrilinear society had its origin in the fact that women are members of the women's society in the village in which they were born as well as in their marital place of residence, and have rights in both. The women's society today is a kind of self-help cooperative that levies monthly dues and gives small credits to women who want to start a business.[8] Similar solidarity-oriented women's organizations exist among the Yoruba.

Though men sell mainly meat and leather goods, women have monopolized the majority of goods. Each town has a women's leader *(iyalode)* whose duty is to represent women before the King and his chieftains. It is one of their main tasks to settle trading disputes with the men. The German researcher H. U. Beier wrote:

> Recently I was able to observe one such conflict. The women who sell *ogi,* a foodstuff which is prepared from corn, had to bring their corn to the mill owner to mill it. These mill owners are men. Women began to complain that the men's price was too high to bring them enough profit in the sale of the *ogi.* The *iyalode* (women's chief) presented a petition to the mill owners, demanding a lower price for the milling. The men refused at first, and then they tried to trade. The *iyalode,* however, called all *ogi* saleswomen out on strike. Women began to grind their corn by hand, and after one week the mill owners yielded unconditionally.[9]

In West and South Africa, primarily, we find a symmetrical political system of the division of power between the sexes, especially in the form of the sacred queen- and kingship.[10] Under the influence of the colonial rule and the subsequent independence movement, many of these political institutions have been destroyed or repressed. Under the male King a female official was head of state, frequently called queen mother or queen sister, although in only a few kingdoms was she the real sister or mother of the King. In some cases the position of the royal functionary was somewhat weaker than that of the King, in other areas a true double kingship existed. In this dualistic division of power the jurisdictions of the highest male and female officials were so intertwined that neither could make fundamental decisions without the other. One example of this balance of power was the Swazi. The French ethnologist Annie M. D. Lebeuf writes:

> Among the Swazi the *indlovukati,* the mother of the king, together with her son, heads the political hierarchy. They each have their own place of residence in separate villages, their own court, their

own officials. Together, they control age groups, assign land, keep law, and preside in religious ceremonies. They support each other in all activities . . . through the separate exercise of power. . . . In legal affairs, for example, the king alone can pronounce the death sentence, but the counselors of the *indlovukati* can appear before the highest court to discuss such affairs, while those sentenced to death can take refuge in their hut. In the same sense, the king controls the army, but the supreme commander is stationed with (the king's) own regiment in the capital city of the queen mother, while she maintains regiments under the leadership of princes in the capital city of the king. She and the king take part in rainmaker rites and in the ancestor cult; she is the keeper of the regalia (royal insignias) but these are ineffective without the collaboration of the king.[11]

Among the Swazi, the Queen represents the elephant, the earth, beauty, the mother of the land. The King, on the other hand, represents the lion, the sun, the great wild animal. From these comparisons it is clear that, unlike many other dualistic systems, these images represent two powers of equal birth.

The government of Ankole consists of three persons who once had the same status.

Among the Lunda, a matrilineal tribe ruled by a patrilinear aristocracy, the King rules with a woman who is picked by his four top dignitaries. She participates in all government affairs, has her own court, her own officials, and tax revenues. Women's organizations exist parallel to men's. Nevertheless, there are mixed societies in which old people of both sexes rule directly in public affairs. Women who are no longer of childbearing age are often elders.

In South Cameroon, among the Bamileke, the mother of the *fong* (chief) is equal to the chief. They receive the same death rites. She has her own palace and her own property, she is responsible for the planning and execution of all the agricultural work performed by women, she is president of all women's secret societies and belongs, as well, to those of the men, with the exception of the military. However, her status is much different from that of all other women. She has complete freedom and immunity, can conduct trade, select a husband, and commit adultery as she pleases.[12]

The queen mother in the Akan states, now Ghana, held an especially influential position as first counselor to the King. The writings of English governors of the eighteenth century often report that the ruler was completely influenced by the queen mother, who bore the title *ohemmaa*. Repeatedly she assumed command of the army. The clans of the Akan were totemistic and matrilinear; the head of a clan was chosen for life by the adult female and male clan members. At district levels among the Ashanti each village chief ruled with an older woman. The *ohemmaa* functioned as a constant moral control on the King; only she was allowed to censure him and his advisers in public.

She lived in her own palace and held her own court. When a new king was to be chosen, she was consulted. She presented him to the people and took part in the coronation ceremonies.

She maintained her own staff of advisers and was responsible for all questions concerning family life, the status and property rights of women, and the marriage of young women of their clan. Legends tell of numerous examples of the queen mother's efforts toward legislation and reforms for the protection of women.

The queen mother is also construed as daughter of the moon, the King as son of the sun, conceptions probably stemming from the fourteenth century.

In Southern Rhodesia the Manyika were known for their queens and their remarkable influence. The men of the chieftain's lineage were called *wachinda* and the women *wazzari.* It was customary for the *wachinda* to assume the function of district chief. At their death, around the beginning of the nineteenth century, a number of women were chosen as local government chiefs. The legends of origin of women chieftains are told in this way:

> In one religious ceremony the chief of the tribe consulted the great spirit through a medium. The spirit answered that the land of the dead district chief was in need of a female successor. The spirit said, "Let her light her fire there and rule the people. If you appoint a man, then there will be a rebellion." The chief then assembled his counselors and announced the appointment of his daughters as district heads.

In 1940, W. Selwyn Bazelay counted nine female district chiefs who partially still ruled or had been chosen since the end of the nineteenth century. However, they were part of a dying institution, for the majority of them were not replaced at death.[13]

Sierra Leone also has a long tradition of women chieftains. In 1914, of eighty-four regions, ten were governed by women; in 1970, ten out of eighty-one territories were. In 1787 the colony of Sierra Leone was purchased by the British crown in order to take possession of land for returned slaves. The contracting partner to the British crown was Queen Yamacouba, a Sherbro woman who ceded a piece of territory to the British. Around the turn of the century the most powerful woman in Sierra Leone, Madame Yoko, managed to bring fourteen different districts under her personal hegemony. The current successor in her area is also one of the leading members of the Sierra Leone People's Party and was a long-time minister in government.[14]

Carol P. Hoffer, an American anthropologist who in 1969 and 1972 conducted field studies among the Mende and Sherbro women in

Sierra Leone, thinks that the exceptional political careers of women in this patrilinear society can be traced primarily to the female secret society Bundu that initiates young women. The power of the Bundu society is so great that any man who has violated its taboos risks disease and death unless he confesses. He then must undergo a purification ceremony and pay a fine. In addition, a revenge-thirsty wife will use a medicine producing impotence whose secret only the Bundu women know.

Such structures work in a parliamentary system and assure women opportunities for influence. But the institutions of agrarian African societies or a symmetrical government system are not simple to transplant to developed industrial nations. The high status women in these societies have attained can be clearly attributed to the existence of independent women's organizations with their own leadership and communication structures.

Part Eight
Conclusion

31/Toward a Theory of Sexism

The demand for human beings, like the demand for every other commodity, is regulated by their production: it can be accelerated if it proceeds too slowly and retarded if it increases too fast. The propagation of the human race in all countries of the world—in North America, Europe, and China—is dependent upon this demand, this desire for people; this is why the population in one country grows so rapidly, in a second grows so slowly and gradually, and in a third stands completely still.

—Adam Smith

He who is not a father is not a man.

—G. W. F. Hegel

I

Even today, efforts to reconstruct the history of the origin of patriarchal socialization remain rare. Sexist structures relate to the form of economy and all aspects of social development. This indicates the difficulty of formulating a theory that is logically consistent with the development of all these phenomena. What is the relationship between gender and history? What particular conditions and variables shape patriarchy as authorized, institutionalized male power? These are questions that must be answered by a feminist theory.

Patriarchy can be understood as a social system with a norm and value structure that grants men partial or total command over female existence.

The question of whether there has ever been matriarchal socialization has not been settled. Those authors who revived Bachofen's

Mother Right have for the most part simplified things a good deal by deeming the concepts of matriarchy credible, but not offering an explanation as to which conditions might have led to the rise of female-dominated societies and which to their disintegration. This matriarchal socialization can hardly be reconstructed from the mythology of ancient peoples but only through unambiguous archaeological finds.

In developing a feminist theory, however, it hardly makes sense to subscribe to speculation on a phase of matriarchal socialization that might once have existed, while we possess concrete knowledge only of patriarchal socialization. Patriarchy is such a worldwide structure that it cannot have been developed in one single society. Even if one considers the cultural variety in the shaping of sex roles, patriarchal socialization must result from common structural foundations.

In addition to the declarations of the great world religions on the nature of the relationships between the sexes—which still play the most influential role in world opinion—feminism has to deal with several lines of scientific thought on the emergence of relevant sex roles. This is a question of Darwinism and the research trends influenced by him (behavioral research and sociobiology), the sexual theory of Sigmund Freud, and the kinship theory of Claude Lévi-Strauss, and, most influential of all, the theories of Karl Marx and Friedrich Engels.

The assertion of the beginning and the end of the society, which Marxist theory propounds, places it in the immediate vicinity of mythological explanation, extending from the act of creation to the end of the world. Marxism establishes the amount of time within which fundamental contradictions between socialized individuals can emerge—from the disintegration of the early community to the beginning of the new communistic society. Before and after there are no social changes that can stem from the conditions of production and lead to the accumulation of power. In this way, historical materialism denies its own principle of evolution—that is, that all societies are constructed in terms of division of labor and that the tendency to increasingly powerful socialization of individual existence must permanently produce contradictions, each of which ends in new adaptations.

Marxist theory has as a criterion for social development the advance of technological and economic knowledge and, related to this, the constant change shown in social organization. Whether progress is associated with development, and whether the progress justifies the general development, just as the stage of feudalism is allegedly justified by capitalism and this by the trend to socialism contained within it, is the critical question that makes so difficult any classification into highly and lowly developed, more complex and simple social systems. Marxist theory justified the past of a society through its future.

The present-day mode of production could soon end in military or ecological catastrophes. The survival chances for our technological-scientific civilization may be small in proportion to the chances for survival that the economic form being adopted guaranteed to the game hunters over a period of more than a hundred thousand years. Thus, all criteria for the classification of evolution patterns into high and low are relative. A high level of technical knowledge may imply little chance of survival.

The periodization of history established by Stalin in 1938—into a primeval community, a slaveholder society, feudalism, capitalism, socialism, and Communism—makes no direct reference whatever to the history of the evolution of patriarchal structures. The period of primeval society, however, was subdivided into a herd state of human beings and into an early matriarchal community.

This pattern of periodization, though, remains questionable. A slaveholding society in which production is borne almost exclusively by slaves did not exist even in the Roman Empire. The contradictions in which Marxism-Leninism has become entangled through this dogmatic periodization of history stem from the fact that Marxist theory built on two analytical premises. Nevertheless, the more important premise, that insights on conditions of production and the emergence of power can be gained from the concrete study of the division of labor, was increasingly upstaged by the second premise, that power relationships can be reconstructed out of the existence of private ownership of the means of production.

According to the early theory of historical materialism, the subjugation of woman by man also emerged in the transition from the collective economy of primitive peoples to the private ownership of means of production. However, ethnographers' research has long contradicted this theory. Even where no social differences based on possession exist, there are power relationships between the sexes. Today Marxist scholars admit that even at this stage of evolution of the forces of production there can be social inequality between men and women and between the older and the younger generation. But it would be impossible for these contradictions to assume an antagonistic character as in the later class societies. Does this amount to an admission that these contradictions are irreconcilable? And what is their source?

Since the Marxist thesis that relations of dominance develop in connection with private ownership of the means of production does not help to explain domination between the sexes, it is more meaningful to study the relationship of services and counterservices that constitute the division of labor specific to sex.

The concept of labor was developed by Marx in connection with the concept of value. Marx wrote: "He who satisfies his own need through his product does indeed create use value but not a commodity. In order to produce a commodity, he must not only produce use value but also use value for others, social use value." The distinction which Marx finds between use value and exchange value is in fact meaningful only in the case of Robinson Crusoe, whom Marx uses as an example of his theory. Robinson Crusoe is self-sufficient. All goods that he produces are use values—that is, intended for his own use. According to Marx, within the patriarchal family the work was divided without the products becoming commodities. This part of Marx's theory is founded on a fallacy. Already the first division of labor, namely, that between the sexes, leads to an exchange of goods and services. The labor necessary for the production of the next generation is performed chiefly by women. Yet men acquire something comparable to surplus value, which, according to Marxist theory, the capitalist realizes in relation to the wage laborer. This surplus value of division of labor specific to sex lies in the male's claim to the children. Only through this expropriation can women become commodities—to retain the Marxist metaphor.

When Karl Marx observed that labor was the source of the creation of value, he did not realize that one particular kind of work is in itself the derivation of all value. The work of bringing a child into the world up to the age at which these children themselves represent labor power that can be productive and constitute use value is furnished predominantly by the women. On a part of this service—namely, on nursing—they have a monopoly.

If women would reproduce only for their own needs in terms of support and replacement of their own labor, they could limit the work of motherhood to fewer children, as well as limit their part in procuring food. Marxist theory was so one-sidedly oriented toward the production of goods that it did not consider that services have a value—be it a use value or an exchange value—nor did it notice that a surplus value can be developed out of these. However, in a society in which few visible goods are produced besides foodstuffs, the services of others are the only surplus product that can be acquired. Gathering firewood, carrying water, hauling loads, caring for small children and the sick, preparing and watering tuberous roots (a lengthy process)—these were women's wearisome, monotonous, continuing services for the family or the group.

The following presentation will be an attempt to explain the "empowerment" of sexuality—which emerges even before class societies —by means of a hypothesis contending that the economic and ideological structures of patriarchy are grounded in the historical formation of conditions for reproduction.

Social orders are defined by the fact that the human species has fashioned out of sex a lifelong social role that is initiated with birth and extends through the individual's period of reproductive capability. Accordingly, feminist theory would analyze how human society has biologically and culturally reproduced on the basis of sex roles, and which types of division of labor styles, of social organization and dominance, have grown out of these roles.

II

Any approach to evolution theory is in some way characterized by the difficulties encountered in establishing models for the termination of social development. The evolutionists of the nineteenth century conjectured a unilinear course of development applicable for all societies and proceeding from low to high; the Marxists assumed a dialectic one.

Most theories on economic change have concentrated exclusively on the development of tools and technology and the increases in productivity made possible by them. The reproduction of human life was considered one of the biological foundations of the social order. Of course, famous economists such as Smith, Malthus, and Ricardo observed the connection between the size of population and wages, but the actual conditions of reproduction interested them little.

If a feminist theory brings the reproduction process into central focus, this does not imply any neglect of economic perspectives in history but only an attempt to establish its point of reference. Economic conditions and the organized division of labor have developed further from the demands of biological reproduction. Reproduction in labor-sharing organizations is the most important factor of economic life. The creation of the next generation has a double function in human society: one is economic, the other has to do with the giving of meaning to life.

Humans must affirm the reproduction of human life or deny their own existence. In terms of a feminist perspective, the central aspect of human history is not the history of war, technology, or class struggle, but precisely what the German philosopher of history Oswald Spengler contemptuously called "the cultureless history of the progression of generations who never changed"—the history of the species.

Underlying child rearing is a conscious or unconscious reckoning of cost and benefit, which of course comes out different according to the prevailing mode of production. Children can be conditioned emotionally and intellectually, and therefore make the best allies against the dangers of the environment or of other groups. After six or seven years, they are already helpers who fit into the labor-sharing society. Through the control of their marriages, possible alliances between groups or families can be formed, and the children are the guarantors of old-age care.

The usefulness of children consists in the maximization of one's own security. In principle it holds true that the larger the family, the clan, the tribe, or the nation I belong to, and the more young members it has, the greater the security.

This is why men as well as women are interested in having the optimal number of children that can be brought up in the particular environmental conditions and state of technology. But even if the increase in existential security through more children is fundamentally in the interest of both sexes, the degree of the interest is unequal.

For the women each pregnancy—and the labor time related to the care of a small child—means an automatic increase in the amount of work they do. Up until the First World War there were hardly any chances of survival for babies who were not nursed, because, as a result of the ignorance of sterilization, the use of animal's milk was not very successful. The feeding of other foods, which is necessary after the sixth month, depends on the availability of soft foodstuffs and requires spoon feeding by the mother. A woman who nurses totally is committed for about one and a half to two hours of work a day and requires about a thousand additional calories. Because for the man the increase in the number of children does not mean the sort of extensive increase in work that it does for the woman, men, under the conditions of the majority of preindustrial societies, have a stronger interest than women in maximizing the number of children.

This difference in interest on the part of men and women toward the creation of the next generation is a basic constellation of all societies, which favors the development toward patriarchy.

The frequency of pregnancies and the birth rate among hunting and gathering people is low. Birth intervals of four to five years are common. Women are frequently able to decide on the life of the newborn child, although the men are thoroughly oriented to population increase. Their frequent insinuations that the women might kill their children are an indication of this.

In cattle-breeding and agrarian societies, however, the great demand for human labor power leads to a much higher birth rate and encourages the institutionalization of patriarchal structures. The greater the women's reproductive burden, the fewer their chances to acquire influence. The higher the frequency of pregnancies, the more gynecological accidents (mother and infant mortality), the more children are required, so that at least some survive. On account of the security needs of the peasant family to have at least enough surviving children to guarantee old-age care and the continuity of production (in all agrarian societies with a low level of technology) the tendency exists to produce a surplus population.

When Thomas Robert Malthus formulated his famous population principle, he ascribed to humans a powerful biological reproduction drive, a blind passion for procreation that leads to overpopulation. Every population has "the tendency to multiply beyond the limits of the means of support provided by the given economic and social organization." This was "the most invulnerable and important natural law of the entire political economy to date."[1]

However, reproduction rate and sex drive are two different things. The use of contraceptives, coitus interruptus, abortion, sexual abstinence, and child exposure are methods of birth control that can be practiced anywhere. To be sure, modern development has enlarged the spectrum of contraceptives, but the majority of island societies (Japan, and in the Pacific), which were not able to export their population surplus to new territories without difficulty, have practiced contraception, abortion, and child exposure on a large scale even under patriarchal conditions.

The problem of population increase, for which Malthus preached only late marriage age and abstinence, was not a result of the sex drive but of reproduction ideologies and conceptions of morality which provided security for the economic foundations of patriarchy. Views on whether contraception, abortion, and child exposure ought to be used change with the mode of production and the different degrees of patriarchal socialization.

Where child exposure was official birth control, other ideas prevail on the point in time at which the soul enters the child, as in Tahiti, where the child was considered not to have a soul during the first hours after the birth.

Today some scientists are of the opinion that Malthus's population law holds true for agrarian societies, while others argue that the population density basically stays below the maximum environmental limit.

Again and again, however, population growth as the driving force of patriarchal socialization has evidently tended to test the environmental limit. Population increase led either to processes of impoverishment or to innovations in the organization of labor and to increase in productivity.

The quintessence of patriarchy is the male control of reproduction, which is oriented to maximize the security for the individual paterfamilias, the oldest member of the clan, the chieftain, or the men of the ruling social classes.

The only economic systems which favor low reproduction rates are those of hunters and gatherers and the highly industrialized ones. That is why in these societies there are at least chances and tendencies toward equality of the sexes.

III

From the point of view of the biological allotment of tasks, women are the actual subjects of history because they are the manufacturers of the next generation and have an immediate relationship to them. Because men lack this immediate access, they are able to integrate themselves into history only by establishing a relationship to offspring on a social level. But unlike the women, they can hardly create equivalent bonding mechanisms for this purpose. A woman's children, whether male or female, are basically her natural allies. The intimate bond that women and children achieve is based on nursing, feeding, carrying, verbal and nonverbal communication, and constant emotional interplay.

There exists a very strong motive for men to control the generative capability of the woman—her fertility—and her relationship to the next generation. If children and young people were to exhibit an attitude of solidarity toward the mothers only, or were to prefer them, the position of the old men would be in constant danger. From this social weakness and uncertainty of position on the part of the old men stem the strongest motives: to reinforce their position and authority toward the children.

The most important prerequisite for the development of patriarchal institutions in a society consists in the disintegration of the mutual solidarity of mother and child. If men want to win allies in the following generation, they must develop a sex-specific solidarity structure. The control of women requires the suspension of the natural, close relations between the mother and the male child. The boys, in other words, must be convinced above all of the insignificance of motherhood.

On entering puberty or even earlier, boys are subjected to initiation rites and drastic socialization measures. Among the Baruya of New Guinea the alienation of the boy from the mother is a process that lasts over ten years, until his initiation is completed. Not until after this time, when he is already married and has children, is he allowed to speak with his mother again and to eat in front of her. In the initiation of an Indian Brahman son, a last meal together by mother and son was a part of the rite before he became an initiate at about age eight.

The old men shape the identity of the boys by a system of communication and meaning from which they exclude the women. Many of their ceremonies are associated with acts of terror against women and smaller children. The membership in the men's associations, secret societies, or military organizations is dependent upon these initiations.

Puberty rites for girls are lacking in most societies, or they consist of a brief individual observance of the girl's first menstruation. In contrast, the maturity rites for boys are for the most part collective and last over a long period of time or extend over the whole of adult life.

In myth the world view of the initiated is expressed. Myth and religion represent the truth in a society. Like religion and science, myth attempts to deal with the meaninglessness of events and of existence. At the same time, it must corroborate and justify existing conditions in the present. The Africanist Hermann Baumann wrote of the myths that establish rights and duties of the sexes: "Often we must speak here really of myths with a purpose." (Example: the Baktaman, a small tribe of New Guinea who have developed a seven-part secret initiation ceremony, claim that only the sperm of the man is important for the development of the child. Among the Baruya, another tribe of New Guinea, the sun and the man cooperate to produce a child.)

The spiritual control of fertility is the power that the old men offer the young ones. Actually, it is the women who are fertile. They have the children; they plant, weed, and harvest the main foodstuffs. However, through their secret knowledge and their rites, it is the men who control all manifestations of fertility, while the women appear only as the caretakers and attendants of plants, animals, and children. The old men achieve their authority toward the young ones through an ancestor cult that confirms the solidarity of all men with the preceding generation of men and through an interpretation of the relationship of the sexes connected with ideological devaluation of the woman.

Every kinship group possesses as a kind of spiritual property the knowledge of its ancestors. Not until central political institutions have formed is the historical memory tended by specialists of the privileged social class. The legitimacy of the claims to sovereignty are established with the exact knowledge of the family trees.[2] Through the association of cosmological narratives (mythos) and ancestor genealogy (history), and with the help of religion and law, men obtain the exclusive right to explain the meaning of human existence. Thus, they become leaders in the interpretations of meaning for the entire society.

Even though women may not accept all male value judgments, these interpretations nevertheless affect their life through purity rules, taboos, and rituals of conduct toward men which express women's subordination.

The formation of political authorities and the rise of states coincide with the reformation of the systems of religious meaning. It is characteristic that a hierarchy of gods or one divinity stands in the center of the religion. Women are now tolerated as passive believers. However, they are excluded from offices of the cult or are permitted less influential cults of their own.

The structural elements that make solidarity between old men and young possible—to the disadvantage of women—hardly offer women the chance for collective resistance. Even when the bond between son and mother is broken when the son reaches a certain age, his new, superior status still applies to women in general. He dominates his future wife and his sisters. In strictly patriarchal cultures, a mother remains subservient to the son; because the son supports her, her bond to the son is the only possibility of maintaining her social existence. The future daughter-in-law is a stranger who, in a patriarchal system, is usually dominated by her husband's mother.

The early forms of organization of the state developed in areas where population pressure was already high. The class societies arose out of groups competing for the exploitation of a particular optimal environment, like the big river deltas in Babylonia, China, and Egypt. Systematic warfare and the private acquisition of means of production are only a further phase in the patriarchal socialization characterized by constant attempts at growth.

In order to stabilize class societies, the state became the guarantor of paternal power, and the paternal power of the state became the guarantor for the subordinate relations of the classes. The control of the sexual impulses of the individual and the fathers' total control over sons, daughters, and wives served to internally maintain the order of the state.

The stability of state order was dependent upon a rigorous hierarchization and the strict compliance to command and obedience. For this reason, the preindustrial states of patriarchal class lack all the permissive regulations characteristic of the early societies of hunters and gatherers, gardeners, and cattle breeders, in which after a certain time breaches of taboos and infractions of ordinances can once more lead to the deviants' integration. The women's right to divorce and extramarital relations, acceptance of out-of-wedlock children, marriages based on love, and deviant sexual conduct become impossible or are punished with maximum severity.

No family system has attained such complete paternal authority as the Chinese, in which the wife/husband relationship was secondary to the father/son and mother/daughter-in-law relationship. The Chinese peasant family frequently adopted a daughter-in-law when she was only a child. With jesuitic strategy her will was broken until she was assimilated into her father-in-law's family. According to Chinese law, she was not allowed to act independently or to possess property, or to become the head of a family. She had no legal status. In the Confucian and Hindu ideologies, the procreation of a son was a prime religious duty.

Associated with paternal authority were doctrines promoting population increase, recorded in the first assemblies of law in the Near East region long before the Christian era. Sumerian, Assyrian, and Babylonian codices made abortion a criminal offense. According to Hindu law, abortion was one of three crimes, including murdering a husband or a Brahman, that made outcasts of women. A devout Hindu made full use of his wife's fertility. The husband who did not have intercourse with his wife during her fertile period was described in religious literature as an embryo killer.[3]

In the Jewish faith the waste of male semen was seen as delaying the arrival of the Messiah; the Son of David would not appear until all the souls of the unborn were born. A similar concept is found in medieval Christianity: increased fertility would increase the population of heaven.[4]

IV

Since the end of the last century, ethnology has concentrated on the investigation of kinship, descent, and marriage rules, as well as the legal relationships in these systems or the unconscious structures underlying them. Lévi-Strauss, most notably, worked out the similarity of marriage rules and the inherent possibilities of social connection with the respective language structure.[5]

Lévi-Strauss and others overlooked the fact that behind the constitution of marriage rules is concealed the society's unconscious economic reckoning of which mode of distribution of marriage partners, under the given conditions, can attain the greatest efficiency.

Sexuality and fertility have an economic dimension in human socialization that is accommodated through the constitution of marriage rules, both positive (orders) and negative (bans). For example, when the marriage of female and male individuals classified as first cousins is prescribed, as in the Australian Kariera system, then it can be assumed that this method of assigning marriage partners, in relation to demographic size, ecological conditions, population density, and economic form, at the same time represents the most rational and secure form of distributing marriage partners in space and time.

The adoption of a system which prescribes preference marriage with the classificatory matrilateral female first cousins and the classificatory patrilateral male first cousins by the Eskimos under their ecological conditions and low population density would probably condemn them to extinction in a short time. Hence, their marriage rules, which permit any marriage outside the nuclear family, offer a maximum free choice in selecting marriage partners and are optimal for their living conditions.

The critical assessment of marriage markets requires more than just a knowledge of the marriage rules. Alongside data on the mode of production belongs information on the number of participants in the marriage market each generation, their marriage age, time of ménarche and menopause, fertility rate per woman, differential mortality rate of the sexes, monogamy, polygamy, divorce, and remarriage of widows and widowers—that is, demographic information as well as the description of economic services associated with the marriage system, with which it can be understood.

While ideological systems represent indirect reflections of the world and of social experience, the marriage relations fall in the category of a society's conditions of production.

One of the most controversial scientific questions is the rise of the incest taboo. In many societies it is related to such a great circle of people that a general biological basis appears impossible. Thus far it has not been settled whether or not a biologically fixed aversion to incest exists between mother and son, as the observed avoidance of sexual contact among subhuman primates. Unlike other animals living in groups, human beings organize the conditions of their reproduction themselves. All societies have taboos and regulations concerning sexuality and the access to reproduction. The social order is constituted by regulations that determine which persons the members of a sex are allowed to entertain sexual relations with and which not. The most plausible explanation for the incest taboo consists in the necessity to marry outside one's own group. This principle of exogamy prevented groups from dying out. For small groups of ten to thirty members as existed in the beginnings of human society, it must have been a matter of survival to exchange marriage partners. Despite the statistical ratio of the sexes, which is 100 female births to 106 male births, considerable disparities can occur between male and female births in small groups. If there are too many men and only a few women of fertile age, a group which practiced no exogamy was extinct after a few generations.

The advantage of exogamy consists in the organization of marriage markets—that is, of a system in which the local scarcity of a factor (male or female marriage partners) can be equalized on a regional basis. But exogamy also had fatal consequences for women: those societies which practiced female exogamy had higher chances of reproduction than those which practiced male exogamy and followed a matrilocal residence rule.

In matrilocal societies, where the husband has to join the wife's family, the increase of the fertility rate is limited absolutely by the number of women of child-bearing age, for according to this residence rule, no increase in women through marriage is possible. As a result, these societies are more susceptible to crises because they cannot compensate for a loss of female reproducers by sickness or infertility. Matrilocality, however, is the most important base for women's influence in preindustrial societies.

The large number of patrilocal societies, in which the woman must move to the family of her husband, and the small number of matrilocal groups prove that societies with a patrilocal residency regulation were able to increase more dramatically because invested in them is a possibility of increasing reproduction capability, which matrilocality lacks. Patrilocal systems are more stable because they can compensate for infertile wives and increase the number of child-bearing women through the institution of polygamy.

Societies with patrilocal residence rule have better chances of survival and a stronger tendency to population increase. This may be the answer to why the big empires and civilizations of the past were all patriarchies characterized not only by patrilocal residence but also by male inheritance and descendency groups.

The Danish political economist Ester Boserup has pointed out the connection between population density, polygamy, and the differential in employment of female and male labor in the economy. In Africa, where labor, not land, is a scarcity factor, the field work is done by the women.

The resistance of African men to the introduction of the plow and tractor was great everywhere. It meant that they would have to supply far more work. Thus, the transition to agricultural methods requiring intensive labor almost always results only when the land becomes scarce because the population has grown too large.

In traditional African economic systems, where land is not yet private property and is not leased, the institution of polygamy is linked economically with this form of economy. Men with two wives cultivate, on the average, an area twice as large.

The polygamists of Africa invariably demand fertility, but not exactly at any price. The value of female labor and of children is too high to risk their life through a rapid sequence of births. The woman can institute long birth intervals, which mean sexual abstinence for several years after the birth of a child. In this period the man tries to marry a second wife. Because the land has little value—only labor has worth—it is a matter of building as large a family as possible. For it is human capital that benefits the man. Besides, through the bridewealth system, he can strengthen the dependency of his sons, who, in order to buy a wife, must either hire themselves out as workers or else receive from him only the necessary currency. With the bridewealth are acquired the rights over the wife's future children. In many societies payment is stretched out over a long period, until the first children are born. If the bridewealth is not paid in full, the family of the bride keeps the rights to the children from this marriage.

The conditions of production for the polygamists, among whom the men have the capital to acquire wives on the marriage market as labor and child bearers, are revealed in the practice of the Dan—a farming people in the interior of Liberia. The father buys a wife, whom after a time he cedes to the oldest son. The demand for future labor power for the family is so great that children are purchased even when they are still in the mother's womb. In addition, a husband can lend his wives to men who are prepared to work for him in return. If this man severs his ties with his employer, the children whom he has begotten also then belong to the owner of the woman.

Even now, many scholars regard the bridewealth as only a symbolic transfer of goods.

According to one study of marriage contracts among the cattle-breeding Sebei in Uganda, the bridewealth follows the laws of the market.[6] Within a half century the number of cattle included in the bridewealth doubled. Bridewealths declined during the world economic depression at the end of the twenties. The large number of polygamous marriages drove the bridewealth of the Sebei high. The first wife of the son is paid and contracted by the father. The second wife is purchased by the son when he can barely afford it. This is why in the second wife he is looking for the lowest bridewealth contract that he can find. Frequently he takes a divorced woman whose reproductive value is reduced as a result of previous births. Bridewealths for third and fourth wives, on the other hand, are quite high, and only wealthy old men are able to afford additional wives.

The economic foundations of polygamy are wholly comparable to the purchase of labor in the capitalist system. The process of capital accumulation begins with the purchase of the first wife. The product of her labor—crops and children—belongs to the husband. The system also holds additional production incentives for the wife, similar to overtime or to the black market of an industrial society. The wife can reserve a piece of land for herself, a part of which she can use to feed her family, another portion to farm for the local market. Through this surplus work she obtains an income of her own to support herself and her children, for in African marriage systems separation of property prevails.

While slavery, which developed out of the exploitation and trade in prisoners of war, had an extremely varied but for the most part minor share in production within individual societies, it was recognized by the Marxists as an independent mode of production. Polygamous marriage is still not regarded as a mode of production.

On the other hand, Marx and Engels saw very clearly the economic significance of monogamy in European class society. The economy of Asia and Europe is characterized by the use of draft animals, plows, and irrigation systems. High population density, a shortage of land, and thus, in comparison to Africa, distinct caste and feudal structures with tenant farm systems and serfdom—all these factors necessitate more intensive labor in agriculture, which requires the continual investment of male labor in contrast to the seasonal African horticultural economy. This organization of labor gives rise to a different organization of the marriage markets.

In Europe, the dowry system developed from bilateral kinship, which recognized the inheritance claims of the daughters and widows, which, since the Childeric order of succession (in the sixth century), had also extended to land. The inheritance claim of the daughters was later transformed into a cash marriage settlement and movable goods as a dowry to her father-in-law. The dowry is also linked to the bride's virginity, monogamy, and usually also to the indissolubility of the marriage, dogma among the Indians, Chinese, and Europeans.[7] Divorces are sometimes possible, but only on the part of the husband.

Among European nobility the payment of the dowry to the father of the groom was associated with the preparation of a future widow's estate or an annuity to cover the living expenses of the bride in the event of widowhood. The ratio between this sum and the cash dowry constituted the negotiation between the families.[8]

In China the widow could occasionally remarry with the permission of her husband's family. However, her dowry always remained the possession of the husband's family. Through long epochs of Chinese and Indian history, widows were expected to commit suicide.

In African societies, with their intense demand for female labor, the self-extinction of the superfluous dinner guest was not required. The widow was adopted by the husband's brother or could return to her family.[9]

The payment of the dowry assured the accumulation of property in particular classes and castes.

Bride purchases for the lower castes in India and the poor country population also existed. The parents of a poor peasant family required the payment of a bridewealth for their daughter because the women in these families had to perform the heavy field work.

In class societies monogamy fulfilled a different purpose than in the bilateral social systems of the hunters and gatherers. In regions already densely populated, it served to limit the number of legitimate heirs, minimizing the dispersal of land ownership. The equally legitimate inheritance claim of the daughters was transformed by the payment of the dowry into an instrument of patriarchal interests, which could help the family of the bride acquire considerable advantages. Typical in India was the concept of hypergamy, which, in a society strictly divided into rank and caste, made possible a certain social mobility against economic obligations. Those husbands sought were influential members of a higher subcaste who would bring the bride's family protection, political refuge, and increased status. The daughters were not allowed to marry men from a lower subcaste. Thus, the marriage market grew increasingly small the higher the caste. In the high castes of northern India, this led to the slaughtering of daughters; because the fathers could accept brides from lower subcastes for their sons, but could give their own daughter only to a bridegroom from the same or higher rank, the payment of the dowry would have ended in the financial ruin of the father.[10]

In European nobility, similar traits of hypergamy can be detected. The sons of the high aristocracy were more likely than daughters to marry a member of the low nobility and patrician families. Thus, the marriage market for daughters of the European upper class was also limited. Since the middle of the sixteenth century, the great demand for bridegrooms of suitable station drove dowries high. In a period of a hundred years they increased tenfold.[11]

V

While an effort is being made here to show how patriarchy is derived from the conditions of reproduction and the male desire for its control, the American anthropologists Marvin Harris and William T. Divale claimed that war is the primary cause of male supremacy.[12]

They trace the rise of the male domination complex from the population pressure of the gardeners who pursue a slash-and-burn economy in the tropical rain forest, a technique of cultivation which requires a great deal of territory.

The fertility of stationary women, according to Divale and Harris, is higher than that of nomadic gatherers, whose reproduction rate is reduced through late menarche and a long nursing period without substantial additional feeding.

War and simultaneous female infanticide, in the view of Divale and Harris, were "part of a particular human system of population control." The two authors convincingly state that in societies that intensify military activities, the most extreme shift in the sex ratio occurs in favor of boys. From this they draw the bold conclusion that "warfare perpetuated and reproduced itself because it was an effective method of maintaining the limitation on the bringing up of female children." They do not go into the causes leading to attacks and tribal feuds: "For our theory it is not absolutely necessary that the exact cause of the first outbreak of war in a given region be known. On the contrary, it will suffice to show why hordes and village societies tend to perpetuate and escalate war."

The two authors support their thesis—that war linked with female infanticide is an efficient method of population control—with the statistical calculation that a population with a life expectancy of forty-seven will remain stationary if a third of all newborn girls do not reach reproductive age and if each grown woman has on the average three healthy children.

Divale and Harris generalize war as the cause for the development and perpetuation of male domination and sexism in all societies. But even the classical examples of ethnography for societies dominated by women conflict with this generalization. The Iroquois, the ancient Spartans, and the warrior caste of the Nairs in southern India show that, under certain conditions, women in warring societies have economic and sexual rights that they otherwise would not have. Similar instances occurred during the world wars, when many women assumed positions in the economy that had not previously been open to them. Thus, only under certain ecological conditions and in numerically small groups is war a suitable adjustment mechanism for the prevention of overpopulation. In regions that permitted a greater population density, epidemics and hunger caused greater population losses than wars, as European history demonstrates.

Despite the ideologies promoting population growth, which accompanied the formation of states, population-regulating mechanisms were built into all patriarchal systems. The ruling classes claimed a large share of the food production. Wet nurses had usually to abandon their own children to start their profession. By this means a limit was set on the reproduction prospects of the underclasses.

The Chinese government never gave up its fertility demands: indeed, taxes were raised somewhat for unmarried daughters, although in the lower classes the ever-recurring crop failures usually led to famine and to drowning of the newborn children, especially girls.[13] Moreover, the growth rate was tempered by a high mortality rate of both mother and child, due to the frequency of pregnancy. Analysis of medieval records indicates that most men died between the ages of forty and sixty, but most women died between the ages of twenty and forty.[14]

Even now the connection between reproduction and class confrontations and strategies of class struggle has been investigated very little. A propertied class can retain its ruling position over generations only if its reproductive behavior differs from that of the oppressed. The number of members of a ruling class must be kept smaller than that of those ruled, or they jeopardize their position. On the other hand, they cannot number so few that they are unable to occupy certain key economic or military positions. There are many examples of these mechanisms at work. In ancient Rome the legislation on population policy referred almost exclusively to the generative conduct of the upper class, which produced too few children to be able to fill the key positions in the government machinery. Rich Romans had no individual interest in a large number of children but were satisfied to produce few heirs.

In Greece the daughter of a female slave had a greater chance of staying alive than the daughter of a free woman, because household labor was in demand whereas the daughter of the free woman necessitated a dowry.[15]

Monogamy in China did not exclude concubinage and sexual intercourse with female slaves. The number of legitimate heirs of government officials remained small, for the children of the concubines and slave women were not on an equal footing.

Nuns in Europe were recruited almost exclusively from the European nobility. Sons from aristocratic families who entered the clergy reproduced secretly, but their offspring were no more likely to be introduced into the propertied class than were other illegitimate descendants of the aristocracy or of rich bourgeois families.

Generally it was possible only for the oldest son of European nobility to make a marriage agreement, while the other sons were indeed supported in accord with their station, but generally this did not permit them to marry or produce legitimate children. Between 1500 and 1700, 41 percent of the men of the European high nobility remained unmarried; in the nineteenth century at least 31 percent were still not married.[16] The unregistered illegitimate offspring of these groups of noble bachelors increased the population figure of the less privileged classes.

While out-of-wedlock children of the nobility were condemned to the (usually low) socioeconomic status of the mothers, the lords of the manor, when it suited their own interests, made no distinction between maternal or paternal descent. In the late Middle Ages many children from mixed marriages between serfs and free men were subjected to serfdom. This regulation was one of the grievances leading to the German peasant wars.[17]

Under the pressure of rising dowries and the coercion to celibacy for non-inheriting sons, the European nobility was the first class to use birth control. Though before 1700 some indications of birth control are identifiable, the low birth rate among the European nobility after 1700 can be explained only in terms of contraceptive methods or abortion. The mortality rate during childbirth decreased considerably after 1700 as a result of the small number of births per woman.[18] At the same time, fewer births brought a dwindling child-mortality rate, because the better condition of the mother's health had a positive effect on the prenatal development of the child.

By the eighteenth century the women of the French aristocracy had attained the low reproduction rate of the twentieth century, but were able to practice birth control only because men had a strong interest in the reduction of the birth rate.[19]

In the unpropertied classes a similar situation developed in the second half of the nineteenth century. With the first social welfare laws, the prohibition of child labor, and the general introduction of compulsory schooling, the short- and long-range economic interest of the proletarians in a large number of offspring dwindled. Because children no longer represented immediate old-age care for the parents or contributed to income until a much later age, they became a luxury for the unpropertied classes. The simultaneous emancipation of the church, further advanced in the industrial proletariat than in the rural districts, supported the reduction of births.

Socialist theory and Karl Marx in particular understood population movements only as a reflection of the capitalistic economic laws. Marx's thesis was that the accumulation of capital must lead to the increase of the proletariat. Every decrease in the demand for labor as a result of technical progress creates at least temporarily a surplus of workers. That is, by affecting the progressive accumulation of capital through their labor, the working population makes itself superfluous. "This is one of the most peculiar population laws of the capitalistic mode of production." The development of the reserve army and the pauperization of the proletariat are the result of this development.

While Marx viewed the economic process dynamically—as his precise observations of the annihilation of the work place and capitalism's coercion to innovation show—he regarded the natural population movements (increase or decline in birth, mortality) as static. For him increase meant the increase of those who possess no means of production and whose number augments not through too many births but through the concentration movements of capital.

In his book *Woman under Socialism,* August Bebel attacked the use of contraceptives. In the socialist society of the future "unnatural preventive intercourse" would no longer exist. The perspective of the party is illuminated by a rule that originated with Wilhelm Liebknecht: the Social Democratic Party press would accept no advertising that recommended contraceptives.

In 1913, when some socialists discussed the theme "Birth Limitation—A Revolutionary Weapon" and helped popularize the slogan "Birth strike," the leading party representatives balked at this kind of demand. Klara Zetkin said in a meeting that by reducing the number of births "the number of revolutionaries is also reduced . . . The Proletariat must take care to have as many fighters as possible."

Both Rosa Luxemburg, a party leftist, and Eduard Bernstein, an accused revisionist, protested strongly against birth limitation. Rosa Luxemburg: "The social question can never be solved through self-help but only through mass help. Child limitation must be resolutely refused as a means of struggle for the proletariat."

This point of view was assumed by the leading socialists and in time was also retained when the proletariat had already switched to birth limitation.

During the end of the nineteenth century in the working-class districts of the large European cities, despite a slow decline in the number of births, still far more children came into the world than in the quarters of the rich. At the end of the twenties, however, the number of births in the working-class districts was already under the average of the population. In some German industrial cities, the number of abortions was larger than the number of births. The statistics of the health-insurance program also show more abortions than births among women factory workers.

It is only a half truth when historians create the impression that the proletarians gradually improved their situation solely by means of their organized struggle for bourgeois equality and social justice. A portion of this class struggle has taken place in bed and in the back rooms of abortionists, and women were the instruments and also the casualties of these class confrontations. Only by this conduct, which was criminalized through the legislation of the industrial states, have they managed to ward off in the industrial states the total impoverishment that Karl Marx prophesied. Millions of abortions per year have supported the trend to welfare development and first made possible the formation of the middle class, of which these countries today are so proud.

Toward the end of the nineteenth century, when the birth rate of the underclasses first went down, governments in the United States and in Europe reacted by bringing the sanction of criminal law against the unchecked distribution of contraceptives and against abortion.[20]

In the United States around 1870, the advertising, mailing, and

selling—in Connecticut even the use—of contraceptives were subjected to strict regulations or prohibited by Congress. The Supreme
Court did not declare these laws unconstitutional until 1965 and 1972.
In almost every European country, laws were passed against the distribution of contraceptives. Sweden, which had repealed such a law in
1910, became the first country to produce new regulations on sex education and the sale of contraceptives.

In England, before the First World War, life imprisonment was set
as the penalty for pregnant women who attempted abortions; moreover, the mere procurement of abortion materials was penalized by
three years in prison. In Ireland the import of contraceptives had been
a punishable offense from 1935, repealed only in 1973 by the Constitutional Court.

On July 31, 1920, France, where the demographic revolution was
furthest advanced and which has lived in anxiety of the greater fertility of the Germans since the war of 1870–71, passed a law that prohibited the description, distribution, and volunteering of contraceptives
other than condoms.

The French government's family policy and the population policy
of French industrialists, which originated even before the First World
War, were reactions to the trend toward two- or one-child families.
Birth bonuses for the third child, nursing benefits, bonuses for caring
for aged parents, loans at favorable interest rates, relief in the military
service, a cut in inheritance and local taxes—a full catalogue of com-
pensatory measures—were developed by the lawmakers for families
with many children. By 1920, French industrialists had fifty-six family
adjustment funds which granted aid to large families. Individual industries (Michelin, for example) whose enterprises were located in
areas with low birth rates became known for their policies promoting
births.[21] Even the League of Nations, in the twenties, condemned any
use of birth control as a "social menace."[22]

The expansion of political power by the establishment of demographic goals was the basis of Fascist policies in Italy and Germany.
Yet it was not the National Socialists who first placed population policies in the central focus of power politics. The National Socialist goals
emerged from the views of a wide-ranging intellectual current. Euge-
nists, race hygienists, social Darwinists, and population statisticians
since the end of the nineteenth century in all European countries
encouraged the measures that National Socialism put into action.

Women were judged by this movement according to whether they
were enthusiastic enough child bearers to halt the menace of race
death.

The population policy of the Fascists was supposed to be a "psychic policy" to rouse "the will for the child." "Thus, the question of
birth is a question of will. Decline in births is a weakness in will in
the people's biology," wrote director of the German National Statistics
Bureau Friedrich Burgdörfer. Leading National Socialists demanded

a "breeder's attitude." Information on contraception was prohibited; the number of indictments resulting from abortions increased. The penalty for abortion increased, to five years in the penitentiary (in 1933) and penitentiary or capital punishment (in 1943). In Fascist Italy both the advertisement of contraceptives and their sale without a doctor's prescription were punishable. Not until 1971 did the Italian constitutional court repeal these laws.

The Fascist population experiment and the population development of industrial societies after 1945 make it clear that reproduction can be controlled, to some extent, but that the falling tendency of the birth rate could not be reversed by government action. In 1975 the Federal Republic had the lowest birth rate in German history and the lowest in the world, followed by the German Democratic Republic.

VI

The reconstruction of patriarchal socialization undertaken here can only be fragmentary. Even now feminist theory is in its infancy. It is certainly posing the right questions today, but still finds itself in an information vacuum on the connections between the development of sex roles, ideology, demographic growth, division of labor, etc., in the majority of societies, of both literate and nonliterate cultures.

The individual man no longer gains economic power or advantage from a large family. This is why he is no longer a reliable ally of the state, as he was in the days when paternal authority and economic power coincided. Appeals to nationalism or a large population from an emperor or Fascist leader remain relatively ineffective in industrial societies. No one has children out of patriotism.

The patriarchal control of the marriage markets in industrial societies has lessened. The old playing rules of class endogamy have by no means gone out of effect, but they will no longer be regulated by class laws and the granting of marriage permits by the state. To a great extent, freedom of choice exists for marriage partners.

In the twentieth century for the first time in the history of the patriarchal judicial system, the mother, in most divorce cases, is allowed to keep her child. Custody of the children represents no immediate use to the father—if anything, the child is an impairment of his economic status. Thus, the man's interest in reproduction is confined to its function of giving meaning to his life and satisfying his emotional needs. Despite this removal of paternal interests, men do have a material interest in the product of the woman's child-rearing but it lies in the future. A mother who is not gainfully employed and who raises two children works indirectly for her husband's old-age care because the pension systems of the majority of industrial countries define interest and pension claims in terms of the gainfully employed husband, regarded as the breadwinner of the family.

The connection between reproduction and geriatric care rarely exists within the family, but is now regulated through the process of anonymous payments to pension funds, life insurance, etc. In West Germany, for example, the payment of pensions since the collapse of old age insurance after the First World War was characterized by a kind of contract between generations. The gainfully employed population pays for the pensions of those who are retired. But in principle the same thing holds true for other social security systems. The legal pension can then be paid only if the contributions of additional new paying members does not fall below the amount that has to be paid out.

Only since the dwindling population trend have the results of this development been recognized. The jeopardizing of pension funds, cutbacks of schools and educational capabilities, unprofitability of services of all kinds, accelerated urbanization as a result of the thinning out of the population, plus national suicide—these are the catchwords typical of the talk from government.

Since 1968 the feminist movement in many Western countries has fought successfully for abortion. In most countries which permit abortion, not only on medical grounds, the woman makes the decision. In West Germany, though, this was declared unconstitutional on February 25, 1975. Despite the international success that the women's movement has been able to achieve, it must not delude itself into believing with any assurance that rights won with such difficulty will be long-lasting.

Countries which, unlike the Western ones, are dependent on the full depletion of female and male labor, offer a cautionary example for the reduction of female self-determination.

The Soviet Union has already changed its stand on the abortion question twice since 1918. Of the other states of the Eastern bloc five countries today are aiming for a higher birth rate. Prices for contraceptives in one or two countries are obviously related to this objective. Moreover, in 1966 abortion was prohibited in Rumania by a decree that stated that abortion prevented "the natural increase of the population." Titles, orders, and medals are given to mothers of large families in both Rumania and Bulgaria. The same methods applied in the twenties and thirties in countries with shrinking population are tried today. Above all, the economic planners in all industrialized countries plead for higher fertility because they fear a labor shortage, an unfavorable change in the age structure of the employed, a reduction in the consuming of goods and services and in the number of young men recruitable as soldiers.

Both the decline in births in capitalist and socialist industrial countries and the population explosion in developing countries demonstrate the bankruptcy of patriarchal reproduction policies.

Actually, the world economic order depends on the fact that women execute a substantial portion of their labor—namely, the totality of the caretaking and services that they must perform to produce the next generation—in exchange for support by the husband or for nothing.

Although a comprehensive feminist model for overcoming patriarchal socialization can be developed only out of political praxis, some points will be argued here that result immediately from the preceding analysis.

The struggles to end discrimination in professions, for equal pay, for educational opportunities, and for abolition of double standard in the labor market remain short-range strategy if women don't recognize the fact that the responsibilities of reproduction directly reduce their chances for equality in the labor market.

That women draw no income for their labor within the home determines, in part, the exchange value of female labor power in the labor market. Unequal pay is a direct result of the unpaid reproductive services of all women, regardless of whether they perform child raising and housework exclusively or whether they care for children in addition to their professional work.

Their potential capability for reproduction even determines their schooling and choice of profession. Their possible pregnancies govern their employment and chances for promotion. If a woman is already a mother, her possibilities for further professional training, compared to those of men, are seriously limited.

The maternity protection laws, which are celebrated as marks of social progress in capitalist and socialist industrial countries, indicate a grotesquely deficient evaluation of the actual economic use which management and government derive from reproduction. The paid exemption to a woman before and after the birth for the protection of her health is turned into an act of charity.

Birth strike is the most important weapon in women's struggle, but it must be accompanied by a feminist mass strategy, because a declining birth rate also contains risks. Childlessness, as an individual female strategy against patriarchy, would merely lead to the formation of a new elite and a two-class system among women similar to that which existed between some educated cloister inmates of the Middle Ages and the wives confined to childbed. Because many female careers are in the service sector, school and university system, and health care, it is precisely these professional groups that will be most rapidly affected when women bear no more children.

Sexual denial, homosexual relations, childbearing strikes, or the refusal of other female services are already political issues in some industrial countries today. If large feminist organizations can successfully be formed that will be able to coordinate the varieties of refusal and generate focused strikes in women's services and consumption, this will result, for the first time, in opportunities to carry out a social transformation.

Early socialist theory called for the complete socialization of child raising. It is indicative that there is to date no successful public experience of this form of child raising, for even in the Israeli kibbutzim and in China the raising of small children is regarded as a woman's job. Indeed, the practice of public child raising is often contradictory insofar as it transfers the norms that prevail in the production of goods—that is, time saving, rational economies, and functionality—to the care of children.[23] In child-care centers, the ratio of adults to children must be at least 1 to 6. Such an ideal relationship would be so expensive that even socialist experiments would revert to the unpaid child-rearing services of the mothers.

Socialization must demand the full participation of males in all educational, caretaking, and household services necessary for the upbringing and development of the next generation. Any payment for housework and child raising that would commit all women unilaterally to these services must be rejected on principle and could therefore be accepted only in a transitional period and for isolated cases.

All adults who furnish reproductive services—fathers, mothers, or others—must receive direct economic compensation for these expenditures of labor. All government measures promoting such institutions as marriage and family through financial subsidies must be challenged because they reinforce the economic foundations of patriarchy. Family policy programs that try to pay off mothers with charity and welfare types of financial concessions, and working hours off, consolidate the dependency structures of marriage and family instead of liberating the interaction of the sexes from its quality of power and violence.

A radical struggle against the economic foundations of patriarchy is possible only on an international level because, with the complex tangle of the world economy and the growing role of concerns operating multinationally, any attempt to institute drastic redistribution actions in a single country would be bound to fail. In addition, international agreements on reproduction rates would be necessary in order to restrict a baby race between rival neighboring countries, tribes, or competing ethnic groups and members of different religious denominations. It is obvious today that some countries are conducting a policy of biological armament at the expense of women's health that resembles the big power population policy goals of the National Socialists in Germany and Italy.

Every reproduction decision must be based on the free will of the woman concerned. This basic human right of female self-determination should never be renounced in favor of any social authority—be it a democracy, dictatorship, or future Communist utopia. Friedrich Engels, who believed in progress, wrote: "If, however, the communist society ever considered it necessary to also regulate the production of human beings, as they have already regulated the production of things, then it would be precisely they and they alone who would execute this without difficulty." The same optimism and trust in progress is shown by Shulamith Firestone: "Childbearing could be taken over by technology."

A demand like this fosters the belief that the solution of social problems is to come through new technologies. Technology has never solved social problems but only created new ones. While the fulfillment of history that Marx imagined consisted in the perfection of the instruments of production and the resulting freedom from manual and monotonous labor, a tendency to biological perfectionism is already clearly visible today. One need not have Orwellian visions of manipulating human genetic information to predict that new findings in reproduction biology will affect the relationships between the sexes and could perhaps change these relationships drastically to the disadvantage of women.

The difficulty in depriving patriarchal world imagery of its power is apparent in the unsuccessful feminist efforts to create a synthesis between the utopian aspects of Marxism and psychoanalysis. Instead of scrutinizing or deepening the critical rational approach of Marxism, various feminist authors extend Marxism's eschatological vision of freedom by simultaneously suspending the incest taboo.

The concept of cancellation or nullification which Hegel speaks of, embodying the destruction of difference, has a heady attraction, for it is the dogma of myth. It suggests a final goal for history and represents the boundless hope of freedom. Yet, if in the next decades feminism intends to acquire political force, it must renounce this concept of finality. The equitable redistribution of society's wealth and the control of power are goals that can be realized in the long run. But the destruction of difference between the sexes and generations, as envisioned by those who claim that artificial reproduction and the end of the incest taboo promise freedom, originates from a teleological perception of the world that is founded in a lack of contradiction in life, attainable only in death.

Notes

I

1. This as well as following quotations from Katia Mann are taken from her life reminiscences: Katia Mann, *Unwritten Memories*. (New York: Alfred A. Knopf, 1975).

2. Hedwig Dohm, *Die Antifeministen* (Berlin: 1902); cf. *Die Frauenkalender,* nos. 75 and 76 (Berlin, self-published).

3. Emile Durkheim, *The Division of Labor in Society* (Glencoe, Ill.: Free Press, 1949).

4. Dohm, "Die wissenschaftliche Emanzipation der Frau" (Berlin: 1874). Dohm, "Der Frauen Natur und Recht" (Berlin: 1876).

5. Quoted by Adele Schreiber in "Hedwig Dohm als Vorkämpferin und Vordenkerin neuer Frauenideale" (Berlin: 1914). Adele Schreiber belonged to the Left wing of the bourgeois women's movement and was later a Reichstag delegate of the Social Democratic Party in the Weimar Republic.

6. *Frauen-Anwalt,* quoted by Margit Twellmann, *Die deutsche Frauenbewegung, Ihre Anfänge und erste Entwicklung, Quellen 1843–1889* (Meisenheim: 1972).

7. Erfurt Platform of 1891, point 1, quoted in *Programme der deutschen Sozialdemokratie* (Hannover: 1963).

8. Schreiber, op. cit. The preceding quotations are from Dohm's essays "Der Frauen Natur und Recht" and "Die wissenschaftliche Emanzipation der Frau."

9. Dohm, *Die Antifeministen.*

10. Dohm, "Der Frauen Natur und Recht."

11. Peter de Mendelsohn, *Der Zauberer* (Frankfurt: 1975).

12. Dohm's "Der Jesuitismus im Hausstand," quoted in Twellmann, op. cit.

13. Quoted by Schreiber, op. cit.

14. A. Hofmann, ed., *Der Kladderadatsch und seine Leute 1848–1898* (Berlin: 1898).

15. Dohm, "Der Frauen Natur und Recht."

16. Ibid.

17. Dohm, *Die Antifeministen.*

18. Schreiber, op. cit.

19. Dohm, "Die Mütter" (Berlin: 1903).

20. Katherine Anthony, *Feminism in Germany and Scandinavia* (New York: Russell, 1977), p. 220.

2

1. Jakob Burkhardt, *Weltgeschichtliche Betrachtungen* (Krefeld: 1948).

2. Golo Mann, *Deutsche Geschichte des 19. Jahrhunderts* (Frankfurt am Main: 1958); *The History of Germany Since 1789,* trans. Marian Jackson (New York: Praeger, 1968).

3. Ibid.

4. Ibid.

5. Golo Mann, *Deutsche Geschichte des 20. Jahrhunderts* (Frankfurt am Main: 1958).

6. Hans Ebeling, *Die Reise in die Vergangenheit,* vol. 4 (1972).

7. *Die Frau im 19. Jahrhundert* (Berlin: 1898).

8. Hannah Arendt, *Rahel Varnhagen: The Life of a Jewish Woman* (New York: Harcourt Brace Jovanovich, 1974).

9. Quoted by Irmgard Tanneberger, *Die Frauen der Romantik und das soziale Problem* (Oldenburg: 1928).

10. Gottfried Salomon-Delatour, ed., *Die Lehre Saint-Simons* (Neuwied: 1962).

11. Johann Gottfried Herder, *Ideen zur Philosophie der Geschichte der Menschheit (Reflections on the Philosophy of the History of Mankind),* vol. 1, Univ. of Chicago Press, 1968, p. 66.

12. J. G. Fichte, *Gesamtausg der Bayerischen Akademie der Wissenschaften,* vol. 1, pt. 4 (Stuttgart: 1970).

13. *Collected Works,* vol. 1, pt. 4.

14. Franz Mehring, *Karl Marx* (Berlin: 1967).

15. Quoted by Margit Twellmann, *Die deutsche Frauenbewegung, Ihre Anfänge und erste Entwicklung, Quellen 1843–1889* (Meisenheim: 1972).

16. Cauer, op. cit.

17. *Geschichte der deutschen Frauenbewegung*, eds., Emmy Beckmann and Elisabeth Kardel (Frankfurt: 1955).

18. Renate Möhrmann, *Die andere Frau, Emanzipationsansätze deutscher Schriftstellerinnen im Vorfeld der 48er Revolution*, unpublished dissertation (1975).

19. Cauer, op. cit.

20. *Die deutschen Frauen und der Bismarckkultus* (Leipzig: 1894).

21. Quoted by von Streitberg, op. cit.

22. *Deutsche Geschichte des 19. Jahrhunderts.*

23. Von Streitberg, op. cit. Johanna Loewenherz, "Wird die Sozialdemokratie den Frauen Wort halten?" (Neuwied: 1895), p. 7.

24. *Untergang des Römischen Reiches Deutscher Nation.* Gutenberg Book Guild ed. (Frankfurt: n.d.).

25. Quoted by Bodo Von Borries, "Frauen in Schulgeschichtsbüchern—zum Problem der Benachteilung von Mädchen im Unterricht," *Westermanns Pädagogische Beiträge*, no. 11, 1975.

26. Quoted by Renate Möhrmann, op. cit.

27. "Women in U.S. History High School Textbooks," *Social Education*, vol. 35 (March 1971).

28. Mentioned by Aileen S. Kraditor, *Up from the Pedestal: Selected Writings in the History of American Feminism* (New York: Quadrangle Books, 1968).

29. *The Rise of the City: 1878–1898* (New York: Macmillan, 1933), p. 434.

30. Ibid., p. 156.

31. (New York: Macmillan, 1927), pp. 377–378.

32. Kraditor, op. cit.

33. Trecker, op. cit.

34. Ibid.

35. *Histoire de France contemporaine*, 10 vols. (Paris, 1920–22).

36. (New York: Octagon, 1974), p. 119.

37. Ibid., p. 225.

38. *Material Progress and World-wide Problems, 1870–1898*, F. H. Hinsley, ed. (1962), pp. 197 ff. (Cambridge, Eng.: Cambridge University Press, 1962).

39. *War and Peace in an Age of Upheaval: 1793–1830*, chapter 4, "Revolutionary Influences and Conservatism in Literature and Thought" (Cambridge, Eng.: Cambridge University Press, no date), pp. 96 ff. and 115.

40. Vol. 2, p. 17.

41. *Römische Geschichte*, Vol. 1 (Munich: 1976).

42. Ibid., vol. 2.

43. *Manual of Political Economy* (Kelley, 1969).

44. *The Course of World History*, vol. 2 (Munich: 1970), pp. 186 ff.

45. "On the Influence of the Woman on History" (1956), p. 24.

46. Quoted by Cauer, *Die Frau im 19. Jahrhundert* (Berlin: 1898).

47. Ibid.

48. *Gedanken und Erinnerungen* (1927).

49. Adolf Hitler, *Mein Kampf* (New York: Houghton Mifflin, 1971), pp. 14–15.

3

1. Léopold Sédar Senghor, "Prayer to Masks" and other poems in Gerald Moore and Ulli Beier: *Modern Poetry from Africa* (Penguin, 1963).

2. Herder, op. cit.

3. Jakob Grimm, *Teutonic Mythology* (Peter Smith, Massachussetts, n.d.).

4. Reinhold Bruder, *Die germanische Frau im Lichte der Runeninschriften und der antiken Historiographie* (De Gruyter, 1974).

5. Ibid.
6. Ibid.
7. *Die Familie* (Stuttgart: 1882).
8. Otto von Bismarck quoted by Gisela von Streitberg, *Die deutschen Frauen und der Bismarckkultus* (Leipzig: 1894).
9. Op. cit.
10. Op. cit.
11. Quoted by Lily Braun, *Memoiren einer Sozialistin* (Munich: 1922).
12. Bruder, op. cit.
13. "Frauenlandsturm," in *Frauenkapital,* no. 33 (1914).
14. Ibid., no. 32.
15. Op. cit.
16. Eduard Bernstein, ed., *Dokumente des Sozialismus,* vol. 5 (Berlin, 1905).
17. *Die Polarität im Aufbau des Charakters. System der konkreten Charakterkunde* (Bern and Munich: 1966).
18. *Gesammelte Schriften,* vol. 3 (Berlin: 1918).
19. *Die Frauen und der Krieg* (Leipzig: 1915).
20. *Aus Leben und Wissenschaft* (Stuttgart: 1896).
21. Günther Stökl, *Russische Geschichte* (Stuttgart: 1965).
22. Op. cit.
23. Eduard Pelz on the women in the U.S. in *Frauen-Anwalt,* vol. 6, no. 5 (1875–76), quoted by Twellmann, op. cit.
24. E. F. W. Eberhard, *Feminismus und Kulturuntergang,* 2nd ed. (Vienna and Leipzig: n.d.).
25. Quoted by Alfred Kind, *Die Weiberherrschaft in der Geschichte der Menschheit* (Vienna and Leipzig: n.d.).
26. Ibid.
27. Quoted by Joachim C. Fest in *The Face of the Third Reich,* trans. Michael Bullock (New York: Pantheon, 1970).

4

1. *The Origin of the Family, Private Property, and the State* (New York: International Publishers, 1942), pp. 46–47.
2. Quotations in Mathilde Vaerting, *Die weibliche Eigenart im Männerstaat und die männliche Eigenart im Frauenstaat* (Karlsruhe: 1921).
3. Manfred Schroeter, ed., *Der Mythos vom Orient und Occident, Aus den Werken von J. J. Bachofen* (Munich: 1926).
4. Ibid.
5. Karl Meuli, ed., *Johann Jakob Bachofen's gesammelte Werke,* 2 vols. (Basel: 1948).
6. Schroeter, op. cit.
7. Ibid.
8. Ibid.
9. Meuli, op. cit.
10. Schroeter, op. cit.
11. J. J. Bachofen, *Myth, Religion, and Mother Right,* trans. Ralph Manheim (Princeton: Princeton University Press, 1967), p. 151.
12. Schroeter, op. cit.
13. Bachofen, op. cit.
14. Ibid., pp. 152–53.
15. Schroeter, op. cit.
16. Ibid.
17. Bachofen, op. cit., p. 130.
18. Ibid.
19. Meuli, op. cit.
20. Ibid.
21. Ibid.

22. Schroeter, op. cit.
23. Ibid.
24. Meuli, op. cit.
25. Op. cit., p. 12.
26. Ibid.
27. Ibid., p. 10.

5

1. *Briefe an Freunde* (Altona: 1810).
2. Ibid.
3. Elizabeth Gould Davis: *The First Sex* (Penguin, 1972); Evelyn Reed: *Woman's Evolution: From Matriarchal Clan to Patriarchal Family* (New York: Pathfinder Press, 1975).
4. Quoted by Abram Kardiner and Edward Preble: *Wegbereiter der modernen Anthropologie* (Frankfurt: 1974).
5. Quoted by *Die Frau* (1905–06).
6. Cf. E. E. Evans-Pritchard, *Social Anthropology* (London: 1951); W. Schmidt, "Entstehung der Verwandtschaftssysteme und Heiratsregelungen," *Anthropos,* vol. 47 (1952); Franz Boas, *Das Geschöpf des sechsten Tages* (Berlin: 1955).
7. (New York: Henry Holt & Co., 1907).
8. Ibid.
9. Ibid.
10. G. Guhr, "Ur- und Frühgeschichte und ökonomische Gesellschaftsformationen," *Ethnographische-Archäologische Zeitschrift,* vol. 10 (Berlin, 1969).
11. S. A. Tokarev, "50 Jahre sowjetische Ethnographie," *Ethnographische-Archäologische Zeitschrift,* vol. 10 (Berlin, 1969).
12. Franz Boas, op. cit.
13. Ibid.
14. Karl Marx, *Capital,* vol. 1 (New York: International Publishing Co., 1967).
15. Cf. F. G. G. Rose, "Die Familie und die Periodisierung der Urgeschichte," *Ethnographische-Archäologische Zeitschrift,* vol. 9 (Berlin, 1968).
16. Ibid.
17. *The History of Human Marriage* (London: Macmillan, 1891).
18. Rose, op. cit.
19. Quoted by Rose, op. cit.
20. "Über die Periodisierung der Urgeschichte," *Ethnographische-Archäologische Zeitschrift,* vol. 8 (Berlin, 1967).
21. Rudolf Feustel, "Die Ur- und Frühgeschichte und das Problem der historischen Periodisierung," *Ethnographische-Archäologische Zeitschrift,* vol. 9 (Berlin, 1968).
22. Ibid.
23. *Die Stellung der Pygmäenvölker in der Entwicklungsgeschichte der Menschen* (Stuttgart: 1910).
24. 5th ed. (New York: Liveright, 1970), p. 62. 1st ed., 1924.
25. Ibid., p. 78.
26. *Social Structure* (New York: Free Press, 1965), pp. 24 ff.

6

1. *Social Evolution* (Peter Smith, n.d.), pp. 64–5.
2. *Male and Female: A Study of the Sexes in a Changing World* (New York: Greenwood, 1977).
3. Childe, op. cit., p. 89.
4. "Mutterrechtliche Züge im Neolithikum," *Anthropos* (1963–64, 1968–69).
5. Ibid.
6. (New York: Alfred A. Knopf, 1962), pp. 112–13.
7. *Das Patriarchat* (Frankfurt: 1975).

8. Ibid.

9. *Woman's Evolution: From Matriarchal Clan to Patriarchal Family* (New York: Path Press, 1975).

10. (New York: Atheneum, 1977).

11. Reed, op. cit., p. 73.

12. *The Imperial Animal* (New York: Dell, 1972).

13. Karl J. Narr, ed., *Ancient History*, vol. 1.

14. Hermann Helmuth, "Kannibalismus in Paläanthropologie und Ethnologie," *Ethnographishe-Archäologische Zeitschrift*, vol. 9 (Berlin, 1968).

15. George Peter Murdock, op. cit., p. 188.

16. Ibid., p. 190.

17. Erika Bourgignon and Lenora S. Greenbaum, *Diversity and Homogeneity in World Societies* (New Haven: HRAF Press, 1973), p. 54.

18. Mentioned by Claude Lévi-Strauss, *Elementary Structures of Kinship* (Beacon Press, 1969).

19. See Erhard Schlesier, *Die Grundlagen der Clan-Bildung* (Göttingen: 1956).

20. *Das Mutterrecht* (Vienna-Mödling: 1955).

21. Ibid.

22. Murdock, op. cit.

23. Bourgignon, Greenbaum, op. cit., p. 53.

24. Ibid., pp. 82 ff.

25. Op. cit., pp. 218 ff.

26. See A. Köhler, "Verfassung, soziale Gliederung, Recht und Wirtschaft der Tuareg" (1904).

27. "The Conditions Favoring Matrilocal versus Patrilocal Residence," *American Anthropologist*, vol. 73 (1971), pp. 571–94.

28. Christian Sigrist, "Regulierte Anarchie" (Olten and Freiburg im Breisgau: 1967); also, T. O. Beidelman, "The Matrilineal People of Eastern Tanzania" (London: 1967).

29. "Vaterrecht und Mutterrecht in Afrika," quoted by Schmidt, op. cit., p. 64.

30. Denise Paulme, ed., *Women of Tropical Africa* (Berkeley, Calif.: University of California Press, 1963).

31. Ibid.; see also Adam Kuper, "The Social Structure of the Sotho-Speaking Peoples of Southern Africa," *Africa*, vol. 45, no. 2 (1975), pp. 139–49.

7

1. A. P. Elkin, *The Australian Aborigines* (New York: Longmans, 1961).

2. See Paul Schebesta, *Die Negrito Asiens* (Vienna-Mödling: 1954), and Martin Gusinde, *Die Twiden, Pygmäen und Pygmoide im tropischen Afrika* (Vienna-Stuttgart: 1956).

3. A. A. Abbie, *The Original Australians* (London: 1969), p. 69.

4. "Women and Their Life in Central Australia," *Journal of the Royal Anthropological Institute*, vol. 63 (1933), p. 208.

5. For example, Martin Gusinde, *Urmenschen im Feuerland, vom Forscher zum Stammesmitglied* (1946).

6. Elkin, op. cit., pp. 142 ff.

7. Op. cit., p. 240.

8. Ibid.

9. Ronald M. Berndt and Catherine H. Berndt, "Sexual Behavior in Western Arnhem Land" (New York: Johnson Reprint, 1951), p. 155.

10. Ibid.

11. Op. cit., p. 162.

12. Ibid.

13. Ibid.

14. Róheim, *Psychoanalysis and Anthropology* (New York: International Universities Press, 1968), p. 91.

15. *Aboriginal Woman, Sacred and Profane* (London: 1939). Gordon Press, no date.

16. Op. cit., p. 52.
17. Ibid., p. 52.
18. Ibid., p. 53.
19. Op. cit.
20. "The Position of Women in Primitive Societies and in Our Own," Fawcett Lecture, October 25, 1955, Bedford College, University of London.
21. "Functions and Limitations of Alaskan Eskimo Wife Trading," *Arctic,* vol. 23 (1970), pp. 26 ff.
22. Ibid., pp. 28 ff.
23. Ibid., pp. 30 ff.
24. Kate Millett, *Sexual Politics* (New York: Doubleday, 1970); Shulamith Firestone, *The Dialectic of Sex* (New York: Morrow, 1974).
25. Morton H. Fried, *The Evolution of Political Society: An Evolutionary View* (New York: Random House, 1968), pp. 76 ff.
26. (New York: Beacon Press, 1969).
27. Ibid.
28. Ibid.
29. Ibid.
30. Vol. 2 (Johnson Reprint, n.d.), p. 288.
31. *Das Mutterrecht* (Vienna-Mödling: 1955).
32. Westermarck, op. cit.
33. Ibid.

8

1. Jomo Kenyatta, *Facing Mount Kenya* (New York: Vintage, 1962).
2. *Schöpfung und Urzeit des Menschen im Mythos der afrikanischen Völker* (Berlin: 1936).
3. *Urmenschen im Feuerland, vom Forscher zum Stammesmitglied* (Berlin: 1946).
4. "The Myth of Matriarchy: Why Men Rule in Primitive Society." In Michelle Zimbalist Rosaldo and Louise Lamphere, eds., *Woman, Culture and Society* (Stanford, Calif.: Stanford University Press, 1974).
5. Ibid., p. 273.
6. Op. cit.
7. Berndt, op. cit.
8. Cf. Edmund Leach, Claude Lévi-Strauss (Munich: 1971); see also Georges Charbonnier, "Conversation with Lévi-Strauss," (New York: Viking Press, 1970); as well as E. Nelson Hayes and Tanya Hayes, eds., "Claude Lévi-Strauss: The Anthropologist as Hero" (Cambridge, Mass.: MIT Press, 1970).
9. Cf. Johann Georg Waich's *Philosophisches Lexikon* (Leipzig: 1775).
10. "Der Pabst über die Ehe," a collection of papal proclamations, Josef Müller, S. J., ed. (Innsbruck: 1958).
11. Op. cit.

9

1. Quoted by Olga Worobjowa and Irma Sinelnikowa, *Die Töchter von Marx* (Berlin: 1965), cf. also Fritz Raddatz, *Karl Marx: eine politische Biographie* (Hamburg: 1975).
2. Alice S. Rossi, ed., *The Feminist Papers: From Adams to Beauvoir* (New York: Bantam, 1974).
3. Quoted from *A Declaration of Sentiments.* Reprinted in *Up from the Pedestal: Selected Writings in the History of American Feminism,* edited and with an introduction by Aileen S. Kraditor (New York: Quadrangle Books, 1968), pp. 184–86.
4. See Juliette Lamber, *Idées Anti-Proudhoniennes sur l'amour, la femme & le marriage* (Paris: M. Levy Frères, 1868).
5. Raymond Lee Muncy, *Sex and Marriage in Utopian Communities: Nineteenth Century America* (Bloomington/London: Indiana University Press, 1973), p. 220.

6. Ibid., pp. 221 ff.

7. L. Ungers, *Kommunen in der neuen Welt* (Cologne, 1972).

8. Norman E. Himes, *Medical History of Contraception* (New York: Gamut Press, 1963), p. 224.

9. Ibid., pp. 239 ff.; Annie Besant was a supporter of the population theory of Malthus and tried to persuade her socialist friends of the necessity of contraception as a remedy against poverty and child labor.

10. *An Essay on the Principle of Population* (New York: Norton, 1976).

11. Quoted by August Bebel in *Charles Fourier—Sein Leben und seine Theorien*, 4th ed. (Stuttgart: 1921).

12. Op. cit., *Origin of the Family*, p. 67.

13. *Der Briefwechsel zwischen Friedrich Engels und Karl Marx, 1844 bis 1883*, vol. 2 (Stuttgart: 1913).

14. Ibid.

15. Ibid.

16. *Communist Manifesto*.

17. Ibid.

18. Engels, op. cit., p. 64.

19. Ibid., p. 64.

20. *Karl Marx, Werke-Schriften-Briefe*, vol. 4 (Darmstadt: 1962).

21. Ibid.

22. Karl Marx, *Capital*, translated from the fourth edition by Eden and Cedar Paul, with an introduction by G. D. H. Cole, vol. 1 (London and New York: J. M. Dent & Sons, Ltd. and E. P. Dutton & Co., Inc., 1962).

23. Quoted from *Der Vorbote*, 1866, by Werner Thönnessen, *Emancipation of Women: The Rise & Decline of the Women's Movement in Germany* (Urizen, 1976), p. 20.

24. August Bebel, *Woman under Socialism*, translated from the 33rd ed. by Daniel De Leon with a new introduction by Lewis Coser (New York: Schocken, 1975), p. 9.

25. Ibid., p. 9.

26. Engels, *Origin of the Family*, p. 58.

10

1. *Die Jugendgeschichte einer Arbeiterin, von ihr selbst erzählt.* Intro. by August Bebel (Munich: 1909).

2. Ibid.

3. Ibid.

4. "Wird die Sozialdemokratie den Frauen Wort halten?" (Neuwied: 1895).

5. Op. cit.

6. Susanne Hillmann, *Zum Verständnis der Texte in Rosa Luxemburgs Schriften zur Theorie der Spontanität* (Hamburg: 1970).

7. Ibid.

8. (Munich: 1922).

9. Op. cit.

10. *Zur Geschichte der proletarischen Frauenbewegung Deutschlands* (Berlin: 1958).

11. Op. cit.

12. Quoted by Luise Dornemann, *Clara Zetkin, Leben und Wirken* (Berlin: 1973).

13. Cf. Adeline Berger, "Die zwanzigjährige Arbeiterinnenbewegung Berlins" (Berlin: 1889); Minna Cauer, *Die Frau im 19. Jahrhundert* (Berlin: 1898).

14. Eleanor Marx-Aveling and Edward Aveling, *Die Frauenfrage* (Berlin: 1973).

15. *Aus Leben und Wissenschaft* (Stuttgart: 1896).

16. *Neue Horizonte für Liebe und Leben* (Vienna and Leipzig: 1922).

17. Op. cit.

18. Op. cit.

19. *Erlebtes—Erschautes* (Meisenheim: 1972).

20. Heymann and Augspurg, op. cit.

21. Anna Blos, ed., *Die Frauenfrage im Lichte des Sozialismus* (Dresden: 1930).

22. Ibid.

23. Heymann and Augspurg, op. cit.

24. Ibid.

25. Camilla Jellinek, *Die Strafrechtsreform und die §§ 218 and 219 St GB* (Heidelberg: 1908).

26. Ibid.

27. *Jahrbuch der Sozialdemokratischen Partei Deutschlands* (1947, 1950–51).

II

1. Bäumer, "Die Frauenbewegung als internationale Erscheinung," *Die Bötcherstraße,* vol. 1, no. 5 (September 1928).

2. Gertrud Bäumer, in *Jahrbuch der Frauenbewegung* (Leipzig and Berlin: 1916.)

3. *Die Frauen und der Krieg* (Leipzig: 1915).

4. Ibid.

5. Elisabeth Altmann-Gottheiner, ed., *Jahrbuch der Frauenbewegung,* "Heimatdienst im ersten Kriegsjahr" (Leipzig and Berlin: 1916).

6. Josephine Kamm, *Rapiers and Battleaxes: The Women's Movement and Its Aftermath* (London: Allen & Unwin, 1966).

7. J. Stanley Lemons, *The Woman Citizen: Social Feminism in the 1920s* (University of Illinois Press, 1973), p. 7.

8. Werner Thönnessen, op. cit.

9. I follow essentially the interpretation of Marie Louise Degen: *The History of the Woman's Peace Party* (Baltimore: Johns Hopkins Press, 1939), p. 31.

10. Heymann and Augspurg, op. cit.

11. Ibid.

12. Ibid.

13. Quoted by Degen, op. cit.

14. Heymann and Augspurg, op. cit.

15. Lida Gustava Heymann, *Frauenstimmrecht und Völkerverständigung* (Leipzig: Verlag Naturwissenschaften, 1919).

16. Ibid.

17. *Neue Horizonte für Liebe und Leben* (Vienna and Leipzig: 1922).

18. Degen, op. cit.

19. Ibid.

20. UN paper, World Conference for the International Women's Year, 1975, in Mexico City.

21. Ibid.

22. Heymann and Augspurg, op. cit.

23. German Bundestag, 222nd Session, July 10, 1952.

12

1. *Abhandlungen und Aufsätze,* vol. 2 (Leipzig: 1915).

2. *Neue Horizonte für Liebe und Leben* (Vienna and Leipzig: 1922).

3. (New York: Kraus Reproductions, 1971), pp. 327 ff.

4. Carrie Chapman Catt and Nettie Rogers Shuler, *Woman Suffrage and Politics: The Inner Story of the Suffrage Movement* (Seattle and London: University of Washington Press, 1970), p. 163.

5. Ibid., p. 339.

6. (University of Illinois Press, 1973), pp. 109 ff.

7. Ibid., p. 109.

8. Ibid., pp. 110 ff.

9. Ibid., p. 86.

10. Ibid., p. 109.

11. *Notable American Women: 1607–1950: A Biographical Dictionary* (Cambridge, Mass.: Harvard University Press, 1971), pp. 284 ff.

12. Emmy E. Werner, "Women in Congress 1917–1964," *Western Political Quarterly,* vol. 1, no. 1 (1966), pp. 16–30.

13. *Die Suffragettes* (Weimar: 1912).

14. *Im Alter die Fülle* (Tübingen: 1956).

15. Marie-Elisabeth Lüders, *Fürchte dich nicht: Personliches und Politisches aus mehr als 80 Jahren, 1878–1962* (Cologne and Opladen: 1963).

16. (Gotha: 1920).

17. Julius Duboc, *Fünfzig Jahre Frauenfrage in Deutschland* (Leipzig: 1896).

18. Heymann and Augspurg, op. cit.

19. Ibid.

20. Ibid.

21. Op. cit.

22. Nationalversammlung, 17th Session, February 28, 1919.

23. Nationalversammlung, 13th Session, February 21, 1919.

24. *Die Frau in deutschen Staat* (Berlin: 1932).

25. National Versammlung, 58th Session, July 16, 1919.

26. Ibid.

27. Op. cit.

28. Op. cit.

29. Emmy Wolff, ed., *Jahrbuch des Bundes deutscher Frauenvereine 1928–1931* (1928–1931) (1932).

30. Werner Thönnessen, op. cit. p. 162.

31. Ibid., p. 144.

32. UN Conference on the International Woman's Year (Mexico City: 1975), Paper E Conf. 66 (3).

33. Cf. Esmeralda Arboleda Cuevas, "Women in Latin America," UNESCO paper, 1975; Rounaq Jahan, "Women in Bangladesh," paper for the Ninth International Congress of Anthropological and Ethnological Sciences (Chicago: August 1973).

34. *The Traffic in Women and Other Essays in Feminism,* reprint from 1917 (New York: Times Change Press, 1971), p. 63.

13

1. *Social Structure* (New York: Free Press, 1965), p. 7.

2. Ibid.

3. Bridget O'Laughlin, "Mediation of Contradiction" in *Woman, Culture and Society,* Michelle Z. Rosaldo and Louise Lamphere, eds. (Stanford University Press, 1974), p. 307.

4. "Comparative Data on the Division of Labour by Sex," *Social Forces,* vol. 15 (1937), pp. 551 ff.

5. *Diversity and Homogeneity in World Societies* (New Haven: HRAF Press, 1973).

6. *Social Structure,* p. 7.

7. *Male and Female* (New York: Alfred A. Knopf, 1953), pp. 170 ff.

8. Quoted by Judith K. Brown in "Leisure, Busywork, and Housekeeping," *Anthropos,* vol. 68 (1973).

9. Ibid.

10. Peggy R. Sanday, "Toward a Theory of the Status of Woman," *American Anthropologist,* vol. 75 (1973), p. 1696.

11. H. Aufenager, "Women's Lives in the Highlands of New Guinea," *Anthropos,* vol. 59 (1964).

12. Susan Brownmiller, *Against Our Will: Men, Women and Rape* (New York: Simon & Schuster, 1975), p. 286.

13. *Birth and Childhood Among the Arabs* (New York: AMS Press, 1975), p. 46.

14. "On the Modesty of Women in Arab Muslim Villages: A Study in the Accommodation of Traditions," *American Anthropologist,* vol. 70 (1968), pp. 671 ff., esp. p. 682.

15. Louis J. Luzbetak, *Marriage and the Family in Caucasia* (Vienna-Mödling: St. Gabriel's Mission Press, 1951), pp. 150 ff.

16. Op. cit., pp. 1682 ff. *Die weibliche Eigenart im Männerstaat und die männliche Eigenart im Frauenstaat* (Karlsruhe: 1921).

17. Franz Eichinger, "Frauenarbeit bei den tibetischen Nomaden im Kokonoagebiet," *Anthropos*, vol. 50 (1955).

14

1. Arnold Gehlen: *Der Mensch* (Berlin: 1940).
2. "Vom Einfluβ der Frau auf die Geschichte" (Munich: 1956).
3. Ibid.
4. Georg Simmel, "Zur Philosophie der Geschlechter. Das Relative und das Absolute im Geschlechterproblem," *Philosophische Kultur* (Leipzig: 1919).
5. *The Second Sex*, H.M. Parshley, trans. and ed. (New York: Alfred A. Knopf, 1953), p. 63.
6. Ibid., pp. 63–4.
7. Elisabeth Blochmann, "Das 'Frauenzimmer' und die 'Gelehrsamkeit' " (Heidelberg: 1966).
8. Autorenkollektiv, *Grundlagen des Marxismus-Leninismus* (Berlin: 1960).
9. *Origin of the Family*, pp. 147–48.
10. August Bebel, *Woman Under Socialism* (New York: Laker News Press, 1904), cf. pp. 338–39.
11. Ibid.
12. Ibid., p. 344.
13. Ibid., p. 347.
14. Erich Fromm, *Marx's Concept of Man* (Ungar, n.d.), p. 178.

15

1. Rolf-Dieter Kluge, "Die Rolle der Frau in der Sowjetgesellschaft" *Osteuropa*, vol. 16 (1966).
2. Alexander Szalai, "The Situation of Women in the Light of Contemporary Time-Budget Research," Background paper to the UN Conference No. E Conf. 66/BP/6 of the International Woman's Year (1975), p. 10.
3. Ibid., pp. 11 ff.
4. Ibid., pp. 13.
5. "Time Spent in Housework," *Scientific American* (November 1974), pp. 116 ff.
6. Op. cit., p. 19.
7. Quoted by Arlie Russell Hochschild, "A Review of Sex Role Research," *American Journal of Sociology*, vol. 78 (1972), p. 1012.
8. "Frauen im Lehrerberuf" (Kaiserslautern: 1974).
9. *Gleichberechtigung im Beruf* (Frankfurt on Main: 1973).
10. *Frauenemanzipation und Sozialismus* (Hamburg: 1973).
11. *China Reconstructs*, vol. 24, no. 6 (June 1975), pp. 17 ff.
12. Op. cit., p. 14.

16

1. *Protokoll des Hauptausschusses des Parlamentarischen Rates*, 17th Session, December 3, 1948.
2. *"Gewerkschaftliche Beiträge zum Frauen Lohn-Problem,"* no. 5 (Cologne: 1962).
3. Hartwig Bülck, "Die Lohngleichheit vom Mann und Frau als internationales Rechtsproblem," *Recht der Arbeit*, vol. 5 (January 1952).
4. Op. cit.
5. Ibid.
6. *Newsweek* (November 4, 1974).

7. "Die Stellung der Frau in der Gesellschaft von Heute," *Deutsches Rotes Kreuz,* vol. 10 (1957).

8. Internationale Arbeitskonferenz 60. Tagung, Report viii (1957).

9. Ibid.

10. Cf. *Brigitte,* "Gleichberechtigung—und wie sie wirklich aussieht."

11. Internationale Arbeitskonferenz, op. cit.

12. Ibid.

13. Women's Rights Resolution of the 24th Regular Congress of the UAW (June 2–6, 1974), Los Angeles.

14. *The 51% Minority* (Pittsburgh: KNOW, Inc.).

15. "The Declining Status of Women," *Social Status,* vol. 48 (1969–70), pp. 183ff.

16. Bártová, op. cit.

17. Magdalena Sokolowska, *Frauenemanzipation und Sozialismus* (Hamburg: 1973).

18. *Die Zeit,* no. 7 (February 7, 1975).

17

1. Hermann Heinrich Ploss and Max and Paul Bartels, *Woman; an Historical Gynecological and Anthropological Compendium* (London: Heinemann, 1935); Rosa Mayreder: *Zur Kritik der Weiblichkeit,* 3rd ed. (Jena and Leipzig: 1907).

2. Martha Vicinus: *Suffer and Be Still: Women in the Victorian Age* (Indiana University Press, 1972), p. 146.

3. *Intelligenz* (Munich: 1975).

4. Hildegard Krüger, "Das Bild der Frau im Spiegel neuerer Literatur," *Gewerkschaftliche Monatshefte,* vol. 10 (1959).

5. Ashley Montagu, *The Natural Superiority of Women* (New York: Collier Books, 1974), p. 79.

6. Ibid., p. 80.

7. Ibid.

8. Ibid., p. 186.

9. Ibid., p. 187.

10. *Das Patriarchat* (Frankfurt: S. Fischer, 1975).

18

1. Op. cit., pp. 71 ff.

2. Quoted by Karl H. Bönner, *Die Geschlechterrolle* (Munich: 1973).

3. Quoted by Ploss and Bartels, op. cit.

4. Georg Simmel, "Das Relative und das Absolute im Gechlechterproblem," *Philosophische Kultur* (Leipzig: 1919).

5. Karl J. Narr, "Der Frühmensch: Halbtier oder Homo religiosus," lecture before the Protestant Academy of Herrenalb (1975).

6. Paul Schebesta, *Die Negrito Asiens,* vol. 1 (Vienna-Mödling: 1952).

7. Ann Crittenden Scott, "Closing the Muscle Gap," *Ms.* (Sept. 1974), p. 50; Anthony Smith, *The Body* (New York: Avon, 1969).

8. Scott, op. cit.

9. Ibid., p. 49.

10. *The Naked Ape* (New York: McGraw-Hill, 1967).

11. Lila Leibowitz, "Desmond Morris Is Wrong about Breasts, Buttocks and Body Hair," *Psychology Today,* no. 3 (1970), pp. 16 ff.

12. Cf. Claude Lévi-Strauss, op. cit.

13. Sherwood Washburn, ed., *Social Life of Early Man* (London: 1962).

14. S. Eimerl and I. DeVore, *Die Primaten* (Reinbek bei Hamburg: 1976).

15. K. Goerttler, "Morphologische Sonderstellung des Menschen . . .," in H. G. Dadamer and P. Vogler, eds., *Neue Anthropologie,* vol. 2 (Munich and Stuttgart: 1972).

16. "The Potency of the Woman" (Cologne: 1974), p. 204.

17. *Zoologie des Menschen* (Munich: 1971).

18. Smith, op. cit., pp. 169 ff.

19. Julia Sherman, *On the Psychology of Women. A Survey of Empirical Studies* (Springfield, Ill.: Charles C Thomas, 1975), p. 197.

20. Morris, op. cit., pp. 53–54.

21. Eimerl and DeVore, op. cit.

22. Ibid.

23. Ibid.

24. Op. cit., p. 54.

25. Ibid., p. 82.

26. Anne Roe and G. G. Simpson, eds.: *Evolution und Verhalten* (Frankfurt-am-Main: 1969).

27. Suzanne Chevalier and Skolnikoff, "Male-Female, Female-Female, and Male-Male Sexual Behavior in the Stumptail Monkey, with Special Attention to the Female Orgasm," *Archives of Sexual Behavior,* vol. 3, no. 2 (1974), pp. 95 ff; Frances D. Burton, "Sexual Climax in Female Macaca Mulatta," *Proceedings of the 3rd International Congress of Primatology* (Zurich: 1970; Basel: 1971), pp. 180 ff.

28. "My Friends the Wild Chimpanzees," *National Geographic* (1967).

29. Op. cit., p. 161.

30. Nancie I. Solien de Gonzáles, *American Anthropologist,* vol. 66 (1964), pp. 873 ff.

31. Werner Köhler, "Menstruation, Schwangerschaft und Geburt in Afrika," *Wissenschaftliche Zeitschrift der Friedrich Schiller-Universität* (Jena), series 3 (1953–54); George Peter Murdock, "Post-Partum Sex Taboos," *Paideuma,* vol. 13 (1967), pp. 143 ff.

32. Quoted by Evelyn Reed, *Woman's Evolution: From Matriarchal Clan to Patriarchal Family* (New York: Pathfinder Press, 1975), p. 134.

33. Ploss and Bartels, op. cit.

34. "Mutter und Kind bei den Chinesen in Tsinghai," part 2, *Anthropos,* vol. 50 (1955).

35. Quoted by Hedwig Dohm, "Gesichtspunkte für die Erziehung zur Ehe," *Sozialistische Monatshefte,* vol. 2. (1909).

19

1. "The Ontogenesis of Ritualization," *Psyche,* vol. 22, no. 7 (July 1968).

2. "The Psychoanalytical Psychology of Childhood and Its Sources," *Psyche,* vol. 22, no. 6 (June 1968).

3. *Childhood and Society* (New York: Norton, 1964), p. 74.

4. Ibid., p. 66.

5. *Tierjunges und Menschenkind im Blick der vergleichenden Verhaltensforschung* (Stuttgart: 1970), Publication Series of the District Medical Board of Nordwürttemberg, no. 17.

6. "Is Breast Feeding Best?" *American Journal of Clinical Nutrition,* vol. 7 (1959), pp. 259–63; quoted by Sherman, below, p. 215.

7. Sherman, op. cit.

8. Ibid., p. 219.

9. *Angst und Geborgenheit* (Hamburg: 1976).

10. Ibid.

11. Ibid.

12. Ibid.

13. Ibid.

14. *Die Gesellschaft und das Böse* (Munich: 1968).

15. Op. cit., pp. 139 ff.

16. *Child Training and Personality: A Cross-Cultural Study* (New Haven: Yale University Press, 1953).

17. Ursula Lehr, "Die Rolle der Mutter in der Sozialisation der Kinder" (Darmstadt: 1974). The following statements are based on Lehr, who gives an overview and summary of all relevant studies.

18. R. Spitz, "Hospitalism. An Inquiry into the Genesis of Psychiatric Conditions in Early Childhood." In Ruth Eissler et al.; see also, by the same author, *Die Entstehungen der ersten Objektbeziehungen* (Stuttgart: 1960) and *Vom Säugling zum Kleinkind* (Stuttgart: 1967); Lehr, pp. 17–18.

19. *Maternal Care and Mental Health* (Geneva: WHO Monograph 2, 1951).

20. Ibid.

21. Ibid.

22. Cf. "Familienpolitik der Sozialdemokratischen Partei Deutschlands: Entwurf" (1972).

23. Op. cit.

24. Ibid.

25. Ibid.

26. Cf. also Information Service 5/75, edited by the Bundesanstalt für Gesamtdeutsche Aufgaben (National Institute for Pan-Germanic Affairs).

27. Lehr, op. cit.

28. Charlotte Bühler, *Psychologie im Leben unserer Zeit* (Munich: 1962).

29. (New York: Random House, 1965).

30. Quoted by Helmut Meier, *Deutsche Sprachstatistik,* 2nd ed. (Hildesheim: 1967).

20

1. Hedwig Dohm, "Der Frauen Natur und Recht," *Zur Frauenfrage zwei Abhandlungen über Eigenschaften und Stimmrecht der Frauen* (Berlin: 1876).

2. "Ehe und Kind im abflußlosen Gebiet Ostafrikas," *Arkiv für Völkerkunde,* vol. 4 (Vienna: 1949).

3. *The Dispossessed* (London: Jonathan Cape Ltd., 1959).

4. Napoleon A. Chagnon, *Yanomamö: The Fierce People* (New York: Holt, Rinehart & Winston, 1968).

5. Louis J. Luzbetak, *Marriage and the Family in Caucasia* (Johnson Reprint 1965).

6. Op. cit.

7. Ibid.

8. Elisabeth Gould Davis, *The First Sex* (New York: Putnam's, 1971), p. 254.

9. Hans Fehr, "Die Rechtstellung der Frau und der Kinder in den Weistümern" (Jena: 1912).

10. Ibid.

11. *Die Familie* (Stuttgart: 1881).

12. Dohm, "Der Frauen Natur und Recht," op. cit.

13. In Helen Lange: *Wie lernen die Frauen die Politik verstehen?* (Berlin: 1912).

14. Op. cit.

15. "A Madman's Defense," in Betty Roszak and Theodore Roszak, eds., *Masculine Feminine: Readings in Sexual Mythology & the Liberation of Women* (New York and Evanston: Harper & Row, 1969), pp. 10 ff.

16. Josephine Kamm, *Rapiers and Battleaxes* (London: Allen & Unwin, 1966).

17. "Die Stellung der Frau in Sunnitischen Islam" (Berlin: 1968).

18. Hilma Granqvist, *Birth and Childhood Among the Arabs* (Helsinki: 1947).

19. Gisela Helwig, *Frau '75. Bundesrepublik Deutschland—DDR* (1975).

20. German Press Agency Report 265, 15 March 1976; Erin Pizzey, "Scream Quietly or the Neighbors Will Hear" (London: 1974).

21. House of Commons, *Report on Violence in Marriage,* vol. 1 (London: 1976).

22. Houses for battered women exist in Amsterdam and in various cities in the U.S. One Berlin women's group is also planning a project of this kind.

23. House of Commons, op. cit.

24. *Child Problems Among the Arabs* (Ekenäs, Finland: 1950).

25. Richard T. Antoun, "On the Modesty of Women in Arab Muslim Villages: A Study in the Accommodation of Traditions," *American Anthropologist,* 70 (1968).

26. Max Bauer, *Deutscher Frauenspiegel,* vol. 1 (Munich and Berlin: 1917).

27. D. M. Stenton, *The Englishwoman in History* (New York: Macmillan, 1957), p. 83.

28. Ian Young, *The Private Life of Islam* (London: 1974).

29. Op. cit., pp. 14 ff.

30. Op. cit.

31. *Married Life in an African Tribe* (Evanston, Ill.: Northwestern University Press, 1966).

32. *Gesamtausgabe*, vol. 1 (Stuttgart: Bavarian Academy of Sciences: 1970).

33. Ibid.

34. "Zur Philosophie der Geschlechter. Das Relative und das Absolute im Geschlechterproblem," *Philosophische Kultur* (Leipzig: 1919).

35. "Women in Bangladesh" (Dacca: 1974). Quoted by Alfred Kind, *Die Weiberherrschaft in der Geschichte des Menschen*, vol. 1 (Munich: 1913), p. 381.

36. *Sexualstraftäter* (Stuttgart: 1971).

37. Georg Gerbner, "Communication and Social Environment," *Scientific American* (September 1972), pp. 153–61.

38. Quoted by Franz Schöler, "Blondinen bevorzugt, Hollywood und die Frauen," broadcast on Hessian Radio, January 25, 1968.

21

1. (Munich: 1972).

2. "Die Beurteilung der orgastischen Kapazität der Frau und ihrer Störungen aus psychoanalytischer Sicht," *Psyche* (January 1969). The psychoanalysts' reluctance to consider empirical research is discussed by Fleck (pp. 58 ff.), who mentions that the "results of years of research by Masters and Johnson . . . were published in 1962, but thus far have been little noted by analysts."

3. *Human Sexual Response* (Boston: Little, Brown, 1966).

4. Ibid.

5. "Jugendsexualität—Tatsachen und Folgerungen," *Zeitschrift für Sexualforschung* vol. 1, no. 2 (1950).

6. Op. cit.

7. Johann Georg Waich, *Philosophisches Lexikon*, 4th ed. (Leipzig: 1775).

8. A. A. Shandall, *Sudan Medical Journal* 5 (1967).

9. (Hamburg: 1974).

22

1. *Aus Mehemed Ali's Reich, Dritter Teil: Nubien und Sudan, Vom Verfasser der Briefe eines Verstorbenen* (Stuttgart: 1844).

2. W. Helck, E. Otto, eds., *Lexikon der Ägyptologie*, vol. 1 (Wiesbaden: 1975); cf. Hermann Grapow, *Kranker, Krankheiten und Arzt* (Berlin: 1956).

3. Quoted by Ploss and Bartels, *Das Weib in der Natur- und Völkerkunde*, 5th edit. (Leipzig: 1897).

4. WIN (Women's International Network), vol. 1, no. 4 (October 1975).

5. WIN first appeared in 1975 and has published material on this subject regularly.

6. Henny Harald Hansen, "Clitoridectomy: Female Circumcision in Egypt," *Folk*, vols. 14/15 (1972–73).

7. Quoted by WIN, op. cit.

8. (Paris: 1972), reproduced according to the passages published in WIN, vol. 1, no. 4 (October 1975).

9. "Circumcision and Infibulation of Females: A General Consideration of the Problem and a Clinical Study of the Complications in Sudanese Women," *Sudanese Medical Journal*, vol. 5, no. 178 (1967).

10. *Facing Mount Kenya: The Tribal Life of the Kikuyu* (New York: Random House, 1962), pp. 132 ff.

11. Ibid., p. 162.

12. (New York: Doubleday, 1972).

13. "Women and Their Life in Central Australia," *Journal of the Royal Anthropological Institute,* vol. 63 (1933).

23

1. Firestone, op. cit.

2. Ibid.

3. *Süddeutsche Zeitung,* March 13, 1974.

4. Vol. 3 (October 1966), pp. 4 ff.

5. (Penguin, 1972), p. 112.

6. Ibid., pp. 110 ff.

7. Gordon Rattray Taylor, *The Biological Timebomb* (New York: New American Library, 1969).

8. Ibid.

24

1. *Hellenistic Civilization,* rev. by Tarn and G. T. Griffith (Cleveland and New York: Meridian Books, The World Publishing Co., 1964), p. 101.

2. Ibid.

3. "A Social and Ecological Analysis of Systematic Female Infanticide among the Netsilik Eskimo," *American Anthropologist,* vol. 73 (1971).

4. M. N. Das, "Female Infanticide among the Bedees and the Chouhans: Motives and Modes," *Man in India,* vol. 36, no. 4 (1956).

5. Ibid., cf. also, M. N. Das, "Movement to Suppress the Custom of Female Infanticide in the Punjab and Kashmir," *Man in India,* vol. 37 (1957).

6. Angelina Pollak-Eltz in *Anthropos* (1963–64, 1968–69).

7. Ploss and Bartels, op. cit.

8. Population Division of the Department of Economic and Social Affairs, 1974, UN paper for the international women's conference in Mexico City, June 19–July 1, 1975, E/Conf. 66/3/Add.3.

9. Quoted by WIN (Women's International Network) (Lexington, Mass.: 1975), vol. 1, no. 2, p. 54.

10. Cf. R. Jungk, J. H. Mundt, eds., *Hat die Familie noch eine Zukunft?* (Munich, Vienna and Basel: 1971).

11. Charles F. Westoff and Ronald R. Rindfuss, "Sex Preselection in the United States: Some Implications," *Science,* vol. 184 (1974), p. 633.

12. Sherman, op. cit.

13. Westoff and Rindfuss, op. cit.

25

1. *Psychologie im Leben unserer Zeit* (Munich and Zürich: 1962).

2. (New York: Holt, Rinehart & Winston, 1961), p. 128.

3. (New York: Doubleday: 1958), p. 48.

4. Karl H. Bönner, ed., *Die Geschlechterrolle* (Munich: 1973).

5. *Zur kognitiven Entwicklung des Kindes* (Frankfurt on Main: 1974).

6. Ibid.

7. Spencer K. Thompson, "Gender Labels and Early Sex Role Development," *Child Development* (June 1975), vol. 46, no. 2.

8. Op. cit.

9. Ibid.
10. Ibid.
11. Ibid.
12. Ibid.
13. Ibid.
14. Ibid.
15. Ibid.
16. Ibid.
17. "Black Is Beautiful: A Re-examination of Social Preference and Identification," *Journal of Personality and Social Psychology,* vol. 16, no. 3 (1970), pp. 398–402.
18. Op. cit.
19. Ibid.
20. Ibid.
21. Ibid.
22. Cf. John Money and Anke Ehrhardt, *Man and Woman, Boy and Girl: Differentiation and Dimorphism of Gender Identity from Conception to Maturity* (Baltimore: Johns Hopkins University Press, 1973).
23. Ibid.
24. Ibid.
25. Ibid.
26. Ibid.

26

1. Quoted by Helmut Meier, *Deutsche Sprachstatistik* (Hildesheim: 1967).
2. *Frühe politische Systeme* (Frankfurt: 1974).
3. *Philosophy of Right,* trans. T. M. Knox (London: Oxford University Press, 1942).
4. Ibid.
5. Ibid.
6. Ibid.
7. Ibid.
8. Ibid.
9. "Symbolische Bedingungen der Sozialisation" (Düsseldorf: 1974).
10. Richard T. Antoun, "On the Modesty of Women in Arab Muslim Villages," *American Anthropologist,* vol. 70 (1968), p. 675.
11. Ernst Moritz Arndt, *Briefe an Freunde* (Altona: 1810).
12. *The Sorrows of Young Werther* (New York: Holt, Rinehart & Winston, 1949).
13. Op. cit.
14. Karoline S. J. Milde, *Der deutschen Jungfrau Wesen und Wirken,* 12th ed. (Leipzig: 1899).
15. German Press Agency, August 13, 1975.
16. *Conundrum* (New York: Harcourt Brace Jovanovich, 1974), p. 82.
17. Ibid., pp. 152 ff.
18. *Die Welt* January 2, 1976.
19. *Wie Frauen werden . . . , Werde, die Du bist* (Breslau: 1894).
20. *Monster* (New York: Random House, 1972), p. 82.

27

1. *Die nominalen Klassifikationssysteme in den Sprachen der Erde* (Mödling/Vienna: 1925–6).
2. Ibid.
3. "Abhandlung über den Ursprung der Sprache" (1772).
4. Royen, op. cit.
5. Ibid.
6. Ibid.
7. Ibid.

8. Ibid.

9. *Die Familie* (Stuttgart: 1882).

10. Royen, op. cit.

11. Ibid.

12. Ibid.

13. Ibid.

14. Ivan Morris, quoted by Robert Jay Lifton, ed., *The Woman in America* (Beacon Press, 1965), p. 30.

15. Charles H. Berlitz, "A Linguist Observes," *Perceptions Module 6* (New York: 1975).

16. Ibid.

17. Georg von der Gabelentz, *Chinesische Grammatik* (Berlin: 1953).

18. W. Schmidt, *Die Sprachfamilien und Sprachenkreise der Erde* (Heidelberg: 1926).

19. "The Origin of Grammatical Gender," *Lingua*, vol. 8 (1959); cf. W. W. Arndt, "Non-random Assignment of Loan Words: German Noun Gender," *Word*, vol. 26, no. 2 (August 1970), pp. 244 ff.

20. Edward B. Harper, "Fear and the Status of Women," *Southwestern Journal of Anthropology* (Albuquerque: 1969), pp. 90 ff.

21. Royen, op. cit.

22. Berlitz, op. cit.

23. Granqvist, op. cit.

24. G. W. F. Hegel quoted by Golo Mann, *Deutsche Geschichte des 19. Jahrhunderts* (Frankfurt: 1958), p. 101.

25. *Soul on Ice* (New York: McGraw-Hill, 1968), p. 75.

26. Quoted by Hedwig Dohm, "Gesichtspunkte für die Erziehung zur Ehe," *Sozialistische Monatshefte* (1909), vol. 2.

28

1. Fung Yu-lan, trans. by D. Bodde, *A History of Chinese Philosophy*, vol. 1 (Princeton, N.J.: Princeton University Press, 1952), p. 383.

2. E. Helck and E. Otto, *Lexikon der Ägyptologie* (Wiesbaden: 1975).

3. Fung Yu-lan, op. cit., pp. 386 ff.

4. Hermann Baumann, *Das doppelte Geschlecht* (Berlin: 1955).

5. Georg von der Gabelentz, *Chinesische Grammatik* (Berlin: 1953).

6. Baumann, op. cit.

7. Ibid.

8. Hermann Müller-Karpe, *Handbuch der Vorgeschichte*, 2 vols. (Munich: 1968).

9. Mircea Eliade, *The Quest: History and Meaning in Religion* (Chicago: University of Chicago Press, 1969), p. 139.

10. Baumann, op. cit.

11. "Marriage and Malevolence: The Uses of Sexual Opposition in a Hindu Pantheon," *Ethnology* (1972).

12. Eliade, op. cit., pp. 150 ff.

13. Baumann, op. cit.

14. Ibid.

15. Op. cit., p. 125.

16. Ibid., p. 287.

17. Hegel's *Frühe politische Systeme*

18. *Jenaer Realphilosophie* (1805/6).

19. Ibid.

20. Ibid.

21. Ibid.

22. Hegel, *Philosophy of Right*, p. 114.

23. G.W.F. Hegel, *The Phenomenology of Mind*, trans. J. B. Baillie (New York and Evanston: Harper & Row, Publishers, Inc., 1967), p. 477.

24. Frank Wiedemann, *Hegel* (Reinbek bei Hamburg), p. 43.

25. Hegel, *Philosophy of Right*,

29

1. *Sexual Politics* (New York: Avon Books, 1971), pp. 17–30.
2. Act I, Scene 1.
3. Hermann Baumann, *Das doppelte Geschlecht* (Berlin: 1955).
4. Ibid.
5. *The Decline of the West,* vol. 1 (New York: Alfred A. Knopf, 1945).
6. *Gesund und angenehm, Die Frau von morgen—wie wir sie wünschen,* Friedrich M. Huebner, ed. (Leipzig: 1929).
7. Quoted by Karl Stern, *Die Flucht vor dem Weib* (Salzburg: 1968).
8. Hermann Baumann, op. cit.
9. Cf. Mercea Eliade, *The Quest: History and Meaning in Religion* (Chicago: 1969), pp. 139ff.
10. "Child Problems among the Arabs" (Ekenäs, Finland: 1950), p. 47.
11. P. Royen, *Die nominalen Klassifikationssysteme in den Sprache der Erde* (Vienna/Mödling: 1925–26).
12. Op. cit.
13. *Das Phänomen der verkehrten Welt in der griechischrömischen Antike* (Klagenfurt: 1970).
14. Ibid.
15. Max Bauer, *Deutscher Frauenspiegel,* vol. 1, (Munich and Berlin: 1917).
16. Edward B. Harper, "Fear and the Status of Women," *Southwestern Journal of Anthropology* (Albuquerque: 1969), p. 83.
17. H. Aufenanger, "Women's Lives in the Highlands of New Guinea," *Anthropos,* vol. 59 (1964).
18. Lawrence Kohlberg, *Zur kognitiven Entwicklung des Kindes* (Frankfurt on Main: 1974).
19. Aufenanger, op. cit.
20. Cf. Hermann Baumann, op. cit.
21. Ibid.
22. Cf. Norbert Mylius, "Ehe und Kind im abflußlosen Gebiet Ostafrikas," *Archiv für Völkerkunde,* vol. 4 (Vienna: 1949).
23. *African Religions and Philosophy* (London, New York: Praeger, 1969).
24. Johann Frick, "Mutter und Kind bei den Chinesen in Tsinghai," pts. 1–4, *Anthropos,* vols. 50/51 (1955–56).
25. Erik Midelfort, *Witchhunting in Southwestern Germany 1562–1684* (Stanford University Press, 1972), p. 184.

30

1. *Women in Development* (Bibliography by American Association for the Advancement of Science) (1975).
2. Hermann Baumann, *Das doppelte Geschlecht* (Berlin: 1955).
3. M. Devulder, "Rituel Magique des Femmes Kabyles," *Revue africaine,* 2nd and 3rd trimesters (Algiers: 1957).
4. Mircea Eliade, *The Quest: History and Meaning in Religion* (Chicago: 1969), p. 134.
5. Henri Labouret, "Situation materielle, morale et coutoumière de la femme dans l'ouest-africain," *Africa,* vol. 13, no. 2 (April 1940).
6. Judith van Allen, "Sitting on a Man: Colonialism and the Lost Political Institutions of Igbo Women," *Canadian Journal of African Studies,* vols. 6 and 2 (1972), pp. 165–81; Sylvia Leith-Ross, *African Women* (AMS Press, 1978).
7. Ibid.
8. Adaoha C. Uzoma, *Viertelsjahresberichte, Probleme der Entwicklungsländer,* no. 44 (Bonn: 1971).
9. *Présence africaine* (Paris: 1955).

10. An overview of this is given by Annie M. D. Lebeuf: "The Role of Women in the Political Organization of African Societies" in Denise Paulme, ed., *Women of Tropical Africa* (Berkeley: University of California Press, 1963).

11. Ibid., pp. 99 ff.

12. All examples mentioned appear in the Lebeuf article.

13. "Manyika Headwomen," *Nada* (The Southern Rhodesia Native Affairs Department Annual) (1940).

14. Carol P. Hoffer, "Mende and Sherbro Women in High Office," *Canadian Journal of African Studies*, vols. 6 and 2 (1972), pp. 151–64.

31

1. Thomas R. Malthus, *An Essay on the Principle of Population* (New York: Norton, 1976).

2. Rüdiger Schott, "Das Geschichtsbewußtsein schriftloser Völker," *Archiv für Begriffsgeschichte*, 12 (1968).

3. S. Chandrasekhar, *Abortion in a Crowded World* (Seattle: University of Washington Press, 1974).

4. John T. Noonan, Jr., *Contraception* (Cambridge, Mass.: Belknap Press of Harvard University Press, 1965), p. 50.

5. *Structural Anthropology* (New York: Basic Books, 1963).

6. Walter Goldschmidt, "The Bride Price of the Sebei," *Scientific American* (July 1973).

7. Jack Goody and S. J. Tambiah give a detailed presentation of bride price and dowry in Africa and Eurasia and the dissemination of polygamy and monogamy in *Bridewealth and Dowry* (Cambridge University Press, 1973). Out of 176 patrilinear societies of Africa, 154 have the bride price and 10 the service marriage; not one has the dowry.

8. Lawrence Stone, "Heirat und Ehe im englischen Adel des 16. und 17. Jahrhunderts," *Comparative Studies in Society and History: An International Quarterly*, vol. 3 (1960–61), pp. 182 ff.

9. T'ung-Tsu Ch'Ü, *Law and Society in Traditional China* (Paris, La Haye: 1961).

10. See chapter 24: "Female Genocide." Cf. Max Weber, *Gesammelte Aufsätze zur Religions-soziologie II, Hinduismus und Buddhismus* (Tübingen: 1921).

11. Lawrence Stone, op. cit.

12. "Population, Warfare, and the Male Supremacist Complex," *American Anthropologist* 78 (1976).

13. Sylvie Gay Sterboul, "Confucius, ses disciples et la population," *Population* 29 (1974).

14. Carlo M. Cipolla, Knut Borchardt (eds.), *Bevölkerungsgeschichte Europas (Mittelalter bis Neuzeit)* (Munich: 1971).

15. William Tarn, *Hellenistic Civilization*, 3rd ed. (London: Methuen, 1966).

16. Sigismund Peller, "Births and Deaths among Europe's Ruling Families since 1500," in D. V. Glass and D. E. C. Eversley, eds., *Population in History* (London: E. Arnold, 1965).

17. Walter Müller, "Freiheit und Leibeigenschaft—Sociale Ziele des deutschen Bauernkrieges?" *Revolte und Revolution in Europa* (Munich: 1975).

18. Sigismund Peller, op. cit.

19. "The Population of France in the Eighteenth Century" in D. V. Glass and D. E. C. Eversley, op. cit.

20. Hans Harmsen, *Praktische Bevölkerungspolitik* (Berlin: 1931).

21. Hans Harmsen, *Bevölkerungsprobleme Frankreichs* (Marburg: 1927).

22. Jan Stepan and Edmund H. Kellogg, *The World's Laws on Contraceptives*, Law and Population Monograph Series, no. 17 (1974). "The Transportation of White Women to German Southwest Africa, 1898–1914," *Race*, vol. 12, no. 3 (1971). Daniel Gasman, *The Scientific Origins of National Socialism* (London, New York: American Elsevier, 1971), pp. 98–100. *Geburtenschwund. Die Kulturkrankheit Europas* (Heidelberg, Berlin, Magdeburg: 1942). *Die Abortsituation in Europa und in außereuropäischen Ländern* (Stuttgart: 1967). Her-

bert Heiss, op. cit. Milos Macura, "Population Policies in Socialist Countries of Europe," *Population Studies* 28, p. 3. Ibid.; see also Alena Heitlinger "Pro-Natalist Policies in Czechoslovakia," *Population Studies* 30, p. 1.

23. Kurt Bader, Gerd Otte, Detlef Stoklossa, *Handbuch für Kindertagesstätten* (Hamburg: 1977); *Corporations and Child Care: Profit-making Daycare, Workplace Daycare—and a Look at the Alternatives* (Cambridge: Women's Research Action Project, 1974).